ENTER-TAINING Ideas

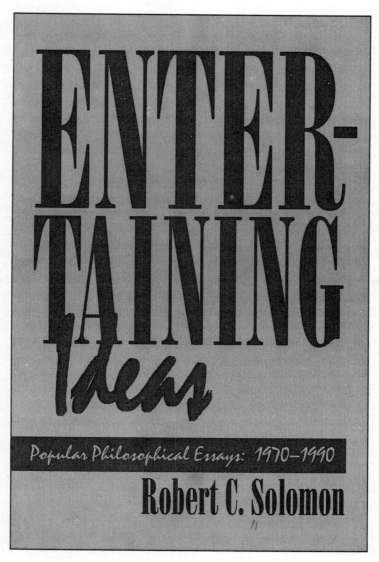

ENTER-TAINING Ideas

Popular Philosophical Essays: 1970–1990

Robert C. Solomon

PROMETHEUS BOOKS
Buffalo, New York

Published 1992 by Prometheus Books

96 95 94 93 92   5 4 3 2 1

Library of Congress Cataloging-in-Publication Data

Solomon, Robert C.
    Entertaining ideas: popular philosophical essays, 1970–1990/by Robert C. Solomon.
        p.   cm.
    The essays were originally published in different newspapers and popular magazines, 1970–1990.
    ISBN 0-087975-753-1 (alk. paper)
    1. Philosophy. 2. Ethics. 3. Social ethics. I. Title.
B73.S65   1992
100—dc20   92-7918
                                                            CIP

Printed in the United States of America on acid-free paper.

for Sam, Pushkin
Beefeater
Lou and Fritz

Contents

8   Contents

Introduction

Philosopher in the Midst

Philosophy, I have always believed, is one of the most enjoyable activities in the world, comparable to food and sex in both its urgency and intensity. Even as a child, I entertained myself by entertaining ideas, and now I entertain others. Of course, it is possible to get carried away with the activities of the mind, obsessed and even gluttonous with speculation and analysis. And, as in any form of indulgence, one can expect the critics, censors, and guilt-mongers to come down hard. On the one hand, they say, "philosophy is a waste of time." On the other, they insist that "philosophy is dangerous." As an activity that is intensely enjoyable, readily available, both profoundly self-absorbing and, done in pairs or groups, extremely intimate, it is particularly prime for condemnation. It is "not practical." It is "not productive." It is "too abstract." It is oblivious to "the real world." But when so many voices converge in proscription of an activity so entertaining and natural, that alone should peak our interest. Ideas can be fun.

The most effective censors, however, are those who would keep philosophy for themselves, turn it into a profession, a "discipline," convert its language into code-words and jargon, deny its joys, and turn play into pain. Philosophy thus moves from its readily available role as enjoyable mental entertainment and exercise to a set of difficult technical skills learned only at great effort and expense in graduate school. After a public lecture at a university just last week on the subject of "love," a woman who was not an academic but had seen notice of the talk in the newspaper expressed her considerable enthusiasm, enjoyment, and personal gratitude, but then added, "but what does this have to do with philosophy?" "This is philosophy,"

11

I replied, and she looked at me as if I had proven that yes, there is a Santa Claus after all.

Why do philosophers insist that their subject is so serious, so difficult, so un-fun? Like ascetics, anorexics, and some reformed alcoholics, they mistake fun with frivolity and temperance with abstinence. Perhaps they are obsessed with being "professionals." Perhaps they just miss the point. Philosophy, like taste and tenderness, requires a certain temperament and cultivation. It is akin to a sense of humor (which it much resembles), knowing how to stretch the imagination almost to the breaking point but recognizing some absurdity in doing so. Philosophy is fun, and philosophy is for everyone. The very word means "love of wisdom," love not drudgery, wisdom not technical cleverness. But given what passes for philosophy in today's curriculum, one would never get that idea. On the other hand, philosophy rendered playful and nontechnical is denounced as "popular" or, to be even more derogatory, "pop."

Philosophy is nothing but thinking, sometimes for oneself and by oneself, but more often with others and for others. It is thinking about everything and anything. There are no bounds to its dilettantism. Indeed, philosophy is best not only when tempered with real life and about real life, but when it *is* real life, real life elevated to the realm of thought and reflection, real life digested and pondered and understood rather than simply lived through, or as some would say, experienced. But experience without philosophy, as one of our most famous philosophers has insisted, is blind. Philosophy divorced from experience, however, is empty. Philosophy may be one of the necessities of life, but it is also not the whole of life. It is to be put in its place, and its place is in the midst of things.

In the following essays I have tried to cross over the boundaries of my "profession" to address some real issues and real people in plain language. Most of the essays were originally published in newspapers and popular magazines rather than professional journals. Perhaps many of the essays and their subjects do not count as philosophy at all, but in stolen paraphrase of any number of nineteenth-century artists and twentieth-century hacks, since I'm a philosopher it must be philosophy. My aim is to make philosophy accessible to everyone, so that all can enjoy a certain kind of reflection, intended to provoke argument and intimacy as well as understanding.

The topics included range from particular philosophers and large questions about religion, society, and ethics to very personal questions about sex, love, and emotion. As I look back over my twenty-odd years in this subject, and the years before that as well, I find two recurring themes. The first is the neglected importance of emotions in philosophy and the general contempt for what is called "sentimentality," not only among intellectuals but in "civil" society generally. Many of the following essays, accordingly, have to do with the emotions and the "appetites" rather than the more hallowed philosophical faculty of rationality. It is in and through our emotions and our desires, not just in the dispassionate discourses of reason, that our best and most powerful ideas emerge. The second is the importance of pluralism and the need for mutual dialogue and tolerance instead of the dogmatism and intellectual imperialism that has so long ruled our history as well as our thought. I have always been bothered by the extreme provincialism that defines modern philosophy—even if in the name of human reason—and I am increasingly aware of the need to embrace the philosophies of the world, if only to provoke our own humility. The two themes come together in a continuing attack on a particularly abstract and arrogant conception of "human nature," and that is, perhaps, why I am so concerned about the small things in life and so cavalier toward some of the more "profound" questions of philosophy. The following essays are intentionally polemical but, I hope, never pedantic. After all, I am writing for people and about the subject I love. If you get bogged down, please move on to another essay. Above all, I have tried to be entertaining, for entertaining ideas is what philosophy is all about.

Part One

On Philosophy

1

A Plea for Philosophy

In the Fall of 1806, in the college town of Jena in what we now call Germany, a young professor named Hegel and his students were getting ready for classes. He was finishing a book; they were doing, well, what students usually do the last few weeks of summer—drinking a lot of beer, catching the last glimpses of the summer sun, separating themselves from what seemed to be a promising September romance.

But that year the university would not open. Napoleon's troops were already near the city, and you could hear the cannonade from the steps of the university library. And yet the shared sense of both professor and students was exuberance and excitement; any anxiety they felt was more than compensated by the expectation of a new and better world.

By way of contrast, I asked my own students at the University of Texas how they would characterize their own times. The answers were less than inspiring. The word that appeared most often was "dull," although words such as "crisis" and "apocalypse" punctuated every other sentence. True, it was a cold, gray day, which is always emotionally disastrous in normally sunny Austin, but the tenor of those answers, in contrast to the nineteenth-century exuberance we had just been reading about, was alarming.

Consider, I suggested, the modern analog to Hegel and his students' situation: A foreign army perched on the borders of Texas, perhaps already

Variations of this piece appeared in *The Los Angeles Times* on July 8, 1979, and in *The Austin American-Statesman* in 1980, © Austin American-Statesman. It is reprinted here in edited form by permission of the publishers.

spilling over the plains of West Texas; the world as we know it is about
to come to an end, to be replaced by who knows what. In those circumstances
Hegel and his students felt what can only be called inspired, if also qualified,
cheerfulness.

But in a period of relative calm and still unmatched prosperity, my
students could only express despair, "the absurdity of life" several of them
called it. Their reasons? Dollar-a-gallon gasoline and the prospect of a less
than exciting career.

They agreed, of course, that such is not the stuff of tragedy, even
throwing in the Ayatollah and the prospect of a Reagan presidency. But
what was the difference? What did those Germans have 175 years ago
that we do not that allowed them to face the destruction of society and
their own careers with an attitude of hope and confidence in what was
then so innocently thought to be "the perfectability of humanity"?

What Hegel had was philosophy, and so did his students. They flocked
to his classes not because he was a dynamic lecturer (he was tedious, at
best), but because he had *ideas*. Ideas give our lives perspective. Ideas define
our place in the universe, our relation to other people, allow us to see
through the habits and expectations of everyday life to the substance of
life itself and its meaning. Our minds need ideas the way our bodies need
food, some larger sense of order and purpose that the routines of job and
family and recreation cannot give us. We are starved for visions, hungry
for ideas.

What is ironic, of course, is that we are *the* society of ideas. Our
nation is built on ideas, in the Declaration of Independence, the Constitution,
and in our perennial confidence in the importance of free speech and debate.
On a lesser level, we now find our bookstores stocked with philosophies,
the soothing platitudes of the New Age, and the religion of self-realization.
Our teenagers join cults not just to find friendships, but to gain a vision
and a sense of meaningfulness they have not found at home or in school.
We parrot ideas that are two hundred years old, but we've forgotten how
to think about them. Much of the sense of free speech that many people
feel is based on the ultimately cynical view that ideas, after all, are nothing
to worry about.

We pretend that we are a practical nation, without the need of philosophy. "But you'll never be practical without it," wrote G. K. Chesterton,
in response to a "practical" man of his own generation. "The decline of
speculative thinking betrays an inherent weakness in a society," wrote the
great philosopher Alfred North Whitehead, but he was not just tooting
his own professional horn. It is true that ideas, as well as the bread-and-
butter issues of history, are what move nations, and lack of ideas sometimes

destroys them. We need once again in this country what Walter Lippman called a *public* philosophy, which does not mean a singular viewpoint but rather a shared sense of debate and enthusiasm.

The problem is not that people today are incapable of critical thinking. Most of the Texas students I meet are cynical about almost everything anyway. But this is most of all true of those students who are searching desperately for meanings, whether through religion or Marxism, who adopt simple slogans in place of real ideas, encouraged to do so by the whole of a culture for whom any declaration of more than a jingle or a bumper sticker is considered tedious, and any concern that doesn't promise virtually instant gratification is considered pointless. And so our children join the cults, leap to conclusions, and turn to the Mickey Marxists of the radical left and the "looking out for number one" ideologies of the right. Who can blame them? What are we providing as alternatives?

At a time when legislators are casting a wary glance at universities, and deans are desperately promising anything short of miracles in defense of "the liberal arts," the argument is, in fact, extremely simple: *Ideas give life meaning.* They provide perspective and purpose and see through the phony obsessions of an overconsuming, status-conscious, and appearance-minded society. In these days of relative scarcity, we can't promise our students the jobs they all want; we can't quick-fix the economy or force better programming onto the television networks. But we can give them ideas and a broader point of view, a kind of satisfaction with life that mere acquisition and success alone cannot provide. Ideas don't cheapen with inflation, they don't cause cancer, and they can't be taxed. They require no large monthly payments and neither rust nor break down nor lose their value before they're paid for. Sam Keen has often said that you can't get enough of what you never wanted in the first place. There is so much of what we really do not need and do not want, and what we need, when we come right down to it, are a few good ideas.

2

Becoming a Philosopher

In the Fall of 1963, I was a medical student at the University of Michigan, Ann Arbor, bored to tears with the tedious memorization, disturbed by the hospital wards, and unmoved (unlike my classmates) by the promise of a vast and well-deserved income later on. Across campus, a young philosophy professor was making waves and a nationwide reputation (even a profile in *Esquire* magazine). His name was Frithjof Bergmann, and his "Philosophy in Literature" course (Philos. 412) was something of a campus phenomenon. A young woman I knew suggested to me that I attend the class, which not so inconveniently conflicted with my Gross Anatomy lectures. (The information was all in the book or in the cadaver, so the lectures were superfluous.) I did not need persuasion, and I became (silently, in the back) a regular auditor in the class. (I also got a B+ in Anatomy, in case it matters.)

It was already the end of November, and the world was in turmoil. John Kennedy, who had not long ago appeared on the steps of the Michigan Union to announce the formation of the Peace Corps and for whom I had campaigned in college, had been murdered in some city I had hardly heard of in an Edna Ferber state known mainly for oil, nuts, and cowboys. Twelve thousand miles away United States Marine "advisors" were getting increasingly bogged down in an undeclared war whose seriousness I was

From *In Love with the Love of Wisdom: On Becoming a Philosopher*, edited by Robert Shoemaker and David Karnos (New York: Oxford University Press, 1992). © 1990 by Robert C. Solomon.

just beginning to appreciate. And I was plodding through my chosen "career" in cardiology as if I were walking into a black hole. It was about that time in the semester, too, when Frithjof (then "Professor Bergmann") was warming up to one of his favorites, a German exile and eccentric named "Nietzsche." I remember reading *On the Genealogy of Morals* in particular with the (now familiar) feeling that I was participating in some very special, very private, very personal liberation. This had none of the immediate consequences often promoted by Nietzsche's detractors. I attempted to break no moral or social taboos and desecrated no churches. Neither my dating behavior nor my attitude toward the law significantly altered. What did change, and I think it was "once and for all," was my sense of enthusiasm about my own life. During a period of profound personal unhappiness, national confusion, and international intrigue, I nevertheless felt "clarified."

It was early December when the lectures on Nietzsche reached what (in retrospect) were their climax in the idea of "eternal recurrence": the wild notion that everything that has happened, including the whole of one's own life, has happened innumerable times before and would happen indefinitely many times again. (In Gross Anatomy they had just reached the hips—it was a full year course.) As a lifelong science student, I found the physical hypothesis of recurrence nothing less than laughable, but the *moral* impact was an entirely different matter. Bergmann emphasized and dramatized the implications of that "terrible thought" so persuasively that my memory of that particular class is a brilliant blur, much like the memory of a most wonderful romantic evening or, I suppose, a true believer's memory of the moment of conversion. Bergmann was going on about the idea of repeating the days and hours and minutes of one's life, this very minute in particular, over and over again, quoting Nietzsche's demon, "would you not throw yourself down and gnash your teeth, and curse the demon that spoke so? Or have you once experienced a tremendous moment in which you would answer: 'You are a god and never did I hear anything so divine!' "

I thought about this moment itself, already so recursive and convoluted as I thought of myself thinking this thought about thinking this thought about thinking this thought forever, but I have never been all that fascinated by the self-referential paradoxes that fascinate so many of my colleagues. I did wonder, for just a moment, whether Nietzsche thought about the eternal repetition of his own aphorism. But what I mainly thought—or rather, what thought overwhelmed me—was that the scope and enthusiasm of this very moment was such that I would gladly have answered the demon (who still speaks with Frithjof's voice to me), "Yes! I'll take this recurrence!" I remembered, however, that not just this wonderful moment but all of my moments, including the histology lab at 7:30 that morning and the physiology lecture to follow, would be repeated a virtually infinite number of times. I spent the rest of the lecture dwelling on that awful hypothesis, and at 3:00 that afternoon I walked into the dean's office in the medical school and resigned. (By missing the second half of anatomy, I never did find out what's below the hips.)

There is currently a scholarly dispute in Nietzsche circles, in which the very notion that Nietzsche intended to change lives has been thrown open to question. He is depicted as something of a proto-deconstructionist, an end-of-the-line metaphysician, an isolated writer who sought to create for himself a persona, an "author" who would be as noble, exciting, even dangerous, as the sickly, lonely writer was not. Bernd Magnus has rescinded his old defense of "Nietzsche's Existential Imperative" with eternal recurrence as its core, now insisting that eternal recurrence is an "impossible" thought, and Alexander Nehamas has argued with great flair that Nietzsche did not intend to give "moral advice" or tell us "how to live." These are two dear friends but I must say (as I have often said) that they are, in my own experience, just plain wrong. It is true that Nietzsche does not tell us to be kind to strangers or to join the military or to quit medical school, but he does something far more powerful and effective, as the best philosophers always do. He throws us back into ourselves (and into our times, too) and teaches us to "see" a whole new way, or many ways. His philosophy is not that delight in the logic of counterfactuals and self-referential paradoxes that draws us away from our lives but rather that uncompromising reflection that is always personal and, if the word makes sense in this context, practical. It concerns hard decisions, one's place in history, and the construction of a self one can be proud of. It is not just a game or—worse—a career. It is an invitation to live, and if the form of the invitation is often vacuous ("Become who you are") its meaning is not. I understood that before I became a "scholar," when I walked into that dean's office and (fifteen minutes later) marched over to the dean of Arts and Sciences and announced my intention of becoming a philosopher. I hope that my attempts to be scholarly never allow me to lose the awareness that, even when what I say is vacuous, I may well be changing lives, including my own.

Of course, no "existential" decision happens in a vacuum. I had always been a brooder, a talker. I loved to argue, to push the perverse sides of an argument, to imagine new worlds and convince my playmates that they were or could be "true." I could talk my way out of—or into—almost anything. (As a diminutive juvenile gang leader in elementary school, I earned the street name, "the mouth.") Now that I look back on the narrative of my life, I can easily construct an almost linear path from birth to philosophy, expressed for many years through my fascination with science and only briefly sidetracked by a deviation through misplaced professionalism. (Of course, in medical school I had an equally plausible narrative about having always wanted to be a doctor.) In high school I had had a similarly euphoric philosophical moment, during a lecture on Parmenides and Heraclitus, given by a history teacher, Robert Hanson (whom I've never succeeded in tracking down). I later had another such experience (this one aided by a now-controlled substance) in which I comprehended—"embraced" would be a better word—the previously incomprehensible thought of Hegel. My life, in this construction, has been punctuated with philosophy, coupled with the meta-thought that it all could have gone another way. The narrative may be imaginary but it is not fictitious, and I now have a great deal of difficulty thinking of myself as anything but a philosopher. And I can honestly say, I have never once regretted it.

3

A Pronoun Is a Small World

Encyclopedists and dictionary makers earn their living with the more cumbersome and impressive words in the language, but our most important words turn out to be the smallest, short sounds with no distinctive substance. Great works of metaphysics turn on such words as "if," "all," "not," and, of course, "to be." British philosopher Bertrand Russell once wrote one of his most influential essays on the word "the," and with Alfred North Whitehead set the tone for the whole of twentieth-century Anglo-American philosophy with a treatise on "and," "or," "not," and "if-then." A recent German philosopher had no trouble filling 400 pages expounding on "as if." And the whole of modern thought might be argued to turn on the shortest word in the English language, "I."

Among the little words that define our language, however, the most powerful are the tiny words called personal pronouns. Verbal battles may be fought over such lofty concepts as freedom and democracy, but the great wars of history have almost all been fought over "mine" and "ours," as well as "us" and "them." Pronouns as such don't have meanings; they betray a perspective; they reflect a position. They distinguish "we" from "him," "her," and "them"; they point backward—"I." They distinguish the sexes as a matter of basic grammar and carve up the political world in a word or two. They define our psychology, whether the "I-you" of face-

This first appeared in the *Chicago Review* 29, No. 4 (Spring 1978), and in shortened form in *The Austin American-Statesman,* April 9, 1985, © Austin American-Statesman. It is reprinted here in expanded form by permission of the publishers.

to-face encounters, the "I-it" ("id-ego") of Freudian theory, the "me-he" of schizophrenia, the "they" of paranoia, the "we" of self-righteousness, or the "they" of anonymity (as in "they say that . . .").

Grammar books tell us, misleadingly, that pronouns act as short substitutes for names of people, places, and things. But the difference between "May I offer you a cigarette?" and "May Robert C. Solomon [referring to the speaker] offer Simone de Sartre [who is spoken to] a cigarette?" is not just a matter of convenience and brevity. Tolstoi on occasion uses the device of having characters so refer to themselves (as in "Prince V. is now going to eat his dinner," spoken by Prince V.) in order to show outrageous pretentiousness or incipient insanity. Personal pronouns are not substitutes for names; they are prior to them. A name is of no use to someone who cannot already distinguish "I" from "he." Learning one's name is not the beginning of self-consciousness; learning the meaning of "I" is, and the former presupposes the latter. (My dog knows his name, in some sense; I'm not so sure that he knows that it is *his* name.)

What is peculiar about the pronouns, the grammar books tell us, is the fact that they do not rigidly refer; they are not names as such. Their meaning shifts from context to context, speaker to speaker. If I say, "I am stronger than you are" and you say to me, "I am stronger than you are," we are not agreeing.

Anthropologists tell us of cultures that, for the lack of a pronoun, live a social life inconceivable to us. Some lack the personal pronoun "I." Calculating selfishness, accordingly, is unknown to them. They cannot even describe it. Some cultures lack the second person "you," referring to anyone of their group as "I" and anyone else as "he" or "it." Languages very close to ours lack the neuter gender (French, for example) that we find awkward when forced to sexualize objects which in English would be "it."

Indeed, our own grammatical rule, that mixed or indefinite genders should always employ the male gender ("if anyone is . . . , would he . . .") has rightly been under fire for its covert logical sexism, and it might well be said, as Christopher Lasch argued in his *Culture of Narcissism,* that our entire culture has placed too much emphasis on the "I," often contraposed against a too impersonal "them," to the neglect of the "we." Indeed, the starting point of modern philosophy, according to virtually every philosopher, is Descartes's famous dictum, "I think, therefore I am." But what if he was wrong?

Small grammatical distinctions make enormous metaphysical differences. Jules Feiffer has a classic cartoon in which a male braggart spends seven frames uttering "me, me, me," but yawns when his female companion bares her soul in a single "I." The personalities, the relationship, and much of "he-she" relations are dissected in two pronouns. The difference between "they" and "them" may mean the difference between a sense of victimization and a sense of disgust, a difference exploited, for instance, in Joyce Carol Oates's novel on bigotry, titled *Them*. The tone and the impact of a book may wholly depend on the author's choice of dominant pronouns, "I" or "we" or "he" or "she," far more than the choice of plot and actual characters.

The pun from "I" to "eye" in English is revealing; an eye sees, but rarely sees itself. So too, it is the I that sees, but rarely sees itself as I. And yet we assume so readily that every "I" is the center of a universe, the core of the individual, when in fact the "I" is no more an essential part of our world than the artist is part of the paint or the camera part of the photograph. Indeed, when we do look at ourselves, we are much more likely to find a "he" or a "she" or part of a "we" than an "I." In fact, when philosophers have looked for Descartes's famous "I," they discovered that it doesn't exist. Instead we create it with a word.

Academics systematically delete the "I" from their studies, preferring "we" (thus shifting the blame) or even "it" (as in "it is the case that . . .") Who will stand up for what is said?

The whole language of science also deletes the "I" and concerns itself wholly with "it." But what would knowledge be like if (as some physicists have claimed) the "I" is ineliminable, and the "it," perhaps only an illusion?

What do Texans know that New Englanders do not, when they refer to their collected friends as "you-all"?

Why do we call some pronouns ("me," "him," "them") "accusative"?

Pronouns, not the more substantial words of our language, set up our world. We are overly impressed by encyclopedias, and accept too lightly the fact that dictionaries have little to say about the littlest words. Webster's might define "it" as "the neuter pronoun of the third person, used as a substitute for a neuter noun, as an indefinite nominative for an impersonal verb, and as a demonstrative." But we know better. What does it mean, for example, when, in certain children's games, we label each other "it"? But then, the dictionary itself is but an "it," and so it cannot have the authority to tell us, in its impersonal terms, what we mean by those very personal words with which we refer to ourselves.

4

Remembering Spinoza

In the current and apparently continuous wave of moral and religious hysteria, not to mention the brutal sectarian violence throughout the world today, it would be fit to celebrate—quietly—the birthday of one of Europe's greatest thinkers—Baruch (Benedictus de) Spinoza.

Spinoza is not one of those great names who changed history with a single idea, who inspired millions or made a discovery and later was remembered as the father of some new bomb or cure. He was not a hero, in any sense; he didn't ever really *do* anything, in the usual sense.

And yet, ever since he was "discovered" in Europe, almost a century after his death in 1677, he has moved and inspired thousands and thousands of individuals, most of whom learned about him by accident, browsing through some library.

What Spinoza did is what we all try to do from time to time; he tried to get his life in order, understand its significance, and rationalize his unhappiness. But unlike most of us today, he insisted on doing it all by himself, instead of accepting the ready-mixed prescriptions for piety combined with selfishness, which then, as now, were popular.

Consequently, he was thrown out of Amsterdam, the most "liberal" city in Europe. He was not burned or branded, like more spectacular religious martyrs. He was simply condemned to a life of loneliness.

From *The Los Angeles Times,* November 24, 1981, and reprinted in *The Houston Chronicle* and *The Jewish Exponent* on the same date. It is reprinted here in edited form by permission of the publisher.

Spinoza was born in 1632; his Jewish parents escaped the Spanish Inquisition by fleeing to Holland, in search of religious tolerance. The central point of Spinoza's philosophy, accordingly, was mutual toleration and understanding. He decried the attempts of every sect to declare itself the "true" religion, and he developed a conception of God that could be common to us all, from our own, quite different perspectives. The problem was, his God was not the prescription God.

Spinoza was one of those rare religious thinkers who believed that one could understand and give meaning to life without imposing one's particular beliefs on everyone else. It is a view that has never been fashionable, except in name. But this is not, as most critics complain, because people are "by nature" dogmatic or prejudiced or full of suspicion. The problem is that it is extremely difficult to believe that your own belief is not the true one, for to consider the alternatives of equal value seems at the same time to conclude that your belief is false. How can one have a firm, rationally justified belief, and yet accept differences and alternatives?

Spinoza insisted that God includes all of us and our beliefs, and asks of us only understanding. There are no privileged positions or perspectives, only the limitations of our personal outlooks and our lack of understanding. Suppose, Spinoza suggests, we imagine a worm, living in a corpuscle in the blood of the body of some great being; it sees its corpuscle as the whole of reality, and would insist, if asked, that this view was the "true" one. But now suppose we, too, are like that tiny worm, trying on occasion to see beyond our corpuscle, but most of the time living off the blood of our tiny corner of the universe, assuming that all the rest is—or should be—much the same. We can never observe the universe as such, but we, unlike the worm, can understand our small part in it and imagine its place in the whole.

Spinoza's philosophy, and his conception of God, ultimately comes down to just this: The cosmos is a single "substance," and this, nothing outside of the cosmos, is what we call "God." We are each part of God insofar as we are "modifications" of that one infinite substance. This means that what we call our individuality, our individual persons, are arbitrary distinctions, and insidious, for they make us think of ourselves as separate and opposed, instead of as a single cosmic unity. We confuse our individual perspectives for the truth, when the truth is nothing but the whole, God or the universe as such.

In Spinoza's time, as in our own, outright war was waging within and between religions, each making its claim to the Truth and attacking the heresy or stupidity of the others. Spinoza was devout but rejected orthodoxy, resulting in his expulsion from his own community. There may be many religions, he argued, but religion is ultimately one, embracing them all. Devotion is not partisan or sectarian but its very opposite, personal humility and an appreciation of a singular cosmic unity.

In Spinoza's time, as in our own, war was still waging between science and religion, each making its claim to the Truth and attacking the stupidity of the other. But Spinoza, who was as fascinated by the new science as he was devout, would have none of that: God and Nature are one as we are one, and science and religion are one and the same enterprise. Not surprisingly, Albert Einstein was an admirer of Spinoza.

The point of Spinoza's philosophy ultimately is that only with such a vision of unity can we have our beliefs and let others have theirs, confident that our understanding is a crucial part of the whole but at the same time humble in our recognition that others' convictions are crucial, too. We are all part of a single grand concern—Spinoza sometimes calls it "life"— and our differences and disagreements are not cause for antagonism or suspicion but rather the bonds of concern that draw us together.

On Spinoza's 350th birthday, that is a lesson still to be learned, and well worth remembering.

5

The Greatest Story Ever Told

It is the greatest story ever told. It is the story of evolution.

It is not just a theory, as its detractors insist. It is not simply a matter of fact, as its defenders have contended. It is a story—an undeniably true one, a narrative filled with life, death, surprises, mysteries, sex of every imaginable variety, and tragedy too overwhelming to comprehend.

It is far longer in its time and in its telling than any national or religious epic bound by human experience. It has far more variety of characters than any Middle Earth fantasy. And it has far more unity, coherence, and explicability than even the most carefully wrought narrative of tribes or nations.

It is a story that puts us in our proper earthly place—whether or not we are created in God's image. It explains who we are and why we are as we are, in the humbling context of millions of strange and noble beasts that survived hundreds of millions of years longer than we have (so far) and are now inexplicably extinct.

"I think its a helluva lot more important to ask why they were so successful," remarked paleontologist Jack Horner when the *Wall Street Journal* asked yet one more time why the dinosaurs, which occupied a chapter of 140 million years, became extinct.

What is most exciting about the story of evolution is the fact that it is unfinished, both in its telling and in its telos, or "end." Where the

First appeared on Christmas Day, 1983, in *The Los Angeles Times*. Reprinted here in edited form by permission of the publisher.

end of history is concerned, we have only speculation and faith—and more fanciful stories. But where the telling is concerned, there is a mind-boggling challenge for all of us. Few of us have the patience to join Jack Horner hunting for dinosaur nests on the rocks of Montana, but all of us can share the thrill of his and his colleagues' revisions—the suggestion that the dinosaurs were warmblooded and intelligent, for example.

Like the very best stories, the story of evolution forces us to look for ever more detail. It encourages us to make discoveries. It promises us new revelations. It makes us think and wonder every time we trundle through the mysterious landscape that we call "nature"—*how is all of this possible?*

The story of evolution, as everyone knows, was told—but certainly not "made up"—in its classic formulation by Charles Darwin in his *Origin of Species,* just over a hundred years ago. What tends to be forgotten is that the hierarchy of nature was already well established in philosophy by Aristotle and in religion by Genesis. However much one may make of the historically explosive but conceptually artificial debate between the Judeo-Christian creation story and modern biology, the latter probably could never have existed but for the former.

Darwin is classic, but not gospel. Much of what he suggested about "natural selection" has been revised. The phrase "survival of the fittest" has been put aside as trivial. (What is fittest, after all, is what survives.) Stephen Jay Gould of Harvard has replaced the smooth Darwinian scale of evolution (with its occasional "missing links") with a discontinuous and more erratic picture, less consonant with our desire for simplicity but more in tune with our sense of storytelling.

It is worth reminding ourselves that Darwin and most of his colleagues called themselves "natural philosophers," which they generally interpreted as the task of appreciating and understanding God's handiwork in nature. They did not reject Genesis so much as they considered it inadequate in detail. (In what order, and how, for example, did God create the animals on the "day" that was allotted for them?)

If Genesis fails to satisfy us, it is not because it could not be true, nor because of its demands on faith. Rather, it gives us only an outline, lacking in development and detail. It can be appreciated best not with more faith but with the theory of evolution. It is in its *in*completeness that the story of evolution is most exciting, in the demands on our intelligence and our imagination.

"Nature does nothing without purpose" declared the proto-evolutionists Immanuel Kant and Johann Goethe, pious philosopher and poet, respectively. "God does not play dice with the universe," insisted Einstein more recently. Piety and science are not opposed, except in politics. "Natural philosophy" is a religion readily available to all of us, and it is, of necessity, part and parcel of every religion of the earth.

When I was a child, I knew the names of the greatest of reptiles. I could draw them and mold them out of clay. I would imagine myself back in their times, and before, trying to conceive of the beginning of time. My head would spin, a not unpleasant feeling even then. It was a sense of the earth that I try to retain to this day, with that awesome greatness, smallness and tragedy, fragility and humility. At that time in my life it never would have occurred to me that such an awesome, even religious, sense of excitement was not only incompatible with but blasphemous to my faith—though, granted, my sophistication in theological matters was quite limited.

The quarrel over evolution is not a battle of religion against science. It is a battle of ignorance against intelligence. It is possible to believe— even literally—in Genesis and still be awed and curious about God's ways on earth. It is also possible to believe in nothing and yet have the mind of a fungus, devoid of awe and curiosity and interested only in the next acquisition. On one side are those who know not and do not care to know; on the other are those who, even if their own knowledge is modest, know the outline of the story and care very much that the knowledge is there, for their children and for a world that we are desperately trying to make more intelligent and world-aware.

We live and learn in stories, and it is in the richness of our stories that we enrich our lives. The tale begun in Genesis (and earlier) lives on in the rich legacy of Darwin. To think that only the earliest and most primitive version of that story is uniquely true is not to express one's religious convictions; it is, rather, to deny God's own works. However one conceives of God, the epic of the works themselves should not be denied— or distorted—for any of his children.

6

Connections to the World

Arthur Danto is one of the most eloquent philosophers of our time. He is a thinker of magnificent scope and expanse, transcending not only the tired boundaries of "schools" and "methods" in philosophy but the administrative walls that separate disciplines and divide intellectual and cultural sensibilities as well. He is a "renaissance" thinker who has written widely in almost every field of philosophy and, today, he is one of the leading art critics in the country. Years ago, he wrote important and influential books on epistemology, action theory, and the philosophy of history. In 1963, he published a timely book on Nietzsche "as philosopher," initiating much of the serious study that now makes up the continuing flow of high-quality Nietzsche literature. Danto wrote the book on Jean-Paul Sartre for Frank Kermode's now classic "Modern Masters" series, and he has also written a small book on Indian philosophy. A talented print-maker in New York before he became a professional philosopher, Danto continues to write some of the best and certainly most philosophical art criticism and theory in recent American memory (in three books and the *Nation* as well as elsewhere). He is, perhaps, the best we have—a systematic philosopher in an analytic world where, all too often, no problem is too insignificant or isolated; a lover of language both clear and eloquent in an academy where obscurantism substitutes for understanding and passes

This review of Arthur Danto's *Connections to the World* (Harper and Row, 1989) appeared in *Teaching Philosophy* 12, No. 4 (December 1989): 420–23. Reprinted here in edited form by permission of the publisher.

all too easily for profundity; a philosophical enthusiast in a field that increasingly finds itself bemoaning its uselessness and diagnosing its own pathology.

The appearance of a new book by Arthur Danto aspiring to take in the whole of philosophy is, accordingly, a reason for celebration. True to expectations, *Connections to the World* is an enthusiastic, original, clearly and elegantly written book on "the basic concepts of philosophy." It takes an "elevated position" above the "jungle" of lurking logical dangers, preferring "the thrill of wide horizons" to the "short vistas" that make up so much of the field. Indeed, Danto does cover an enormous amount of territory, including such familiar landmarks as Plato's *Republic,* Descartes's "I think, therefore I am," the ontological argument for God's existence, and Wittgenstein's theory of language. But Danto tells us that he is after philosophy "in its entirety," and as such, I think, *Connections* gives us a surprisingly impoverished view of the subject from one of our richest philosophers.

In a telling mix of metaphors, Danto tells us that philosophy, which must "explain the world as a whole," is nevertheless "singular," its basic concepts are "few and fundamental" and the whole subject, accordingly, can be put in a "nutshell." In his discussion of philosophy as a sequence of perpetual beginnings, he leaves no doubt that the entire subject is inevitably tedious, a "cloying sameness," and he compares the seeming multitude of philosophical positions to the Hindu exhaustion with life after many reincarnations. Indeed, this deep skepticism about the usefulness of philosophy in human affairs begins with Danto's opening, fascinating but philosophically depressing (rather Nietzschean) account of cognition as essentially a biological process in which consciousness (much less philosophical reflection) plays virtually no role whatsoever. Discussing Descartes, he comments once again that the "role and place of philosophy is obscure" (p. 147) and this attitude permeates the book. Danto's obvious enthusiasm for philosophy runs strangely counter to his deep reservations about its relevance.

And yet, here is a philosopher who writes philosophically about the battlefield at Gettysburg and the art of Frank Stella, and his book does not contain even a section on art, or for that matter politics or society or religion or ethics. When Danto allows himself an artistic example— e.g., Duchamp's "ready-mades" as an example of "indiscriminables" or his wonderful one-line analysis of the Robert Motherwell painting on his own cover, his prose visibly twinkles with excitement. The other topic that seems to excite his best sensitivity is his dogs. In one charming passage, he notes that dogs should be disciplined immediately because they have such short memories, and any delay will provoke in them a keen sense of injustice. In the final passage of the book, he mentions what Hegel fittingly called the "realm of spirit," "the domain of politics, law, morality, religion, art, culture and philosophy itself." But, Danto tells us, "the bulk of philosophical reflection has not crossed this boundary . . . [it is] dark and difficult *terra incognita* so far as philosophical understanding is concerned, though . . . so far as human understanding is concerned [it is] the most familiar territory of all. It is in the realm of spirit that we exist as human beings" (p. 274). Why is this not philosophy, if not philosophy "in its entirety"? What about Plato and Aristotle, we feel compelled to ask? What about Hegel himself? What about . . . Arthur Danto?

Connections to the World is a rather drastic revision ("grew out of") an older, shorter book, *What Philosophy Is,* published over twenty years ago (1968). Such revisions are always fraught with dangers, especially for a creative thinker who has the great virtue of being able to pick him- or herself up by his or her own bootstraps and rethink everything. There is good reason why Wittgenstein (who declared his early work "definitive") did not try to rewrite the *Tractatus* after he had given up its basic premises, and there are similarly good reasons why Heidegger and Sartre never completed the projected second volumes of their early master works, *Sein und Zeit* and *L'etre et le neant.* Danto's own history is particularly instructive here, for what lies behind *Connections to the World* is indeed something like a Wittgensteinian attempt to rewrite the *Tractatus* in the light of a wholesale change of mind. Arthur Danto was once himself very much an "atomist," a traditional analytical philosopher who believed in foundations and analysis; his epistemology and action books are very much in this tradition. That tradition also involved a rather sharp and not very tolerant distinction between what was philosophy and what was not, and the artist Danto and the philosopher Danto kept pretty much to their mutual "realms." *What Philosophy Is* was a product of that atomistic period, and its structure reflects that limited view of philosophy, or what Richard Rorty now refers to disdainfully as "*Philosophy*" (with a capital "p"). Danto's own conversion from atomism came, appropriately, upon confronting Andy Warhol's *Campbell Soup Cans,* when he realized that the differences between art and plain soup cans—and similarly the problems of philosophy—could not be resolved through any analysis of differences. At that point, Danto became what I would call a neo-Hegelian, a holist for whom context is essential, including not only social and political context but personality as well (e.g., in some of his recent writings on Picasso). Following his conversion, Danto's more recent books and, especially, his criticism in the *Nation,* have become infinitely richer and more expansive. He has left behind "*Philosophy*" and *What Philosophy Is* for "the realm of spirit," and this is where he will make his lasting mark as a philosopher.

In a *Nation* essay (8/21/89), Danto wrote that "it is healthy for art to vacate the position of pure aestheticism in which conservative critics seek to imprison it, and to try to affect the way viewers respond to the most meaningful matters of their lives." So, too, I would argue, with philosophy. So, too.

7

Reaching Out—to World Philosophy

As everyone who has recently set foot in a university or read the editorials of our more cosmopolitan newspapers knows, there is a vigorous attempt in academia to combat the ethnocentrism of the traditional ("male, white European") college curriculum and the implicit chauvinism (if not racism) it represents. In philosophy in particular, it has been all but mandated that as a field of study it should become increasingly conscious of and attentive to other philosophical traditions. Even a casual review of the standard course offerings and dissertation topics demonstrates an embarrassing one-dimensionality, stretching through time from Socrates to Sartre or Quine with nary a mention of Confucius or Narajuna. There is no mention of African philosophy or any African philosopher (except Augustine, whose origins are conveniently ignored), and no Latin American philosophy. No matter what one's position on the politically hot if not explosive topic of "multiculturalism," it must be admitted that the demand for global sensitivity in philosophy is healthy for a subject that has indeed become overly narrow, insulated from other disciplines, and in many quarters oblivious even to its own culture as well as to others.

This piece was written as a review of two recent books on "world philosophy" by Schlomo Biderman and Ben-Ami Sharfstein (eds.), *Rationality in Question: On Eastern and Western Views of Rationality* (E. J. Brill) and David A. Dilworth, *Philosophy in World Perspective: A Comparative Hermeneutic of the Major Theories* (Yale University Press) for *Philosophy East & West,* Fall, 1991. It grew to become the introduction to a book on World Philosophy for McGraw-Hill Book Company. Reprinted with the permission of *Philosophy East & West.*

Coming to appreciate those other cultures and their philosophies is hampered, however, by the very narrow strictures on what deserves the honorific name of "philosophy." For example, the current emphasis on argumentation—often summarized as "rationality"—as the essence of philosophy excludes much of the more poetic and nondisputational wisdom of "non-Western" cultures, and even gives rise to the remarkable suggestion that these cultures are therefore "non-" or "pre-rational." In the East and in the South, the ideas by which people guide their lives are often expressed in song, slogan, and poetry, not disputational prose. But poetry has been banned from philosophy since Plato. In many cultures, philosophy places an overwhelming emphasis on ethics and religion, often expressed in myth and allegory. It is therefore dismissed as philosophy not only because ethics and religion have themselves been relegated to second place since the onset of the obsession with epistemology that began with Descartes and "the New Science," but because myth and allegory have themselves (except for a few canonized examples in Plato) have also been declared to have no role in philosophy. The obsession with logical argumentation and epistemology reached its zenith only recently, with the logical positivists in the era of World War II, when virtually every concern of substance was dismissed as "meaningless." That terrible war may have been global but the philosophy it produced became even more isolated and provincial. Indeed, as recently as last year (1989), one of our best and most broadminded philosophers could write that philosophy has emerged in only two cultures in the history of the world, on the rocky seasides of ancient Greece and in the mountains of India. ("Philosophy has really arisen only twice in the history of civilization, once in Greece and once in India"—Arthur Danto, *Connections to the World* [p. 14].)

Philosophy has been studied, of course, by students from around the globe, but a great many of those graduating philosophers and philosophy teachers who learned their trade in the pubs and tutorials of Oxbridge returned to their native cultures and taught, in essence, the same one-dimensional British philosophy, especially the supposedly "neutral" philosophy of logical positivism, along with those few foreign figures and currents that had insinuated themselves into the British curriculum (Descartes, a few eighteenth- and nineteenth-century Germans and, of course, the ancient Greeks and Romans). Local philosophies may have affected the course of instruction in quaint ways, but most culturally specific and significant ideas were dismissed as prerational, intellectually primitive, and unprofessional. Even Buddhism and Confucionism, with credentials as ancient as those of the pre-Socratics and of which we have far more substantial extant texts, have been excluded. And one still hears the claim, in not just a few of our "best" philosophy departments, that the discipline of philosophy is, as a matter of fact if not by way of tautology, that emaciated subject matter which as a matter of anthropological and sociological curiosity has emerged as the standard curriculum in most of our universities and colleges.

One obvious complication with the idea of cross-cultural philosophical education is that, in reading other philosophical traditions we are not only trying to understand other authors, other languages, other ideas. We are trying to embed ourselves in another culture, engage in another life. If Hegel was right, that philosophy is the spirit of its time (and place) rendered conceptually articulate, then understanding a philosophy is necessarily understanding the strains and structures of the culture it expresses and through which it is expressed. This raises deep questions about our ability to read such philosophy. It is not enough to know the language—one can readily enough learn Sanskrit, Swahili, or Chinese if one is sufficiently motivated—nor even to have something more than a tourist's view of the land, its peoples, and customs. One must, it seems, put oneself "in another's skin," to see "from the inside" a life that is as routine and unexceptional to others as our lives are to us, so defined as well as convenienced by technology, the notions of privacy, individual possessiveness, and the separation of the secular from the sacred. It is, therefore, not enough to show that early Indian philosophers developed an epistemology that displayed remarkable similarities to the British empiricists or that certain Buddhists had a concept of self that resembled some arguments in David Hume or Jean-Paul Sartre. In this sense one can grossly misunderstand a philosophy precisely by "understanding" it, that is, by embracing and absorbing a few ideas which seem familiar and ignoring the surrounding mysteries and the underlying structure that (for those who promulgated them) allowed them to make sense.

What we call "world philosophy" isn't a single discipline or way of thinking. It is not variations on a single set of themes, expressed and speculated upon now in an African way, now in a Latin way, now in an Arabic or Persian way, now in the Anglo-American way. (Indeed, what is that?) For the embarrassing fact long submerged in the tyrannical reign of the "history of philosophy"—that exclusionary artifice largely invented by Hegel to embrace all of European philosophy into a single narrative—is that what we call "Western" philosophy isn't really that at all. Even assuming one wants to include Greece in what we now call "the West" it is evident that much of the definitive influence on the great Greeks came from Asia Minor and the Orient, from northern Africa and the migrations of many tribes north and south, east and west. Judaism and Christianity were not, despite their now official designation as such, "Western" religions, nor was Islam, which produced some of the greatest Medieval philosophy. In addition to radical differences in philosophy and culture across the globe, we find almost everywhere we turn (except for a few, soon-to-be-destroyed, long-isolated rain forest or African bush peoples), confluences and influences, ideas swapped along with foodstuffs, satins, and spices (usually for free), amalgamated theories evolved from once-warring myths and ideologies, global philosophy as a long-cooking stew instead of a scattering of "centers" or a worldwide intellectual "human condition."

Of course, there is such a "condition": all people everywhere are born into families and communities; are vulnerable to cuts and burns; suffer pain and illness; and die. They have to eat and sleep; they fear for their lives, for their children, for a few favorite belongings. They have sex. They have parties. And more than occasionally, they think. But, of course, what they think and how they think, as well as what they do at parties, how they enjoy but also restrict their sex life, what they fear, how they suffer, and how they die are all born of sometimes widely different strategies. How do we understand these strategies? How do we put ourselves "into another's skin"? How do we break out of what most of us now believe to be a readily understandable but nevertheless no-longer-justifiable ethnocentric trap to get into another philosophy and another culture? One can always suggest the standard glib solution: Seek out similarities. Appreciate differences. But how does one do this without manufacturing the similarities and glossing over (or, just as bad, exaggerating and celebrating) the differences?

The first part of the answer is to give up the "interplanetary perspective" that is the aspiration of most global philosophers. Those high-flying observations allow clear vision of only those markings and ideas that are already expected or so generic that they are all but uninformative, like touring Paris, Nairobi, and Delhi from a Boeing 747. Nor can one expect to get wholly within other philosophical traditions. One will always be a tourist, at best, in a culture that he or she is merely visiting. What is wrong with much of the world philosophy and multicultural movement today is that it clings to the notion of *teaching* rather than *conversation:* where the former consists of one person or culture lecturing to (or at) another, the latter consists of questions and answers, anecdotes and personal stories, honest disagreements and arguments. Respect for another culture is not the same as uncritical acceptance. Whether the lecture or textbook in question is traditional "white male Western" philosophy routinely promulgating its ways in Oxbridge-type universities in Africa or Asia or the new demand for "equal time" so that Third World societies can lecture white American students on the virtues of alternative cultures and the horrors and guilt of oppression, the mistake remains the same. It is through dialogue and differences that the philosophies of other cultures will emerge, not through systematic exposition. Part of these conversations, of course, will be readings from the great texts of each culture and its past. These are not scriptures but influential voices. They can be disputed not only by foreigners who do not share that framework but by natives who do. Indeed, that is what philosophy ultimately comes to in any culture, not great texts or even great teaching so much as the will to disagree, to question, to seek understanding in place of mere acceptance.

Part Two

Reinventing Humanism

8

The End of Man

In Aristotle's Greece, to be Greek (preferably male, an aristocrat, and an amateur philosopher) was to be human. In Java, according to the anthropologist Clifford Geertz, "to be human is to be Javanese." We may think this objectionable, but at least it is straightforward. It is what I call "the transcendental pretense," the projection of one's own virtues as the defining characteristics of "humanity."

Today, we are far more subtle. We pretend to include everybody, but then proceed to define what is best about "being human" in terms of distinctively European, cosmopolitan, urban, middle-class, and usually male virtues, such as reason, a certain obsession for autonomy, a strong sense of right and wrong, self-control, emotional sublimation, and, most of all, a robust sense of confidence in human progress. Explicitly, this sense of progress may emphasize the wonders of modern science and technology but, you can be sure, there is ample implicit assurance that this material progress is a means to—if not proof of—a certain progress of the Human Spirit as well.

If there is such a phenomenon as human progress—not just the easily demonstrable improvement of gadgets, medical cures, and astronomical theories but the emergence of a moral superiority as well—then it turns out that most of the children of the "family of man" must be less than

This piece first appeared in the popular anthropology journal *Mankind* in June of 1981. It began as a review of Robert Nisbet's *History of the Idea of Progress* (Basic Books, 1980). © Robert C. Solomon.

wholly human, less than fully developed, why not say it—inferior—in certain respects, to those of us who can present the Diner's Club card in our own name. And we call this modern version of the transcendental pretense, this self-congratulatory sense of humanity and human progress, *humanism.*

Not surprisingly, even the most "enlightened" humanists—David Hume in the eighteenth century, for example—have tended to be racists, chauvinists, and sexists. (It was no mere accident of grammar that the authors of his time as well as ours wrote about "humanity" but preferred to shorten their titles to "man.") And today, the French humanist Jean-Paul Sartre has defined "being human" as "being historical," thus excluding whole societies as merely "proto-human." It is our duty, he argues, "to bring them into history," that is, to make them Marxists. Two hundred years ago, this destruction of other societies was called "the advance of civilization." But it is always, "in the name of humanity."

And yet, despite these abuses, humanism is the one philosophical outlook that seems to us above reproach, beyond investigation, just a homey nest of platitudes. It may even be, as David Ehrenfehl has argued, our most popular modern religion. Even those who now deny progress as such, lambasting technology and doubting the beneficence of science, tend to appeal to human potential and to our sense of spiritual development. The writing of human history (now called world history) has become, in effect, the history of history, and even those cynics who see in the past only "one damn thing after another" (in the eloquent phrase of John Masefield) insist that we can indeed *learn* from it, that is, improve ourselves and progress beyond it. To be a "progressive" in politics is to be on the winning side— at least eventually; to be a "humanist" in psychology, even if (especially if) one has nothing to say, marks one a hero against the "dehumanizing" alternatives of technological behaviorism. Who could be against humanity? And so who would be against humanism, except perhaps a handful of fanatical fundamentalists, who would push us "back" (not only in time) to the Middle Ages? When a writer needs an adjective, he or she can do no better than to add the word "human"—as in "human existence"—which seems to commit the author to nothing, but adds a warm glow of universal concern. But does it commit the author to nothing? When I thoughtlessly added the word "human" to the subtitle of a book on emotions a few years ago, it should have occurred to me that the addition was both false and fatuous. I was writing about the emotions of an ill-defined subculture in America, not about the emotions of Eskimos, Polynesians, or Mexican peasants, and *that* was how I came to appreciate the pervasiveness of the pretense.

Now, on the one hand, the concept "humanism" has been well used to attack and correct certain specific abuses in the past. The French and American revolutions, for example, would have been impossible without it. But one need not deny this to appreciate that the same concept in a different context can function dialectically to support some of the same abuses that it once attacked, e.g., the arrogance of thinking oneself superior and a patronizing imperialism toward those who are "less fortunate." Humanism has now become the religion it once warned us against.

It is the promise of progress, however, from Saint Simon to Sartre, that provides the selling point of humanism, its advertising slogans and its rewards. Philosophical wordplay has its limits, but if Christianity could sell a wholly incomprehensible version of universal humanity with its promise of eternal salvation, then humanism could use its purely secular sense of salvation to sell what seemed to provincial Europeans merely a matter of common sense, that all of the members of an easily identifiable biological species were basically the same everywhere, but only had to be "liberated" from ignorance and provincial cultural handicaps. The French philosopher Condorcet (executed during the more progressive years of the French Revolution) presented the sales pitch of secular salvation and humanism as well as anyone:

> How consoling for the philosopher who laments the errors, the crimes, the injustices which still pollute the earth and of which he is often the victim, is this view of the human race, emancipated from its shackles, released from the empire of fate and from that of the enemies of its progress, advancing with a firm and sure step along the path of truth, virtue and happiness.*

Robert Nisbet's *History of the Idea of Progress* is a scholar's book, the kind that deserves sympathetic reviews, the kind of project that once received federal grants. It has a clear and concrete topic, laid bare even in his title. He has a specific antagonist, namely, the philosophers of the "Enlightenment" and their modern disciples, such as J. B. Bury, who have long argued that the idea of progress is a peculiarly modern concept. And he has a simple theme, amply illustrated, namely, that the idea of progress is not a modern idea at all but has its origins in precisely that period most distained by the humanists, in the Medieval Christian conception of Providence, if not even earlier in the supposedly a-historical musings of the Greeks. He argues with considerable persuasiveness that the Christian

---

*Condorcet, *Sketch for a Historical Picture of the Progress of the Human Mind,* quoted from Solomon, *History and Human Nature* (Harcourt Brace Jovanovich, 1979), p. 27.

themes of the unity of the human race and the singularity of time are the presuppositions, not the antagonists, of our modern sense of both humanism and human progress.

In Christian theology, the superficial features of genealogy, culture, and race were considered secondary to the simple fact that to be human meant simply to have a soul, to be a candidate for salvation. Of course, there were debates from the sixteenth century until the nineteenth (though one still hears them now) over the putative souls of savages in America and Africa, but the metaphysical point was undebatable: if one had a soul, one was human. And not incidentally, one was thereby entitled to certain minimal rights. Humanity was but a single "race," rolling (if not exactly running) toward what Augustine called "the City of God," the spiritual goal of that race.

Politically, however, the point of progress and of humanism in general is the "homogeneity" of peoples, or what I have called the transcendental pretense. Nisbet describes the arrogance of this pretense without hesitation; for it is indeed a large part of the history of the idea:

> The point, rather, is the degree to which the faith in human progress became a means of assimilating all the non-Western peoples into a single progressive series reaching its apogee in Western civilization. Belief in progress and its premise of the unity of mankind, drawn from Christianity, made it possible to convert perceived heterogeneity into a conceptualized homogeneity; the homogeneity of a single, temporally ordered progression of all peoples in the world from the simplest to the most advanced—which, of course, to the people of Western Europe meant themselves.*

This disturbing picture of progress does not seem to disturb Professor Nisbet at all, however. For like most scholarly books, this one has a moral theme, an ideological rabbit that pops out only in the very last chapter. Nisbet is a defender of the faith. He is not only tracing the history of the idea of progress through virtually every thinker since Hesiod who might conceivably be mentioned in this context. He is manning the barricades, shoring up a historical lesson whose moral is, that what he calls the "dogma" of progress not only defines the whole history of "the West" but is necessary to our survival as well. Without it, we lose not only our sense of the future but our sense of the past.

Nisbet's moral rabbit turns out to be a familiar and, by now, quite tiresome bunny. For those who do not believe in progress, there is only

---

*Robert Nisbet, *The History of the Idea of Progress* (Basic Books, 1977).

decadence and disillusionment, the "malaise" from which we are currently suffering. He approvingly quotes von Hayek, another defender of the faith, who complains that "sophisticated" writers today hardly dare to even mention progress without quotation marks, that confidence in progress has now become a mark of "a shallow mind."

Nisbet does not quote Christopher Lasch, but he might as well, since he too gloomily writes about our "current disillusionment, retreat to self, and hedonistic materialism"—the only alternative to a sense of progress. In his chapter on the ancients, for example, Nisbet contrasts having "a vision of progress" with being "hopelessly enmired in a pessimism that could see nothing but decline and degradation in the passage of time," an absurd contrast that, needless to say, he uses in the end to characterize our own "modernist void."

Nisbet's view that the idea of progress is necessary requires a rereading of history, for it is only by showing that this idea pervades the whole of our history—rather than just the last two hundred years—that Nisbet can make his case that we'd be nowhere without it. After all, how can we hold onto our longstanding myth about ancient Athenian vitality if they didn't have the idea of progress, too? Thus Nisbet's argument against Bury is not just a difference of historical opinion. It is the groundwork for a long Hegelian windup whose conclusion is that those who reject the idea of progress are rejecting the very essence of human history.

Suppose that we accept Nisbet's thesis that progress was not the innovation of the Enlightenment as a weapon against the Medieval church but rather something of a perennial feature of "Western" thought, a religious dogma of sorts. (Perhaps this is the time to point out that the word "Western," like "humanity," conveniently excludes many of the people within those nominally geographic boundaries.) What this argument for the continuity of the Medieval Christian church and our modern sense of progress would seem to suggest, however, is not only the "nobility and vitality of the idea," as Nisbet continually reminds us, but a far less flattering and more political self-portrait.

Nisbet tells us that one of the premises of the idea of progress is the *superiority* of Western civilization. In fact, it is impossible to even state the idea without including the words "better" or "best," or some similar superlative of self-congratulation. But what is crucial to the argument for progress is that it is a *general* argument, an argument for all "humanity," what Nisbet calls a sense of "singular time," and what European philosophers since Bossuet have generally considered "universal history."

Given a suitably specific and narrow concern—for example, the development of more efficient energy machines or the increase in public literacy in Cuba—talk about progress is perfectly justified and unproblematic. But when the specific turns into the universal and becomes the thesis we all learned in high school—that there is but a single "humanity" and a single path of human progress, which we all share together despite the fact that some of us have done most of the work in blazing the path—the idea of progress becomes insidious. "Underdeveloped" continues to be our fashionable euphemism for humanist retardation, though once it was worse. What used to be "the advance of civilization" was the simple dismissal of whole peoples as inferior—barriers on the road to universal progress—to be removed in the name of "humanity." Thus "progress" presupposed this belligerently defined conception of "humanity," just as humanism was persuasively supported by the idea of progress.

Nisbet and most modern defenders of the faith in progress discuss and dismiss racism as if it were an unfortunate historical distortion, an abuse of the idea of progress rather than one of its essential features. But racism is built into the very idea of "progress," since any attempt to plot the progress of a single unified "humanity" on a single path is going to find that some peoples and cultures are further along and thus "better" than others. And if one takes the concept of progress as seriously as we are supposed to, this gives those who are further along certain self-declared rights and privileges, even if not abused and distorted. Thus Charles Darwin, whose views on evolution inevitably gave a new arsenal of weaponry to the defenders of progress, emerged quite aside from his supposedly descriptive role as biologist to promote the superiority of the Angle-Saxon race. Even the American Founding Fathers found no trouble using their humanism as a source of superiority, despite their explicit appeals to equality, encouraged as they were by European praise as "the hope of the human race" (the exact phrase is from Turgot, but one finds it, too, in Hegel, Goethe, and a hundred others).

The conceptual irony here is that humanism, which we have used for so many centuries to fight for equality in rights and respect for all peoples, can be and is now typically turned to precisely the opposite purpose. Humanism (and egalitarianism) now act as the *premise* for racism, since it is by placing all peoples before a single, inevitably biased but supposedly cross-cultural standard, that some can be judged superior, and others inferior.

Discussions of progress usually begin, as well they should, with examples of progress in the realm of science and technology, where improvements are easily quantified and proven. It used to take three months to get from Boston to Seattle, now it takes seven hours. People used to believe that the world was flat and stationary; we now know beyond a doubt that it is spherical and constantly in motion. It is easy to show that people in reasonably affluent societies now live longer, grow taller, eat better, and don't have to worry about dying of smallpox or syphilis. But there is something of a sleight of hand that follows these easy demonstrations, for throughout the argument for progress, there remains an always-present but only sometimes-stated premise, namely, that these easily quantifiable material and cognitive advances are not themselves the essence of progress but, at best, a means to or an indication of *real* human progress, namely, *spiritual* and *moral* progress.

Thus Nisbet rightly insists, though we might question the terminology, that progress is essentially a "Puritan" conception. Not just science and technology, not even comforts and happiness, provide the content of the idea of progress. But here the notions of "superiority" and things "getting better" start to become hopelessly muddled. The Greeks simply assumed that they were superior, defining this "superiority" in terms of their own virtues. But for us, the tradition traced and celebrated by this progress has universal and "objective" standards; thus the emphasis on science and technology and the slippery shift to the spiritual is essential to the argument. Symptomatically, Nisbet avoids giving us examples of such progress. (Perhaps the murder rates in our urban centers?)

Now science in a sense is defined in terms of progress: scientific explanation is the best account of a given phenomenon *so far*. Similarly, technology sets itself a problem to which the most satisfactory solution so far is, again by definition, progress. But when theorists try to use similar criteria in the arts, for instance, the results are embarrassing. Suzi Gablick, for example, in her *Progress in Art* inevitably restricts her argument to improvement in certain techniques of representation. And it is an argument that falters badly at the first confrontation with a pre-Columbian totem, a Kouros statue, an African mask, or a New Guinea shield. There are always those who have tried to quantify the quality of life, drawing the same vague causal connection between the tangible availability of necessities and comforts and the likelihood of happiness. But freedom from deprivation and disease is one thing, happiness another, and if we were to take a purely quantitative measure of unhappiness, we would surely find that the number of people starving and miserable in the world today far outnumbers their equally miserable counterparts in the past.

Even in science, it must be said, the now dominant argument is that progress there, too, appears only within a fairly restricted "paradigm" and that, within a larger arena, science, too, may have its limits. Thus Gunther Stent, in his *Coming of the Golden Age: A View of the End of Progress,* argues that confidence in science and technology as such is on the wane and has become subjected to the larger demands of culture. Nesbit insists on misinterpreting this view as the rejection of science as such. But even in those contexts within which science can be said without qualification to be progressing, the shift to the Puritan notion of progress—progress in the realm of the spirit—the argument contains far more sophistry than history. Worse still, it shifts the argument, usually without any warning, from the tangible "improvements" that progress can easily promise within a limited framework (e.g., better plumbing, more efficient farming methods) to that intangible sense of superiority that is, I have argued, what humanism and the history of the idea of progress are ultimately all about.

The slippery argument from tangible progress in science to the Puritan's progress has always had its critics. Jean-Jacques Rousseau made his initial reputation among the Enlightenment philosophers with his prize-winning essay in answer to the question "Has the restoration of the arts and sciences tended to purify morals?" Against the prevailing climate of opinion, Rousseau answered no, arguing that modern progress had corrupted if not maimed morality, and, he added, happiness as well. It is only recently that this argument has become widespread among intellectuals, a trend that Nisbet despises. But it is worth pointing out that the attack on the idea of progress is often made in the name of humanism, thus maintaining the pretense. Rousseau, for example, set the tone still followed by such scholars as Levi-Strauss, in appealing to some vague "original" or "natural" human qualities that have been corrupted by our own society. Thus W. R. Inge declared progress a "pernicious superstition" in 1920, and Austin Freeman about the same time declared what is now a platitude, that progress was indeed destructive, and that "even the primitive negro in Africa" is now the superior of "subhuman" Western man. But notice that it is still the same metaphor, except that "up" has changed to "down," "ascent" to "descent," with the same dogmatic assumption that there is such a thing as "human nature," common to all of us, and a singular sense of time. The difference is that, where once we used that argument as a source of extravagant, profound self-congratulation, we now tend to use it as a source of self-contempt. The one is as faulty as the other.

"The end of man" is a phrase that is now circulating in certain intellectual circles, due to the efforts in particular of Michel Foucault. It is a phrase that refers, with a certain unnecessary ominousness, to the end of a pretense, an end to the supposition that there is a single humanity, a single "universal history," a smooth chain of development that is anything more than our own retrospective fabrication. But the phrase also means, and until this century usually meant, the *purpose* of humanity, the goal of human progress. (Thus Hegel's almost always misunderstood pronouncements about the "end of human history," which referred not to a philosophical apocalypse but rather to a certain kind of fulfillment, namely, the ultimate success of humanism.) It is this sense of the end, this idea of progress and humanism itself, which must be brought to an end.

When this is suggested, it is always argued in objection that giving up humanism and the faith in progress will result in utter despair and disillusionment, as if, particularly in America, we cannot give up our presumptuously heroic role as "the hope of the human race" without ceasing to exist altogether. But giving up our sense of superiority does not entail accepting a sense of inferiority. Giving up a sense of progress may instead allow us to put our immediate goals and those of the world into focus.

9

The Awful Truth
(about "Secular Humanism")

Several years ago, I completed a study attacking "humanism," a doctrine that I found oddly bland and arrogant at the same time. It was bland because it affirmed what I thought no one could sensibly deny—that human beings and their well-being are important and worthy of respect. It was arrogant and even dangerous because it tended, in the name of this same "humanity," to ignore the spiritual significance of the earth and its nonhuman inhabitants and, even worse, to impose a single, often provincial standard of what it meant to be "human" on the broad variety of peoples and cultures around the planet.

How disconcerted I was to learn, then, not only that I am a "humanist" myself but that humanism is now a doctrine considered by some to be deeply offensive. To hear the Reverend Falwell tell it, for example, "secular humanism" is the enemy of religion. And to make things ever more confusing, Mobile's learned Judge Hand has recently declared that secular humanism is itself a religion, on the grounds that it is strongly believed by its adherents. This decision has been repeated by courts in the Midwest and is now dutifully repeated by a cadré of unthinking reporters. For the same reason, science has been often declared a religion, along with romance, communism, and football.

This was written at the height of the "Moral Majority" campaign against "secular humanism" in the early eighties and soon after the publication of my book *History and Human Nature,* in which I myself inveighed against "humanism." My more recent thanks to Gordon Gann of Kansas City for his good discussions of humanism.

Whatever the Founding Fathers intended in their insistence on the separation of church and state, they surely did not mean that no one in public service should have inordinate respect for human beings. But neither did they intend that religion should be put so on the defensive. The result is that both religion and humanism are getting a bad name. The truth, however, is that humanism is not the enemy of religion and it should not be defined, as it was by Judge Hand, as the view that "all values are human in their origin."

I think that we should set the record straight, and the historical record shows that humanism, far from constituting an attack on religion, is a movement which in its current forms originated within Christianity. It provided the values and the foundations of Protestantism as well as the anticlerical humanism that flourished in Western Europe during the "Enlightenment" of the eighteenth century. Humanism and religion have gone hand in hand, not without internal conflict, of course, but then, religion itself has not been without its internal conflicts either.

The values of humanism were not created by atheists and antichrists. They emerged over many centuries within the Judeo-Christian tradition. They are shared by believers and nonbelievers alike. Marxists and Christians both presuppose them in their most basic arguments. Humanist values form the foundation of Marx's criticism of capitalism and the Catholic bishops' recent scrutiny of the market economy. The claim that humanism creates values apart from and opposed to religion is simply wrong. It is the Judeo-Christian religious tradition that provides humanist values.

It is true that the eighteenth-century humanists attacked the Catholic Church (a target they now share with many of the groups who are most vocal about the evils of secular humanism). But most of the humanists were also religious. They emphasized the importance of individual faith but did not attack faith. They attacked "superstition," but not religion as such. Indeed, not even Voltaire, the most outspoken critic of the French Enlightenment, denied the existence of God. He despised the church that had turned belief into a matter of blind authority instead of human reason. And the German philosopher Immanuel Kant, probably the greatest single theorist of the Enlightenment, defended the basic beliefs of Christianity in the name of "reason" and "humanity." To think that secular humanism is opposed to religion is, again, just plain wrong.

Judge Hand said that secular humanists insist that all values are human in origin. Secular humanists would agree that they inherit many of their values from the Judeo-Christian tradition, so the disagreement is a theological one, whether or not they also believe in God. A secular humanist might well deny that our values come directly from God. But very few of us get our values "directly from God." We are taught them by our parents, peers, and teachers, who were taught them by their parents, peers, and teachers, and so on. Or one learns them from the Scriptures, a book slowly compiled by many voices and often translated between almost untranslatable languages. Except for those rare souls who receive their moral commandments directly from Heaven—and they tend, statistically, to deviate considerably from the Judeo-Christian norms—we learn our values from one another.

But, the antihumanist will argue, the ultimate origins of our values must be divine, even if, almost inevitably, we receive them second or fifth or ninety-ninth hand. Here, too, there is ample room for confusion, in that many of the most pious believers in history have felt quite strongly that the idea of God imposing laws upon us is antithetical to his gifts of freedom and reason. Others have argued that, whatever their origins, our most basic values are found in our genes, which were also created by God, say the faithful, or have evolved through history as the emergence of collective reason guided by God. It is clear that there are any number of accounts of our knowledge of right and wrong, all of which are quite compatible with both the belief that these are ultimately of divine origin, and that they are not.

Furthermore, there is some confusion between the idea that our values originate with God and the idea that our values are sanctioned by God through divine reward and punishment. The latter idea, it has often been charged, is a childish and degrading view of both humanity and morals, as if the only reason we do what is right is to earn a reward or avoid punishment. To insist that values have their origins in religion is quite different from the idea that good and evil are punished by a divine being. To insist that people have values only because they stand in fear of divine retribution is offensive. One does not have to be a secular humanist to believe that moral behavior is and must be self-motivated.

Secular humanism is the view that values concern human beings and their welfare. It is not a view about the origins of value and need not deny that values have divine origin. A humanist is one who believes in the worth and dignity of the human individual, wherever these values happened to come from. Whether or not they come from God, they find their warrant in human experience. And if they emerge as the crucial ingredients in the Judeo-Christian tradition, that says more about the importance of humanism than it says about the origins of the values themselves. Humanist values are the products of experience and reasonable thinking about values and the attempt of any community to live productively and amicably together; they may be part of our genetic inheritance from those of our ancestors who flourished and survived because their genes instructed them to be cooperative and competitive but not mutually self-destructive.

The question of values is quite distinct from such questions as whether or not one belongs to a church, believes in God, or sends hard-earned money to this or that television preacher. The values we all accept are shared by both theists and atheists, Christian fundamentalists and secular humanists. One may believe in a Supreme Being or not, but we all believe in compassion; love; honesty; generosity; courage; and faith in the worth, happiness, and dignity of the individual human being. The invention of "secular humanism" by the religious Right has contributed to a disastrous misunderstanding of religion, history, and humanism and has no place in the important debates about morals and religion in this country.

10

The End of the Enlightenment

"What is Enlightenment?" asked the philosopher Immanuel Kant, nearly two hundred years ago. His answer suited his profession: "dare to *know,*" he said, as if that insolent and revolutionary turmoil through which we still continue to identify ourselves might be summarized in a philosophy book. But if we were to answer Kant's question today, we should have to say that knowledge is not the defining characteristic of the age. And no less important, we should have to say that the Enlightenment, after nearly three centuries, seems to be over.

"Enlightenment": even the word is self-congratulatory. Those who were among the "enlightened" in France called themselves *philosophes* though many of them knew little of philosophy. They would illuminate the secrets of human existence, clarify the confusion called society, throw light on superstition, lead us out of the shadows of Plato's cave into the sunny realm of truth, and put an end to the "Dark Ages" that preceded them. "Pure insight will resolve the confusion of the world" wrote Hegel, at once an heir and critic of the movement. The *philosophes* declared themselves the spokesmen for all humanity (though some of them had rarely been beyond their *quartier* in Paris). They defended universal reason against the "prejudices" of those who opposed them. They promised a Golden Age, a "new world," though they were armed only with their own noisy

This article was originally written for the now-defunct *Saturday Review,* on the basis of my then just-released *History and Human Nature* (Harcourt Brace Jovanovich, 1979). © Robert C. Solomon.

cleverness and an unprecedented secular optimism tempered by a bitter impatience and cynicism regarding human stupidity in general (so obvious in Voltaire, for example).

The Enlightenment was a historical epoch. And historians, so easily transfixed by double zeroes, conveniently locate it in the eighteenth century, between 1700 and 1800, as if the curtain rang down right on time with Napoleon's rise to power in France. But the Enlightenment in England was in flower in 1650. The Enlightenment (or *Aufklärung*) in Germany did not begin until late in the next century. (Kant's essay on Enlightenment was written in 1784.) But most important perhaps is the span of the Enlightenment in the United States; it began in the eighteenth century, imported directly from England, and it is just now beginning to wane. And that, no doubt, is why it should be of such interest to us.

What Is Enlightenment?

Enlightenment is our creed, our ideology, so inseparable from the "American way of life" that it is difficult for American students to see it merely as a movement, a historical period, or an epoch. Rather, it seems to us to be simply the truth. Its principles are not bound by history or the contingencies of geography. Such concepts as "human rights" and "liberty" are not negotiable, not just cultural artifacts or notions of the historical moment. The Enlightenment may have discovered them, or at any rate given them renewed importance, but Enlightenment did not create them. They belong to humanity, not to a particular historical epoch.

Or, for those who have turned critical, Enlightenment is our ultimate myth, "the American dream." But truth or myth, it is Enlightenment that defines us, with its familiar language of "liberty" and "equality" and "inalienable human rights." It is the promise of a rational world—ruled by reason, common consensus, and debate—and "the pursuit of happiness" that inspires us.

And yet, quite the opposite of the "new world" and the "young country" we sometimes pretend to be, America is rather the world's oldest teenager, fixated in adolescence and an eighteenth-century ideology that is finally proving to be inappropriate. In Europe, the Enlightenment ended centuries ago, perhaps with the French Revolution—a date close enough to 1800 to keep the historians happy, but in any case by 1850. Much of what is usually considered to be the reaction against the Enlightenment can better be viewed, I would argue, as its continuation, including such "movements" as romanticism, Marxism, and existentialism. For these represent not so much countermovements as compensations, desperate and sometimes degenerate attempts to keep the main pretensions of Enlightenment alive in a world that had already proven them to be naive. History is the continuation of ideology by other means.

As much as we can learn anything from history, we can learn what happened to "our" ideology in the *in vivo* conditions of Europe, where the frontiers had disappeared long before and the myth of open-ended individual opportunity for everyone had only a fleeting plausibility. For these were the unspoken presuppositions of Enlightenment idealism, together with a sense of the "family of man," always difficult to keep in mind in the cultural conflicts of a too-small continent. But it is an ideal that stayed alive in America until a few years ago. By 1850, if not before, some of our present platitudes were already proven falsehoods in Europe.

How one defines the Enlightenment depends on one's intentions, of course. Peter Gay, for whom the Enlightenment provides something of a current ideal and a protection against fanaticism and fascism, defines it as "the spirit of criticism." Carl Becker, with far less sympathy, points to the continuity between the Middle Ages and "the heavenly city of the eighteenth-century philosophers." He concludes that the Enlightenment presented not so much a new world as a continuation of the old one. Critics from the Frankfurt School, who have long seen the dangers rather than the promises of the Enlightenment, tend to argue that the movement is characterized mainly by its rejection of authority and tradition. But, for the most part, the Enlightenment is defined by its luminous principles, in particular, its emphasis on reason, its humanism, and the principles that American school children are taught to recite and fight for.

Historically, however, I think the Enlightenment is best characterized as adolescence—our adolescence. The Eriksonian category is justified by the personality itself, so evident in every country as Enlightenment becomes dominant in public policy. Enlightenment is rebellion, aspiration, and idealism. It is not, contra Kant, so much daring to know as daring to question, to challenge, to argue. Thus it is both what Peter Gay called "the spirit of criticism" and what the critics call "the rejection of authority." But it is also relatively conservative, cautious, at times even reactionary. (David Hume, for example, was an unabashed conservative, even though he was generally acknowledged the "good uncle" of the philosophers, and Voltaire never moved from his belief in the monarchy, no matter how many seeds he may have sown for its destruction.) Like an adolescent trying to "find oneself," the Enlightenment combined rebellion and timidity, insecurity and arrogance, self-righteousness with defensiveness, sometimes even paranoia. (Both Voltaire and Rousseau come to mind, neither of them very hospitable characters.) Their politics were usually more reformist than revolutionary; "liberal" might be the best word for them. There was a lot more noise than action. And in Germany, where political conditions continued to be oppressive, the Enlightenment was almost wholly philosophical, devoid of political action except for some vicarious enthusiasm for the French Revolution, safely some distance away. Thus Kant's characterization of the Enlightenment wholly in terms of knowledge, although he was, from beginning to end, an enthusiast of the French Revolution.

Nuts and Bolts

As a philosopher, I'm tempted to see the structures and movements of history in ideological terms. Of course, it's one-sided, and more nuts-and-bolts historians are rightly disturbed by a theory of modern history that spends more time on a few passages in Kant and Hegel than the whole of the Napoleonic Wars, the Continental system, and the economic vicissitudes of a particularly traumatic period. So let me just say, rather flatly, that one of the preconditions of Enlightenment thinking is indeed a particular political-economic-social situation. The Enlightenment, whatever its own emphasis on "universal humanity" (or, in the sexist parlance of the age, "Man"), was a class movement, the movement of the "middle" classes or *bourgeoisie*. If today "middle class" and "bourgeois" are sometimes terms of abuse, indicating a kind of slovenly and self-righteous conservativism, it was quite the opposite two hundred years ago, when the middle class was the "new" class, vigorously battling for recognition against the entrenched aristocracy and its unearned privileges. And politically, it was not coincidental that the Enlightenment began to flourish in France, under a king (Louis XIV) who encouraged the middle class as a hedge against the power of the aristocracy. On the other hand, it did not flourish in Germany, where Enlightenment was more often than not but a superficial pretense of the petty German princes, who prided themselves on being *avant-garde* but acknowledged virtually none of the ideals of the Enlightenment in their governing. And economically it was a combination of mismanagement and economic opportunity that made the middle class and its business-like efficiency so attractive and also gave it the sense of unlimited possibility, if not in Europe, at least in America. (A bit of self-congratulation we have still not entirely outgrown.) And one should also mention the growth of cities, for it was the existence of London and Paris, in particular, that made the Enlightenment possible, and of course the Industrial Revolution, which provided the promise as well as the weapons for the middle-class reform of the material world. But how these conditions came about and how they have changed is not my philosophical business, except for my obligation to clearly acknowledge their importance. That done, let me move back to the ideas; they (not Marx's "iron laws") provide the inspiration of history.

The Politics of Abstraction

More than any other movement in history, perhaps, the Enlightenment was composed of abstractions—philosophical principles and metaphysical pretensions. The principles of "liberty" and "equality," for instance, are abstractions whose interpretations still perplex us. The very concept of "humanity," one of the key words of the Enlightenment, is an abstraction, glossing over all individual and cultural differences as so many superficial eccentricities and asserting with unwarranted confidence the essential similarity of all peoples, their common "human nature"—another abstraction. The central concept of "reason" is an abstraction, an uncomfortable synthesis of human faculties as diverse as the ability to do arithmetic and the willingness to obey the law, where what is "rational" is often what I believe as opposed to "prejudice," which is what you believe. And less obviously, the concept of the individual, apparently so concrete, is an abstraction, too, wrenched out of context and treated as an integral whole. And this family of abstractions, sometimes summarized as "human rights" or, more generally, as "humanism," provides the ideological skeleton of the Enlightenment, explains much of the "logic" of the French Revolution and its aftermath as well as the conceptual dynamics of the cold war, the end of the American dream, and our continuing philosophical confusion vis-à-vis the "Third World." "Irrationality" and "barbarism" are often refusal to accept the Enlightenment principles that we presuppose as the universal truth.

The ideology of the Enlightenment has always been "bourgeois," if we can separate that much-abused word from the sneer that often accompanies its mention. As such, it has always been the ideological weapon of a particular class—though the size of that class varies markedly—huge in America, where the Enlightenment has endured so long, tiny in nineteenth-century Germany and Russia, where it made its most abortive appearances. But the way the weapon works is to deny its narrow interests and to speak wholly in terms of humanity and human rights. The strategy of the French during the eighteenth century was clear enough: they used the slogan "liberty, equality, and fraternity" to state their claims against the aristocracy above them. And although there were scattered but celebrated attempts to defend the rights of the "lower" classes "below" them

(Voltaire's defense of Jean Calais is a favorite example), the recognition that the same claims might be made against the relative affluence of the middle class was slow in coming, suddenly forced upon the bourgeois lawyers of the revolutionary National Assembly by that new entity "the people" whom their philosophy had created.

Armed with the idea that all men [sic] are created equal, the philosophers demanded equal privileges and rights formerly restricted to the aristocracy. The fate of the rest of "humanity" did not really concern them. In fact, apart from the correction of the grossest abuses, the Enlightenment philosophers were unabashedly elitist. Voltaire considered "the people" rather as "the rabble," and even Rousseau was far less the democrat and populist than subsequent misreadings (or nonreadings) have made him out to be. All the talk about "humanity," in fact, was and is little more than a projection of self-interest onto an abstraction whose existence and worth was unquestionable, just as God had been only a few years before.

The Dogmas of "Humanism"

Though Enlightenment was not nearly so "godless" as its critics have made it out to be, the Enlightenment did succeed in creating its own religion, humanism. It is often assumed that humanism is intrinsically antagonistic to Christianity and the church. I think a more accurate assessment would see the two as a continuity (in fact, most Christians today would insist that Christianity *is* humanism, not opposed to it). Enlightenment ideology learned some of its best tricks from the church, not least, the ideological power of a theory of "humanity," which, on the one hand, saw all human beings as essentially the same, and thus ripe for conversion, and on the other, treated each individual as a separate soul, in need of salvation. The ideology of humanism, usually attributed to the Enlightenment and, before that, the Renaissance, in fact had its origins much earlier. The virtues of *humanitas* had achieved full recognition already in the twelfth century, in the hands of such orthodox Christian scholars as St. Anselm, who saw each individual as the whole of humanity writ small, and in less orthodox thinkers like Abelard, who argued the importance of individual conscience as the key to salvation, centuries before the Reformation.

Humanism rests on two dogmas: first, the existence of humanity as a single entity, a metaphysical doctrine that, despite its apparent obviousness, was by no means a matter of experience but of pretentious assertion. (Who knew, in the eighteenth century, much less in the twelfth, what the varieties of cultures might prove to be?) Second, there is the belief in the importance and the "rights" of the individual, in Christianity the individual soul, in more secular thinking the individual person, with his or her consciousness, conscience, and feelings. In fact, the two dogmas support one another, since it is the individual who gives substance to the abstraction "humanity," and it is the idea of a universal human nature that gives significance to the abstraction "the individual." After all, the Enlightenment philosophers argued, what is it that gives dignity to the individual if not his or her existence as a human being?

Why do I say that individuality is an abstraction? For that matter, why is humanity an abstraction? Perhaps I can make part of my argument clear by pointing out what this pair of abstractions leaves out, namely, everything in between. On the one side, there is the vacuous individual, shorn of all personal and cultural characteristics: on the other side is a pretentious universal, oblivious to all cultural and individual differences. Put them together and what you see is a view of people in which family, community, and culture are at best of secondary importance. This is perhaps understandable, coming from a group of philosophers who were virtually all male, mostly bachelors, and often on the lam from country to country, but it is hardly a fair representation of "human nature." The great philosophers of the Enlightenment saw no need to develop an adequate view of human relationships, once they had developed a theory of universal reason, human nature, and morality. The family was the context from which one had escaped to make one's way in the world, and culture consisted of provincial prejudices which kept people from seeing the larger picture, namely, the whole of humanity. The ideal was to be "cosmopolitan," above such provincialism. In fact, most of what made up the day-to-day substance of human existence was simply ignored by the philosophers of the Enlightenment, in the name of "humanity," for what made a person human, they said, was nothing less than the universal characteristics of rationality, freedom, and rights. No wonder the French Revolution, following these same philosophers, found it so easy to disrupt everyday life without mercy, so long as the promised return would be liberty, equality, and fraternity.

The Enlightenment did not deny human differences, of course. And not all of the philosophers were equally brutal in their rejection of family, friends, community, and culture. But their shared ideal was to overcome all of these, to reinstitute the family on a cosmic level, to make the community a world community. But in order to do this, the philosophers of the Enlightenment had to make an enormously arrogant presumption, which I have called, the "transcendental pretense": "transcendental" (the word comes from Kant) because it presumed a universal essence of all humanity, a "pretense" because it was assumed, without argument, that the best and most developed example of this universal essence was to be found in middle-class, mostly male, decently educated and particularly verbal European self-styled philosophers. Most of them had given up the concept of the Christian soul, but they held onto the view, so self-righteously advanced by Rousseau in his *Confessions,* that "deep down," there is a basic human goodness, covered up if not corrupted by the artifacts and prejudices of modern society.

The idea of universality was expressed in one of the most interesting and, until recently, one of the most enduring doctrines of the Enlightenment: faith in a universal language. Leibniz, the precocious German philosopher, imagined a "calculus" in which all problems could be expressed and solved. It was argued, or assumed, in a dozen different ways, that all languages were essentially the same, that phonetics might differ and so might vocabulary but meaning and reference remained constant. Today, it is becoming increasingly clear that none of this is so; that language to a large extent defines its world and that literal translation to other languages may indeed be impossible. And so, too, then, might the mutual understanding of the various cultures that different languages define. The current adequacy of Enlightenment thinking, in this regard, might well be summed up in the failure of *esperanto,* the universal language that once was believed to signify the end to international misunderstandings and unintelligible cultural differences.

(Two Vikings are discussing the fate of the world over beer. One says, "If we're ever going to understand one another, we all have to speak the same language." To which the other replies, "Sure, but how are we going to teach everyone in the world to speak Danish?")

The End of Enlightenment

Perhaps it could have happened earlier, but our ideology is floundering at the borders of Palestine and at almost all points south and east of the Mediterranean, in every ghetto in the world, even in seemingly similar neighborhoods where differences have come to outweigh cross-cultural identities. At the beginning of the Enlightenment, the Baron de Montesquieu wrote a popular text called *The Persian Letters.* Its strategy, very much in anticipation of the overall strategy of the Enlightenment, was to look at France through the eyes of two exotic Orientals, as a way of criticizing and parodying his own country. But to do so, he supplied his exotic Orientals with remarkably Western and in fact enlightened attitudes, the assumption being, of course, that all people are essentially the same and that enlightenment anywhere reflects the same basic human principles and human nature.

It was a popular pretense. Voltaire used it all the time. Kant didn't write parodies but he accepted the technique, and he wrote a set of powerful "critiques" in which he described in the most impressive philosophical prose ever known the middle-class consciousness of a peculiarly pious, self-righteously moral and enthusiastic amateur scientist, and projected this as the transcendental nature of human consciousness as such, "the human mind." Hegel came to recognize as Kant did not the importance of cultural and ideological differences: "forms of consciousness" he called them. But he, too, looked forward to the day, which he saw as his philosophical duty to announce, when all of these differences would be resolved and synthesized into one single all-encompassing conception of the human spirit. Marx also began his theories with an idea of "man" as a "species-being," a creature whose nature was universal and scientifically discernible, and Marxists ever since have had a hell of a time trying to expand Marx's limited mid-century view of a peculiarly European situation to apply with some semblance of intelligibility to cultures that share none of those features: e.g., in "Maoism," a particularly inappropriate if not unintelligible philosophical position adopted nevertheless by several recent generations of European and occasionally American intellectuals.

Romanticism, whether of the 1830s European variety or the 1960s "counterculture" American style, may have made much noise about the rejection of Enlightenment thinking (just as the Enlightenment philosophers made so much noise against the *ancien regime* that supported them). But Romanticism shared with the Enlightenment its belief in humanism and the transcendental pretense. Not surprisingly, the great Romantic philosophers —Schelling and Schopenhauer, for example—found their point of departure in Kant. But where Kant and the French philosophers (most of them anyway) looked to universal reason as the key to human nature, the Romantics, following Rousseau, looked to intuition and fellow-feeling, to religion and adventure. And even existentialism, for all of its bluster against rationality and its emphasis on individual choice and commitment, begins with the essence abstraction of the individual and attributes to him or her a human essence, whose nature is to be free to choose. (A point that is perversely hidden by the nominal thesis, popularized by Sartre, that "there is no human essence.")

The Enlightenment is still with us, of course, and I for one find it difficult if not impossible to imagine what kinds of concepts will replace our sometimes admirable but in any case pretentious appeals to universal human rights and human nature. Actually, I shudder to think about it. But this much is clear to me: the Enlightenment pretense that all peoples are essentially the same and different cultures and languages merely superficial is no longer plausible. The liberal (or today's libertarian) fantasy of groups of autonomous individuals who freely choose their lifestyles limited only by the principle that they don't interfere with the rights of others too easily assumes that tolerance and self-absorption must be part of the ideology of every such group. The militancy of modern religion, at least, should have proven to us that the fantasy is impossible. The simple political categories, the optimism of material abundance across the ocean, and the sense of unlimited opportunity that originally fed the Enlightenment and has always fed "the American dream" is a thing of the past, revitalized (or raised from the dead) only on occasion to sell books and to support flagging political campaigns.

But neither is this to say that "our way of life is in danger," or that our belief in individuality, out hopes for a peaceful world, our willingness to defend human rights, and our aspirations to be happy have to be given up in the face of this latest if belated twist of the *Zeitgeist*. But I'd have to disagree with Meg Greenfield, one of our best down-to-earth ideologists, who proposes that we "return to our eighteenth-century roots—the humanistic and rational sources of our society and our success." To the contrary, I would argue that it is our persistent unwillingness to ever look beyond those roots that is responsible for what she calls "the pickle" we're in. In terms of ideas, America is just beginning to enter the twentieth (or perhaps the nineteenth) century and a multicultural world in which we can no longer conceive of ourselves as merely a "melting pot." It's about time for that kind of enlightenment.

11

Existentialism: An Introduction

"I am not an existentialist." So insisted Albert Camus and Karl Jaspers, two of the most famous existentialists. So, too, growled Martin Heidegger, with existential indignation. But if I were asked, I suppose that I would have to say, if awkwardly, "I am an existentialist." At a time when American philosophy is well on its way to becoming a respectable branch of cognitive science and a mandated prerequisite for law school, I find myself quaintly worrying about the meaning of life, the significance of feelings, and about who or what I am. In an age when philosophers have finally become professionals instead of street-corner kibitzers, I stubbornly believe that philosophy ought to speak to ordinary, intelligent people about personal worries, reflections, and experiences. It's embarrassing to be so out of style.

It is a commonly accepted half-truth that existentialism is a revolt against traditional Western rationalistic philosophy. It is also a demonstrable half-truth that existentialist philosophy is very much a continuation and logical expansion of themes and problems in Descartes, Kant, Hegel, Marx, and Husserl. But two half-truths provide us with less than the truth. Existentialism is not simply a philosophy or a philosophical revolt. Existentialist philosophy is the explicit conceptual manifestation of an existential

This selection is the Introduction to my anthology titled *Existentialism,* which was first published by McGraw-Hill as a Modern Library book © 1974. It is prefaced by the beginning to a more recent introduction to my *From Hegel to Existentialism,* published by Oxford University Press in 1987. Both are reprinted in edited form by permission of the publishers.

attitude—a spirit of "the present age." It is a philosophical realization of a self-consciousness living in a "broken world" (Marcel), an "ambiguous world" (de Beauvoir), a "dislocated world" (Merleau-Ponty), a world into which we are "thrown" and "condemned" yet "abandoned" and "free" (Heidegger and Sartre), a world that appears to be indifferent or even "absurd" (Camus). It is an attitude that recognizes the unresolvable confusion of the human world, yet resists the all-too-human temptation to resolve the confusion by grasping toward whatever appears or can be made to appear firm or familiar—reason, God, the nation, authority, history, work, tradition, or the "other-worldly," whether of Plato, Christianity, or utopian fantasy.

The existential attitude begins with disoriented individuals facing a confused world that they cannot accept. This disorientation and confusion are some of the by-products of the Renaissance, the Reformation, the growth of science, the decline of church authority, the French Revolution, and the growth of mass militarism and technocracy. In philosophical terms, the new stress on "the individual" provides the key themes of the Enlightenment, the "Age of Reason," the philosophical rationalism of Descartes, Kant, and Hegel. In these authors, however, the theme of individual autonomy is synthesized and absorbed into a transcendental movement of reason. But in a culture that harps so persistently upon the themes of individual autonomy and freedom, there will always be individuals who carry these to their ultimate conclusion. Existentialism begins with the expression of a few such isolated individuals of genius, who find themselves cut adrift in the dangerous abyss between the harmony of Hegelian reason and the romantic celebration of the individual, between the warmth and comfort of the "collective idea" and the terror of finding themselves alone. Existentialism is this self-discovery. Its presupposition is always the Cartesian *"I am"* (not the *"I think"*).

So long as we think of philosophy as a set of (what we hope are) true propositions, we will continue to be tempted by notions that philosophy can be a "science," that there is a *correct* way of doing it, that a philosophical judgment or body of judgments can be *true*. If instead we allow ourselves to think of philosophy as *expression,* these rigid demands seem pointless or vulgar. Yet we surely do not want to reduce philosophy to *mere* expression, to autobiography or poetry, to "subjective truth" or psychic discharge. Although it is an expression of personal attitude, a philosophical statement is better compared to a piece of statuary than to a feeling or an attitude. Philosophers are conceptual sculptors. They use their language to give a shape to their prejudices and values, to give their attitudes a life of their own, beyond the philosophers, for the grasp of others. A philosophical statement, once made, is "in the world," free of its author, open to the public, a piece to be interpreted; it becomes universal. But "universal" does not mean "universally true." Philosophical genius lies not in the discovery of universal truth, but in the seductiveness with which one molds personal attitudes as universals for others. Philosophers build insight onto insight, illustration into argument, join metaphysical slogan to concrete observation, perhaps using themselves as examples, their entire age as a foil. Nevertheless, the philosophy is never merely a personal statement; if it is the individual who has made existential philosophy possible, it is also the case that existentialism has deepened our individualism. Nor is philosophy ever merely an epiphenomenon of cultural attitudes; it gives them shape and direction, creates them as well as expresses them.

Existential philosophy, perhaps like all philosophies, typically finds itself going in circles, trying to prove axioms with theorems, converting premises into methodological rules, using repetition and restatement for argument and illustration for proof. Here "the individual" appears as a conclusion, there as the presupposition, and there again as the rule. The existential attitude finds itself in syndromes, interpreting a feeling as a mark of identity, converting an insight about oneself into an interpretation of the world, resolving self-doubt by exaggerating the self in everything. The existential attitude is first of all an attitude of self-consciousness. We feel separated from the world and from other people. In isolation we feel threatened, insignificant, meaningless, and in response, we demand significance through a bloated view of self. We constitute the self as a hero, as an offense, as a prophet or anti-Christ, as a revolutionary, as unique. As a result of this self-exaggeration, the world becomes—whether in appearence or reality —more threatening. So we attack the world, discovering, with both despair and joy, that its threats are themselves without ultimate meaning, that there are no moral facts, no good and evil, that "the highest values devalue themselves," and that the human world is typically, even essentially, a hypocritical world. And so we are self-righteously the creator of meaning, which heightens our role as absurd hero, prophet, revolutionary, "underground man," rebel, saint, or buffoon. Then there is at least slight paranoia: us against the others, the authorities, the public, the herd, the bourgeoisie, the pharisees, the oppressors.

As the world becomes more threatening, we are thrown into an exaggerated concept of self all the more; and as we become more self-conscious, the world becomes increasingly "his." Then we begin to feel impotent in the face of the responsibility for "our" world; it becomes more apparent how indifferent the world is, how contingent its events, how utterly absurd. We feel isolated from others, and in desperate loneliness we seek camaraderie, through rebellion, through art, through writing existential philosophy. In the existential syndrome every tension increases self-consciousness, every increase in self-consciousness exaggerates the irresolvable tension with the world that is always there. As existentialists become more sophisticated, as their feelings become formulated into ideas, as the existential attitude becomes philosophy, it becomes a mantra for similar attitudes in others. When those attitudes finally manifest themselves in the sardonic irony of Kierkegaard, the utter loneliness of Nietzsche's Zarathustra, the pathetic spitefulness of Dostoevsky's underground man, the struggle against nausea and "bad faith" in Sartre, the struggle for the heights in Camus's Sisyphus, these attitudes are no longer personal syndromes but universal meanings that we can accept as our own.

According to many existentialists, every act and every attitude must be considered a choice. Yet the existential attitude itself is apparently not chosen. We find ourselves in it. Dostoevsky tells us that self-consciousness is a "disease"; Nietzsche adds, in his discussion of "bad conscience," that it is "a disease—but as pregnancy is a disease." Although many existentialists speak of the universality of "the human condition," this universality is itself a view from within an attitude which is less than universal. Most existentialists, no less than Descartes, Kant, and Hegel, take self-consciousness to be the home of a universal first truth about all of humanity. But self-consciousness itself is not universal, although once we become self-conscious, we cannot go back, no matter how we deny ourselves, drug ourselves, *leap* or *fall* away from ourselves (the terms, from Kierkegaard and Heidegger respectively, carry their evaluations with them). In *Utilitarianism,* John Stuart Mill argues for "quality" of pleasures by contrasting the dissatisfied Socrates with a satisfied pig. The first is preferable, Mill argues, because Socrates has experienced both Socratic pleasures and pig pleasures and he, like other men, has chosen to remain Socratic. Actually Socrates had no choice. He could act like a pig but he could not enjoy himself as one. Socrates could no more imagine the self-less indulgence of pig pleasure than the pig could appreciate the arguments of Plato's *Apology.*

Once expressed, the existential attitude appears as a universal condition, but only to those who can understand it. It is a peculiarly Western attitude, and talk of "the human condition" is as presumptuous as it is overdramatic. Perhaps that is why, for many of us, Hermann Hesse is convincing, even in the wild fantasies of the magic theater, but lyrically unpersuasive as he attempts to capture the selflessness of his Eastern Siddhartha. If we begin by understanding Siddhartha's quest, it is because we, like Hesse, understand quests. However, we may well have difficulty understanding the peace and satisfaction of Siddhartha's repetitive routine as a ferryman. Of course we, like Hesse, can moon for that selflessness as a dream, a nostalgia for something lost. But for us, even selflessness is something viewed self-consciously, something that would have to be striven for by each of us as an individual. The existential attitude is not universal, and existential philosophy is not a truth about the human condition. As Camus says, for many of us it is simply a necessity.

Most of us have experienced this existential attitude at several points in our lives. A threat of imminent death, or even a passing thought of our own mortality, is sufficient to wrench us out of our current involvements—even if but for a moment—and force us to look at our lives. Like Sartre's characters in hell in *No Exit,* it is perhaps our private dream to see our own funeral, to see life after its completion. In life, however, there can be no such viewpoint, as Kierkegaard complains against Hegel, since "at no particular moment can I find the necessary resting place from which to understand [my life] backwards." Inevitably the thought of death prompts existential questions. What have I done? Who have I been? What have I wanted to be? Is there still time? But anxiety of death is only one preface to existential anxiety. As Camus tells us, "at any streetcorner the absurd can strike a man in the face."

Imagine yourself involved in any one of those petty mechanical tasks that fill so much of each day's waking hours—washing the car, boiling an egg, changing a typewriter ribbon—when a friend appears with a new movie camera and, without warning, says "Do something!" as the camera whirls. A frozen shock of self-consciousness, embarrassment, and confusion comes over you. "Do something!" Well, of course you were doing something, but that is now seen as insignificant. And you are doing something by just standing there, or perhaps indignantly protesting like a housewife caught in curlers. At such moments we appreciate the immobilization of John Barth's Jacob Horner, that paralyzing self-consciousness in which no action seems meaningful. In desperation we *fall* back into an everyday task, or *leap* into an absurd posture directed only toward the camera. In either case, we feel absurd. We remain as aware of the camera as of our actions, and then of our actions viewed by the camera. It is the Kantian transcendental deduction with a 16mm lens: there is the inseparable polarity between self and object; but in this instance the self is out there, in the camera, but it is also the object. A *sum* (not a *cogito*) accompanies our every presentation. "How do I look?" No one knows the existential attitude better than a ham actor.

Enlarge this moment, so that the pressure of self-consciousness is sustained. Norman Mailer, for example, attempted in *Maidstone* a continuous five-day film of himself and others which did not use a developed script, leaving itself open to the "contingencies of reality." His problem was, as ours now becomes, how to present oneself, how to live one's life, always playing to the camera, not just as one plays to an audience but as one plays to a mirror. We enjoy making love, but always with the consciousness of how we appear to be enjoying ourselves. We think or suffer, but always with the consciousness of the "outer" significance of those thoughts or sufferings. A film of one's life: would it be a comedy, a tragedy, thrilling, boring, heartrending? Would it be, as Kierkegaard suggests, the film of "a life which put on the stage would have the audience weeping in ecstasy"? Would it be a film we would be willing to see? Twice? Infinitely? Or would eternal reruns force us to throw ourselves down and gnash our teeth and curse this Nietzschean projectionist? And who would edit this extravagant film of every detail—of yet undetermined significances—of our life? How would the credits be distributed? We find ourselves in our own leading role—the hero, the protagonist, the buffoon. John Barth tells us that *Hamlet* could have been told from Polonius's point of view: "He didn't think he was a minor character in anything."

What does one do? "Be yourself!" An empty script; "myself" sounds like a mere word that points at "me" along with the camera. We want to "let things happen," but in self-conscious reflection nothing ever "just happens." We seize a plan (choose a self), and all at once we demand controls unimaginable in everyday life. Every demand becomes a need, yet every need is also seen as gratuitous. During the filming of *Maidstone,* Mailer was attacked by one of his "co-stars" (Rip Torn), and his candid reaction exploded the film's pretense of reality. No one can be an existential hero and also accept fate, yet no one is more aware of contingencies. Camus tells us that Sisyphus is happy, but perhaps he is because his routine is settled. He can afford to have scorn because his mythical reality is entirely structured within its predictable contingencies. Could Sisyphus remain the absurd hero if he were alive? How much does Camus's absurd hero and the existential attitude require the routine and leisure of the bourgeoisie? Perhaps there are no existentialists in foxholes.

The hero? The buffoon? Do any of us really think of ourselves that way? As Odysseus, Beowulf, James Bond, Woody Allen, perhaps not. But as the center, the one who endows all else with meaning, that is an attitude we recognize easily. Yet at the same instant we recognize ourselves as pelted by meanings, "sown on our path as thousands of little demands, like the signs which order us to keep off the grass" (Sartre). The existential attitude is the constant confusion of given meanings and our own. As this confusion becomes better formulated, we begin to suspect both. Today, I am Dr. Pangloss, and the world is spectacular; yesterday I was a Schopenhaueran fecal monist, grumbling over a fine wine in a rotten world. Each day values are given to me, but each day I find changes to explain how yesterday's differing values depended on differences in the world. (Yesterday I was there, now I'm here; yesterday she was friendly, today she insulted me.) My friends assure me, typically, that what has changed is only me, and that yesterday's depression was a symptom of a very real problem. It is today that is the illusion; my happiness is merely another symptom of my problem. But the values remain a problem, outside of me. Then, the exaggerated insight: It is all me (mine). No one can begin in the existential attitude without feeling sometime the hero, the megalomaniac (Nietzsche: "I am dynamite"). But again, one need not, should not, take this attitude for the truth. The realization that "I am the world" is a necessary step in the awakening of self-consciousness. In the existentialists' self-aggrandizing sense, perhaps we have never existed if we have never once seen ourselves as everything.

What is self-consciousness? According to some recent existentialists, there is no *self* as such. And what is consciousness? "It is nothing," Sartre tells us, and for Heidegger it is scarcely worth mentioning. We look at paradigm cases: a person is self-conscious because of the camera, or "he is self-conscious about his baldness." To be self-conscious is to be embarrassed, to be ill-at-ease. Or is that a peculiarly American paradigm? Descartes sees self-consciousness as nothing but our immediate awareness of our own existence. Hegel is centrally concerned with self-consciousness in his master-slave parable, but self-consciousness in Hegel carries with it a sense of dignity, pride, autonomy. We might well suspect that semantics is here becoming an ethology as well. What we begin to see, in our movie-making example, as well as in Descartes and Hegel, is that self-consciousness is neither a subject aware nor an awareness of an object (the self) so much as it is a motivation, an attitude that illuminates the world as well as the individual in the world. Self-consciousness is not, strictly speaking, awareness of self, for there is no self. Rather, self-consciousness in the existential sense is this very recognition that there is no self. The self is an ideal, a chosen course of action and values. Self-consciousness does not add anything to the world or to consciousness; it is neither a Lockean "turning back on itself" nor a Cartesian reflective substance. Self-consciousness robs the world of its authority, its given values, and self-consciousness robs consciousness of its innocence. Self-consciousness is not a premise or an object for study. Rather, it is the perspective within which existentialism attempts to focus itself.

Self-consciousness has much to do with our feelings, but a feeling does not have an identity or a direction before it is already made self-conscious. For one who is not yet self-conscious, a feeling can be a cause of behavior.

In one who is self-conscious, a feeling is but an obscure text that requires an interpretation, and that presupposes a set of values. In one and the same situation I might be ashamed or embarrassed, depending on my own sense of responsibility; angry or afraid, depending on my sense of value; indignant or amused, depending on my sense of morality. We always find values as "given," in everyday tasks, by "the public," but existential self-consciousness puts all such "givens" into question. We can no longer turn to religion. Even Kant—who was no existentialist—destroyed its authority and reduced it to a mere "postulate" of morality. So, we create a criterion; we "leap" to a set of values, to a life of our own. Camus calls this "philo-sophical suicide," for every such attempt to adopt a value is at the same time a pretense that the value is justified. However, we cannot simply rest in the existential attitude of the absurd, any more than we can relax in Hegel's dialectic. Kierkegaard's "leap," like the lie in Kafka's *Trial*, becomes for existentialism a universal principle.

The existential attitude, as we have been describing it, is not merely a piece of psychology, much less psychopathology. Existential statements are at once both personal and general. Personal, however, is not auto-biographical. The same Kierkegaard who complains of the lack of passion in his age is thus described by a friend: "There is nothing spontaneous about him: I am surprised he can eat and sleep." The Nietzsche we might have met in Sils Maria in 1886 was surely not the Dionysian epic hero we picture from his writings. This is not hypocrisy. It is the mark of these great philosophers that their personal discomfort could be so brilliantly transformed into matters of universal concern and inspiration. Kierkegaard describes himself as a "stormy petrel" (a bird that appears "when, in a generation, storms begin to gather") and as "an epigram to make people aware." Nietzsche often feared that he would be considered either a saint or a buffoon. (Hesse remarked that "a nature such as Nietzsche's had to suffer the ills of our society a generation in advance"; his personal suffering was at the same time "the sickness of the times themselves.") And Camus gives us, not just *his* feelings of alienation, but "an absurd sensitivity that is widespread in our age." If these feelings are not universal, neither are they exceptional. What is exceptional is their expression in these authors, their ability to provoke others who hold these still unformed and unex-pressed existential attitudes as personal failures and not yet as philosophical insights. Kierkegaard and Nietzsche wrote only for "the few": Camus and Sartre write to generations. Nevertheless, in each case the philosopher is the *provocateur,* not simply striving after merely the truth, but after converts as well.

One might object that this sketch of the existential attitude and its philosophical expression has failed to give a definition of existentialism. But existentialism is not a dead doctrine to be bottled and labeled. It is a living attitude that is yet defining and creating itself. As Nietzsche warns us in his *Genealogy of Morals,* "Only that which has no history can be defined." And Sartre, rejecting an invitation to define his existentialism, says, "It is in the nature of an intellectual quest to be undefined. To name it and define it is to wrap it up and tie the knot. What is left? A finished, already outdated mode of culture, something like a brand of soap, in other words, an idea" (*Search for a Method*). Although we might develop a working definition of one or another aspect of one or another twentieth-century existentialist "movements," existentialism is but a growing series of expressions of a set of attitudes which can be recognized only in a series of portraits. Existentialism is not a movement or a set of ideas or an established list of authors. It is an attitude which has found and is still finding philosophical expression in the most gifted writers of our times. But little more needs to be said *about* existentialism, for nothing could be further from the existential attitude than attempts to define existentialism, except perhaps a discussion about the attempts to define existentialism. The important thing, as small as it sounds, is to *be.*

12

What's Wrong with Sentimentality?

"A sentimentalist is simply one who desires to have the luxury of an emotion without paying for it."

—Oscar Wilde, *De Profundis*

What's wrong with sentimentality? That question already indicates a great deal about a century-old prejudice that has been devastating to ethics and literature alike. According to that prejudice, it goes without saying that there is something wrong with sentimentality, even if it is difficult to "put one's finger on it." To be called "sentimental" is to be ridiculed, or dismissed. Sentimentality is a weakness, it suggests hypocrisy. Or, perhaps it is the fact that sentimental people are so . . . so embarrassing. How awkward it is talking or sitting next to someone weeping or gushing, when one is oneself dry-eyed and somber. And isn't it a well-confirmed fact that sentimentalists have poor taste, and sentimental literature is tasteless, cheap, superficial, and manipulative, verbal kitsch? Such mawkish literature jerks tears from otherwise sensible readers, and sentimentalists are those who actually enjoy that humiliating experience. Perhaps that is why Oscar Wilde thought that sentimentalists were really cynics. ("Sentimentality is merely the bank holiday of cynicism.") Or, perhaps what bothers us is that sen-

This piece grew out of my thinking about compassion and why so many people feel uncomfortable with it. It was first published as a much longer piece entitled "In Defense of Sentimentality?" which appeared in *Philosophy and Literature* 14 (1991): 304–323.

timental people indulge themselves in their feelings instead of doing what should be done. It is said that the problem is that sentimentality and sentimental literature alike give us a false view of the world; they distort our thinking and substitute a "saccharine" portrait of the world in place of what we all know to be the horrible realities. Perhaps sentimentality even leads to brutality or fascism, as Milan Kundera famously argues in his *The Unbearable Lightness of Being*. But even where sentimentality is a harmless diversion—a Daphne du Maurier novel on a sad Saturday after-noon—it seems to be all but agreed that sentimentality is no virtue even if it is not, like cruelty and hypocrisy, intrinsically vicious. Something is wrong with sentimentality; the only question is, what is it?

I want to argue that there is nothing wrong with sentimentality. Of course, like any quasi-ethical category, it admits of unwarranted excesses, hypocritical abuses, and is prone to various pathological distortions. But the prejudice against sentimentality, I want to argue, is ill-founded and in fact is an extension of that all-too-familiar contempt for the passions in Western literature and philosophy. Our disdain for sentimentality is the rationalist's discomfort with any display of emotion, warranted as well as unwarranted, appropriate as well as inappropriate. It is as if the very word "sentimentality" has been loaded with the connotations of "too much": too much feeling and too little common sense and rationality, as if these were opposed instead of mutually supportive. It is as if sentimentality and its sentiments are never warranted and always inappropriate. The word has come to be used as the name of a deficiency or a weakness if not, as some critics have written, a malaise. But I take sentimentality to be nothing more nor less than the "appeal to tender feelings," and though one can manipulate and abuse such feelings (including one's own), and though they can on occasion be misdirected or excessive, there is nothing wrong with them as such and nothing (in that respect) wrong with literature that pro-vokes us, that "moves" us to abstract affection or weeping. Sentimentality is not an escape from reality or responsibility, but, quite to the contrary, provides the precondition for ethical engagement rather than serving as an obstacle to it.

Historically, one could trace the fate of sentimentality to the parallel fates of the "sentiments" and their apparently doomed plea for ethical legitimacy in what was once called "moral sentiment theory." The sentiments have had a bad time in Anglo-American moral and social philosophy for well over a century, and sentimentality has been held in contempt for just about the same period of time. During at least some of the eighteenth century, morality was thought to be a matter of proper feeling, and senti-mentality, accordingly, was something of a virtue. But Immanuel Kant did away with "melting compassion" as an ingredient in ethics once and for all before 1800 in a single sarcastic comment in the *Groundwork* ("kindness done from duty . . . is practical, and not pathological . . . residing in the will and not in the propensions of feeling, in principles of action and not of melting compassion"). Indeed, the offensive epithet "sentimentalist" has not long been a term of abuse: just two hundred years ago, when Schiller referred to himself and his poetry as "sentimental" (as opposed to Goethe's "naive" style), he had in mind the elegance of emotion, not saccharine sweetness and the manipulation of mawkish passions. But in 1823, Southey dismissed Rousseau as a writer who "addressed himself to the sentimental classes, persons of ardent and morbid sensibility, who believe themselves to be composed of finer elements than the gross multitude." This charge of elitism was soon to be reversed: hitherto a sentimentalist would have distinctively *inferior* feelings. If Rousseau's audience was objectionable early in the century because it believed itself to have "finer" feelings, the object of Oscar Wilde's scorn (the young Lord Alfred Douglas) was attacked as a "sentimentalist" for his fraudulent and contemptible passions. By the end of the century, "sentimentalist" was clearly a term of ridicule.

I suggest that the status of "sentimentality" went into decline about the same time that the sentiments lost their status in moral philosophy, and that the key figure in this philosophical transformation was Immanuel Kant. But Kant's unprecedented attack on sentiment and sentimentalism was at least in part a reaction, perhaps a visceral reaction, not only against the philosophical moral sentiment theorists (whom he at least admired) but against the flood of popular women writers in Europe and America who were then turning out thousands of widely read potboilers and romances that did indeed equate virtue and goodness with gushing sentiment. It is no secret that the charge of sentimentalism has long had sexist implications as a weakness which is both more common (even "natural") and more forgivable in women than in men, and one might plausibly defend the thesis that the moralist's attack on sentimentality cannot be separated from the more general Victorian campaign in pseudoscience and politics against the rising demand for sexual equality. But in the purportedly nonpolitical, genderless world of philosophy, sentimentalism was forced into a confrontation with logic and became the fallacy of appealing to emotion instead of argument. In ethics, to be accused of "sentimentalism" meant that one had an unhealthy and most unphilosophical preference for heartfelt feeling over hardheaded reason.

Sentimentalism more generally became a matter of moral bad taste, a weakness for easy emotion in place of the hard facts and ambiguities of human social life, and the literature that provoked and promoted such emotions became itself the object of moral—not only literary—condemnation. Not surprisingly, a prime target for such a charge were those same women's novels—and the emotions they provoked—which were and still are dismissed as "trash" by the literary establishment. But though designated "sentimental rubbish" by their detractors, some of these novels achieved unprecedented success, not only in terms of popularity but moral and political influence as well. Harriet Beecher Stowe's much-demeaned *Uncle Tom's Cabin* was not only the first American novel to sell a million copies but perhaps the most politically influential book in postcolonial American history.

What is wrong with sentimentality? William James depicts a wealthy society matron who weeps at the plight of the characters on stage while her waiting servants freeze outside. There is a similar story about Rudolf Hess weeping at the opera put on by condemned Jewish prisoners during the Holocaust. Such stories demonstrate that sentimentality divorced from life may reflect a particularly despicable or dangerous pathology, but it is not sentimentality as such that is at fault in these two famous cases but rather its utter inappropriateness in the context in question. Sentimentality is rarely the symptom (much less the cause) of moral deficiency. We can agree that certain sentiments and sentimentality can be inappropriate and excessive without granting that sentiments and sentimentality are immoral or pathological as such, and we can similarly agree that sentimentality in literature can be inappropriate and excessive without granting that sentimentality marks a deficiency in literature or in the reader who responds to it. It is simply not true, as more than one great cynic has claimed, that sentimentality betrays cynicism. It is rather that sentimentality betrays the cynic, for it is the cynic and not the sentimentalist who cannot abide honest emotion.

I want to defend sentimentality as an expression of and an appeal to the tender emotions. If the tender emotions (e.g., pity, sympathy, fondness, adoration, compassion) are thought to be not only ethically irrelevant but ethically undesirable (in contrast to hardheaded practical reason, for example) then it is not sentimentality that should be called into question but rather the conception of ethics that would dictate such an inhuman response. Indeed, it is difficult to see how strong sentiments could constitute a weakness unless there is already operating some powerful metaphor that views our sentiments as alien and the integral self as a will that is supposed to contain or control them but fails to do so. So, too, sentimentality seems to be self-indulgence if one is seen to indulge in personal emotional weaknesses. One could thus view the reader as the willing victim of the emotionally manipulative author, as an alcoholic is the willing victim of that first drink.

Sentimentality is "giving in," and a preference for sentimentality suggests a perverse willingness to make oneself vulnerable. Sentimentality thus becomes a form of self-indulgence. In a famous discussion of kitsch and sentimentality in *The Unbearable Lightness of Being,* Milan Kundera writes:

> Kitsch causes two tears to flow in quick succession. The first tear says: How nice to see children running on the grass!
>
> The second tear says: How nice to be moved, together with all mankind, by children running on the grass!
>
> It is the second tear that makes kitsch kitsch.

The charge is that we have tender emotions in order to feel better about ourselves. Kundera, of course, is concerned with a particular kind of political propaganda, which intentionally eclipses harsh realities with emotion and uses sweet sentiments to preclude political criticism. To be sure, sentimentalizing fascism is one of the clearest possible examples of the "inappropriate" uses of sentimentality, but it does not follow that this is the true nature of sentimentality or that sentimentality is cynical or bad in itself. We can readily share Kundera's concern for the use of kitsch as a cover for totalitarianism, but there is nothing intrinsically wrong with our being moved by the children playing in the grass and then by our further being moved by our being moved. The "second tear" is not self-indulgence but what would normally be called "reflection." Why should reflection be tearless, unless we are wedded to an indefensible divorce between reason and the passions, the latter wholly self-absorbed and without reason, the former a merely "ideal spectator," wholly dispassionate and wholly without feeling?

The most common charge against sentimentality is that it involves false emotion. But what is it for an emotion to be false? It is not enough that the emotion is "vicarious." The fact that an emotion is vicarious (in some sense "second-hand") does not mean that it is not a real emotion or that it is not an emotion of the morally appropriate type. Sympathy for a fictional character in a novel is nevertheless genuine sympathy. Horror provoked by the grisly view of an apparently decapitated cat on a movie screen is real horror, perhaps accompanied by real disgust and real nausea, no matter that the viewer knows it to be another one of Hollywood's many tricks and the special effects man to be a cat lover. Indignation about the maltreatment of blacks in *Uncle Tom's Cabin* is rightful indignation, whether or not the character evoking sympathy and the situation provoking indignation are actual or modeled after an actual character and situation. Nor is an emotion "false" if it is divorced from action. It is the nature of some emotions, e.g., grief, to be cut off entirely from effective action and open only to "adventitious" (though more or less appropriate) expression. Self-indulgence in an emotion may make it "false" in the sense that one exaggerates either its importance or its effects, but it is not the emotion itself that is false. So, too, excessive self-consciousness of one's emotions may well lead to the suspicion that an emotion is overly controlled or "faked," but emotional self-consciousness is not itself fraudulent but rather an important philosophical virtue. A thoroughly righteous emotion (such as indignation) may well be self-conscious without in the least undermining its claims to legitimacy.

One prominent suggestion is that sentimentality yields "fake" emotions because the object of the emotion is not what it claims to be. It is *displaced.* Sentimentalists only pretend to be moved by the plight of another; they are really reacting to a much more personal plight. Sentimentalists sob their way through a "tear-jerker" novel, but they are really weeping for a just-lost lover, a dying aunt, a recent and humiliating reprimand at work. This is different from the charge that the emotions involved in sentimentality are vicarious, that is, based on fictional situations or situations that (though real) are not one's own. Vicarious emotions have (in some complex sense) unreal objects, but the emotion is nevertheless directed toward those objects. Displaced emotions only seem to be directed toward their putative objects when in fact they are directed elsewhere. Thus there is a suggestion of hypocrisy in the displacement charge that is not at all evident in the claim that sentimentality is vicarious.

Many emotions are displaced. (Indeed some extreme Freudians and symbolists would claim that all are.) Displacement has nothing special to do with sentimentality, and does not generically make an emotion false. A man gets angry with his boss at work and comes home and yells at his misbehaving kids. His anger is displaced, but it is nevertheless not the case that "he isn't really angry at his kids," even if it is true that, in a more mellow mood, he would tolerate their screaming without such explosive irritation. Another is shattered when his lover leaves, but the very next week he falls madly in love with a woman who seems remarkably like the one who just made her exit. "Love on the rebound" is a form of displacement but, again, one cannot hastily conclude that it is therefore false. What gets presupposed in such discussions is a kind of quantitative zero-sum or qualitative unidirectional assumption such that an emotion can "really" have but one and one only object. If the man is really angry at his boss he cannot also be angry at his kids, and if the other is still in love with the first woman, then he cannot also be in love with the second. But there is no reason to accept such monotopical restrictions on our emotional life, and if sentimentality is to a considerable extent a phenomenon of displacement (Why else would we respond to some of those novels and movies?) then it should be credited with enriching and enlarging our emotional lives. It would be a nightmare, not a matter of integrity, if we could direct our emotions only at their primary objects, if we could not express and satisfy ourselves with secondary, derivative, and fictional objects as well.

One longstanding argument is that sentimentality is objectionable and its emotions false because it is *distorting*. Mary Midgley, for instance, argues (in "Brutality and Sentimentality") that, "the central offense lies in self-deception, in distorting reality to get a pretext for indulging in *any* feeling." Discussing the maudlin death of Little Nell in Dickens's *Old Curiosity Shop* (which Oscar Wilde insisted he could not read without laughing), Midgley claims,

> Dickens created in little Nell and various other female characters a figure who could not exist and was the product of wish-fulfillment—a subservient, devoted, totally understanding mixture of child and lover, with no wishes of her own. This figure was well-designed to provoke a delicious sense of pity and mastery, and to set up further fantasies where this feeling could continue. One trouble about this apparently harmless pursuit is that it distorts various expectations; it can make people unable to deal with the real world, and particularly with real girls. Another is that it can so absorb them that they cannot react to what is genuinely pitiful in the world around them.

Sentimentality, she argues, centers around the "flight from, and contempt for, real people." In literature, characters like Dickens's Nell or Harriet Beecher Stowe's Little Eva are one-dimensional, inspiring an excessive purity of emotion. These girls don't do any of the nasty things that little children do. They don't whine. They don't tease the cat. They don't hit each other. They don't have any blemishes on their perfect cuteness. They are, accordingly, false characters and our feelings are distorted.

But the reply to this is that all emotions are distorting in this sense. Anger looks only at the offense and fails to take account of the good humor of its antagonist; jealousy is aware only of the threat and not of the wit and charms of the rival; love celebrates the virtues and not the vices of the beloved; envy seeks only the coveted object and remains indifferent to questions of general utility and the fairness of the desired redistribution. But why call this "distortion" rather than "focus" or "concern"? And what is the alternative: never having a nice thought without a nasty one as well? What is wrong with sentimentality is not a matter of distortion of reality for the sake of emotion, for all emotions construct a perspective of reality that is specifically suited to their concerns.

There are, of course, ways of carving up the world, ways of selecting the sweet from the surrounding circumstances, that are indeed falsifying and dangerous. We can sentimentalize the situation of the Southern plantation slaves before the Civil War or the virtuous motives of terrorists. We can sentimentalize mischievous children who are bound for reform school (or worse), or all mammals that are on farms or in experimental laboratories. Gwynne Dyer warns us, in his terrifying study of war, against the temptation to "sentimentalize war." It is obvious that in such cases we are already in ethical territory, but what is at stake here is the mode of categorization, not sentimentality. One might (and many do) reach the same results through the affectless application of principles. It is not the nature of the feelings that characterize such problematic cases of "sentimentality" but rather the inappropriate or even dangerous way of misperceiving an ethically loaded situation. So, too, we should react to the example of the Jewish prisoners' opera. It was not Hess's weeping that is damnable but his evil ability to focus on a single, narrow aspect of a situation that ought to inspire horror and revulsion (not sentimental emotions) in any civilized human being.

Mark Jefferson (in his 1983 essay, "What's Wrong with Sentimentality?") offers us an example—a very telling example—of how sentimentality can become a danger to morality. In E. M. Forster's *Passage to India* the English fiancee (Miss Quested) becomes sentimentalized as the symbol of "the purity, bravery and vulnerability of English womanhood." Her alleged attacker (Dr. Aziz) is complementarily cast as "lust-ridden and perfidious" (along with his people). But I would argue that the point made here has much more to do with chauvinism and racism rather than with sentimentality, and it has little of that innocence of feeling that constitutes sentimentality. There is a confusion here between the alleged innocence of Miss Quested and the innocence of the emotions felt about her. There is also an ambivalence about the relationship of sentimentality and action, for it is not sentimentality that provokes (directly or indirectly) the vilification of Aziz and his people, and the "simple-minded sympathies" bestowed upon Quested are hardly an example of sentimentality. Here, again, I think we see the danger of that zero-sum sense of emotion, manifested in a confusion between idealization on the one hand and a dichotomizing conflict on the other. One need not, in celebrating the virtues of an Englishwoman, imply or conclude anything unflattering about the non-English. Competitive winners may entail the possibility of losers and praise may entail the possibility of blame, but there are many forms of idealization that do not entail such contrasts.

It is discomfort with the tender affections, I am convinced, that is the ultimate reason for the stylish attack on sentimentality. Philosophers have long felt uncomfortable with emotions and passion in general (especially those that Hume called "violent"), but the attack on sentimentality, though an obvious symptom of this discomfort, is not so much an attack on emotion as such (angry indignation and bitter resentment have never gone out of style in Western intellectual life) but the "sweet" sentiments that are so easily evoked in all of us and so embarrassing to the hardheaded. It is probably not irrelevant that the higher classes of many societies associate themselves with emotional control and reject sentimentality as an expression of inferior, ill-bred beings, and it is easy to add the now-familiar observation that male society, in particular, has held such a view, rejecting sentimentality as an inferior, "feminine" emotion. Sentimentality is supposed to be undignified—as opposed, for example, to coldblooded respect, devoid of feeling. But, of course, that depends on what one means by "dignity," and I would suggest that there is more human dignity rolling around with a baby or a puppy than in the proud arrogance of "being above such things."

It is true that such sentiments "distort" reality and it is true that they do so in the service of their cautious and obviously self-serving cultivation of certain pleasant emotions. Telephone advertisements pressing us to "reach out" to a grandmother or a grandson or a long-absent friend may be annoying because they are so crassly commercial, but it is not the strong, tender feelings evoked that ought to be the target of our disdain. Somewhat similar public service announcements for Save the Children Foundation and CARE provoke similar feelings without the accompanying disdain, and it seems perfectly right and proper for them to do so. How else should one appeal for donations to feed a starving family or inoculate a stricken village against the ravages of disease? By appealling to our abstract sense of duty?

Nostalgia is a form of sentimentality, and given the unfortunate fact that most of our experiences are at least tinged with unpleasantness, nostalgia requires considerable effort in the selecting, editing, and presenting of memories. This does not mean that the memories are false or falsified, however, although that may be sometimes the case. To remember grandpa on what may have been his one healthy and happy day in a decade is not to have a false memory, and to remember with fondness and laughter together the half-dozen tiny tragedies that almost wrecked the wedding and consequently the marriage is not falsification. Nostalgia as sentimentality is the ability to focus or remember something pleasant in the midst of what may have in fact been tragedy and horror: for example, old soldiers fondly remember the camaraderie of a campaign and forget the terror, bloodshed, and death that surrounded them. But why should this be cause for attack and indignation? If it were used as a defense of war, to "sentimentalize war," perhaps, but that is not its usual purpose, and a preemptive general strike hardly seems called for.

What I am suggesting is that the attack on sentimentality is wrongheaded and possibly worse, a matter of self-deception or serious self-denial. (That, of course, is just what the critics say about sentimentality.) The usual attack on sentimentality is, I am convinced, too often an attack on innocence and the innocent enjoyment of one's own tender and therefore "soft" emotions. Allowing ourselves to become teary-eyed about the tragic death of an impossibly idealized girl does not make us unable to deal with the real world but rather activates our sensitivity to lesser as well as equal actual tragedies. There is always the aberrant case of the parents who go goo-goo–eyed over the child they physically abuse, but again, it is a grotesque mistake to conflate such inappropriate and pathologically inconsistent sentimentality with the brutality that goes with it. The sum-total vision of our emotional economy, according to which we have only so much sympathy to spend, is a particularly ill-considered and corrupting doctrine. It is true that a single trauma can exhaust our emotional resources, but it is unlikely that reading about Little Nell or Little Eva and experiencing "melting compassion" will do that to us. Indeed, it is precisely the virtue of sentimentality that it stimulates and exercises our sympathies without straining or exhausting them. So considered, sentimentality is not an emotional vice but a virtue.

13

Confessions and Memoirs:
The *Ad Hominem* in Philosophy

"Gradually it has become clear to me what every great philosophy so far
has been: namely, the personal confession of its author and a kind of involuntary and unconscious memoir."

—Nietzsche, *Beyond Good and Evil*

How personal can and should philosophy be? Nietzsche (among others)
insisted that a philosopher should "be an example." Is this so? Should
the difference between what one teaches and what one does make a difference to the soundness of what is taught? Is there a place for autobiographical material in a philosophical essay? To make a point? To offset
criticism? To win sympathy? To establish one's credentials? And what about
using personal facts about other philosophers to make a point? Socrates'
marriage or, for that matter, his trial and death? Augustine's or Rousseau's
Confessions? Kant's bad taste in art? Sartre's rather extravagant pharmaceutical habits? And, notoriously, what about the use of *ad hominem*
arguments, against which we warn our introductory students? Is the fact
that someone is a communist or a homosexual (the two most common

Originally written as part of a talk for a conference on "Nietzsche and the Judeo-
Christian Tradition," held at Baylor University in Waco, Texas. The full version
of this paper is to be published by Cambridge University Press in 1993 in a volume
on *Nietzsche* by Bernd Magnus. © Robert C. Solomon.

textbook examples) an argument against their opinions? What about the
fact that someone is a libertarian, a Quinian, a deconstructionist? An in-
trovert, a sociopath, a claustrophobe, a hypocrite? Is hypocrisy, for example, an argument against the skeptic, not Pyhrro who evidently acted it
through but, say, Hume who found his own speculations "ridiculous" or
Peter Unger who seems to know his way around lower Manhattan despite
his claim that "nobody knows anything"? This has bothered me for virtually
my entire career in philosophy. (Is that too personal?) What is the place
of the personal in philosophy, and where (if anywhere) are *ad hominem*
arguments legitimate philosophical moves?

These questions have become more urgent, not just for me, but for
a great many philosophers. Some feminists have argued with vehemence
against various male biases in philosophy, all of them perpetrated in the
name of gender (and other sorts of) "neutrality." The fact that these philosophers are men, they insist, is essential to understanding the nature of
their arguments and their positions, especially those that are called "original"
(as in John Rawls's famously "neutral" account of justice). So, too, Third
World philosophers and their advocates (e.g., Tom Auxter in his comments
on Richard Rorty after the Twelfth Inter-American Conference on Philosophy in Guadalajara) have insisted that culture counts in the evaluation
of a philosophical argument, if only because it has been so thoroughly
bracketed by "mainstream" (i.e., Anglo-American) philosophers. Annette
Baier has been arguing for some years now that ethics, in particular, not
only invites but requires some more or less autobiographical statement
concerning the range of moral experience of the author, and the burgeoning
field of "virtue ethics," while it need not be autobiographical and certainly
can be just as technical and impersonal as traditional Kantian ethics or
utilitarianism, seems to invite more personal and even impertinent inquiries.
When an ethicist writes on some formulations of the categorical imperative,
his or her home life or political opinions seem not to matter. But when
that same ethicist writes about courage or loyalty or integrity, we are naturally
curious. "Is he?" or "Isn't she?" Enquiring minds want to know.

It is often said that such questions and concerns are simply irrelevant
to the philosophical topics under consideration, and sometimes, indeed,
often this is the case. An irate competitor calls a modal logician an "idiot"
and a "charlatan." A critic dismisses Heidegger for his now-confirmed un-
repentant Nazi sympathies, and similarly dismisses Jacques Derrida for his
admittedly limp and embarrassing defense of him. A conservative logician
dismisses the work of another because he voted for Dukakis, while another
female philosopher refuses to read the work of a colleague because the
latter once had an affair with her husband. But, of course, such dismissals

are rarely if ever *justified* in such terms; they are at most *explained* (and almost always by others) in such terms. But irrelevant insults and gratuitous egotism can be dismissed on quite independent grounds, namely, "irrelevancy," and not because they are personal or autobiographical. One person accuses another of fraud or pandering. But here we expect to be further told the nature of the fraud, and presumably it will lie in the proof or presentation of proof itself and not, for example, in the author's last income tax report. What kind of explanation or understanding or revelations can we expect here? Sometimes just anecdotal: e.g., familiar stories of great decision theorists who simply cannot make up their minds, defenders of determinism who refuse to take responsibility, libertarians (in the free-will problem) who use it as an instrument of "bad faith" to procrastinate indefinitely and insist that "they can do it anytime they choose to." Amusing, but hardly philosophically convincing. So, too, the great pessimist Arthur Schopenhauer's fine dinners and brutal treatment of his landlady, whom he once threw down the stairs. Does that help us understand his philosophy?

An *ad hominem argument,* as everyone learns in any Introductory Logic or Basic Composition course, is an attack directed "against the person" instead of addressed to his or her thesis or argument. To do so is to commit an elementary albeit "informal" fallacy, and it is frowned upon almost as routinely as it is actually used, in philosophy as in politics and virtually every other human endeavor where people care more about winning the argument than obeying the rules of academic etiquette. But are ad hominem arguments fallacies? Do they ever provide fair grounds for rejecting or at least being suspicious of the views or opinions of a person? The answer to the second question is, "of course they do," and the answer to the first is, at least, "not always." To recognize someone as a compulsive liar is to be suspicious, at least, of their most sincere-sounding pronouncements, and to recognize that someone has a personal interest or investment in a case (e.g., a scientist hired by the Tobacco Institute to disprove the link between smoking and cancer) is, again, to be deeply suspicious of the supposed "objectivity" of the research, no matter how painstakingly pure the experimental methodology. It is true, of course, that such suspicions do not show such pronouncements or the conclusions of such research to be false, but the entanglement of truth and method, knowing and the knower, is such that the ad hominem argument is often—at least as a practical matter—conclusive. The thesis may in fact be true, but in the absence of other arguments from other, less suspicious parties, we are no longer willing to listen.

Exactly what is an ad hominem argument? In one of the leading textbooks, Howard Kahane (*Logic and Philosophy* [2d ed.] p. 240) gives the usual formulation: "an attack on the person rather than the argument."

But, he adds, it is not always a fallacy. Lawyers who attack the testimony of an expert witness and question his or her moral character, argue ad hominem, though not fallaciously. But why should "expert" witnesses be the exception? Insofar as anyone makes any pronouncement, is he or she not subject to similar suspicions, or even more so? After all, what supposedly makes an "expert" (in theory if not in practice) is his or her "objectivity" and "disinterest." (The fact that experts in a court of law are often hired and paid by one side or the other obviously compromises their "disinterest" if not their "objectivity.") And for those of us who do not claim to be "experts" but may nevertheless speak as such on any number of occasions, ad hominem arguments are often devastating, not least of all the generic, "Oh, you think you know everything." The crucial difference between an expert and us, in fact, is not only knowledge but context: the opinion of the expert carries weight. It has consequences. Our everyday opinions about politics, religion, and the weather, on the other hand, may start an occasional fight and compromise a friendship or two but they remain, whatever else, our opinions, without the more general recognition that provides weight as well as conviction. (I defer comment on how philosophers fit into this scheme, as philosophical influence and philosophical "expertise" are obviously very different phenomena.)

Michael Scriven (*Reasoning,* p. 228) seems to agree with the exception for "experts," and with the legal context again in mind he distinguishes the "reliability, consistency, and credibility" of a witness, three concerns where criticism of his or her moral character may be "appropriate." But why, again, should it be that with an "expert witness," ad hominem arguments are tolerable but not in general? Paul Feyerabend, no doubt, would be quite happy with this bit of anti-authoritarian discrimination, but why should experts be singled out for ad hominem abuse? Why should legitimate *ad hominem* arguments be confined to the courtroom and excluded, presumably, from the philosophy seminar? In William Halverson's *A Concise Logic* (p. 58), he gives us the standard view that "rational discussion requires that views be considered on their own merits, no matter who may happen to hold or express them. The fallacy of arguments against the person occur when someone who wishes to oppose a certain view attempts to discredit the person who holds the view rather than assess the merits of the view itself." Halverson does not bother to qualify or question the scope of the alleged fallacy, and in this we may take him to be providing us with the standard, traditional view. He also gives us a particularly appropriate example: "Don't waste your time studying the philosophy of Nietzsche. Not only was he an atheist but he ended his days in an insane asylum." Halverson goes on to distinguish *abusive* arguments, aimed at one's character or arousing negative feelings against him (her) on the part of the audience; *circumstantial* arguments, aimed at the context and therefore probable personal motivation; and *tu quoque* or "you too" arguments, which shift the focus from the accused to the accuser. All three, of course, have been levied against Nietzsche (1. He was crazy [abusive]. 2. He lived in a family of Protestant women [circumstantial]. 3. And wasn't *he* as filled with *ressentiment* as anyone" [tu quoque]?) If ad hominem arguments are acceptable in the court of philosophy, wouldn't they apply with devastating effect on that self-appointed "expert" in moral psychology, Friedrich Nietzsche?

Nietzsche's own philosophy is certainly "the personal confession of its author," whether or not it is "involuntary" or "unconscious." It would be a crass inconsistency for him to claim otherwise (though he could, I suppose, try to capitalize on "so far" and claim himself as the first exception). Nietzsche's philosophy is not mere confession (nor a confession overloaded with accusations), but it is—and this is essential—a *personal engagement*. The key to his ad hominem strateg(ies) is some similar claim concerning every philosopher (or, at least, every "great" philosopher, leaving room for exception in the case of those scholarly hacks whose expression of self is limited to their loyalty). A philosophy expresses the outlook of the philosopher and defines (sometimes misleadingly) his or her engagement with the world and relations with other people. A critique of the philosophy entails criticism of the philosopher, and vice versa. (This is why philosophers have to be so good at protecting their arguments; it is also why they are so vulnerable to and adamantly against ad hominem attacks.) So, too, it makes perfectly good sense, indeed it is necessary, to see Nietzsche's own philosophy as "expression" if not "confession," perhaps even as "memoir," though it is not only this, and his arguments against others are not compromised by this. Indeed, the very idea of an ad hominem argument, properly understood, is to identify the self with its ideas and evaluate these together. What is presupposed here—though Nietzsche argues for it from time to time—is a remarkably rich conception of the self, as opposed to the minimal, emaciated merely "transcendental" self presupposed by so many philosophers from Descartes to Kant to Rawls. (Rawls calls it "the unencumbered self," that is, "unencumbered" by emotions, desires, personality, or character.) What Nietzsche presumes here is a substantial self (Kant would trivialize it as "empirical"), which cannot be distinguished from its attributes, attitudes, and ideas. An ad hominem argument, accordingly, does not only "explain" the fact that *this* person holds *that* belief (though it does this, too); an ad hominem argument *identifies* the thought and the thinker. This may be overstating the case, but for Nietzsche it is clear that he did not distinguish between an attack on an idea and an attack on the person who proposed it, and he repeatedly insisted that his ideas were very much his own, indeed, he envisioned himself *as* his ideas, but without leaving the rest of his substantial if sickly self behind.

Other philosophers have suffered, of course, but few have spread it across their pages so vividly. One can see Wittgenstein wrestling with himself through his admittedly tortured notes and pages, but he doesn't make a big deal of it and turns us away from the author just as insistently as Nietzsche turns us toward him. So, too, one can now see in retrospect the enormous suffering concealed by Spinoza in the pseudo-formality of his *Ethics,* but the work itself is anything but "personal." Nietzsche's great virtue was precisely that he refused to separate the philosophy from the philosopher; he refused to pretend, with Wittgenstein and Spinoza and so much of the philosophical tradition, that there was indeed a "truth of the matter" that was independent of the thinker, the *person* who pursued that truth. What Nietzsche's "style" signifies, first and foremost, is the insistence on the essential role of *personality*—or what in ethics is usually called *"character"*—in philosophizing. The first person voice is not, for him, a mere presentational device, a rhetorical anchor (as in Descartes's *Meditations*) for a chain of thoughts that could (and were intended to be) entertained by anybody. Nietzsche's continuing emphasis on his own uniqueness —one of his more obnoxious stylistic obsessions—is important not for its megalomania but for its more modest message that there is always a particular person behind these words, these books, these ideas. Nietzsche is no idealized philosophical author whose existence is wholly absorbed by his books. He was and is, first and foremost, a personality, a unique and unforgettable voice filled with passion and personal enthusiasm and loathing. It is for this reason—the absence of protracted argument and self-imposed tedium and other such symptoms of philosophical rationality—that he is often dismissed as a philosopher and accepted, if only grudgingly, as a poet, a sage, a *literato.*

But why *should* philosophy be the impersonal, supposedly rational, and so often tedious discipline that it has become in recent decades? Why should we insist—as graduate school education is designed to insist—on writing that ideally could be written by anyone, devoid of personality or passion, betraying nothing whatsoever of its author? This is my primary concern in reading Nietzsche, and it is why I have come to see his ad hominem approach as much more than an argumentative strategy or a rhetorical device. An ad hominem argument, we are told, is an argument against the person, aimed at one's character, circumstances, or motivation. But why shouldn't philosophy do just this? At what point did philosophy get defined as the impersonal concern with arguments and ideas devoid of character or personality? Socrates often talks this way, but his own behavior in the Platonic dialogues belies it at every step. It is the feisty character of Socrates that we celebrate and remember rather than his often poor arguments and his very hard to define (or find) ideas. We have to look at who a philosopher is as well as at what he or she says, and we should be impressed (or not) by the philosopher-philosophizing and not just by the philosophy alone.

The extreme version of this personalist philosophy is: Why shouldn't a philosopher be, first of all, an example, with everything riding on this and this alone? Was Socrates, for instance, really all that virtuous? However bad some of his arguments or merely clever his sophistry, shouldn't we rest our case, as Plato does in the *Crito* (admittedly, an early work), on the behavior of the man himself? But that, perhaps, is asking too much of us dull academics, and it is certainly demanding more of poor Nietzsche than he was capable of giving us. A more modest but, it seems, not much less revolutionary suggestion these days is that philosophy should dispense with its obsession with reason, its insistence on the dispassionate and impersonal, and get back to those Socratic (not Platonic) questions about the self and the soul and the passions, though it must be said that Socrates' own self-scrutiny (as opposed to his irony) in this regard was not always as critical or self-effacing as it should have been. Why do we so emphasize the abstract, the a priori, the impersonal? Our subject is supposed to be "the love of wisdom"—but I see very little loving and not much wisdom. What happened to Platonic *eros,* that intellectual curiosity that was first of all *enthusiasm*? Whatever happened to the *person* who does philosophy, hidden behind all of these anonymous locutions, "it can be argued that" and "if it is the case that" and the occasional professorial "we" that is no one in particular but rather (in Heidegger's terms) the "das man" of academic philosophy? But, of course, it is not just "the philosopher" that concerns us here. It is, perhaps more importantly, the reader as well. The point of philosophy is not to prove but to provoke, and the aim of the philosopher should not be so much to "make a case" as to make us think and "see." Philosophy is first of all personal engagement, and the unrelenting personal probing of Nietzsche's philosophy forces us to face up to ourselves, often by making us indignant or angry. Socrates does it in his dialogues, but we are always one step removed; Nietzsche actually does it *to* us, and we are engaged—ad hominem—along with him.

In recent social philosophy, a great deal of effort and intelligence has gone into the formulation, elaboration, and defense of a number of rather ingenious but very abstract theories of *justice,* ideal schemes according to which the wealth of society should be distributed (or not distributed, as the case may be). There is, for example, the intricacies of John Rawls's redistributive principles and the invisible hand argument behind Robert Nozick's insistence on the minimal state. What is almost entirely missing from both accounts is any adequate notion of individual *merit,* the common-sense idea that a person ought to get what he or she *deserves.* (Rawls actively attacks this idea; Nozick circumnavigates it.) These notions, of course, invite something more than abstract rationality and the complications of game theory—namely, strictly empirical considerations of personal worth. And as for the theories of justice themselves, is it really a matter of irrelevance who it is that promotes them and for what motives? The obvious contrast here is Socrates, particularly in Plato's *Republic.* He did not just define and argue for justice (though he did this, too, of course): he *showed* what it meant to be just, above all. As justice gets elevated to an ideal in philosophy—the perfect blueprint for society or a constitution in the sky (the language of "grounding a theory" betrays the metaphor at work here)—what gets lost is the ancient idea of justice as a personal virtue, the idea of a person *being just* rather than simply believing in one or another a theory of justice. Plato thought this, and so did Aristotle. And so, too, did Nietzsche. Justice isn't an abstract ideal but rather a personal virtue, and some of the best arguments for justice hide some of the most mean-spirited attitudes and provide masks for some of the most unjust political personalities. The proof is in the putting.

It has been argued (e.g., by Rawls) that being just, having sentiments of justice, is one's disposition to behave in accordance with a theory (preferably his) of justice. But this, I propose, is quite backward: if one does not share what I do not doubt to be Rawls's own profound sense of compassion and sensitivity to the inequities that surround him in Cambridge, Massachusetts, or wherever, then the ingeniousness of his argument—however presented as if in deductive form—will have no impact whatever. A similar claim has often been made, of course, about such arguments as Saint Anselm's ontological proof for the existence of God. If you don't feel it to start with, there's nothing there to prove. But, anyway, this is the idea. The important concepts in philosophy don't operate on their own, in some Platonic heaven. They are from the start culturally constructed and cultivated and insofar as they have any meaning at all that meaning is first of all *personal*—not private, much less personally created but personally *felt,* steeped in and constitutive of the character of the person in question. So much for the alleged ad hominem "fallacy": the fallacy, to the contrary, is supposing that a philosophy or its arguments can be cut away from their moorings in the soul of the individual and his or her culture and treated, as they say, under the auspices of eternity.

One will notice that I wish to be just to the Germans: I do not want to break faith with myself here. I must therefore state my objections to them. . . . How much disgruntled heaviness, lameness, dampness . . . how much *beer* there is in the German intelligence! (Nietzsche, *Twilight of the Idols*)

Part Three

Thinking about Emotions

14

Rationality, Emotions, and Culture

Most philosophical discussions of "rationality" make me rather irritable (which is not to say, "irrational"). All too often, we find that learned philosophers exercise great ingenuity to establish what they in fact all began by agreeing, that rationality is that virtue best exemplified by philosophers. True, rationality as ultimately conceived might dispense with the philosopher altogether and become pure thought thinking about itself, but short of this divine purity, the philosopher, merely finite as he or she may be, becomes the measure of rationality. All other putatively rational creatures, from the squid to the dolphin and the ape, from "primitive" and "developing" societies to the ancient cultures of the Orient, are more or less rational insofar as they are or are not capable of doing what philosophers in the Western tradition do so well—articulating abstract concepts, gathering evidence and mustering argument, reflecting on the meaningfulness of what they say, disputing with those who raise objections against them, and demonstrating beyond a doubt that this or that thesis is indeed an a priori truth—despite the pig-headed refusal of certain less than fully rational colleagues to acknowledge this. Western philosophers from Aristotle to Gadamer and the deconstructionists have thus delighted in distinguishing their own rational discourse from the unreflective language of the "vulgar" and contrasting their own philosophically sophisticated societies from those

This was originally written for a conference on "Rationality, Emotions, and Culture" held on Mount Abu, Rajasthan, in January of 1991. The full version was published in *Philosophy East & West* (1992). Reprinted by permission of the publisher.

whose inferior place on the evolutionary ladder is exemplified by the fact that they have not yet produced an Aristotle or a Hegel, much less a Derrida. The concept of rationality that emerges from these discussions, accordingly, tends to be ethnocentric and chauvinist as well as overly complex and obscure, laden with metaphysical baggage (e.g., "logocentrism") and extremely intellectualized with an excessive emphasis on what is supposedly uniquely human, not just the use of language but of languages capable of self-reflection and, accordingly, self-undermining. The irony here, of course, is that the most advanced demonstrations of rationality tend to be precisely those that raise the paradoxical conclusion (not to be taken all that seriously) that we are not rational after all.

Rationality, I want to argue, has been abused by philosophers. It has been obscured, ambiguities and equivocations have been plastered over, ever more technical meanings have been invented and then undermined (e.g., Baysian and other concepts of maximization in decision theory), and ever more stringent criteria have been applied to guarantee that, in the last analysis, no one could possibly qualify as a rational agent unless he or she had pursued at the minimum a baccalaureate, if not a Ph.D. in philosophy. Nor is this strictly a Western inflation of the currency of reason. In a detailed analysis of the Sanskrit concept of *Pramana*, J. N. Mohanty, one of the world's best Sanskrit scholars as well as an accomplished Husserlian phenomenologist, has argued, for example, that rationality must be conceived not only in terms of a philosophical view but also requires a "theory of evidence, rational justification, and critical appraisal . . . and also a theory of these theoretical practices" (Schlomo Biderman and Ben-Ami Scharfstein, eds., *Rationality in Question: On Eastern and Western Views of Rationality* [Leiden: E. J. Brill, 1989], p. 219). So, too, philosophers since Socrates (who may or may not have had such a "theory" himself) have made philosophical reflection the hallmark of rationality. Needless to say, this eliminates from candidacy a great many cultures for whom self-reflection and self-criticism has not been encouraged or developed, for whom the theory of knowledge is not an interesting or an intelligible set of questions, for whom "justification" is a matter of authority and not intellectual autonomy. Nor would such a notion of rationality apply to virtually any species of "higher" animal, no matter how intelligent. ("What will philosophers do when they teach an ape to speak?" Oxbridge philosopher G. E. M. Anscombe was once asked. "They'll up the ante," she replied.)

By way of correction, I want to shift the conversation about rationality away from theory, reflective self-understanding, and justification and back to some more elemental aspects of human (and nonhuman) life. Once rationality is removed from its philosophical pretensions and relegated to a more commonsensical search for "living well," it is not at all clear that a great many animals and supposedly "simple" people will not emerge as far more rational than a great many philosophers. Most animals (it is falsely claimed "all") abstain from killing their own kind; few animals exemplify the extensive greed and imprudent self-destruction so evident in the recent ecological accomplishments of humanity. And many societies that have lived for centuries without "high" technology now serve with some reason as romanticized models of harmonious living—a model of rationality that may lack *Realpolitik* but nevertheless reminds us where the criteria for rationality ought to be sought—not in intelligence and ingenuity alone but in living well. Once we have put in its place the self-reflective overlay superimposed on the good life by such philosophers as Aristotle and Socrates, who insisted absurdly that "the unexamined life is not worth living," it becomes quite evident that a happy, rational life may be readily available to those who do not display any predilection or talent for philosophy or reflection whatever. Indeed, on the other side of the coin, we should remember that Dostoevsky, Kierkegaard, and Unamuno as well as a number of iconoclastic ancient philosophers both Greek and Oriental insisted that rationality is above all anxiety and suffering; "consciousness is a disease." Nietzsche remarked (in his *Gay Science*) that reflective consciousness becomes philosophically interesting only when we realize how dispensable it is.

To say that rationality is at best optional and at worst pathological is, however, much further than I would like to go here, but I do want to call into question the various overly sophisticated conceptions of rationality that have been the source of much philosophical concern, and suggest instead that we ought to be concerned with a much more modest conception of rationality, or what in the simplest philosophical parlance means "living well." Rationality is not necessarily fully articulate or disputational. It is rather, I want to suggest, best captured in the thesis that rationality is *caring about the right things*. My thesis, accordingly, is that it is not reason but rather our emotions and affections that mark the limits of rationality, not from the "outside" (like barbarians at the gate) but from the "inside," as determinate of rationality itself. But such a shift implies that reason is not, as is so often assumed (or even defined as such), universal and necessary. It is based on the contingencies of the human condition and the circumstances of particular cultures and situations. Emotions are for the most part culturally determined (though they, like reason, have often been claimed to be universal, but by way of shared biology). So, too, rationality is shaped and distinguished by culture. Thus when philosophers sing the praises of rationality, it is not always clear what they are praising, apart from, as Bertrand Russell wryly put it, our "ability to do sums." The very notion of "rationality" is typically ethnocentric, where it is an explicit part of an ethos at all, but this is not to say that reason—and our emotions—cannot have some kind of "objectivity."

When "rationality" means *reasonableness,* it is typically contrasted with emotionalism and "irrationality." If our concern is the idea of living well and wisely, this contrast issues in a conceptual disaster. We do not praise but are highly suspicious of people who are cold and calculating; *Star Trek's* Dr. Spock, for example. (A common theme of horror movies, such as *Invasion of the Body Snatchers,* is the depiction of otherwise "normal" humans whose status as monsters is marked by their lack of emotion.) In Camus's best-known novel, *The Stranger,* the odd central character is distinguished most of all by his lack of emotion: no grief upon his mother's death; no disgust in the presence of his pimp, chauvinist, slimeball neighbor Raymond; no love in his intimate conversations with his girlfriend Marie; no fear in the presence of a potential assassin with a knife; no regret for a murder that might easily have been avoided. But it is this lack of emotion (which many of my students find "cool," even heroic) that makes Meursault "an inhuman monster wholly without a moral sense" in the words of the overzealous prosecutor at his trial. It is our emotions that make us human. To be reasonable is to have the right emotions and to be rational includes having the right emotional premises.

And yet, throughout the history of philosophy, we find a portrait of the human soul or psyche in which the emotions play at best an inferior (at worst a devilish) role. It is a portrait that is well summarized in the image of a *"Steppenwolf,"* poeticized early in this century by the East-West writer Hermann Hesse, as half-human, half-beast. The human half gets characterized in terms of rationality, the bestial as the irrational, the emotional, the uncivilized, the primitive. The two halves are at war with one another, although a few philosophers have expanded the duality into a trinity and others have suggested musical metaphors such as "harmony" —typically of the wise master/obedient slave variety. (Aesop: reason should be the master of the passions. Hume: reason is and ought to be the slave of the passions.) But the antagonism remains and even in Hume emotion is relegated to the realm of the "impressions" and is denied intelligent status (despite his very sophisticated model of the causal role of ideas in emotion). My argument here, briefly stated, is that emotions already "contain" reason, and practical reason is circumscribed and defined by emotion. (Nietzsche: "as if every passion didn't contain its quantum of reason!") Our emotions *situate* us in the world, and so provide not so much the motive for rationality—much less its opposition—but rather its very framework.

The concepts and judgments that make up our emotions in turn constitute the criteria for rationality as well. If an offense is worthy of anger, it thus becomes rational (that is, warranted) to be angry about it; if one argues that it is even more rational (for example, more effective in terms of self-esteem or common prudence) *not* to get angry, that only shows, I want to suggest, how firmly entangled are the life of the emotions and the various meanings of rationality. Indeed, rationality begins to look more and more like emotional prudence, presupposing, of course, the right emotions. This doesn't mean the "control" of the emotions, much less their suppression. It rather underscores the emotional grounding of rationality. I want to reject the now-prevalent idea that rational criteria are simply the presuppositions of emotion or the external standards by which emotions and their appropriateness may be judged. That would leave standing the idea of a rational framework *within which* the emotions may be appropriate or inappropriate, warranted or unwarranted, wise or foolish. I want to suggest, rather, that emotions constitute the framework(s) of rationality itself. Of course, a single emotion does not do this, any more than a single correct calculation makes a student intelligent. A single emotion (or even an entire sequence of emotions) may be dictated by character, the circumstances, and the overall cultural context, but altogether our emotions (appropriate to the general circumstances) dictate that context (as well as that character). A truly "dispassionate" judgment is more often pathological than rational and detachment more likely signals alienation than objectivity. Heidegger's pun-like conception of *mood* (*Stimmung*) as our mode of "being tuned" (*Bestimmen*) to the world is instructive here, both because of its welcome shift in emphasis from detached knowing to holistic personal caring (*Sorge*) but also because of the not insubstantial fact that he emphasizes moods—which are general, defuse, and devoid of any determinate object— rather than, for example, love, an emotion whose character is marked first of all by its particularity and attachment. But what is important about both moods and emotions is the fact that they thoroughly permeate our experience and they are not, as several honorable ancient views would have it, interruptions, intrusions, or brief bouts of madness that get in the way of the otherwise calm and cool transparency of rational objectivity.

The idea that emotions as such are not rational thus begins with a basic misunderstanding of both the nature of emotions and the nature of rationality, and the idea that emotions as such are irrational is a confusion of certain sorts of specialized procedures, appropriate perhaps to the seminar room and the negotiating table, with rationality as such. But even in the seminar and at the negotiating table, it is caring that counts first of all, and as a matter of strategy, it is obvious that even as a negotiating tool emotion is often appropriate and, when well used, effective. Love is some-times said to be irrational because it overevaluates the beloved. But here as always we should be very suspicious: Is the enthusiastic idealization of someone about whom one cares a great deal a falsification and thereby irrational, or is it part and parcel of any intimate connection, recognizing another as more important than others ("to me") and being engaged in life rather than a merely disinterested, dispassionate spectator? So, too, with almost all of the emotions, including many of those which have typically been dubbed "negative," even "sins," one must be very careful about dis-missing their admittedly biased vision of the world as merely "subjective" or "irrational," for what is the alternative—not caring at all (*apatheia*), no affections or offenses whatever? Maybe the alternative is no commit-ments or attachments: the dubiously "rational" approach to a life without loss suggested by various ascetics and religious thinkers, e.g., the Arab phi-losopher al-Kindi in the ninth century. These are the targets of Nietzsche's renowned attack on the hypocrisy of asceticism in his *Genealogy of Morals,* where he claims that ascetics (like everyone) seek power and self-assertion but obtain it, as it were, backwards, by stealth and self-denial. But what sort of person would be incapable of anger or any sense of "getting even" when offended, not as a matter of strategy or in pursuit of higher goals but just by virtue of "reasonableness" alone? A person with pathologically low self-esteem, or a saint might qualify, but are not saints to be characterized precisely by their very rarity and, perhaps, irrationality. (Consider Dos-toevsky's well-known candidate, Prince Mishkin in *The Idiot.*) And even then, are not most of our saints recognized as such not by their cosmic indifference but rather by their extreme *caring*—about their people, about their religion, about the very rationality (certainly not to be confused with the "objectivity") of the world? Caring about the right things—one's friends and family, one's compatriots and neighbors, one's culture and environment and, ultimately, the world—is what defines rationality. It is not reason (as opposed to emotion) that allows us to extend our reach to the universal but rather the expansive scope of the emotions themselves. What we care about is defined by our conception of the world, but our conception of the world is itself defined by the scope and objects of our emotional cares and concern.

Not only is every emotion structured by concepts and judgments, most of them learned (at least in their details and applications), but every emotion is also engaged in a strategy of psychological as well as physical self-preservation. Thus it is readily understandable that emotions should first of all emerge as self-interested, even selfish, then concerned with kin and kinship rather than a larger sense of community, chauvinistic rather than cosmic. But part of cultivation, or "civilization," is internalizing the larger concepts of history, humanity, and religion, conceptions of morality and ethics that go beyond provincial self-interests. But this is not to say that the emotional nature of these concerns is replaced by something more abstract and impersonal; the emotions and the personal themselves become more expansive. Emotions are not just "reactions," and although they undoubtedly have an evolutionary history that precedes the arrival of the human species by hundreds of millions of years, they have evolved not only along with but hand in hand with the evolution of reason and rationality, which means in part an awareness of the larger human and global context in which all of our fates are engaged and our interests involved. There is, however, nothing particularly human about emotion as such (a dog or a horse can be as rightfully angry or sad as a person), although there are particularly human emotions, for instance romantic love and moral indignation. Indeed, some of those particularly human emotions—religious passion and scientific curiosity, for instance—are precisely the passions which are typically designated as proof of our rationality.

15

Anthropology and the Emotions

Among the Utkuhikhalingmiut ("Utku") eskimos of the Canadian Northwest Territories, anger is a genuine rarity. In her book *Never In Anger,* anthropologist Jean L. Briggs suggests that even in circumstances that we would find intolerably frustrating or offensive, the Utka do not get angry. Where we would be resentful or furious, the Utku are merely resigned.

Among the Ifaluk of Micronesia, murder is unknown, and the most serious incident of aggression last year, according to Catherine Lutz who has been studying them, was when one man touched another's shoulder. He was subjected to a severe fine.

The Tahitians were described 200 years ago by one of Captain Cook's officers as "slow to anger and soon appeased." Today, psychiatrist-turned-anthropologist Robert Levy finds that, even after centuries of European fantasies and interference, they are still slow to anger and soon appeased.

Sitting in rush-hour traffic on Storrow Drive in Boston, by way of contrast, one finds that anger is neither rare nor slow nor easily appeased. Indeed one would not be readily refuted in the hypothesis that ire is, in the heterogeneous and transient subculture that defines Boston traffic today,

Initially developed for an interdisciplinary conference at the Social Science Research Institute in New York, this piece formed the first part of "Getting Angry," which was later published in *Culture Theory,* edited by Schweder and Levine (Cambridge University Press, 1984). This brief version is from *"Onward," The Austin American-Statesman,* May 21, 1985. © Austin American-Statesman. Reprinted by permission of the publisher.

the dominant passion of life. Flying through rush-hour traffic in New Delhi, by way of contrast again, one is struck by the emotional calm in the midst of vehicular (and camel) chaos.

It is often said, by way of both profundity and platitude, that people are, "deep down," all the same. Customs, laws, governments, mating rituals, table manners, and religious beliefs may vary from culture to culture, but emotions, at least, are the same from Samoa to lower Manhattan, with variations appropriate to traffic and circumstances.

The idea that emotions are the same the world over is brought home in many ways. For example, one of my friends was in Vietnam during the worst days. When he first arrived, he once watched a group of young Vietnamese women burst into peals of laughter when they were shown photographs of a recent bomb explosion in their town, an explosion that had killed or maimed a dozen children, some of them presumably relatives. Needless to say, my friend was startled and perplexed.

The incident seemed to confirm the worst propaganda: the idea that the Vietnamese were temperamentally indifferent to suffering and thus so different from us as to be "inhuman." A few months in Saigon, of course, taught my friend a very different lesson, that the women's laughter was not an expression of amusement but of horror and grief. The mode of expression was unfamiliar but the emotion expressed was all too common.

Gardiner Lindzey summed up the leading version of this old idea in 1954 when he insisted that "emotions, as biological events, are the same the world over." Sociobiologist Edward O. Wilson, often quoted in such matters, locates the emotions in the "lower" and least variable parts of the brain. But brains and biology are not all there is to emotions.

It is an idea that dies hard, but contemporary anthropologists are on the attack. Anthropologist David Schneider of the University of Chicago writes, "As a fully paid up member of the cultural relativist position, I must deny that in any sense can 'emotions be the same the world over.' "

"Not only ideas but emotions, too, are cultural artifacts," wrote Princeton anthropologist Clifford Geertz, once again propounding a theme he has pursued for many years. "Complete rubbish," replied Cambridge dean of anthropologist Edmund Leach, thus opening up a new round of hostilities in the perennial debate about the nature of "human nature."

Richard Schweder of the Center for Human Development in Chicago suggests that the battle lines are once again forming between the "enlightenment" humanists, who emphasize universal reason and minimize the cultural significance of emotions, and the "romantic rebels," who emphasize both the importance and the diversity of emotions. On the side of the rebels is a world of new research on emotion that shows that our passions are not just "natural" but culturally determined, part of our education just as much as etiquette, literature, and religion. If this is so, then emotions may vary as much as languages and customs, and the fact that we have the same kind of brains no more means that we have similar feelings than a common body shape requires us to all dress the same. Emotions, too, may be a cultural accoutrement.

Emotions clearly have a biological substratum, which does not entitle us to conclude that we are biologically all the same. One of the most well-verified facts about the human brain is its malleability to learning and experience, and though it is true that certain "lower" (note well!) components of the brain are less malleable than the "higher" cerebral centers, it is simply a fallacy to conclude that because the former are necessarily involved in emotion (damage to those parts of the brain result in serious affective disorders) the nature of emotion is to be found wholly there and not as well in the same quarters as cultivation and civilization.

There is, in addition to our (more or less) shared biology and our diverse cultures, such a thing as the "human condition": the fact that all of us are born into families; are vulnerable to pain, disease, and death; the fact that we need and want to be with other people; and, the most significant single fact of all, that we all *know* these things (no matter how we may resist or rationalize). So, too, we all share a (more or less) common physiology, we all speak some language or other, and we all have some sense of self and others—whether in accordance with extreme American individualism or extreme communitarian tribalism. But beyond this sparse outline of humanity it is the differences that seem to us significant, not so much the gross similarities. It is the *meanings* of our emotions that count, and these meanings—which mean the emotions themselves—are cultivated in different ways in different circumstances providing different frameworks of what is rational and what is not. Consider the difference between a society obsessed with efficiency and productivity and one more impressed with social harmony, a society that celebrates the eccentric or exceptional individual and one that demands conformity and consensus. The "human condition" may remain the same, but the concept of rational action will be very different indeed and the conditions for mutual understanding possibly quite difficult.

Emotions, in other words, are part and parcel of the structure of a society, indeed, they are more "in" the social realm than they belong to the much-touted private realm of personal experience so glorified by Descartes and many overly introspective empiricists. Emotions evolve along with a way of life, according to which some activities are encouraged, others forbidden; some things are said to be delightful, others repulsive; some people are attractive and to be admired and courted, others are to be shunned or made fun of. Thus fear of snakes, or mice, or thunder may be rational in some societies but not in others, and "falling in love" will be sanctioned and encouraged in some cultures and not in others. Ambition is to be praised in most of America, but it is a target of scorn and contempt in much of the world (as in Shakespeare's contemptuous characterization of Cassius, in *Julius Caesar*.) David Hume once said, "Reason is and ought to be slave of the passions." But Hume overly separated the ends (emotions) and the means (rationality), as if emotions were not themselves already strategies and as if rationality were nothing but a calculative strategy and not itself already situated and defined in an emotionally defined social context. What counts as "rational," accordingly, is based on a system of such emotional premises which, as Hume suggested, provide the "ends" that any system of rationality must serve. It is culture that defines both what counts as rational and what is a legitimate emotion.

It remains and should remain an open question (not to be solved in an armchair) whether there are rational or emotional (or rational-emotional) structures that transcend and cross cultures and whether there are standards or measures (e.g., "utility") by which alternative rational-emotional structures can be evaluated. In the broadest of terms, "the human condition" would seem to provide the possibility of such a measure, based upon the universality of the uncertainty (if not fear) of pain and death, the protection people must provide for their children, and the fear and then resentment of public humiliation. But one can find wide variations on all of these themes and all of them may be denied by a misleading rationality which pretends to detach itself from all such contexts and attachments, justified by the atrocious philosophical presumption that if it can't be rationally demonstrated then it must be rationally doubted.

Our emotions provide a socially constructed "conceptual framework" in which the forms of engagement and caring emerge as the dominant *Gestalten*. It is within the bounds of engagement—being part of a community (even as the local oddball)—and by presuming one's care and concern for other people (even if what one cares about is mainly one's own reputation) that the rules of rationality are constructed to protect and preserve a set of emotional practices. Hume's famous claim that by reason alone he would prefer the destruction of half the world to the pricking of his finger shows just what is wrong with an emotionally detached conception of reason. Contra Kant, practical reason begins with caring, fearing, hoping, and even hating. Emotions are not the masters of reason nor are they reason's slaves. The dichotomy is a false one, and with it our conception of rationality has become impoverished.

16

Justice and the Passion for Vengeance

"There is no denying the aesthetic satisfaction, the sense of poetic justice, that pleasures us when evil-doers get the comeuppance they deserve. The impulse to punish is primarily an impulse to even the score. . . . The satisfaction is heightened when it becomes possible to measure out punishment in exact proportion to the size and shape of the wrong that has been done."

—Arthur Lelyveld

"The criminal law stands to the passion of revenge in much the same relation as marriage to the sexual appetite."

—Fitzjames Stephens

However problematic its current role in justice may be, there is no doubt but that vengeance is the original passion for justice. The word "justice" in the Old Testament virtually always refers to revenge. Throughout most of history the concept of justice has been far more concerned with the punishment of crimes and the balancing of wrongs than with the fair distribution of goods and services. "Getting even" is and has always been one of the most basic metaphors of our moral vocabulary, and the frightening emotion of righteous, wrathful anger has been the emotional basis for justice just as much as benign compassion. "Don't get mad, get even"—whether

---

This piece began as a lecture in Australia and became part of my book titled *A Passion for Justice* (Reading, Mass.: Addison-Wesley, 1990). © 1990, by Robert C. Solomon. Reprinted by permission of the publisher.

or not it is prudent advice—is conceptually confused. Getting even is just an effective way of being mad, and getting mad already includes a generous portion of revenge.

This is not to say, of course, that getting even is therefore legitimate or the action of revenge always justified. But to seek vengeance for a grievous wrong, to revenge oneself against evil: that seems to lie at the very foundation of our sense of justice, indeed, our sense of ourselves, our dignity and our sense of right and wrong. Even Adam Smith writes, in his *Theory of the Moral Sentiments,* "The violation of justice is injury . . . it is, therefore, the proper object of resentment, and of punishment, which is the natural consequence of resentment." We are not mere observers of the moral life; the desire for vengeance seems to be an integral aspect of our recognition of evil. But moral life also contains—or can be cultivated to contain—the elements of its own control, a sense of its limits, a sense of balance. Thus the Old Testament instruction that revenge should be *limited to* "an eye for an eye, a tooth for a tooth, hand for hand, foot for foot, burning for burning, wound for wound, stripe for stripe" (Exodus 21:24-5)—the concept of *Lex Talionis.* The New Testament demands even more restraint, the abstention from revenge oneself and the patience to entrust it to God. Both the Old and New Testaments (more the latter than the former) also encourage "forgiveness," but there can be no foregiveness if there is not first the desire (and the warrant) for revenge.

Vengeance is not just punishment, no matter how harsh. It is a matter of emotion. It is not a matter of obligation or rationality but neither is it opposed to a sense of obligation (e.g., in family vendettas and matters of honor) or rationality (insofar as rationality is to be found in every emotion, even this one). Vengeance presupposes "getting even," putting the world back in balance. It is not just the urge to harm. And here emerges a question that philosophers have been much too quick to answer: Is this sense of "balance" or "retribution" a function of emotion or must it be an idea, a rational principle? Kant, of course, immediately opts for the latter, dismissing the former virtually altogether. Vengeance is assumed to be wholly without measure or reason, devoid of any sense of balance or justice. Vengeance, unlike justice, is said to be "blind" (though it is worth reminding ourselves which of the two is depicted in established mythology as blindfolded). Vengeance, it is said, knows no end. It is not just that it gets out of hand; it cannot be held "in hand" in the first place. And, of course, we can agree that there is danger in vengeance. It is by its very nature violent, disrupting the present order of things in an often impossible attempt to get back to a prior order that has itself been violently disrupted. Such an impossibility breeds frustration and violence. And violence typically leads to more violence. An act of revenge results in a new offense to be righted. And when the act is perpetrated not against the same person who did the offense but against another who is part of the same family, tribe, or social group (the logic of "vendetta"), the possibilities for escalation are endless. Accordingly, the limitation of revenge through institutionalization is necessary. But it does not follow that vengeance itself is illegitimate or without measure or of no importance in considerations of punishment. To the dangers of vengeance unlimited it must be added that if punishment no longer satisfies vengeance, if it ignores not only the rights but the emotional needs of the victims of crime, then punishment no longer serves its primary purpose, even if it were to succeed in rehabilitating the criminal and deterring other crime (which it evidently, in general, does not). The restriction of vengeance by law is entirely understandable; but, again, the wholesale denial of vengeance as a legitimate motive may be a psychological disaster.

These preliminary comments are intended to unearth a number of bad arguments against vengeance (which are often generalized into even worse arguments concerning "negative" and violent emotions as a unified class):

1. *Vengeance is (as such) irrational, and, consequently, it is never legitimate.* Only a moment's reflection is necessary to realize that we all recognize (whether or not we recognize at the time) the difference between justified and unjustified revenge. Vengeance is not just the desire to harm but the desire to harm *for a reason,* and a reason of a very particular sort. To flunk a student because he has an orange punk hairdo or because he disagreed with one's pet theory in class is not justified, but to expel him for burning down the department library is another matter. But what about the fact that sometimes, while in the "grip" of revenge, we fail to recognize or properly exercise the reason and warrant for our vengeance? The point is the word "sometimes," for there is nothing essential to vengeance that requires such failure. In indisputably rational contexts decision makers mistake a means for an end, or become so distracted in their pursuit of the end that they neglect or simply miss the most appropriate means. In vengeance one can also get caught up in the means, or obsessed and distracted by the end, but the logic of "reasons" and appropriateness is nevertheless present as a standard. Accordingly, the question is not whether vengeance is ever legitmate but, rather, when it is legitimate, when are those standards and reasons in fact appropriate and warranted.

2. *There is no "natural" end to it.* But, of course, there is. The idea that vengeance leads to a total loss of inhibition and control ignores the built-in and cultivated satisfactions of revenge, and seems to confuse the potential escalation of mutually vengeful acts with the fact that a single

act of vengeance typically has its very specific goals and, consequently, its own built-in standard of satisfaction. *Ivan the Terrible,* Part I (after the slaughter of the innocents): "Even beasts are rational in their anger." We recognize the built-in satisfactions of vengeance in our notion of "poetic justice," the central theme of many if not most of the movies produced today. When that satisfaction is not provided, e.g., in Woody Allen's brilliant but perverse *Crimes and Misdemeanors,* we find ourselves extremely uncomfortable.

3. *Vengeance is always violent.* The blood-thirsty acts of the Dirty Harry character or the Ninja assassin may hold dramatic sway over our fantasies, but the more usual act of revenge is a negative vote in the next department meeting, a forty-five–minute delay in arriving to dinner, or a hurtful comment or letter, delivered with a vicious twist of phrase, perhaps; rarely is it the twist of a blade, except, of course, metaphorically. Given the current tendency to inflate the meaning of words and numb our sensitivities to moral differences, one might argue that such acts do indeed constitute "violence," but to do so certainly drains the substance from this standard objection against vengeance. And, on the other side of the argument, even many of those who reject vengeance, accept "retribution" so long as it is in the name of cool legal justice rather than hot revenge. It is here that Kant, in a famous (or infamous) passage, suggests that, were the world to end tomorrow, we should nevertheless execute all condemned criminals today, not for vengeance but as a matter of practical reason, of course.

4. *It takes the law "into our own hands."* (The use of "in hand" metaphors seem to abound in such discussions.) It is worth noting that historically, punishing the perpetrator for almost any offense against an individual, from an obscene gesture to rape and murder, rested with the family, and it was considered not only inappropriate but unjustifiable intrusion into private matters for the state to step in. It is a relatively recent development—and an obviously very political move—that punishment of such crimes should have become the *exclusive* province of the state. Moral objections against vengeance and the desire for public order seem to me to have far less to do with this than the usual arrogance of the state in abrogating individual rights and its desire for control. Indeed, it is a point worth pondering that major crimes against the person are, in law, crimes against the state. When current criminal law reduces the victim of such crimes to a mere bystander (assuming that the victim has survived the crime), the problem is not that in vengeance we take the law "into our own hands" but rather that without vengeance justice seems not only to be taken out of our hands but eliminated as a consideration altogether.

Current concerns with punishment, even those that claim to take "retribution" seriously, seem to serve the law and sanction respect for the law (or reason) rather than the need for justice. Not that the law and respect for the law are unimportant, of course, but one should not glibly identify these with justice and dismiss the passion for vengeance as something quite different and wholly illegitimate.

The notion of retribution or retaliation lies right at the heart of the question of punishment (indeed, it has often been argued that it is just another word for "punishment"), and it has long held the dominant position against its rival theories, which emphasize deterrence and rehabilitation respectively. (For example, Gregory Vlastos: "the institutional basis of punishment is not to relieve vindictive feelings but to minimize wrongs.") It is not that retributivists need deny the importance or desirability of deterring crime or changing the character or at least the behavior of criminals. It is just that such activities, no matter how well-intended or conceived, do not count as punishment. It is often pointed out that courts in fact always use discretion and mercy, and it is therefore false that in practice, "the punishment fits the crime" (i.e., that guilt and nothing but guilt justifies infliction of punishment). Since ancient times, there has been Socrates's oft-repeated objection that punishment is the return of evil for evil and so never legitimate, no matter how horrendous the crime. More recently, A. S. Neil has argued, "I think that the deterrent argument is simply a rationalization. The motive for punishment is revenge—not deterrence." In the realm of technical philosophy, it is sometimes charged that retributivist theory, at least in some of its formulations, is really based upon utilitarian considerations. But the argument is that, as a general guideline for punishment, retribution and only retribution will do; any real retributivist will insist that retribution is, in effect, good in itself, not a means to further ends (deterrence or reform). However often retribution may be called "barbaric," no matter if it is "the most unfashionable theory in philosophical and other circles" and "frequently dismissed with contempt," the idea continues to hold powerful sway over us. As Kant put it, "Only the law of retribution (*jus talionis*) can determine exactly the kind and degree of punishment," so long as (Kant adds) such a determination is made in a court of justice and not in private judgment. It is this sense of what Kant calls "equality" that counts, the punishment "fitting" the crime. If a man has committed a murder, Kant argues, he must die; "there is no substitute that will satisfy the requirements of legal justice. There is no sameness of kind between death and remaining alive even under the most miserable conditions."*

---

*I. Kant, *Philosophy of Law,* trans. Hastie (1889).

In some ways, the conflict between retributivist and various utilitarian theories of punishment is a false one. The fact is that any competent judge weighs guilt, deterrence, and the possibility of rehabilitation together and is not constrained or tempted by the philosopher's need to seize one side of a multifaceted issue. But this is not the question here. It is rather the idea that retribution forms the conceptual core, the *sine qua non,* of punishment and, therefore of justice. And, given that argument (or something like it), our question is whether vengeance is or is not this conceptual core of retribution. No matter how hard the defenders of retributive theory may strive to distinguish and separate vengeance from retribution, the merely and dangerously emotional from the rational and legal, the legitimate claims and concerns of the one are the legitimate claims and concerns of the other. And what defines both of these claims and concerns is a series of metaphors, too often thrown together as one, and too often treated as if they were not metaphors at all but literal truths. (Let me say from the start that I have nothing against metaphors—some of my best philosophical friends are metaphors. But when a theory presents itself as a product of Practical Reason, we have a right to expect something other than poetry.) I want to comment on four of these here:

1. The *"debt"* metaphor: to punish is to "repay" a wrong. There is some dispute (for example, in Nietzsche, *On the Genealogy of Morals,* Essay II) whether the notion of legal obligation preceded or grew out of this idea of a debt; but with regard to punishment, the metaphorical character of "repayment" is quite clear. The suggestion that there is an implicit contract (whether via Hobbes and Locke or Plato's *Crito*) is just to repeat the question, how the metaphor of repayment can be rationally justified. To link it with the other metaphors, punishment neither "balances the books" nor "erases" the wrong in question, as repayment of a debt surely does. The "debt" metaphor, by the way, is not restricted to capitalist societies; "debt" is not the same as "consumer debt," and applies to the New Guinea custom of giving a pig for a wrongful death as much as it does to the problem of paying off one's credit card. Debt, in most societies, is a moral measure rather than a monetary arrangement.

2. The *"fit"* metaphor is the popular idea that the punishment should "fit" the crime. (W. S. Gilbert's *Mikado*: "an object all sublime/make the punishment fit the crime.") Punishment must "fit" the crime, we are told, going back to the easy formulation of the *lex talionis.* But as many opponents and critics of retributivism have pointed out, such punishments are administered—or even make sense—only in a very limited number of crimes (e.g., intentional murder). But even then, as Albert Camus has famously pointed out,

For there to be equivalence, the death penalty would have to punish a criminal who had warned his victim of the date at which he would inflict a horrible death on him and who, from that moment onward, had confined him at his mercy for months. Such a monster is not encountered in private life.*

Defenders of retributivism gladly weaken the demands of "fit," suggesting, for instance, that it provides only a general measure, that the crucial concept here is one of "proportion"—so that petty theft is not (as it once was) punished with the harshness of a violent crime. With this, of course, we all agree, but "proportion," too, misleadingly suggests quantification where there often is none, and it, too, summarizes rather than solves the problem of punishment. To be sure, it is somehow "fit" to trade a life for a life (or more accurately, "a death for a death"), but is it just? There are so many qualifications and extenuating circumstances concerning intentions, risk, and appropriate caution that qualify each and every case. Does the singular image of "fit" make sense? (Of course, we recognize the *lack* of fit: witness our horror, e.g., when Afghan tribesmen summarily execute [by beheading] the hapless tourist involved in an automobile accident, even one which [were the driver to have made an insurance claim] might have been proclaimed "faultless.") In eighteenth-century British law, responsibility for the white population of Australia is astonishingly exemplary of lack of fit, as were the punishments meted out to those who arrived.

3. The *"balance"* metaphor: punishment makes things "even" again. It is through punishment that one "gets even." In epic literature, it is by punishing the villain that one "balances the forces of good and evil." One problem is that this moral balance is often simply equated, in the crudest utilitarian fashion, with a balance of pleasure and pain, as if the application of an amount of pain to the villain equal to the amount of pain he or she has caused (which is not the same as the amount of pleasure gotten from his crime) balances the scales. (We should remember again the standard allegorical figure of justice, this time with her scales.) Where the crime is strictly pecuniary, it might seem that balance (like the repayment of a debt) might be literally appropriate, but this, of course, isn't so. One can pay back the amount of money stolen or otherwise taken, but this does not yet take into account the offense itself. As soon as one must pay back even an extra penny, the literalness of the "balance" again comes into question. Granted, the original sum has been repaid, but now what is the "cost" or the "price" of the crime? Again, my point is not that the metaphor

---

*A. Camus, "Reflections on the Guillotine," in *Resistance, Rebellion and Death* (trans. J. O'Brien, 1961).

of "balance" isn't applicable or revealing of how we think about justice, but it underscores rather than solves our problems.

4. The *"erasure"* metaphor: the idea that we can "annul the evil" through punishment. Vendetta cultures talk about "bloodmarks" (also "blood debts") not as a sign of guilt but rather of unrevenged wrong. But can we undo a crime—for instance, rape or murder—in any sense whatever? In financial crimes, again, one can "erase" the debt by paying it back, but one cannnot erase the crime itself. For example, how does one erase the terror suffered in an armed robbery, even if the money were to be politely returned? ("Here you are, Miss; I'm a student at the local police academy and I wanted to experience what the criminal felt like.") Indeed, how does one measure the fear that one suffers in such crimes, even if there is no "harm done" in any of the usual senses?

What I am arguing here is not that retributivism is wrong or unintelligible but rather that it is wrongly presented as a theory or a set of principles when it ought to be treated as the expression of revenge. Of course, retribution can be turned into a theory (no one would accuse Kant of mere metaphor mongering), but retributivism, I want to argue, is primarily a set of concepts and judgments embodied in a feeling, not a theory. Perhaps it was overstated in the majority opinion of the United States Supreme Court in *Gregg* v. *Georgia* (1976): "the instinct for retribution is part of the nature of man, and channeling that instinct in the administration of criminal justice serves an important purpose in promoting the stability of a society governed by law. When people begin to believe that organized society is unwilling or unable to impose upon criminal offenders the punishment they 'deserve,' then there are sown the seeds of anarchy—of self-help, vigilante justice, and lynch law." But at least the emotion of vengeance was taken seriously and not merely sacrificed to the dispassionate authority of the law. Retributive justice, however rationalized, is not as such a purely "rational matter"—but neither is it thereby "irrational" either. Most of the arguments that have been advanced against vengeance could, with only slight modifications, be applied to the standard notions of retributive justice as well, which is not surprising if vengeance and retributive justice are in the end identical. But it is perhaps not just a question of whether revenge is rational or not, but whether it is—at the bottom of our hearts as well as off the top of our heads—an undeniable aspect of the way we react to the world, not as an instinct but as such a basic part of our worldview and our moral sense of ourselves that it is, in that sense, unavoidable.

I have not tried here to defend vengeance, nor have I provided a real argument to the effect that retributivist theories must always be about vengeance (nor does this seem to me to be so). My claim is that vengeance deserves its central place in any theory of justice and, whatever else we are to say about punishment, the desire for revenge must enter into our deliberations along with such emotions as compassion, caring, and love. Any system of legal principles that does not take such emotions into account, which does not motivate itself on their behalf, is not—whatever else it may be—a system of justice.

17

The Philosophy of Horror, Or, Why Did Godzilla Cross the Road?

Among the various virtues of Noel Carroll's *Philosophy of Horror* is the delightful reminder that philosophy—even old-fashioned Ithaca-style conceptual analysis—can be fun. The book reflects (one hesitates to speculate how many) hundreds (thousands?) of hours engaged in what the author (only partially tongue-in-cheek) describes as "research," initiated no doubt in late-night Saturday sessions in front of his parent's black-and-white television as a teenager and continuing, so he tells us, into the bonds of marriage and tenure. These teenage habits have now been elevated to a "method," the method of "random viewing" (p. 54). How else could one expect to gain a fair representation of the several hundred so-called horror films put on celluloid since Murnau's *Nosferatu* in 1922, not to mention the several hundred H. P. Lovecraft short stories and science-fiction-type horror novels that filled in the time between movies and very likely during high school classes as well? Carroll is indeed a dedicated scholar. His book is a delight to read, an excuse to recapture and enjoy one's own adolescent ghoulish Grendelphilia.

The horror genre is, no doubt, as old as stories around the fire in Cromagnon times, tens of thousands of years before the first film depiction of *The Golem* shortly before World War I. There were "Gothic" novels before there were Gothic movies, and before them the Medievals had more

A critical review of *The Philosophy of Horror* by Noel Carroll (Routledge, 1991) in *Philosophy and Literature* 16 (1992). Reprinted here in edited form by permission of the publisher.

119

than their share of horror stories, which Carroll too readily dismisses "because people actually believed them." I want to argue that the connection between horror and belief is much more intimate than this, and the horror of a period really does reflect what people are actually afraid of. Before the explicitly depicted horrors of Hell and damnation there was Petronius's *Satyricon* and the many monsters of the *Odyssey;* the horrifying manifestations of Shiva and Kali; the malevolent goddesses of the Solomon Islands; the monster Grendel in *Beowulf;* the later perversities of Merlin in *King Arthur;* the many devils of Bali; and the real-life, raccoon-sized but plenty fearsome devil of Tasmania. I think Carroll is just plain wrong— or too much in a hurry to get to his main subject of movies—to insist that the horror genre begins during and as a reaction against the Enlightenment. I think that he is therefore mistaken in limiting his analysis to the admittedly peculiar experience of sitting in a theater or in front of a television watching one of a large but carefully delimited set of mostly inferior and culturally pointless films. There is something to be said for his casual suggestion that horror novels depicting the "unnatural" presupposed the Enlightenment conception of an orderly nature, and I agree with him that the usual Manichean account of horror and much of Romanticism as the "dark side" of the Enlightenment depend on an image that is at once inaccurate and obscure. But what Romanticism really represented does not seem to be of any interest to Carroll, including its proclivity for original "Gothic" (i.e., Medieval) and ancient pagan mysteries and monsters. What happened in the eighteenth and nineteenth centuries is but part of a somewhat cyclical story that goes back to pre-biblical times, beginning no doubt when a few clever cavemen (or, more likely, cavewomen) scared the pelts off some of the youngsters, no doubt invoking the possible presence of prehistoric monsters that were by no means fictional at the time.

At the same time, horror has often been linked with comedy, and the shriek of horror is never entirely distinct from hysterical laughter. Despite its predictably more somber origins in Germany, the horror film in America has almost always been tied up with comedy. In fact, the first Hollywood horror film was a spoof (Leni's *Cat and the Canary*) and it was not long before Abbott and Costello and the Three Stooges were sharing the screen with Dracula, Frankenstein's monster, and Lon Chaney, Jr. Roger Corman made his reputation with a sequence of films that were much more ludicrous than they were frightening (notably, the original version of *Little Shop of Horrors,* recently remade as a Lower East Side play in New York and then a trendy film with Rick Moranis and Steve Martin). The (sub-)genre of "*schlock-*horror" has continued to be one of lesser Hollywood's most prolific productions, and many (if not most) of the horror films produced in the last forty years have been obviously intended as laughable as well as (or rather than) terrifying. This is to say nothing of the rubber-suited Japanese monsters or the truly gifted horror-comedies of Tim Burton (*Beetlejuice, Edward Scissorhands*), Roman Polanski (*Fearless Vampire Killers*), or George Hamilton as a remarkably sun-tanned Dracula in *Love at First Bite*.

Horror holds a special place in the meeting of philosophy, psychology, and sociology (not to mention biology and the other sciences that are twisted to its purposes). What is horror? Using horror fiction as a paradigm has its limitations, and even within the genre, it matters a great deal whether one takes as an example *Jaws, King Kong, The Blob, Night of the Living Dead, Friday the Thirteenth*, or (Carroll's own apparent favorite) *The Exorcist*. There is also horror in "real life"—gawkers at the scene of an accident; the shock with which one watches a loved one, totally "out of character," stage a tantrum or fly into a drunken rage; the horror with which one gazes at the remaining stub of one's bloody little finger after an accident with a sharp implement; or the packed courthouse in Milwaukee for the arraignment of a serial killer. It is not just the distinction between fiction and life I want to question here, a distinction too often obscured by other scholars who seem comfortable with neither. It is, rather, the nature of horror—and the nature of emotion as such—that I want to call into question. Carroll defines horror in terms of the emotions it causes, and it is the nature of this emotion—as well as the boundaries of the genre that provoke it—that interest me here.

A second question is, What is the object of horror? This "ontological" question has been around at least since Coleridge, who provided a memorable phrase as well as an interesting answer to it. "The willing suspension of disbelief" was Coleridge's explanation of how we could allow ourselves to be absorbed in fantasy. "Why should we fear fictions?" is the alliterative way Ken Walton put it in his book, *Mimesis as Make-Believe*. But I want to be careful here, for there is a quicksand of philosophical questions. When we ask, "What is the object of horror?" is that in fact the proper question, or is that rather shorthand for a more general question about the nature of a kind of experience in which the "object" is but an abstracted focus? Is it fear that we feel when we are watching a horror film? Or is that already misplacing the question and misunderstanding the nature of the emotion involved? The standard way of putting the question, "How can we be afraid of something that we know does not exist?" is tantalizing and thought-provoking but ultimately stultifying. Either the answer is "we are not afraid," which seems utterly false, or "we really do believe in its existence," which defies common sense. "Well, then, why don't you run out of the theater?" is Carroll's sensible response.

A third question has to do with the nature of the experience of horror. Quite apart from the status of the horrible object, what is it *like* to be horrified? Here, in particular, much depends on the nature of emotion and the theory or theories of emotion one entertains. One persistent account of emotion takes an emotion to be a physiological disturbance caused by cognition, which has its advantages and disadvantages. The most obvious advantage is that it places proper attention on the role of "beliefs" (or some sort of "cognition") in the role of emotion in general and horror in particular. The main disadvantage is that it puts too much attention on the sheer physiology of the experience, and in particular the shivers and shudders that are typically provided (even promised) as part of the price of horror-movie admission. Indeed, Carroll defines the horror-experience, in part, as disgust, an exceedingly visceral sensation (and arguably not an emotion at all). But horror and the emotion of art-horror caused by and definitive of horror is, nevertheless, a disturbing and unpleasant experience, which leads us quite naturally to a fourth and last question: Why are we are willing to subject ourselves to an experience that is intrinsically disgusting and unpleasant? (There was something sanctimonious about the complaint that was voiced by not a few critics of *Jaws* (I), namely, that the film was "manipulative." What else would they have gone to the theater for?) We are "willing," in Coleridge's phrase, whether or not we willingly suspend our disbelief. (The angry reactions of an unwitting companion who accompanied you in the belief that the movie would be a romance or an adventure story, should make the point.) But why do we do it at all? Teenage males may do it to prove their bravado and insensitivity, and their semi-willing girlfriends may go along as an excuse to engage in the submissive helpless behavior that modern feminism years ago bred out of them, but the image of tenured professors (admittedly mostly male) sitting up late at night, watching once again the transformation of one of the many Jekylls into one of the many Hydes or one of so many mummies stagger back to the vault reminds us that there is something more to be explained here than youthful machismo (or the desire to live those years again).

Part of the answer to the "why?" question, of course, will have to do with the fact that the horror (art-horror) that Carroll discusses is explicitly and straightforwardly fictional. If there really were a blob of slime, giant ants, a werewolf, or a vampire coming at us, we would surely not sit there glued to our seats (with or without our hands in front of our faces) waiting to see what will happen. We would, presumably, run away in terror. Nor can we understand the fascination for horror in terms of any simple "as if" explanation. Carroll early on presents us with a "thought-experiment" (one of many) in which a friend or acquaintance tells us a story with all of the ingredients of a horror story, but giving us the sense that it is a true story. Carroll points out that, when we find out that it is only fiction, we are not horrified or amused but rather indignant. It is here in particular that Coleridge's phrase, "the *willing* [or at least knowing] suspension of disbelief" obviously comes into play. (Carroll does not discuss Orson Welles's 1938 radio broadcast of *War of the Worlds;* in this context, it's an odd omission.) But the answer to the final question leads us back to the first: What is horror, such that we actually enjoy it? It also leads to the second: Why should the object of horror horrify us, given that we know that it is merely fictitious?

Within the genre of horror movies—which for self-evident technological reasons did not begin before this century—there is also a multifaceted history that deserves some attention. It is not insignificant that the genre and all of the early classics began in Germany, despite the fact that the technology was developed in the United States and France. It is not incidental that America followed the (defeated) Germans into the genre only several years after the war, and then with a spoof rather than horror and suspense. It is no doubt worth noting how "celebrity-bound" the American pictures and their never-ending sequels became. Boris Korloff and Bela Lugosi became so identified with the parts they played that a viewing of *The Mummy* or *Frankenstein* or *Dracula* or any of their many variations became more like spending a few hours with an obnoxious but familiar relative rather than subjecting oneself to horror. Carroll carefully notes the affinities and differences between the horror genre and science fiction, but he does not bother to note how relatively recent the science-fiction craze is and how it transformed the horror film in the fifties. It is no coincidence, of course, that the amalgam coincided with publicly televised nuclear testing, the cold war and, with Sputnik in the late fifties, the first glimmer of space exploration. It is also a significant fact that so many of the films made today are what Carroll correctly but disgustingly identifies as "splatter films," movies whose primary and sometimes sole distinction are the gruesome special effects depicting bodies being mutilated in any number of ways, typically by "monsters" who are homicidal human psychopaths. These are quite different from the films made through most of the period Carroll discusses, and it will not do simply to dismiss them as degenerate or overly disgusting examples of the genre. They say something very real about what we fear—and aspire to—today.

What is horror? A lot depends on how we circumscribe the scope of our examples. What is included, and what is not? There is the usual inchoate blob or green slime, the biologically probable monster or rather monstrous shark in *Jaws;* the sentimental if somewhat chauvinist giant ape in *King Kong;* the various vomiting, head-turnings and quasi-Christian demonology of *The Exorcist;* and the slasher maniac in *Halloween.* Then there are the more or less clearly ideologically loaded "cold war" threats of mind-control (or, perhaps, total takeover), like *The Invasion of the Body Snatchers* and the various warnings against the unknown powers and effects of nuclear energy, notably in the guise of the various test-site desert critters grown to house or warehouse size (*Them!* or *Gila Monster*). There is the more general set of warnings about the abuses and dangers of science that date back to the book (not just the movie version) of *Frankenstein,* though that was not that novel's main moral purpose. One can, accordingly, trace the history of narratives warning against the abuse of one's powers (whether magical, mythical, or alchemical) back to the medieval and oriental enchanters and enchantresses who became caught up in their own wizardry to the ancient story of King Midas, a horror story that certainly ought to have significance in the world of Wall Street today. And there are horror movies without monsters at all, and certainly without the "unnatural" monsters discussed by Carroll. Slasher and splatter movies—the current favorite—are concerned with an all-too-real horror of contemporary life, the serial killer. Arthur Conan Doyle's *Hound of the Baskervilles* was one of the most frightening stories and later movies I remember (at least the Basil Rathbone version), but, though there were hints of the unnatural, the hound in question turned out to be a perfectly mortal but particularly ferocious dog. (One might contrast the metaphysical acrobatics in a story like Stephen King's *Cujo,* or the magical [and sexually loaded] transformations of Irena in *Cat People.*)

The answer to our second question—What is the object of horror?—might simply be summarized as a monster, something unnatural and impure that provokes fear and disgust in an audience. But fear seems to presuppose belief—the belief that the monster is (could be) real—so how can this be possible? Either one has the emotion and therefore the belief as well or one does not have the belief or the emotion. This is one of Carroll's "paradoxes of the heart," but I find it not to be a paradox at all. Notice that I have carefully avoided using *fear* as the name of the emotion in question, unlike Carroll and Kendall Walton and most other writers on the topic. There is a reason for this. I do not think that horror is the same as fear, and I do not think that the beliefs or presuppositions are the same for the two emotions. There is no problem if this distinction is respected.

"Why should we fear fictions?" asks Kendall Walton. His answer is that we do not fear fictions, because we do not believe in them. We rather experience make-believe fear—which is not fear—as part of our make-believe game in response to a make-believe monster. Daddy pretends to be a monster, and his three-year-old daughter is delighted to go along with the pretense, screaming and running around the living room but not for a moment terrified. So, too, audiences flock by the thousands to see mummies and monsters on the screen but only pretend to believe and, consequently, pretend to be afraid. I believe that Walton's analysis is charming and makes a good deal of sense for many of the arts and much of fiction, but it does not capture what Carroll cites as the definitive feature of horror, and that is the emotion. I think that Carroll is right to insist that the emotion experienced as horror is genuine and not pretend emotion at all. That emotion is not fear but horror, and the difference between them is not, as Carroll insists, the fact that horror involves disgust and the unnatural while fear need not. Nor is it that fear is directed at some real external threat while horror is stimulated by fictions. Consider Walton's three-year-old playing the game of "Daddy's a monster" with her father. That game consists, for the most part, of a great deal of activity—gestures, shrieks, and what in football would be called broken field running. Throughout the game, one expects a broad smile on her face and a sparkle in her eyes. The shrieks are sounds of joy, not terror. Walton is no doubt correct; she does not feel fear. But I would add that she does not feel make-believe or quasi-fear either. Carroll misses this point as well; he confuses fear with physiological feelings and sensations produced by adrenalin. The truth is, she is not afraid at all.

But what if she were to believe, for just a moment, that her father really was out to hurt her, or actually had been transformed? (This happens, and typically marks the abrupt end of the game.) The running stops, and so does the shrieking, which is replaced by a scream. She will most likely be frozen in place, aghast in horror. Immediately, Daddy drops all monstrous pretenses and consoles his hysterical child. The game is over, but the horror lingers. What essentially changed was not just a belief, namely, the belief that Daddy was playing a game. Indeed, it was probably over-cognizing the transformation to suggest that she came to believe, if just for a moment, that her father really was out to hurt her. A more appropriate phrase would be, "the thought occurred to her" or "for a fraction of a second it seemed." The difference between a belief and a thought or a "seeming" is of critical importance here, but, first, I want to develop the equally important distinction between fear and horror. It is not primarily a difference in belief.

In fear, one flees. One can pretend to fear, accordingly, by pretending to flee, a vigorous activity in which there may be little visible difference between pretense and reality. In horror, on the other hand, there is passivity, the passivity of presence. One stands (or sits) aghast, frozen in place, or "glued to one's seat." Of course, one can be frozen (or "paralyzed") by fear, but that is when fear becomes horror. Horror involves a helplessness which fear evades. The evasive activities of fear may be pointless, even self-defeating, but they are activities nonetheless, activities that can be feigned. Horror is a spectator's emotion, and thus it is especially well-suited for the cinema and the visual arts. But notice, then, that the ontological problem has all but disappeared. For while it makes all the difference whether the object of one's fear is real or a fiction, it makes little or no difference whether the object of horror is real or imagined. The bleeding body on the midnight asphalt of Interstate 35 is an object of horror in just the same sense that the bleeding bodies of the cinematic victims of imaginary monsters are objects of horror.

What changes, with the occurrence of the thought, could well be the mental move from the belief that Daddy is not to the belief that Daddy is a monster, but it is not, consequently, the shift from fear to horror. There never was any fear. And when the thought occurred, the apparent monstrosity of the situation, the hopelessness of "getting away" from one's own father, threw the child into a state of horror, not fear. To be sure, it was not a state that was chosen, much less a pretense or the object of a game. (That is why she was "thrown" into it.) But she could have chosen it, or one like it, and in a few years, she probably will. She could pay her six dollars, sit down in front of the screen where any one of a number of "Father-is-a-monster" films is being shown, and quite voluntarily experience, in safety, the same horrifying experience that once momentarily traumatized her as a child (though she may well have forgotten or suppressed that).

To say that it is the thought that identifies the object of horror is a deep insight that Carroll, with his anti-Freudian bias, may choose to pass over. But Ron Rosenbaum, a once-upon-a-time Harold Bloom student, has no such hesitation, and he rightly identifies the thought—rather than an actual external threat—as the hallmark of horror as opposed to fear. But "the thought" needs an explanation, and it is not merely, as it may have seemed above, a mere transient occurrence, a momentary "seeming," a brave little onion popping up through the concrete of the mind with no connection to anything around it. Thoughts can be momentary, of course, but they can also be profound, pervasive, even metaphysical.

In his discussion of poetry, Aristotle suggests that poetry (and, of course, philosophy) is superior to history because the latter is concerned only with particulars, the former with universals. Discussing tragedy, Aristotle insists that the object of our horror is, in fact, the universal, though enacted by a particular actor as a particular person in a particular situation. Our emotional response to uninstantiated universals is impoverished, but our emotional reactions to mere particulars is of no interesting significance. Paul Woodruff, for example, suggests that we are all afraid of a particular death—our own or someone close to us—and only awed by the idea of death as such. But a particular death as an exemplar of all deaths (or death itself) is a powerful experience, leaving it open to the spectator to instantiate the universal imaginatively—thinkingly or not—with any other particular with dramatic emotional impact. Watching a convincing peformance of *Oedipus Rex* or *Antigone* is a paradoxically devastating but pleasurable experience. On the one hand, we know that the actor or actress who plays Oedipus or Antigone does not suffer and may be enjoying the role. After the performance, he or she will go out with the cast for some cappuccino and a good night's sleep. On the other hand, we recognize that what we are watching is not just a game of make-believe, not just a troup of performers doing their bit, not just an imitation of tragedy, but tragedy as such. It could happen to you, or to me. The thought, Rosenbaum suggests, is a possibility. But it is not only this. It is a vivid experience of the genuine article.

I want to return, for a moment, to Carroll's apparent infatuation with *The Exorcist,* the film he most often refers to and which he describes in the most detail. Carroll predictably emphasizes the unnatural and impure aspects of possession, and the intention of the producers of that film to disgust us is all too obvious. But here the film cheats—as do its many sequels and offspring (*The Omen,* etc.). It produces disgust by means of merely disgusting scenes and substances—heads spinning, blasphemous obscenity, green vomit—and so distracts us from the deeper implications of possession. Indeed, such visceral digust effectively blocks any such delving into the meaning of the thought of the film—the type, not this mere multimillion-dollar token. Rosenbaum is a veteran deep film diver, however, and he is not distracted from the meaning. It is the horrifying thought of being taken over, having one's mind as well as one's body "snatched." The thought of possession is a mightily disturbing thought, and it motivates some of the best horror of the genre. I would mention in particular here both versions of *Invasion of the Body Snatchers.* The original version, at least, evokes true horror with only a drop of blood, as we all imagine our friends and loved ones suddenly devoid of feelings or tenderness. (Note that it is the fear of possession of others, not oneself, that evokes the horror here.)

I think that Carroll understands this as well. He fully endorses the importance of the imagination in horror, but he restricts his play of the imagination to mere "prospects" and won't draw the larger conclusion. He gives us the plot of *Body Snatchers* (p. 110) but ignores the theme. So, too, he rather blandly mentions as the idea behind *The Exorcist,* "the demonic purpose of possession is not primarily to appropriate the soul of the possessed, but to undermine the faith of all of those who surround and witness the spectacle: to make them doubt and despise themselves . . . ," (pp. 103–104) but then he goes on to appreciate only the particulars of the movie, not the universals behind them. There is no problem about the ontological status of the particulars. The emotion (if not the movie) is not really about them at all.

Mere monsters make pretty lousy horror movies, and the best of the genre tend instead to reflect inward, at some possible transformation. I think that the possession theme alone is not the whole of horror, but neither do I think that disgust and monsters even begin to capture the nature of the genre, however pervasive they may be. Monsters and their carryings-on may provide a great challenge for special effects specialists, and the merely disgusting may attract teenage audiences, but neither have much to do with horror. Where disgust meets horror is in the existential dimension, not the Twilight Zone. Horror is not just confrontation with an object. It is an imaginative confrontation with oneself. Of course, what one imagines may be as straightforward as being bitten by a shark or crushed under one of King Kong's shark-sized toes, but it could also be a peek through the thin veneer of rationality into the far more confusing cauldron of whims, obsessions, and desires below. The object of horror is only an example, and perhaps along with the horror there is the fear of contamination. Indeed, perhaps even vomit and slime have existential dimensions that we have neglected.* In every case, it is the thought that horrifies us. (Saint-Exupery: "Horror is the *memory* of fear.")

Our third question has to do with the nature of the experience of horror. We have already noted the spectator status of horror, its consequent immobility and helplessness in contrast to fear and the role of the thought (rather than any particular) as its object. But this is the place to delve a bit deeper into the nature of emotion in general and horror in particular. For Carroll, much depends on his account of the nature of emotion and, accordingly, on the theory or theories of emotion he entertains. Carroll seems particularly attracted and attached to David Lyons's theory of emotion as a physiological disturbance caused by cognition (Lyons, *Emotion,* Cambridge, 1980). Carroll defines the horror-experience, in part, as disgust, an exceedingly visceral sensation (though arguably not an emotion at all). Indeed, the very

---

*Cf. Jean-Paul Sartre on slime in *Being and Nothingness,* on "Existential Analysis."

word "horror" comes from the Latin *horrere* and the French *orror*, to bristle or to shudder, and it is all too tempting to suggest that horror *is* just this set of sensations. The danger lies in the thesis that horror involves physical agitation without the proper cognitions, and thus our understanding of the nature of emotion is jeopardized. It is not just that cognitions *cause* physical agitation, as psychologist and philosopher William James clumsily suggested a century ago. The physical agitation, the flow of adrenalin, and the physiological and sensational consequences are not, contra James, the emotion. The cognitions in question are essential to the emotion, part of its structure, its content as well as its logical conditions, not simply causes or presuppositions or preconditions. Gooseflesh can be caused by all sorts of conditions, some of them thoughts, some of them the atmospheric conditions of the room. Whether or not the gooseflesh experience is an emotion, and whether or not that emotion is horror, depends upon the thoughts involved. A cold, wet wind from the window will cause gooseflesh and its familiar sensations, but no one would say that those sensations constitute an emotion. The prospect of a passionate love affair prompts the gooseflesh experience, but only a cynic would insist that the emotion in question is horror. (Perhaps horror buffs tend to be cynics.) The gooseflesh experience counts as horror only if its object is horrible. But these thoughts are not merely the cause. They inform and fill the experience. The emotion or the emotional experience is a holistic pattern that includes the body as well as the thoughts. Sartre overdramatizes the point only slightly when he argues (in his essay on *The Emotions*) that the body in emotion becomes affected by way of "magical incantations." True, one can notice, in a moment of horror, the hair standing up on one's neck and one can even pay close attention to the shivers traveling up or down one's spine. But in so doing, one is not paying attention to the emotion, only its physiological cum sensational concomitants. To separate the thought or object from the cause of emotion is therefore to misunderstand the nature of emotion, to eviscerate the emotional experience by making it nothing other than visceral.

So, why do we subject ourselves to that which is disgusting and unpleasant? Why do we seek out horror experiences? I think Carroll is right to be suspicious of the many overly anxious religious interpretations of the horror phenomenon, and I think he is also right to reject the overarching ideological interpretations that have become so popular since semiotics came to rule the (art)world. But his own answer to the paradox is, I must say, deeply disappointing. Having rejected the likelihood of a comprehensive and profound hypothesis, such as religion and ideology promise, he retreats to what I would consider a purely aesthetic account, where (dare I say it here?) aesthetics is sometimes to popular culture as patriotism is to scoundrels—a last refuge. Carroll suggests that we find pleasure in the plot, the rhetorical framing of horror, and its narrative form. Art-horror is "an aesthetic contrivance," and monsters are simply "natural subjects for curiosity." What horror is really about is the "unknowable," and "disgust is the price one pays for the pleasure of their disclosure." But this doesn't explain horror, not even art-horror, and Carroll himself notes fatal weaknesses. He does insist that there is a "qualitative difference in the kind of curiosity" involved in horror, but that is surely weak stuff indeed after nearly two hundred pages of vampires, werewolves, demonic possessions, giant reptiles, shattered and twin personalities, smog monsters, and the Golem (the Jewish answer to Frankenstein). And when we turn from art-horror to horror as such, the purely aesthetic account is surely implausible. The observers at an accident aren't simply gawkers who seek out an aesthetic experience.

Carroll rejects ideology and religion as accounts of horror, and he rejects Freudian analysis, predictably, as "not comprehensive enough," but it is not clear that he offers us anything of substance to take their place. Perhaps, as Carroll himself has argued, the ambition of an all-embracing theory—even of a single genre—is overreaching. Perhaps we should settle for some accounts of horror in terms of religious impulses, others in terms of ideological hopes and fears, and still others in terms of frustrated or forbidden sexual impulses. And as I earlier suggested, I think that Carroll neglects the very important connection between horror and humor.

Freud theorized a great deal about wish-fulfillment, but he described and talked much more about fear-fulfilment in his clinical studies and self-analyses. Horror is fear-fulfilment, evoking thoughts that are horrible. The revolting and disgusting is attractive in its own right, not because we crave the disgusting much less because it is the price of curiosity, but because it reminds us of something essential about ourselves. Horror is our way of facing up to the world, even if the horror in question is fictitious. We live in a sanitized society in which even criminal executions have been whittled down to a clinical, private injection. Carroll insists that horror is directed at the unnatural, but I would argue that horror itself is natural, and we as a society have done our best to deny it. Carroll talks about "narratives of disclosure," but what I am suggesting is that the disclosure is self-disclosure, reminding us of our most basic vulnerabilities. Aristotle, in opposition to Plato, defended the theater as preparatory for the emotions and for life. By confronting ourselves with the extremes of life in the theater, we open ourselves to the contingencies of life in the world.

18

The Logic of Emotions

Emotion has almost always played an inferior role in philosophy, often as antagonist to logic and reason. Even David Hume, one of the few great philosophers to give emotion its due, sharply distinguished passion from reason and set them at odds with each other. Where he differed from other philosophers was his argument that "reason is and ought to be the slave of the passions," rather than the other way round. It is also worth noting that Hume's analysis of emotion is wholly derivative of his more general epistemological theories, with considerable damage to his view of emotion. The same must be said of Descartes; with his compatriot Malebranche, he considered emotions as "animal spirits," clearly inferior products of the psyche. Leibniz considered emotions to be "confused perceptions." And we all know Kant's famous (or infamous) degradation of the emotions as "pathological," at least in the context of practical reason. Along with this general demeaning of emotion in philosophy comes either a wholesale neglect or at least retail distortion in the analysis of emotion. My aim here is to help correct this neglect and distortion and return the topic of emotion to the very heart of philosophy, as it is in human nature. I want to argue that the emotions have a logical structure that is no less fascinating and no less analyzable than the logical structures of "reason."

This essay was originally presented at an American Philosophical Association symposium and published in the journal *Nous* 2 (March 1977). Reprinted by permission of Basil Blackwell.

Insofar as philosophers have taken the trouble to analyze emotion at all, their attempts traditionally have fallen into one of three overlapping categories. First there is the common-sense view that emotions are feelings, distinct experiences not unlike physical sensations, something like nausea or anxiety. This is reflected in our ordinary talk about emotions ("she hurt his feelings") and it forms the basis of some of the most persistent and respectable philosophical theories of emotion, notably those of Hume and Descartes, according to whom an emotion is a species of idea or impression, like a sensation but whose source is, as they say, "internal rather than external and through the senses."

Second, there is the equally old view that emotions are physiological disturbances of some sort, remnants of an animal psyche or Freudian "it" that we inherit from a more "primitive" (i.e., less reasonable and more emotional) past. The Cartesian-Malebranchian talk of "animal spirits" is part of this theoretical view; so is the medieval psychophysiology of "bile," "spleen," "phlegm," and "gall," whose language has long outlasted its medical plausibility. Poetry abounds in examples borrowed from this theory: consider the hundred metaphors, most of them trite from overuse, about the breaking and bursting of hearts in love, and also the various hydraulic metaphors with which we describe anger as "boiling over," "letting off steam," "penting up rage," and "bursting with anger." Recent attempts to develop a physiological theory of emotion, most famously by William James in America and C. G. Lange in Denmark, are but scientifically respectable versions of a series of theories and metaphors that have been with us since ancient times.

The third set of theories are more recent, but very powerful in Anglo-American philosophy and psychology in particular. I will simply call them "behavioral" theories (avoiding the stricter term "behaviorist"). Wittgenstein's "private language argument," Ryle's attack on the "Cartesian myth," and Watson's polemics against introspectionism have all but eclipsed traditional feeling theories. I began by saying, however, that the three sorts of theories were often overlapping. Thus James, while arguing for an essentially physiological theory, nevertheless found it necessary to include an essential feeling-type element. It is the *experience* of a visceral disturbance, he argued, that *is* the emotion. Many advocates of behavioral theories, at least those who are less than full behaviorists, would not even try to deny a feeling component of emotion; rather, following Wittgenstein, they would simply insist that feeling alone is not sufficient to account for our use of emotion ascriptions, and that, so far as our criteria for identifying emotions are concerned, the feeling is one of those Wittgensteinian wheels that has nothing to do with the mechanism.

The objections to each of these theories are so voluminous and well-known that it is neither possible nor necessary to repeat them here. The feeling theory in particular has suffered from decades of relentless criticism, particularly from behavioral theorists. I believe I can safely begin by saying that, in its traditional forms, it has been thoroughly discredited. This is not to insist that emotions do not involve feelings. It might even be argued that emotions essentially involve feelings, such that one could not be said to have an emotion unless, under certain circumstances, and at least occasionally, one experienced one of those mildly discomfortable sensations of constriction and flushing so graphically described by James and others before him. But this is not all there is to having an emotion. Even if it were essential to having an emotion, it would not be at all interesting.

The classic rebuttal of the physiological theory is W. B. Cannon's attack on the James-Lange theory. Citing a series of experiments that are still being repeated (always with an air of surprised discovery), Cannon showed that different emotions were accompanied by exactly the same physiological symptoms, and that the same emotion might, in different circumstances, have very different physiological accompaniments. Most philosophers, of course, would argue this conclusion in a more *a priori* way; Aristotle knew perfectly well when he was angry or jealous, for example, and he didn't even have a concept of the central nervous system. This argument is too short, but the conclusion is hard to avoid: that our concept of emotion, which does not differ so much from Aristotle's, does not turn on our knowledge of physiology.

The behavioral view is far more difficult to attack, mainly because there are so many versions of it and their claims so variable as to what will and will not count as "behavior." Once the relevant behavioral dispositions are numerous enough and covert behavior and verbal reports are included, it is hard to see how such theories could be refuted. But this much has been made clear in recent work: there is something extremely peculiar about the behavioral view when it comes to identifying emotions in one's own case, and the variety of behavior expressive of a given emotion is so vast that under appropriately unusual circumstances a person might do anything whatever to express an emotion. But even the term "expression" betrays the problem—that there is something else, namely, the emotion, which is expressed. But what is this "something else"?

In my view, all three of these theories, whether separately or combined, make the same pair of mistakes. First they confuse relatively inessential aspects of emotion for its essence. One can be angry without feeling anything in particular, without doing anything in particular, and without displaying any physiological symptoms of a unique syndrome for that emotion. While it might be argued that feelings, tendencies to behave in certain ways, and certain physiological syndromes usually or even always accompany particular emotions, none of these—nor all of them taken together—tells us anything very important about the nature of emotion. The second mistake points to what is missing. All three of these theories ignore what might be called *subjectivity,* one's own viewpoint and what one experiences— other than sensations and the like—when he or she has an emotion. This is even true of the feeling theory, insofar as the "feelings" so considered are restricted to the physical feelings of constriction, flushing, palpitation, etc. Phenomenologists have made much of this subjective viewpoint, and it is accordingly to them and their theory of *intentionality* that we turn to take the major step away from all three traditional theories.

Husserl did not invent the concept of intentionality, of course, and he hardly applied it at all to emotions. The scholastics used the concept centuries earlier, and they did so apply it. Heidegger, following both Husserl and the scholastics, avoided the term but used it in his analysis of moods. Max Scheler developed an explicitly intentional theory of emotion in his work on sympathy and value in ethics (*The Nature of Sympathy*). Jean-Paul Sartre gave the idea its best expression so far in his little essay on the emotions in the late thirties. In England and America, similar suggestions appeared, for example, in Anthony Kenny's *Action, Emotion and Will.* The intentionalistic theory of emotions, as mental acts and as propositional attitudes (mental activity directed at some putative claim or state-of-affairs), had never received the attention it deserved. Both Hume and Descartes had labored over the idea that emotions have objects, but neither of them escaped from a strictly *causal* view of the relationship between emotion and object, largely because of their commitment to a feeling view of one kind or another. This confusion still persists today, but rather than argue against it here, I will spell out the ramifications of the intentionalistic theory.

A topic that has received some attention in recent years is the connection between emotions and *belief.* For psychologists, this has signaled an important breach in the traditional noncognitive assumptions about emotions. For philosophers, it has raised a problem: How is it that an emotion can be logically tied to a propositional attitude? If emotions are feelings, or bodily states, or even dispositions to behave, this connection is surely mysterious. But if emotions are themselves propositional attitudes, and if they are themselves very much like beliefs, then the connection is not at all mysterious. In fact, it is obvious.

Both Gilbert Ryle and Ludwig Wittgenstein attacked the feeling theory of emotion, although neither had very much to say about emotion as such.

(Ryle's chapter on "Emotion" in *Concept of Mind* talks about everything but emotion.) What emerged from both of their attacks was a renewed emphasis on the circumstances of emotion, though neither philosopher pursued the idea that it is a person's *view* of his or her circumstances which is essential to emotion. Errol Bedford, following this tradition, renewed the attack on the feeling view, again suggesting a quasi-behavioral view in its stead.* But his classic paper added an important twist; *evaluations* became a crucial ingredient in the analysis of emotion. George Pitcher used this same idea to argue a thesis much closer to the intentionalistic theory that I want to defend; he claims that emotions themselves are evaluations.† I believe this to be a bit too simple, just as the intentionalistic thesis itself, as it is usually stated, is too dependent upon more general intentionality theses and therefore extremely skimpy on insight into emotions in particular. But they are on the right track.

"Emotions are judgments." That is oversimplified, but it is a quick way of introducing the theory I want to defend. The term "judgment" is extremely intellectualistic. I intend it to be, for the brunt of this theory is the total demolition of the age-old distinctions between emotion and reason, passion and logic. Emotions are not the brutish, unlearned, uncultured, illogical, and stupid drives that they are so often argued to be. To the contrary, they are extremely subtle, cunning, sophisticated, cultured, learned, logical, and intelligent. There is more intelligence in resentment than in the routine calculations of syllogizing; and there is far more strategy in envious Iago than in thoughtful Hamlet. The cunning of reason, when you see what Hegel means by it, is almost always the cunning of emotion.

I take the concept of "judgment" in much the same way that Kant did, in a constitutive way, as a rule for interpreting experience. I do not want to advance any claims, as Max Scheler did, about "the emotional a priori"; but I do want to follow the Kantian trend of his theory in insisting that our emotions are interpretive judgments. Jean-Paul Sartre argues a similar theory when he says that emotions are "magical transformations of the world." You can see why it is so important to distinguish this theory from the traditional feeling theory. In some hopelessly loose sense, both make emotions out to be part of "experience," but what is important is that emotions are not sensations of constriction or flushing, but constitutive interpretations of the world.

---

*"Emotion," reprinted in Calhoun and Solomon, *What Is an Emotion?* (Oxford, 1984).

†Also entitled "Emotion," *Mind* (1965).

It should be evident that by "judgment," I do not necessarily mean "deliberative judgment." Many judgments, for example, perceptual judgments, are made without deliberation. (One might call such judgments "spontaneous" as long as "spontaneity" isn't confused with "passivity.") But it is equally important to appreciate the degree to which many emotions are deliberative judgments. We literally "work ourselves up" to anger or love. We do not always do so, but whether deliberative or "spontaneous," getting angry or "falling in" love are things that we *do*, judgments that we make about our world.

If emotions are judgments, then of course they are intentional. But this also explains, in an easy way, the logical connections between emotions and beliefs. Emotional judgments, like any judgments, have presupposition and entailment relationships with a large number of beliefs, many of which are not in any sense a part of the emotion itself. This also allows us to see what is so right in Bedford's introduction of evaluations into emotion ascriptions, and how Pitcher was partially justified in identifying emotions and evaluation. I say "partially justified" because emotional judgments are not only evaluations, but a great many different kinds of judgments, only some of which are straightforwardly evaluative. The intimate connection between emotions, beliefs, and evaluations also allows us to explain, as the traditional theories cannot, the fact that we often talk about emotions as being "warranted" or "unwarranted," "reasonable" or "unreasonable," "justified" or "foolish." Like any judgment, an emotion is susceptible to any number of epistemic and ethical objections and corrections.

What distinguishes emotions among judgments (for not all judgments are emotional)? Emotional judgments are marked by their importance to us, by the fact that our self-esteem is at stake in them. It is important that the propositional content of the judgment need not be self-involved, but only that self-esteem be tied up with that judgment. For example, a microbiologist may become extremely emotional in his judgments about mitochondria, but only insofar as he has invested his self-esteem in his theory, identified with it, and has come to see its acceptance or rejection as an acceptance or rejection of *him*. Anger, as I want to analyze it, is a set of judgments of accusation, an indictment for a personal offense, for example, an insult. I might make a similar set of judgments to the effect that what someone has said is insulting and offensive, but without being angry. What constitutes the anger is my judging *that I have been insulted and offended*. It is my "taking it personally" that makes this set of judgments *anger*.

We can now see how the three traditional theories enter into our account. Although we *make* judgments, we surely do not make our feelings or our physiological states in anything like the same sense. But when we make an emotional judgment, our involvement and excitement is such that it stimulates a physiological reaction, the pumping of hormones such as adrenalin or noradrenalin, for example, with the resultant sensations and feelings. Whenever an emotion is of any considerable intensity, such physiological and sensational consequences naturally follow. But notice that they follow only "naturally," that is, causally, and not logically. There is nothing essential to the emotion about them, even if they are common to every intense emotion. But the emotion is the judgment, and the intensity of the emotion is the personal significance of the judgment: how much it effects our self-esteem and thereby how urgent it is, not the intensity of the accompanying feelings. (One can always produce those with a shot of adrenalin.) Intense feelings are the effect of intense emotions, not their essence.

The relationship between emotions and their behavioral "expression" is far more complicated than the usual post-Humean causal-versus-conceptual debate would indicate. It is true, beyond a doubt, that a person who has a certain emotion will tend to behave in certain ways under certain circumstances. Perhaps that is even a logical truth. But why should a person with *this* particular emotion tend to behave in *those* particular ways? Behavioral disposition theories are remarkably quiet on that issue. Are these merely cultural contingencies, or are they in fact part of human psychological nature? Or is it possible that there is a logical connection between emotions and their expressions? But despite all of the talk about such "logical connections," it has yet to be shown that they exist. Look at the connection between anger and violent action, for example. Surely that is more than a cultural curiosity. (The appropriateness of some particular violent response may be: a harsh word may be far more punitive than physical violence in some societies.) But given the theory that emotions are judgments, the nature of this connection is evident; if anger is a judgment of accusation, then its connection with punishing is clear. In general, the expression of an emotion is dictated by the logic of the judgment. The indictment of anger requires an act of retribution. The caring of love requires acts of concern and tenderness. The vengefulness of resentment requires acts of strategic retaliation.

I admitted to an oversimplification in the too-brief slogan, "emotions are judgments." Judging, even in the most personal matters, may not have sufficient motivating power to explain the intimate connection between emotions and what James rightly calls, "the urge to vigorous action." Furthermore, the notion of judgment by itself does not tell us why our emotions are so often involved in intricate schemes and filled with the cunning so obvious to every novelist, if not to philosophers and psychologists. Accordingly, it is important to add that every emotion is also a system of desires and intentions, hopes and wishes, or what I call the *ideology* of emotion. Thus in anger, it is essential that there is a desire, no matter how unworkable, to punish. Here is the full connection between emotion and expression. It is not simply a causal connection, for the desire is built into the emotion itself. But since desires and intentions are often not easily separable from the actions they inspire, the distinction between emotion and expression begins to break down as well. This is the central insight of the behavioral theories, which spoil their advance only by then trying to sacrifice the emotion altogether, saving only (what is left of) its expression.

A theory is only as good as its development. The three traditional theories, however attractive in the abstract, all collapse when faced with the task of analyzing particular emotions. It is worth noting, for example, how quickly Hume and Descartes introduce considerations wholly foreign to their theories when they begin such analyses. What is now required, therefore, is a detailed analysis of the logical structures of a wide range of different emotions in view of the theory that emotions are judgments and ideologies. What we shall find is that emotions turn out to be far more logical, far more complex, far more sophisticated, and far more a part of reason than most philosophers have ever imagined.

19

Are the Three Stooges Funny? Coitainly! (or When Is It O.K. to Laugh?)

"Everything is funny so long as it happens to someone else."

—Will Rogers

"Rire est le propre de l'homme" ("to laugh is fitting to man"), wrote Rabelais. Of course, he never saw the Three Stooges. Would they have given him second thoughts? Can you imagine raunchy Rabelais watching Curly or Shemp doing the dying chicken? Trying to appreciate bowl-coiffured Moe pulling Larry's rag mop of hair, slapping him down while calling him a moron? Of course, Rabelais's countrymen today think that Jerry Lewis is the funniest thing since the invention of the baguette, so there is reason to suppose that an appreciation of idiocy is well settled into the Gallic gene pool. But these are also the people who elevated *logique* to the status of an art, and the juxtaposition is instructive. Although philosophers have long made much of the supposed fact that human beings are the only creatures who "reason," it seems to be just as plausible (with some of the same exceptions) to insist that we are just as unique in our silliness. We are fundamentally creatures who laugh, and these two familiar human

This essay was prepared for a symposium on the Three Stooges at the Toronto meeting of the Society for Popular Culture, November of 1990. The session was organized and directed by Jon Solomon, also a participant and a lifelong Stooges fan. © Robert C. Solomon.

functions, reason and humor, are intimately tied together. The bridge between them, as Mark Twain once suggested, is embarrassment.

The Three Stooges have caused considerable embarrassment in their fifty years of success and popularity. Their humor is chastised as being childish, violent, vulgar, and anti-feminist. (Their first film, by way of evidence, was entitled *Women Haters.*) Consequently, relatively few women find them funny, perhaps because their older brothers acted out one too many Stooges antics at their expense. Stooge appreciation also takes time, the time to convert idiotic madness into familiar ritual. Educators, rarely Stooge fans themselves, pontificate about their bad influence. The Soviets once wanted to use the shows "to show how Americans had been brutalized . . . in the name of fun." Few adults in their chosen professions would dare attempt a Stooges gesture at risk of being terminally dismissed, but most men carry the secret knowledge around with them, and, in a wild fit of catharsis, display a telltale Stooges gesture when the door closes and the boss is out of view. I only hesitate to suggest that it is one of the most basic bonds between men, and and it is far more elemental than the mere phrase "a sense of humor" could ever suggest.

Impropriety is the soul of wit, according to Somerset Maugham, and few wits since the Romans have ever been more improper than the Stooges. But the comedy of the Three Stooges is not just rudeness personified. The comedian John Candy says of the Stooges that "the magic was their subtlety." Film critic Leonard Maltin insists that "their art was artlessness." The Stooges were ideal for television, and that was where they made their mark. Their films were originally made and distributed as "shorts" to precede feature-length movies, but the Stooges found and still find their largest audience on the small screen. There is nothing special about television humor except, perhaps, that it is so condensed and concise, and it is shared by so many people, across generations and social classes. It lacks, of course, the audience participation that one might enjoy or suffer in a live theatrical or vaudeville performance. There is a drop in the intensity of humor in the conversion of live stage to television screen (e.g., the televised sessions of "Evening at the Improv") which cannot be explained by appeal to censorship alone. It is, however, that loss of the immediacy that allows stand-up comics to be intimate that allows the Stooges to be safely sealed, like miniatures in a box from whom the audience is safely protected. Within their little box, the Stooges are the heirs of ancient forms of humor, from the theater of Aristophanes and Plautus to the Commedia del Arte and then modern vaudeville, where they started, with their unique combination of wit, slapstick, insult, skill, tomfoolery, and stupidity. But their humor and their message, drawn from those ancient sources, are refreshingly up-

multiple stabbing of Caesar. In another theater Othello strangles his struggling but innocent wife. This is called tragedy. (No one laughs.) Nor does anyone comment that the actor playing Caesar isn't really bleeding, or that Desdemona will go out for a cappuchino after the performance. The "willing suspension of disbelief," as Coleridge famously coined it, is alive and well here. No one is "really" hurt so we can allow our emotions their free "make believe" reign. Why, then, is the equally feigned petty violence of the Three Stooges in question as comedy? Perhaps because it wildens the kids, but then, doesn't everything? But it is not the word "violence" that best captures the Stooges mutual abuse of their various foils and of each other. It rather falls into the category of ritual humiliation. The Stooges' humor is the humor of humiliation, taking it as well as dishing it out, but one misses the point if he or she sees humiliation as the end in itself. It is humiliation to end all humiliation, for once one accepts oneself as a Stooge, the slings and arrows of outrageous fortune are nothing but fodder for another joke or gesture.

Laughter may indeed be the "best medicine" as one of our more prestigious periodicals proclaims, but laughter at what? We make a rather harsh distinction (at least in polite discourse) between "laughing *at*" and "laughing *with*," and rule number one of our ethic of humor is not to laugh at the misfortunes of others. And yet, most of what we find funny in the Stooges is just that, a foolish and frustrated Curly carrying a block of ice up fifteen flights on a hot summer day, Moe wearing a mask of paint or flour, an innocent bystander deprived of his wig, a customer who leaves the shop with a gigantic hole in his pants, a room full of sophisticated diners hit by a battery of pies and, even worse, allowing themselves to join in. And then, of course, there is the usual: Moe's ritualized double eye-poke, Curly's equally practiced hand block, and Moe's counter-feign. Then Curly's cry and hyperkinetic dance of pain and indignation. (One should not underestimate the importance of sound in undermining the seriousness of the Stooges' violence: the kettledrum stomach punch, the violin pluck eye-poke, and the rachet ear twist.) "That's not funny," decry the righteous, but they're wrong.

Henri Bergson hypothesized that humor blocks normal emotion, but I think that the opposite is true. It is the sympathetic laughter we enjoy at the Stooges' alleged expense that makes us aware of our own best and least pretentious emotions. Pride, envy, and anger all disappear. That sense of status that defines so much of our self-image dissolves. Accordingly, Plato urged censorship of humor as well as poetry to preserve the good judgment and virtue of the guardians of the republic. I would argue to the contrary that laughter opens up the emotions and it is good humor that makes good judgment possible.

The philosophy of humor is a subject that itself tends to be all-too humorless. But that is perhaps because it does not appreciate the extent to which it is itself a ludicrous topic, and my basic belief in these matters is that the basic meaning of humor and "a sense of humor" is ultimately laughter *at oneself*. But for this to be meaningful the laughter will have to be "low humor" and folly rather than wit and learned cleverness that are the hallmark of humor, quite the contrary of those examples preferred by the most contemporary theorists. Philosophers, in particular, appreciate cleverness, preferably based on some profound linguistic or ontological insight. Freud, by contrast, preferred elephant and fart jokes, but then he was looking for a diagnosis rather than a good laugh. (Did Freud chuckle as he was writing his *Wit and Its Relation to the Unconscious*? Or did he rather insist on maintaining that famous stone face of disapproval, even in the solitude of his study?) The Stooges, by contrast again, were always laughing at themselves, and they invited us to do so, too, with the understanding that we were laughing at ourselves as well. Their shorts are often cited as paradigms of bad taste but have nevertheless dominated television from its earliest days and continue to influence and be imitated by the most talented comedians today. They are not particularly clever or chauvinist or brutal but they provide a mirror for our own silliness—if only in our laughing at them.

But why are the Three Stooges funny? They would seem to provide an obvious case of *laughing at*. Watching the Three Stooges, what we seem to experience is what the Germans (wonderfully humorous people) describe as *schadenfreude*—the enjoyment of other people's pain and suffering, deserved or undeserved. Are we really so cruel? We might note here with some wonder that it is so easy to be funny when there is something to laugh at but hard to be funny when praising or admiring. Critic John Simon is hopeless when (rarely) he likes something. His reviews are memorable when they are offensive. Why? It does not seem to matter whether or not they are deserved. If they are deserved, of course, we can have a clear conscience in laughing, but we find ourselves laughing at insults even when they are not fair. The Stooges, on this easy account, set themselves up to be ridiculed. Their humor is a gift, allowing us to feel wittily superior.

Since ancient times, according to John Morreall in his book on laughter, one can discern three dominant conceptions of humor. First, there is the *superiority* theory, assumed by Plato and Aristotle, in which laughter expresses one's feeling of sophistication, wisdom, and superiority over the poor slob who would get himself entrapped in such a situation. Obviously such humor would be appealing in aristocratic societies or any society that has a more or less clearly delineated inferior class. According to Albert Rapp, in his *Origins of Wit and Humor,* the original laugh was probably a roar of triumph for the victor in a fight. Roger Scruton, who is not unsympathetic to aristocratic thinking, has hypothesized that humor involves devaluation.

The Three Stooges would seem to fit perfectly into this conception of humor, for what losers have ever made themselves more lowly, more ridiculous, more prone to ridicule? In a world in which everyone has the right not to be offended and where everything is becoming offensive, humor by way of superiority is too often inappropriate, "politically incorrect." Laughing at the Stooges, however, is OK. The problem, however, is that we do not just laugh at the Stooges, and much of their humor depends on the humiliation of others. Superiority theory doesn't quite work. One doesn't walk away from the Stooges feeling superior, but, rather, released and relieved.

The second conception might be called the *relief* theory. It was most famously advocated by Freud, and it renders laughter akin to sport in safely expressing violence and, of course, forbidden sexual impulses. If you can't *do it,* in other words, at least you can laugh about it. But such laughter, so understood, is not just laughing at; it is also a vicarious form of activity, "the world as play." We laugh because the Stooges do what we would like to do, act as we would like to act, not sexually to be sure but as fools, clowns beyond humiliation, humiliating those whom we would also love to humiliate: e.g., pompous doctors, overbearing matrons, "tough" bosses, and crooked politicians. Humor thus becomes a devious expression of *resentment,* and the release and relief we feel is nothing less than the catharsis of one of our most poisonous emotions. There is something suspicious, however, about a theory that makes laughter out to be a weakness, a leak in one's psyche, so to speak, and directs itself mainly to one's hostile or immoral thoughts of others. One cannot disprove such a theory, of course, but we should be very cautious about accepting it. Three Stooges' humor does not feel particularly vicious, and those who complain that it seems so are easily dismissed as those who have not allowed themselves to "get into it."

Finally, there is the *incongruity* theory, defended by Kant and Schopenhauer among others and described by the Danish existentialist Kierkegaard as "comedy as painless contradiction." What makes this theory attractive is that it dispenses with any notion of "laughing at" and looks to the language and the humorous situation as such for a clue to the humor. Humor is our reaction to things that don't fit together. We laugh at stupidity not because we feel superior to it but because the juxtaposition of actions and events surprises us. Linguistic incongruity, for example, is, of course, the favorite conception of humor in academia, where facility with language is a special virtue and puns, wordplay, and cleverness are readily appreciated. Similarly, John Morreall suggests that humor involves a "pleasant psychological shift," such as when one is caught off guard. There are, to be sure, any number of unexpected and unusual psychological shifts required to follow the typical Stooges plot, and incongruity is central to much of their humor. But the incongruity theory does not explain why the Stooges get better and better with repetitive viewing, and why imitation is part and parcel of Stooges spectatorship. It also sells the Stooges short, prettifies their humor, and ignores or denies its bite. The humor of the Stooges is the humor of mutual humiliation, not mere incongruity or surprise, but neither is it merely relief of our own frustrations or the sense of superiority that comes from laughing at someone else.

No one, to my knowledge, has advocated what we might call the *inferiority* theory of humor, laughter as the great leveler, beyond contempt or indignation, antithetical to pretention and pomp. Sitting on the sofa watching *Malice in the Palace* for the twenty-seventh time, we allow ourselves to fall into a world of miniature mayhem in which we feel as foolish as they are. We enjoy these petty plots of ambition, ire, and revenge, and not because we feel superior to them or use them for our own catharsis much less because, on the twenty-seventh viewing, we are in any way surprised. Why should we not? Do we still have to pretend with the critics that our own natures are not similarly petty, vengeful, and, viewed from the outside, uproariously slapstick. Larry, Moe, Shemp, and Curly capture the silly side of human nature just as surely as Macbeth and Hamlet represent the tragic side, but we can easily understand why the critics would prefer to ennoble themselves with the latter while rejecting the former. Satire and parody may be much more effective for developing individual thought than tragedy and self-righteousness, and in order to avoid the supposed bad taste of enjoying the Three Stooges we encounter the much greater danger of taking ourselves too seriously.

Voltaire once commented that, to combat human misery, we require hope and sleep. It was the moralist Immanuel Kant, of all people, who corrected Voltaire by suggesting that in addition to hope and sleep as palliatives for human misery we should also count laughter. But Kant, I presume, would not have found Moe's eye-poke or Curly's clucking chicken to be laughable, and Kant's idea of a good joke would no doubt fall flat on television today. Kant, like most intellectuals, thought that a joke should be profound. For the Stooges and their fans, repetitive, mindless silliness was the way to humor. Philosophers, as people of reason, have always found laughter and humor suspicious. As far back as the *Philebus,* Plato warned against the dangers of humor as he had chastised the falsification of poetry in the *Republic,* and he urged censorship to protect the guardians of the the republic from the distortions and distractions of laughter. Aristotle—despite his lost treatise on comedy which provides the theme of Umberto Eco's *The Name of the Rose*—shared many of Plato's reservations about comedy. And despite the proliferation of comedy among the "low arts" throughout the ages, comedy as such was never held in high regard. Humor and the Comedia del Arte were strictly the province of the masses, the *hoi polloi.* The most famous "comedy" of the Middle Ages, appropriately, was a thoroughly somber poetic journey through Heaven and Hell, neither place known for its humor.

Among many faults recently raised against the "Western tradition" since Plato—its sexism, racism, Eurocentrism, scientism, technophilia and obsession with control, hyper-rationality, myopic universality, asexuality and denial of the body, ecological meanspiritedness and wastefulness—surely must be included its lack of humor, its utterly solemn seriousness. Recent defenses of that tradition, e.g., in the fighting words of Alan Bloom, only make that fault even more glaring, and Third World and feminist critics, however right on the money, seem only to make it worse, more humorless, more deadly serious, more depressing. Socrates was, first of all, a stooge, a clown, a champion of intellectual slapstick. (Aristophanes gets it right in *Clouds.*) By contrast, Wittgenstein suggested that an entire philosophy could be written entirely in jokes, although he himself seemed incapable of telling one. Perhaps the most successful if controversial philosopher joking today, Jacques Derrida, makes his best points with puns, historical wisecracks, and self-deprecating humor (charms often lacking in his traditionally serious, even pugnacious students, who take Derrida's well-aimed jokes as a serious "methodology"). Against the wisdom of the age, I would say that humor, not rationality, is the key to tolerance and peace. Nothing is so important in philosophy or anywhere else as not taking oneself too seriously.

"Rebukes are easily endured, but it is intolerable to be laughed at. We are quite willing to be wicked, but we do not want to be ridiculous."

—Moliere

Part Four

About Love

20

"Violets are Red, Roses are Blue": A History of Love

"All you need is love," sang the Beatles, declaring once again what pundits and greeting cards have been saying for centuries. "God is love" writes John in his gospel and "Love IS" scribbles Gertrude Stein—and who could disagree with her?

We have elevated love—romantic love—to absolute status. It is "the answer" (to what question?). It is, wrote Disraeli, "the principle of existence": it is "the key to the gates of happiness" proclaimed Oliver Wendell Holmes. Two and a half millenia ago, Plato first raised *eros* into a God; ever since we have been taught to think that it is "divine." And not surprisingly, we have come to believe that love is increasingly impossible. "Modern man finds himself incapable of love" writes Rollo May; but in fact, perhaps, it is our idea of love that has become impossible, not love.

Against this tradition of bloated, "divine" love, the modern reaction is cynicism. Adults dismiss it as adolescent. Adolescents are embarrassed by it and deride it as childish. Children are bored by it. Freudians diagnose it as nothing but lust. Marxists equate it with prostitution. Some feminists

This Op-Ed piece originally appeared the day before Valentine's Day (1982) in *The New York Times,* and later appeared in modified form as the introduction to Stanley Marcus's miniature book, *Love* (Dallas: Somesuch Press, 1983). References are to Irving Singer's *The Nature of Love,* Vol. III, and Francesca Cancian's *Love in America,* reviewed in *The Philadelphia Inquirer* (Sunday, November 29, 1987). © 1982 by The New York Times Company. Reprinted by permission.

equate it with rape. Serious people see it as irresponsible frivolity. Frivolous people view it as tediously serious. And many of us, in tune with our favorite American metaphor, think of love as a *game,* to be played as skillfully as possible.

The two sides of this schizoid view live in painful coexistence. We still "believe in" love; we worry whether it is possible. We spend years of our lives looking for it, working for it, holding onto it, getting trapped by it, losing it, getting over it, always wondering whether indeed we have really found it. Or if "it" in fact is not merely one of those neurotic substitutes—need, insecurity, infatuation, (co-)dependency—that our pop psychiatrists are always warning us about.

By way of contrast, love among the Greeks—Socrates' unpopular views aside—was a perfectly human, agreeable, tangible passion. No mysteries, no pieties, no cynicism. Plato begins his great *Symposium,* for example, with the lament that no one ever bothers to sing love's praises, which probably was just as well. When Aristotle discusses love and friendship, he makes it clear that they constitute but one set of virtues among many, one component of "the good life," along with having a good sense of humor, a fair sense of justice, a good reputation, an adequate income, and the ability to handle one's share of wine. He would have seen "all you need is love" as an incomprehensible joke. And love is no more "divine" than wine.

Because love was taken for granted among the Greeks, scholars often hesitate to call their *eros* "romantic love" at all. Indeed, "romantic love," the love-students now agree, only begins to show itself in the twelfth century A.D., in France (of course) with the rise of chivalry and a peculiar group of poets called "the troubadors." It was the troubadors, in particular, who created the imagery of the beautiful woman on a pedestal (quite literally, often, in a tower high above their heads.) It was the troubadors who introduced to the world the virtue of *languor*—protracted but metaphysically meaningful sexual frustration. According to the not very accurate legend, the idea was to delay the physical consummation of love for as long as possible, since they already knew—along with many a modern teenager—that the passion of love sometimes ceased abruptly, and the poetry, too. The fact was that many of these courtly affairs were indeed consummated, but they were impossible in another sense because in many cases one or both parties were already married or promised (to someone else). Courtly love also involved elaborate rituals, personal charm and eloquence, even poetry. It is, at least to that extent, something we might do well to emulate today.

It was also in twelfth-century Italy that "Platonic love" was invented, for which Plato should not wholly be blamed. Love without sex, and ultimately, the love of God; this was the ideal. Not the casual sex and companionship of the Greeks. Not the ordinary love of a man for a woman, which Plato thought "vulgar" and Christians considered "profane," much less the love of a man for a man, which about this time began to be considered "unnatural." "Love" became a passion impossible to be enjoyed, then suffered in rare moments, unless of course it could be translated into religious passion, "true love," which also had the advantage of being unrequited.

Romantic love as such did not really appear until perhaps the seventeenth or eighteenth century. It required, among other things, the improving "liberation" of women, an increasing equality that could be found only rarely even among the most privileged classes in the courtly twelfth century. It also involved the development of our modern conception of "the individual," which began, again, in the Middle Ages and culminated in the Enlightenment and the Romantic philosophy of modern times. It involved another inward turn and a new appreciation of the beauty of the emotions (and love in particular) for their own sake, or what Robert Stone has nicely called "affective individualism." And, perhaps most of all, it required the propagandizing of love into the burgeoning middle classes by way of "romance" novels. We might think of them as "potboilers" today, but back in the eighteenth century they conveyed a truly revolutionary message, that young women actually had a choice about whom to have as a husband. The basis of this choice need not be economic or social or practical (though these were rarely lost sight of) but based on their own feelings and emotions. Respect for individual passions became the social condition for love.

Perhaps it's because we're so fond of saying "love is forever" that we tend to think of love as eternal, the same for all people at all times and in all places. Love as we know it, however, is a historically and culturally determined passion, developed only in the last few centuries as the product of socialization and ideas about sex, marriage, the equality of the sexes, the place of emotion in human life, and the nature and meaning of human life in general.

The history of love is an undervalued area of study, in part because we're so resistant to seeing it as historical, because the history of an emotion takes great skill to uncover, and because the history of sex and scandals is much more titillating and financially rewarding. But love offers a special and fascinating history, involved not only with sex but with the details of social and emotional life and the way we think of ourselves.

Understanding the origins of romantic love allows us to see—contrary to our "love-is-everything" mythology—not only how this peculiar passion came into our world but also why it emerged, what purpose and functions it served and still serves. For love is not natural (it is not unnatural either). It is the cultural product of a certain kind of society. It fulfills a function, a function that was already filled for the Greeks but not for the Medievals of the twelfth century. That function was to provide some emotional social glue, to a society that was otherwise falling apart.

The twelfth century, as any high school student of European history can tell you, was the century of the crusades. The husbands and fathers of France were away to the wars; the women were unprotected. The kings and great nobles were away from their domains; the traditional structures of society were disintegrating. And in this absence of protection and authority, something remarkable happened; warrior knights, who had previously been bound by oath to particular lords, now became free agents (knights errant) free to choose the objects of their devotion. And the ladies (indeed, the modern notion of "lady" was just coming into existence) became the objects of devotion, instead of mere daughters, wives, and mothers. As much as we may disdain the idea now, eight hundred years later, women were suddenly valued for their "charms," instead of their economic functions. And this, it turns out, became the definitive step in women's liberation, in their ability to choose in turn for themselves. Like the knights, and the devoted troubador poets, the ladies of the manor had the new right to choose their champions—on the basis of their personal feelings.

What made this possible—what made romantic love necessary—was the breakdown of traditional social bonds and loyalties. Feudal society was crumbling, and with it the usual expectation, and the "natural" bonds of family and feudal law. In other words, relationships between men and women became a matter of choice; mobility became a matter of necessity. New attachments, not prearranged according to family and political preferences, became essential. And to this end, a passion was born. Indeed, the scholars of the period sometimes refer to the "discovery of affection." So, too, the notion of personality emerged, distinct from social and public roles and status. A person began to count as "an individual," in part because there was no longer a sufficient web of fixed social relationships to define her or him in any other way.

But now we can understand what is essential to romantic love: not the pathetic longing of frustrated poets, not the pretentions of divinity with which these feelings were sometimes rationalized, not the intrinsic degradation of women that has been charged by some feminists, not the timid gloss over nasty sexual lust that has been diagnosed by the Freudians. What is essential to romantic love is the formation of bonds of personal attachment in the absence of established interpersonal identities.

(Sometimes romantic love flourished *in spite of* established bonds, as in Romeo and Juliet, Tristram and Isolde, etc.) The bonds need not be openly sexual; they need not involve what we usually call "intimacy" (another peculiarly modern invention). But what is essential is that they can be formed almost instantly (or at least within weeks or months) between virtual strangers, to provide anew the interpersonal connections between us that our excessively mobile and restless society continuously insists on disrupting.

We can easily appreciate—in this somewhat cold and entirely unromantic portrait of love—why romantic love should be so important to us; but we can also appreciate its limitations. Love for us has become an option, but it is by no means our only option, much less "everything." The twelfth century also witnessed the birth of a "cult of friendship"—mainly among monks—to serve much the same sorts of needs served by romantic love, without the "profanity" of sexual desire. Friendship still can serve that function, and it is perhaps a comment on our obsession that, in our elevation of romantic love, we have so demeaned our concept of friendship. (Indeed we sometimes call a person a friend though we have only just met, with the usual exchange of pleasantries.)

Throughout history, marriages have rarely been based on love. Courtly love maintained that love and marriage were all but incompatible, a view that persisted into modern times with Montaigne and Stendhal. Shakespeare and the Shelleys tried to reconcile them, but the doubts persisted, and they still provoke some of the hardest questions of our time. In this century, Bertrand Russell continues to doubt the compatibility of romance and stable marriage, and Denis de Rougement raises the conflict between "conjugal" and "passionate" love to a new level of antagonism. Tom Robbins plaintively asks, "How do we make love last?" and scholar Irving Singer asks how to make romantic love continue into marriage. He replies that love is itself the search for a long-term relationship and marriage, not just completion but the continuance of it.

Francesca M. Cancian has been interested in the vicissitudes of love and marriage in America today (though most of her studies seem to involve Southern California couples, not, I would think, a very trustworthy sample). Her newest book (*Love in America*) concerns a conflict between love, on the one hand, and what she calls "self-development" on the other. The freedom enjoyed by Americans in the last thirty years or so has been so considerable that previously unthinkable options—unmarried cohabitation; women's remaining single or childless; professional wives and mothers— are not only possible but almost routine. Roles for men and women have become remarkably flexible as well as confused. The result, according to many scholars and social critics, is a loss of "commitment," a weakening of intimacy, the disappearance of love.

Cancian's thesis is that this painful diagnosis may not be justified. Between the traditional restrictive roles for women and the very modern sense of mutual commitment Cancian finds a third possibility, which she summarizes as "mutual interdependence." Many Americans, she writes, "believe that to develop their individual potential, they need a supportive, intimate relationship with the spouse or lover. They see self-development and love as mutually reinforcing, not conflicting."

Moreover, the old distinction between "feminine qualities," such as submissiveness, dependency, and emotion, rather than rational and "masculine qualities," such as self-confidence, independence, "cool" logic, is giving way. It is the separation of the family from economic production that separated male and female roles. (The previous 3,000 to 50,000 years of sex discrimination don't enter into Cancian's account.) By the middle of the eighteenth century, the "patriarchal household" had all but disintegrated, and the distinction between warm, personal private life and cold, competitive public life was well under way. Scouting the magazines of the period, Cancian shows us how the complementary ideologies separated and became virtually separate worlds. The feminization of love was the outcome. Not surprising, many women turned to female friends to share a world that they could not share with their husbands.

The twentieth century allowed men and women to regain more equal footing as women began to work for wages and both men and women began to place a high value on intimacy and self-development. But the inequality and estrangement of the past continue to dog the present.

So what is love, and what does it mean to us today? It is time to put an end to the popular concept that love is "eternal." Our conceptions of love are a recent experiment, and it is not yet clear whether love is here to stay. Despite the unbridled optimism of some of our more mainstream music, love is not always good, or enough, or healthy. (Blues and country music tend to be closer to the truth.) It has rightly been objected that love, in its emphasis on the very private further disintegrates the public bonds that hold us together, and the reality of fully equal and non-oppressive relationships is still an ideal on the horizon and not a matter of fact. Love is, to be sure, one of the good things in life. But we are just now inventing—or reinventing—love, and its history is far from over.

21

The State of Unions

"Man is a network of relationships," wrote Saint-Exupery, "and these alone matter to him." And yet, our vision of ourselves is quite otherwise. We tend to define ourselves as "individuals"; we get away from everyone else and break up marriages to "find ourselves." We talk about "reaching out to someone" and our psychiatrists remind us constantly about "the prison of our loneliness," from which love and friendship represent refuge and escape. The popular philosopher of selfishness Ayn Rand announces with a sense of discovery that each of us is born into the world alone and responsible to ourselves alone. But even as biology, this is simply false. Our first grand entrance is inevitably staged at least *á deux,* and the delivery room is usually considerably more crowded than that.

We look at relationships as supplemental, as external links between ourselves and others, and for that reason, inevitably, we misunderstand them. The fact is that we are not atoms floating in a social void, waiting for a "chemical attraction" between us so that we can form molecules. That image has been popular for years, from Goethe's "elective affinities" to Gilbert and Sullivan ("hey diddle diddle with your middle/class kisses it's/a chemical attraction, that's all.") But it is bad chemistry, as well as bad psychology. The bonds are already formed; the places are only waiting to be filled. We *are* our relationships, and nothing else without them.

Freud was not being perverse when he announced that every one of

---

This piece appeared on Valentine's Day (1980) in the "Images" section of *The Daily Texan.* It is reprinted here by permission of the publisher.

157

158 Part Four: About Love

us falls in love again and again with our parents; the expectations and attractions we learn as infants do indeed stay with us through life, though presumably modified and even reversed far more than Freud sometimes used to think. But Freud, too, was captured by the fraudulent image of the self as an atom—or in his *Introductory Lectures*—as an amoeba, alone in the world, reaching out and absorbing others, occasionally being absorbed in turn. Accordingly, the upshot of so much of Freud, and the whole of modern literature in turn, is an image of relationships as essentially strained, troubled, tragic, and mutually defensive. They are an unwelcome necessity, brought about by the nature of "reality," which interrupts and renders once and for all impossible the self-satisfied life we supposedly enjoyed in our first few minutes or hours, complete within ourselves.

The violent upshot of this atomistic or amoeboid image has been given its best philosophical presentation in the early works of the French existentialist Jean-Paul Sartre. Relationships, Sartre simply says, are essentially *conflict*. Sartre also begins with the traditional isolated, self-absorbed notion of self (borrowing heavily from Descartes's classic statement of the image, "I think, therefore I am"). But if *I* am, what about the others? They are obstacles, threats, occasionally instruments, or raw materials for my creation of my own self. Other people infringe on my freedom, try to make me into what they want and expect, instead of encouraging what I want and aspire to. And in love, which would seem to be the antithesis of conflict, this competition and antagonism reaches its peak; sex and romance are merely means, Sartre argues, to turn the other person "into an object," to command their approval and defuse their ability to interfere with us. Sex, in particular, is nothing but a weapon in a war, and love is just the ultimate in arms.

Sartre's theory, if taken at face value, would be enough to keep us out of bed for a month. (In fact, of course, Sartre succeeded in maintaining one of the most admirable relationships of the century, with his equally gifted companion Simone de Beauvoir.) But what Sartre once argued (he since changed his mind) only follows quite naturally from the overly individualistic model in which we all think of ourselves, as first of all individuals, only secondarily defined in our bonds with other people. If self comes first, then conflict will indeed be the perennial threat, if not the essence, of human relationships.

But there is another model, an ancient and by no means disagreeable model of selfhood, in which loneliness and conflict play no such tragic role, in which the bonds between us are taken as primary rather than secondary, in which loneliness is recognized as a temporary aberration instead of "the human condition." We refer to this second conception, for instance, when we say in a moment of unimaginative romance "we were made for each other." It is the metaphysical model hidden behind the outmoded hypothesis that "marriages are made in Heaven." (As a sociological theory, this has been seriously challenged by the divorce statistics; but as a philosophical model, it still has much to recommend it.)

The most dramatic and also amusing illustration of this second view of relationships, in which we are "made for each other," is a short story told by Greek playwright Aristophanes in Plato's dialogue, *The Symposium*. Asked to tell his fellow drunken dinner guests about the nature and origins of love, Aristophanes invented a wonderful tale, in which we were each long ago "double-creatures"—two heads, four arms, and four legs (the rest of the biology remained somewhat obscure)—complete with enormous intelligence and arrogance (or *hubris*). To teach us a lesson, Zeus struck us down and cleft us in two ("like an apple," Aristophanes tells us) so that each resulting half-person now spends his or her life "looking for the other half." That, Aristophanes concludes, is the origin of love, not the search of one complete and isolated individual for another but the urge for each of us incomplete creatures to reunite with someone who is already part of us. The fable is pure fiction, but the point is profound. Relationships are primary, and selfhood emerges only within them and in their terms. They begin not when two people first meet but, in an important sense, with the very beginning of our species. "I think therefore I am" is ultimately a falsehood; the real truth is, "we are," and it is only in that context that our relationships (of one sort or another) can really be understood, not just as occasional conveniences but as the essential basis of a satisfying life.

22

"The Game of Love"

"Let me say—why not?—that yellow is the color of love."

—Gilbert Sorrentino, *Splendide-Hotel*

We'd known each other for years; and for months, we were—what?—"seeing each other" (to choose but one of so many silly euphemisms for playful but by no means impersonal sex). We reveled in our bodies, cooked and talked two or three times a week, enjoying ourselves immensely, but within careful bounds, surrounded by other "relationships" (another euphemism), cautiously sharing problems as well as pleasures, exorcising an occasional demon and delighting each other with occasional displays of affection, never saying too much or revealing too much or crossing those unspoken boundaries of intimacy and independence.

Then, we "fell in love." What happened?

There was no "fall," first of all. Why do we get so transfixed with that Alice-in-Wonderland metaphor and not just that one but a maze of others, obscuring everything: what is a "deep" relationship, for example? And why is love "losing" yourself? Is "falling for" someone really "falling for"—that is, getting *duped*? Where do we get that imagery of tripping, tumbling, and other inadvertent means of getting *in*-volved, *im*-mersed,

---

This piece originally appeared as a chapter in my book, *Love: Emotion, Myth and Metaphor* (Doubleday, 1981; Prometheus Books, 1990) and in first serial in *Psychology Today,* October 1981. A shorter version appeared in the *Austin American-Statesman.*

and *sub*-merged in love, "taking the plunge" when it really gets serious? If anything, the appropriate image would seem to be openness rather than depth, flying rather than falling. One makes love (still another euphemism, this one with some significance), but our entire romantic mythology makes it seem as if it happens, as if it is something someone suffers (enjoying it as well), as if it's entirely natural, a need and something all but unavoidable.

We look at love, as we look at life, through a series of metaphors, each with its own language, its own implications, its own biases. For example, if someone says that love is a *game,* we already know much of what is to follow: relationships will be short-lived. Sincerity will be a strategy for winning and so will flattery and perhaps even lying. ("All's fair. . . .") The person "played with" is taken seriously only as an opponent, a challenge, valued in particular for his or her tactics and retorts, but quickly dispensable as soon as someone has won or lost. There is no getting hurt, only "being a poor sport," no future, only winning and losing. "Playing hard to get" is an optimal strategy, but "being easy" is not immoral or foolish so much as playing badly, or not at all.

On the other hand, if someone sees love as *"God's gift to humanity,"* we should expect utter solemnity mixed with a sense of gratitude, serious-ness, and self-righteousness that is wholly lacking in the "love-is-a-game" metaphor. There is no frivolity here. Relationships will tend to be long-lasting if not "forever," fraught with duties and obligations dictated by a gift that, in the usual interpretations, has both divine and secular strings attached.

The game metaphor is, perhaps, too frivolous to take seriously. The gift-of-God metaphor, on the other hand, is much too serious to dismiss frivolously. Not surprisingly, these love metaphors reflect our interests elsewhere in life—in business, health, communications, art, politics, and law, as well as fun and games and religion. But these are not mere figures of speech; they are the self-imposed structures that determine the way we experience love itself. For that reason, we should express reservations about some of them.

One of the most common metaphors, now particularly popular in social psychology, is the *economic* metaphor. The idea is that love is an exchange, a sexual partnership, a trade-off of interests and concerns and, particularly, of *approval.* "I make you feel good about yourself and you in return make me feel good about myself." Of course, exchange rates vary—some people need more than others—and there is a law of diminishing returns; that is, the same person's approval tends to become less and less valuable as it becomes more familiar. (This law of diminishing returns, which we experience as the gradual fading of romantic love, has been explored by the psychologist Elliot Aronson of the University of California at Santa Cruz. His theory has been aptly named by the students "Aronson's Law of Marital Infidelity.") In some relationships, the balance of payments may indeed seem extremely one-sided, but the assumption is, in the words of Harvard sociologist George Homans, that both parties must believe they are getting something out of it or they simply wouldn't stick around.

The economic model has much to offer, not least the fact that it gives a fairly precise account of the concrete motivation of love, which is left out of more pious accounts that insist that love is simply good in itself and needs no motives. But the problem is that it too easily degenerates into a most unflattering model of mutual buying and selling, which in turn raises the specter that love may indeed be, as some cynics have been saying ever since Marx and Engels, a form of covert prostitution, though not necessarily—or even usually—for money. "I will sleep with you and think well of you or at least give you the benefit of the doubt if only you'll tell me good things about myself and pretend to approve of me."

It may be true that we do often evaluate our relationships in this way, in terms of mutual advantage and our own sense of fairness. The question "What am I getting out of this, anyway?" always makes sense, even if certain traditional views of love and commitment try to pretend that such selfishness is the very antithesis of love. But the traditional views have a point to make as well, which is simply that such tit-for-tat thinking inevitably undermines a relationship based on love, not because love is essentially selfless, but because the bargaining table is not the place to understand mutual affection. Love is not the exchange of affection, any more than sex is merely the exchange of pleasure. What is left out of these accounts is the "we" of love, which is quite different from "I and thou." This is not to say that fairness cannot be an issue in love, nor is it true that all's fair in love. But while the economic exchange model explains rather clearly some of the motives for love, it tends to ignore the experience of love almost altogether, which is that such evaluations seem at the time beside the point and come to mind only when love is already breaking down. It is the suspicion, not the fact, that "I'm putting more into this than you are" that signals the end of many relationships, despite the fact that, as business goes, there may have been "a good arrangement."

A powerful metaphor with disastrous consequences that was popular a few years ago was a communication metaphor, often used in conjunction with a relating metaphor, for obvious reasons. Both were involved with the then-hip language of media and information theory: "getting through" to each other and "we just can't communicate any more" gave lovers the unfortunate appearance of shipwrecked survivors trying to keep in touch over a slightly damaged shortwave radio. The information-processing jargon ("input," "feedback," "tuning in," and "turning off") was typically loaded with electronic-gadget imagery, and good relationships, appropriately, were described in terms of their "good vibrations." Like all metaphors, this one revealed much more than it distorted, namely, an image of isolated transmitters looking for someone to get their messages. It was precisely this milieu that gave birth to Rollo May's *Love and Will* and his concern that people had rendered love impossible. Love was thought to be mainly a matter of self-expression—largely but not exclusively verbal expression. Talk became enormously important to love; problems were talked over, talked through, and talked out. The essential moment was the "heavy conversation," and talk about love often took the place of love itself. Confession and openness (telling all) became the linchpins of love, even when the messages were largely hostility and resentment.

Psychotherapist George Bach wrote a number of successful books, including *The Intimate Enemy* (with Peter Wyden), that made quite clear the fact that it was expression of feelings, not the feelings themselves, that made for a successful relationship. On the communications model, sex, too, was described as a mode of communication, but more often sex was not so much communicating as the desire to be communicated with. Sex became, in McLuhan's jargon, a cool medium. And, like most modern media, the model put its emphasis on the medium itself (encounter groups and the like), but there was precious little stress on the content of the programming. Not surprisingly, love became an obscure ideal, like television commercials full of promise of something fabulous yet to come, hinted at but never spoken of as such. The ultimate message was the idea of the medium itself.

A very different model is the *work* model of love. The Protestant ethic is very much at home in romance. (Rollo May calls love the Calvinist's proof of emotional salvation.) And so we find many people who talk about "working out a relationship," "working at it," "working for it," and so on. The fun may once have been there but now the real job begins, tacking together and patching up, like fixing up an old house. This is, needless to say, a particularly self-righteous model, if for no other reason than that it begins on the defensive and requires considerable motivation just to move on. Personal desires, the other person's as well as one's own, may be placed behind "the relationship," which is conceived of as the primary project. Love, according to the work model, is evaluated for its industriousness, its seriousness, its success in the face of the most difficult obstacles. Devotees of the work model not infrequently choose the most inept or inappropriate partners, rather like buying a rundown shack, for the challenge. They will look with disdain at people who are merely happy together (something like buying a house from a tract builder). They will look with admiration and awe at a couple who have survived a dozen years of fights and emotional disfigurements because "they made it work."

In contrast to the work model, we can turn with a sense of recreation to the *dramatic* model of love, love as theater, love as a melodrama. This differs from the game model in that one's roles are taken very seriously, and the notions of winners and losers, strategy and tactics are replaced by notions of performance, catharsis, tragedy, and theatricality. Roles are all-important—keeping within roles, developing them, enriching them. The dramatic model also tends to play to an audience, real (whenever possible) or imagined (when necessary). Fights and reconciliations alike will often be performed in public, and an evening at home alone may often seem pointless. Some dramatic lovers are primadonnas, referring every line or part back to themselves, but one can be just as theatrical by being visibly selfless, or martyred, or mad. Lunt and Fontaine or Bogart and Bacall might well be models, and lovers will strain without amusement to perfect, for the appropriate occasion, someone else's drawl, insult, posture, or sigh. Unfortunately the dramatic model too easily tends to confuse interpersonal problems with theatrical flaws, to praise and abuse itself in terms that are, appropriately, the vocabulary of the theater critic. The worst that one could say of such love, therefore, is that it's boring or predictable.

Blandness can be just as significant as excitement, and a metaphor may be intentionally noncommittal as well as precise. Thus we find the word "thing" substituted for everything from sexual organs (a young virgin gingerly refers to her first lover's "thing") to jobs, hangups, and hobbies (as in "doing your own thing"). Where love is concerned, the most banal of our metaphors is the word "relating," or "relationship" itself. There's not much to say about it, except to ponder in amazement the fact that we have not yet, in this age of "heavy relationships," come up with anything better. There is a sense, of course, in which any two people (or two things) stand in any number of relationships to one another (being taller than, heavier than, smarter than, more than fifteen feet away from . . . and so forth). The word "relations" was once, only a few years ago, a polite and slightly clinical word for sex (still used, as most stilted archaisms tend to be, in law). People "relate" to each other as they "relate a story," perhaps on the idea that what couples do most together is to tell each other the events of the day, a less-than-exciting conception of love, to be sure. The fact that this metaphor dominates our thinking so much (albeit in the guise of a "meaningful" relationship) points once again to the poverty of not only our vocabulary but our thinking and feeling.

In our extremely individualistic society we have come to see isolation and loneliness as akin to the human condition, instead of as by-products of a certain kind of social arrangement that puts mobility and the formation of new interpersonal bonds at a premium. This individualistic metaphor, which I call the "ontology of loneliness" because it implies some kind of coherent law in the human organism's development, is stated succinctly by Rollo May: "Every person, experiencing as he [or she] does his [or her] own solitariness and aloneness, longs for union with another" (*Love and Will*).

This viewpoint has been developed by the philosopher Ayn Rand into an argument for selfishness: "Each of us is born into the world alone, and therefore each of us is justified in pursuing our own selfish interests." But the premise is false, and the inference is insidious.

Not only in our infancy but also in adulthood we find ourselves essentially linked to other people, to a language that we call our own, to a culture and, at least legally, to a country as well. We do not have to find or "reach out" to others, they are, in a sense, already *in us*. Alone in the woods of British Columbia, I find myself still thinking of friends, describing what I see as if they were there, and in their language. The idea of the isolated self is an American invention—reinforced perhaps by the artificially isolated circumstances of the psychiatrist's office and our fantasies about gunfighters and mountain men—but it is not true of most of us. And this means that love is not a refuge or an escape, either. Our conception of ourselves is always as a social self (even if it is an anti-social or rebellious self).

Our language of love often reflects the idea of natural isolation: for example, in the communication metaphor in which isolated selves try desperately to get through to each other. But this picture of life and love is unnecessarily tragic, and its result is to make love itself seem like something of a cure for a disease rather than a positive experience that already presupposes a rather full social life. Indeed, it is revealing that, quite the contrary of social isolation, romantic love is usually experienced only *within* a rather extensive social nexus. "Sure, I have lots of friends and I like my colleagues at work but, still, I'm lonely and I want to fall in love." But that has nothing to do with loneliness. It rather reflects the tremendous importance we accord to romantic love in our lives, not as a cure for aloneness, but as a positive experience in its own right, which we have, curiously, turned into a need.

Standing opposed to the "ontology of loneliness" is an ancient view which takes our unity, not our mutual isolation, as the natural state of humanity. Our own image of two people "being made for each other" is also an example of the metaphysical model, together with the idea that marriages are "made in heaven" and that someone else can be your "better half." The metaphysical model is based not on the idea that love is a refuge from isolated individualism but that love is the realization of bonds that are already formed, even before one meets one's "other half."

The ontology of loneliness treats individuals as atoms, bouncing around the universe alone looking for other atoms, occasionally forming more of less stable molecules. But if we were to pursue the same chemical metaphor into the metaphysical model, it would more nearly resemble what physicists today call "field theory." A magnetic field, for instance, retains all of its electromagnetic properties whether or not there is any material there to make them manifest. So, too, an individual is already a network of human relationships and expectations, and these exist whether or not one finds another individual whose radiated forces and properties are complementary. The old expression about love being a matter of "chemical attraction" is, scientifically, a century out of date, attraction is no longer a question of one atom affecting another but the product of two electromagnetic fields, each of which exists prior to and independent of any particular atoms within its range. So, too, we radiate charm, sexiness, inhibition, intelligence, and even repulsiveness, and find a lover who fits in. The problem with this view is that it leaves no room for the development of relationships, but makes it seem as if love has to be there in full, from the very beginning.

Today, our favorite metaphor, from social criticism to social relationships, has become the disease metaphor, images of health and decay, the medicalization of all things human, from the stock market to sex and love. Not surprisingly, a large proportion of our books about love and sex are written by psychiatrists and other doctors. Our society is described in terms of "narcissism" (a clinical term), as an "age of anxiety," and as "decadent" (the negative side of the biological process). For Rollo May and Erich Fromm, lack of love is the dominant disease of our times. For others, such as Stanton Peele, author of *Love and Addiction,* love is itself a kind of disease. Some feminists have seized on the metaphor, saying the disease was invented by and carried by men: Ti-Grace Atkinson in *Amazon Odyssey* calls love "a pathological condition." But whether love is the disease or the cure, this model turns us all into patients, and one might ask whether that is the arena for falling of love.

Perhaps the oldest view of love, the pivot of Plato's *Symposium,* is an aesthetic model: love as the admiration and the contemplation of beauty. The emphasis here is on neither relating nor communicating (in fact, unrequited love and even voyeurism are perfectly in order). On this model, it is not particularly expected that the lover will actually do much of anything, except, perhaps, to get within view of the beloved at every possible opportunity. It is this model that has dominated both our theories and our practices of love.

It is this model that provokes women to complain that men put them up on a pedestal, a charge that too often confuses the idealization that accompanies it with the impersonal distancing that goes along with the pedestal. The objection is not to the fact that it is a pedestal so much as that it is usually a very tall pedestal; any real contact is out of the question. Or else it is a very small pedestal, "and like any small place," writes Gloria Steinem, it becomes "a prison."

What is crucial to the contract model is that emotion plays very little part in it. One accepts an obligation to obey the terms of the contract (implicit or explicit) whether or not one wants to. The current term for this ever-popular emasculation of emotion is "commitment." In fact there seems to be an almost general agreement among most of the people I talk with that commitment constitutes love. (The contrast is almost always sexual promiscuity.) But commitment is precisely what love is not, though one can and often does make commitments on the basis of whether one loves someone. A commitment is an obligation sustained *even if the emotion that originally motivates it no longer exists.* The sense of obligation isn't love.

The idea that science itself can be but a metaphor strikes us as odd, but much of what we believe about love, it seems, is based on wholly unilateral biological metaphors. For example, we believe that love is natural, even an instinct, and this is supported by a hundred fascinating but ultimately irrelevant arguments about "the facts of life": the fact that some spiders eat their mates, that some birds mate for life, that some sea gulls are lesbians, that some fish can't mate unless the male is clearly superior, that chimpanzees like to gang-bang, that gorillas have penises the size of a breakfast sausage, that bats tend to do it upside down, and porcupines do it "carefully." But romantic love is by no means natural; it is not an instinct but a very particular and peculiar attitude toward sex and pair-bonding that has been carefully cultivated by a small number of people in modern aristocratic and middle-class societies.

Even sex, which would seem to be natural if anything is, is no more mere biology than taking the holy wafer at High Mass is just eating. It, too, is defined by our metaphors and the symbolic significance we give to it. It is not a need, though we have certainly made it into one. Sex is not an instinct, except in that utterly minimal sense that bears virtually no resemblance at all to the extremely sophisticated and emotion-filled set of rituals that we call—with some good reason—making love. And where sex and love come together is not in the realm of nature either, but in the realm of expression, specific to a culture that specifies its meaning.

There is one particular version of the biological metaphor, however, that has enjoyed such spectacular scientific acceptance, ever since Freud at least, that we tend to take it as the literal truth instead of, again, as a metaphor. It is the idea that love begins in—or just out of—the womb, and that our prototype of love—if not our one true love—is our own mother.

Our models and prototypes of love include not only our parents but also brothers, sisters, teachers in junior high school, first dates, first loves, graduating-class heroes and heroines, hundreds of movie stars and magazine pictures, as well as a dozen considerations and pressures that have nothing to do with prototypes at all. Indeed, even Freud insisted that it is not a person's actual parent who forms the romantic prototype but rather a phantom, constructed from memory, which may bear little resemblance to any real person. But if this is so, perhaps one's imagined mother is, in fact, a variation on one's first girlfriend, or a revised version of Myrna Loy. Why do we take the most complex and at times most exquisite emotion in our lives and try to reduce it to the first and the simplest?

The way we talk about love as an emotion is so pervaded by metaphors that one begins to wonder whether there is anything there to actually talk about. We talk about ourselves as if we were Mr. Coffee machines, bubbling over, occasionally overflowing, getting too hot to handle, and bursting from too much pressure. We describe love in terms of heat, fire, flame—all of which are expressive and poetic, but metaphors all the same. Is love really the sense that one is going to burst, or the warm flush that pours through one's body when *he* or *she* walks into the room? And if so, why do we set so much store by it? It is for this reason, no doubt, that the age-old wisdom about love has made it out to be more than a mere emotion— a gift from God, a visitation from the gods, the wound of Cupid's arrow, the cure for a disease or a disease itself, the economics of interpersonal relations, or even the answer to all life's problems. But then again, maybe we underestimate the emotions.

So what, after all, is love? It is, in a phrase, an emotion through which we create for ourselves a little world—the love-world—in which we play the roles of lovers and create our selves as well. Thus love is not, as so many of the great poets and philosophers have taken it to be, any degree of admiration or worship, not appreciation or even desire for beauty, much less, as Erich Fromm was fond of arguing, an "orientation of character" whose object is a secondary consideration. Even so-called unrequited love is shared love and shared identity, if only from one side and thereby woefully incomplete.

In love we transform ourselves and one another, but the key is the understanding that the transformation of selves is not merely reciprocal, a swap of favors like "I'll cook you dinner if you'll wash the car." The self transformed in love is a shared self, and therefore by its very nature at odds with, even contradictory to, the individual autonomous selves that each of us had before. And yet at the same time, romantic love is based on the idea of individuality and freedom. This means, first of all, that the presupposition of love is a strong sense of individual identity and autonomy that exactly contradicts the ideal of "union" and "yearning to be one" that some of our literature has celebrated so onesidedly. And second, the freedom that is built in includes not just the freedom to come together but the freedom to go as well. Thus love is always in a state of tension, always changing, dynamic, tenuous, and explosive.

Love is a dialectic, which means that the bond of love is not just shared identity—which is an impossible goal—but the taut line of opposed desires between the ideal of an eternal merger of souls and our cultivated urge to prove ourselves as free and autonomous individuals. No matter how much we're in love, there is always a large and nonnegligible part of ourselves that is not defined by the love-world, nor do we want it to be. To understand love is to understand this tension, this dialectic between individuality and the shared ideal. To think that love is to be found only at the ends of the spectrum—in that first enthusiastic discovery of a shared togetherness or at the end of the road, after a lifetime together—is to miss the love-world almost entirely, for it is neither an initial flush of feeling nor the retrospective congratulations of old age, but rather, a struggle for unity and identity. And it is this struggle—neither the ideal of togetherness nor the contrary demand for individual autonomy and identity—that defines the ultimate metaphor of romantic love.

23

Love's Chemistry

I approach this love
like a biologist
putting on my rubber
gloves and white lab coat

—Margaret Atwood, *Power Politics*

It's spring—at last—and a young man's heart supposedly turns to love, a young woman's heart, too, and many not-so-young hearts as well. In fact, hearts don't "turn" at all. Hearts are dumb, busy muscles pumping away in the isolation of the chest cavity. What turns to love, according to the latest science, are chemicals.

The latest chemical to win recognition as nature's love potion is an amphetamine-like substance called phenylethylamine (PEA). Nonscientific types discovered this long ago when they found that eating chocolate is sometimes a boost to love. PEA explains the exhilaration of love, and also its demise. A high can last only so long.

But the still-standard chemistry of love in most quarters holds that romantic love is mainly a matter of hormones. Stanley Schachter at Columbia University argued back in 1962 that all emotions consisted of a state of

This piece first appeared as an aside in *Love: Emotion, Myth and Metaphor* (Prometheus Books, 1990). It appeared in this abbreviated form in "Onward," *The Austin American-Statesman* (May 7, 1985). © Austin American-Statesman. Reprinted by permission of the publisher.

physical arousal brought about by the secretion of epinephrine—an adrenal hormone—along with the appropriate "labeling" of that arousal with the word "love." Elaine Webster, another social psychologist, applied this "arousal-plus-labeling" theory to love, with dramatic results. She writes, "To love passionately, a person must first be physically aroused, a condition manifested by palpitations of the heart, nervous tremor, flushing, and accelerated breathing.

> Once he is so aroused, all that remains is for him to identify this complex of feelings as passionate love, and he will have experienced authentic love. Even if the initial arousal is . . . induced by an injection of adrenaline, once the subject has met the persona and identified the experience as love, it is love. (*Psychology Today*, 1971, 5:1, p. 47)

Being a man of my times, I decided that it would be appropriate to bring the antiquated literature of love up to date. All that old stuff with hearts and souls needs recasting into the modern language of neurochemistry. Accordingly, I envisioned a scene. (The place: the psychology lab at the University of Verona. Time: late afternoon, before the sixteenth century.)

ROMEO: But soft! What light through yonder doorway breaks? It is my Social Psychology 261B professor! O, it is my love! O, that she knew she were!

JULIET: Romeo? Romeo Montague? Wherefore art thou? What manner of student art thou, bescreened in the dark of the hallway, so stumblest in on my office hour?

ROMEO: O, I love thee, Professor Capulet!

JULIET: How camest thou hither?

ROMEO: Down the hall, past the chairman's office, led by love.

JULIET: What is love? [Sighs]
Love is a smoke raised with the fume of sighs;
Being purged, a fire sparkling in the eyes;
Being vexed, a sea nourished with tears.
But what else?
But just a word, and nought else besides.

ROMEO: 'Tis true, I feel a fire and my heart
Poundeth in my bosom; I am sweating profusely
And I am nervous as a laboratory rat. But 'tis
The circumstances and the uncertainty.
Dost thou love me? I must know or I'll frown and be perverse, and most likely flunk thy course.

JULIET: What's in a name? Everything, it would seem. That which we
           call love, by any other name would be something else. [Pause]
               But 'tis hardly appropriate, for thou knowest me not.
ROMEO: I've taken thine every course, and I've loved thee three semesters.
JULIET: And thou hast been in such a state all the while? Thou must
           be exhausted!
ROMEO: My present anguish is fear that thou mayest lower my grade,
           for surely I am none so wrought elsewhile.
JULIET: Dost thou love me? I know thou wilt say "Aye."
           And I will take thee at thy word.
           For that would be but a self-fulfilling prophecy.
           Since thou art so obviously aroused.
ROMEO: O wilt thou leave me so unsatisfied?
JULIET: What satisfaction canst thou have from me in my office hour?
ROMEO: The exchange of thy love's faithful vow for mine.
JULIET: Indeed, I am blushing.
ROMEO: Then call it love, before thou calmest down.
JULIET: I have no joy in this contact,
           It is too rash, too sudden.
           Next time, let's meet for dinner, with flowers and candles.
ROMEO: Irrelevant, I'm afraid.
JULIET: Indeed, I feel a madness most indiscreet
           A choking gall and persevering sweet.
           I'll swear not by the moon, so inconstant,
           Like my visceral disturbances.
           Hark, I hear a noise within.
ROMEO: 'Tis thy belly churning, I heard it from here.
JULIET: But how do I know that it's thou, Romeo?
ROMEO: It matters not, by thine own theory. But label it love, and all
           is well.

24

The Politics of Sleep

It is ironic, at least, that one of the two socially acceptable euphemisms for having sex is "sleeping together." There is probably no activity so antithetical to sleeping, however exhausting and eventually soporific it may be.

Perhaps it is a sign of encroaching middle age, but I now think that a good night's sleep may be a better indication of love and intimacy than even the most passionate evening. Bedtime intimacy can be undone by incompatibility when sleeptime comes along. One cuddles; the other won't. One rolls over; the other complains, or grunts (same thing), or leaves for the safety of the sofa. One wakes up early, ready to go. The other prefers to sleep in, taking full advantage of the already warmed blanket.

Indeed, modern couples who are unintimidated and undaunted by sex fearfully avoid the dangers and humiliations threatened by a night together. One arranges to leave not long after the bewitching—that is, the sleeping hour. One complains that he or she has to get up very early the next morning—to go to work, to catch a plane, to catch up on work, to— it doesn't much matter. It's all an excuse to be left alone. Sleeping together, not sex together, is the testing ground for long-term intimacy. Sleeping together, not sex together, is the most prominent source of misunderstanding and disaster.

Sleeping together, like love itself, says a lot about one's identity, and how one "fits"—quite literally—with another. In my experience, there seem

An earlier version of this piece first appeared in my book *About Love* (Simon and Schuster, 1988). Reprinted by permission of the publisher.

to be two basic types—although perhaps the more imaginative or more experienced could uncover a half dozen more. There are SNUGGLERS and there are SOLIPSISTS. Snugglers relish the presence of another warm body. There are passive snugglers, who crave to be held, and active snugglers, who enjoy holding but resist being held; most snugglers are both active and passive, or indifferent to the distinction. It is enough for them that the other is present, warm, and cuddly. Snugglers can tolerate or adjust to a remarkable amount of rolling, stretching, jerking, groaning, squeezing, and even smacking. Even in their sleep, they recognize this as a small price to pay for love, warmth, and comfort.

Solipsists, on the other hand, can stay awake all night because of a fly in the room. The dog on the rug is OK, so long as he doesn't snort, wag, or move. The cat who tries to leap on the bed is soon thrown out of the room, or the house.

I confess that I am a solipsist, or at least, I used to be. Solipsists may love sex and, indeed, during the sexual act they may hug and allow themselves to be hugged. But, deep down, they want to be alone. One should never be surprised when a passionate lover who has great trouble sleeping suddenly insists that he (or she) "needs space." We have developed all sorts of theories to explain this phrase, but the truth may be that solipsists just want to sleep and wake up alone.

Both snugglers and solipsists will complain rather quickly that their sleeping habits do not betray their real personalities. Solipsists will point out that one might like to sleep alone but nevertheless love intimacy and snuggling. Snugglers will insist that they are in fact quite independent and do not need to hold on or be held onto in order to feel perfectly at home with themselves. I don't believe it. One is never more at home than in sleep, never more oneself, never more free—as Jean-Jacques Rousseau used to fantasize—from the artifices, expectations, and conventions of society.

In sleep we are free, not free to do much that is productive, perhaps, but free if also compelled to insist on the basics—independence or dependency (not such trivia as food, drink, micturation, or love, for these can be provided—up to a point—in dreams). These are the basic ingredients of the self, as Hegel pointed out years ago, as Freudians (in different terms) have argued, too. But whatever the multitude of bad arguments about love and sex and regression to childhood, the obvious truth is that if we ever regress, it is when we sleep, and sleeping together like sleeping alone is primal. One might well need sex for any number of reasons: because it is socially expected, for encouragement, for the challenge, because it is maximal hedonism, for power, or as a way of killing time. But we all need sleep, and how one sleeps is not an expression of that need but rather an insistence on the conditions that foster sleep: the security of another hugging body, or the isolated safety of sleeping alone.

Two snugglers together is the very portrait of bliss: the sort of mawkish scene that became a standard scene for nineteenth-century academic romantic painting. This is true even of two uncompromisingly active snugglers, whose competition for mutual holding may be as active and as satisfying as their sexual snuggling some hours before. (There may be a temporary problem with two passive snugglers, but they quickly realize that their need to be in an embrace is much more pressing than their preference for being embraced.)

Two solipsists can well survive, but preferably in a king-size bed. (Those twin-bedded bedrooms in 1950s movies may not have been prudishness after all; they may have reflected a preponderance of solipsists in the film industry.) There may be nagging doubts at first, for instance, when it is permissible to break away from embrace and set out across the bed on one's own, and there is always the danger that whoever does so first may offend the other—even though he or she is also a solipsist. Feeling neglected is always the bane of the solipsist—even if, in a sense, he or she prefers it. Insomniacs are almost always solipsists.

The real tragedy or farce begins when a snuggler and a solipsist come together. It may begin agreeably enough, with a long and pleasant conversation, interests in common, and no audible disagreements. The embrace does not betray the secret nor give any evidence of the deep incompatibility between them, and the warm comforts of sex do little to give it away. There is no moment of truth, but rather a slow unravelling of illusion, starting perhaps in the exhaustion that follows, but more likely remaining dormant (so to speak) during an initial and most misleading round of sleep, that fifteen minutes to an hour that is the most sound and satisfying sleep of all. It begins when one—the snuggler—reaches around and embraces the other, and is rebuffed, at first gently perhaps but soon with sleepy resentment. Or, it begins when one—the solipsist—rolls over and turns away, leaving the snuggler caressing the air and feeling rejected or—if so inclined—worrying about being found repulsive.

Needless to say, the one thing leads to another, but rarely to sleep. The snuggler tries another embrace; the solipsist mutters and pulls away. The snuggler, confused, wonders what has gone wrong. The solipsist—now beyond the realm of rest and relaxation—may get up and go to the next room, "to think," to drink, but really just to be alone and conclude, angrily, that this person is just too possessive to consider. A self-confident snuggler may then go to sleep, having chalked off the relationship as "too weird" to follow through. A less secure snuggler may well lie awake, plagued with self-doubts, hugging the pillow (or both pillows, the other being unused) to sleep. And since we rarely think of sleep as a romantic issue, the idea of an honest confrontation doesn't even arise.

We have all become artfully articulate about sex as an issue, replacing politics (to which our current views of sex are much akin) but we have little practice or even vocabulary to talk about the intimacies of sleep. As a consequence, more couples hit the skids because of sleeplessness than sexual malperformance. One can excuse and talk about clumsiness or lack of coordination; there is no apology appropriate for incompatible sleep.

To make matters all the more complicated, however, one and the same person can be both a solipsist and a snuggler—at different times, with different partners. This is why sleeping together is so relevant to love. A confirmed solipsist may become a wanton snuggler when he or she is sufficiently in love (and, let me tell you, there is no more magnificent transformation in the world). The many metaphors of lights and fireworks that have been employed to dramatize and poeticize love are nothing compared to the quiet, warm comfort of a converted solipsist. And when two former solipsists find themselves snoring joyfully in each others arms through the night, that is love indeed.

25

Sexual Paradigms

It is a cocktail lounge, well-lit and mirrored, not a bar, martinis and not beer, two strangers—a furtive glance from him, shy recognition from her. It is 1950s American high comedy: boy arouses girl, both are led through ninety minutes of misunderstandings of identity and intention, and, finally, by the end of the popcorn, boy kisses girl with a clean-cut fade-out or panned clip of a postcard horizon. It is one of the dangers of conceptual analysis that the philosopher's choice of paradigms betrays a personal bias, but it is an exceptional danger of sexual conceptual analysis that one's choice of paradigms also betrays one's private fantasies and personal obsessions. No doubt that is why, despite their extraprofessional interest in the subject, most philosophers would rather write about indirect discourse than intercourse, the philosophy of mind rather than the philosophy of body.

In Tom Nagel's pioneering effort there are too many recognizable symptoms of liberal American sexual mythology. His analysis is cautious and competent, but absolutely sexless. His Romeo and Juliet exemplify at most a romanticized version of the initial phases of (hetero-)sexual attraction in a casual and innocent pick-up. They "arouse" each other, but

This essay first appeared as a comment on Thomas Nagel's "Sexual Perversion." The pieces from which it is drawn appeared in the *Journal of Philosophy* 66 (1969), and 71 (1974), respectively, and have been reprinted frequently, most recently in Alan Soble's *Philosophy of Sex and Love,* 2d ed. (Littlefield Adams, 1991). Reprinted by permission of the Journal of Philosophy.

there is no indication to what end. They "incarnate each other as flesh," in Sartre's awkward but precise terminology, but Nagel gives us no clue as to why they should indulge in such a peculiar activity. Presumably a pair of dermatologists or fashion models might have a similar effect on each other, but without the slightest hint of sexual intention. What makes this situation paradigmatically sexual? We may assume, as we would in a Doris Day comedy, that the object of this protracted arousal is sexual intercourse, but we are not told this. Sexuality without content. Liberal sexual mythology takes this Hollywood element of "leave it to the imagination" as its starting point and adds the equally inexplicit suggestion that whatever activities two consenting adults choose as the object of their arousal and its gratification is "their business." In a society with such secrets, pornography is bound to serve a radical end as a vulgar valve of reality. In a philosophical analysis that stops short of the very matter investigated, a bit of perverseness may be necessary just in order to refocus the question.

Sexual desire is distinguished, like all desires, by its aims and objects. What are these peculiarly sexual aims and objects? Notice that Nagel employs a fairly standard "paradigm case argument" in his analysis; he begins,

> . . . certain practices will be perversions if anything is, such as shoe fetishism, bestiality and sadism; other practices, such as unadorned sexual intercourse will not be.

So we can assume that the end of Romeo and Juliet's tryst will be intercourse; we do not know whether it is "adorned" or not. But what is it that makes intercourse the paradigm of sexual activity—its biological role in conception, its heterosexuality, its convenience for mutual orgasm? Would Nagel's drama still serve as a sexual paradigm if Juliet turns out to be a virgin, or if Romeo and Juliet find that they are complementarily sadomasochistic, if Romeo is in drag, if they are both knee-fetishists? Why does Nagel choose two *strangers*? Why not, as in the days of sexual moralism, a happily married couple enjoying their seventh anniversary? Or is not the essence of sex, as Sartre so brutally argues, Romeo and Juliet's mutual attempts to possess each other, with their separate and independent enjoyment only a secondary and essentially distracting effect? Are we expected to presume the most prominent paradigm, at least since Freud, the lusty ejaculation of Romeo into the submissive, if not passive, Juliet? Suppose Juliet is in fact a prostitute, skillfully mocking the signs of innocent arousal: is this a breach of the paradigm, or might not such subsequent "unadorned" intercourse be just the model that Nagel claims to defend?

To what end does Romeo arouse Juliet? And to what end does Juliet become affected and in turn excite Romeo? In this exemplary instance, I would think that "unadorned" intercourse would be perverse, or at least distasteful, in the extreme. It would be different, however, if the paradigm were our seven-year married couple, for in such cases "adorned" intercourse might well be something of a rarity. In homosexual encounters, in the frenzy of adolescent virginal petting, in cases in which intercourse is restricted for temporary medical or political reasons, arousal may be no different even though intercourse cannot be the end. And it is only in the crudest cases of physiological need that the desire for intercourse is the sole or even the leading component in the convoluted motivation of sexuality. A nineteen-year-old sailor back after having discussed nothing but sex on a three-month cruise may be so aroused, but that surely is not the nature of Juliet's arousal. Romeo may remind her of her father, or of her favorite philosophy professor, and he may inspire respect, or fear, or curiosity. He may simply arouse self-consciousness or embarrassment. Any of these attitudes may be dominant, but none is particularly sexual.

Sexuality has an essential bodily dimension, and this might well be described as the "incarnation" or "submersion" of a person into his or her body. The end of this desire is interpersonal communication; but where Sartre gives a complex theory of the nature of this communication, Nagel gives us only an empty notion of "multi-level interpersonal awareness." Presumably the mutual arousal that is the means to this awareness is enjoyable in itself. But it is important that Nagel resists the current (W.) Reichian-American fetish for the wonders of the genital orgasm, for he does not leap to the facile conclusion that the aim of sexual activity is mutual or at least personal orgasm. It is here that Nagel opens a breach with liberal sexual mythology, one that might at first appear absurd because of his total neglect of the role of the genitalia and orgasm in sexuality. But we have an overgenitalized conception of sexuality, and, if sexual satisfaction involves and even requires orgasm, it does not follow that orgasm is the goal of the convoluted sexual games we play with each other. Orgasm is the "end" of sexual activity, perhaps, but only in the sense that swallowing is the "end" of tasting a Viennese torte.

There was a time, and it was not long ago (and may come soon again), when sexuality required defending. It had to be argued that we had a right to sex, not for any purpose other than our personal enjoyment. But that defense has turned stale, and sexual deprivation is no longer our problem. The "swollen bladder" model of repressed sexuality may have been convincing in sex-scared bourgeois Vienna of 1905, but not today, where the problem is not sexual deprivation but sexual dissatisfaction. The fetishism of the orgasm, now shared by women as well as men, threatens our sex lives with becoming antipersonal and mechanical, anxiety-filled athletic arenas with mutual multiple orgasm its goal. Behind much of this unhappiness and anxiety, ironically, stands the liberal defense of sexuality as enjoyment. It is one of the virtues of Nagel's essay that he begins to overcome this oppressive liberal mythology. But at the same time he relies upon it for his support and becomes trapped in it, and the result is an account that displays the emptiness we have pointed out and the final note of despair with which he ends his essay.

Liberal sexual mythology appears to stand upon a tripod of mutually supporting platitudes: (1) that the essential aim (and even the sole aim) of sex is enjoyment; (2) that sexual activity is and ought to be essentially private activity; and (3) that any sexual activity is as valid as any other. The first platitude was once a radical proposition, a reaction to the conservative and pious belief that sexual activity was activity whose end was reproduction, the serving of God's will or natural law. Kant, for example always good for a shocking opinion in the realm of normative ethics, suggests (in his *Metaphysics of Morals*) that sexual lust is an appetite with an end intended by nature, and that any sexual activity contrary to that end is "unnatural and revolting," by which one "makes himself an object of abomination and stands bereft of all reverence of any kind." It was Sigmund Freud who destroyed this longstanding paradigm, in identifying sexuality as "discharge of tension" (physical and psychological), which he simply equated with "pleasure," regardless of the areas of the body or what activities or how many people happened to be involved. Sex was thus defined as self-serving, activity for its own sake, with pleasure as its only principle. If Freud is now accused of sexual conservatism, it is necessary to remind ourselves that he introduced the radical paradigm that is now used against him. Since Freud's classic efforts, the conception of sexuality as a means to other ends, whether procreation or pious love, has become bankrupt in terms of the currency of opinion. Even radical sexual ideology has confined its critique to the social and political *abuses* of this liberal platitude without openly rejecting it.

The second platitude is a holdover from more conservative days, in which sexual activity, like defecation, menstruation, and the bodily reactions to illness, was considered distasteful, if not shameful and to be hidden from view. Yet this conservative platitude is as essential as the first, for the typically utilitarian argument in defense of sexuality as enjoyment is based on the idea that sex is private activity and, when confined to "consenting adults," should be left as a matter of taste. And sex is, we are reminded by liberals, a natural appetite, and therefore a matter of taste.

The platitude of privacy also bolsters the third principle, still considered radical by many, that any sexual activity is as valid as any other. Again, the utilitarian argument prevails, that private and mutually consensual activity between adults, no matter how distasteful it might be to others and no matter how we may think its enthusiasts to be depraved, is "their own business."

Nagel's analysis calls this three-part ideology to his side, although he clearly attempts to go beyond it as well. The platitude of enjoyment functions only loosely in his essay, and at one point he makes it clear that sexuality need not aim at enjoyment. ("It may be that . . . perfection *as sex* is less enjoyable than certain perversions; and if enjoyment is considered very important, that might outweigh considerations of sexual perfection in determining rational preference.") His central notion of "arousal," however, is equivocal. On the one hand, arousal is itself not necessarily enjoyable, particularly if it fails to be accompanied with expectation of release. But on the other hand, Nagel's "arousal" plays precisely the same role in his analysis that "tension" (or "cathexis") plays in Freud, and though the arousal itself is not enjoyable, its release is, and the impression we get from Nagel, which Freud makes explicit, is that sexual activity is the intentional arousal both of self and other in order to enjoy its release. On this interpretation, Nagel's analysis is perfectly in line with post-Freudian liberal theory.

Regarding the second platitude, Nagel's analysis does not mention it, but rather it appears to be presupposed throughout that sexuality is a private affair. One might repeat that the notion of privacy is more symptomatic of his analysis itself. One cannot imagine J. L. Austin spending a dozen pages describing the intentions and inclinations involved in a public performance of making a promise or christening a ship without mentioning the performance itself. Yet Nagel spends that much space giving us the preliminaries of sexuality without ever quite breaching the private sector in which sexual activity is to be found.

The third platitude emerges only slowly in Nagel's essay. He begins by chastising an approach to that same conclusion by a radical "skeptic," who argues that sexual desires are "appetites": "Either they are sexual or they are not; sexuality does not admit of imperfection, or perversion, or any other such qualification" (7). Nagel's analysis goes beyond this "skepticism" in important ways, yet he does conclude that "any bodily contact between a man and a woman that gives them sexual *pleasure* [italics mine], is a possible vehicle for the system of multi-level interpersonal awareness that I have claimed is the basic psychological content of sexual interaction" (15). Here the first platitude is partially employed to support the third, presumably with the second is implied. Notice again that Nagel has given us no indication of what distinguishes "sexual pleasure" from other pleasures, whether bodily pleasures or the enjoyment of conquest or domination, seduction or submission, sleeping with the president's daughter, or earning thirty dollars.

To knock down a tripod, one need kick out only one of its supporting legs. I for one would not wish to advocate, along with several recent sexual pundits, an increased display of fornication and fellatio in public places, nor would I view the return of "sexual morality" as a desirable state of affairs. Surprisingly, it is the essential enjoyment of sex that is the least palatable of the liberal myths.

No one would deny that sex is enjoyable, but it does not follow that sexuality is the activity of "pure enjoyment" and that "gratification," or "pure physical pleasure," that is, orgasm, is its end. Sex is indeed pleasurable, but, as Aristotle argued against the hedonists of his day, this enjoyment accompanies sexual activity and its ends, but is not that activity or these ends. We enjoy being sexually satisfied; we are not satisfied by our enjoyment. In fact, one might reasonably hypothesize that the performance of any activity, pleasurable or not, which is as intensely promoted and obsessively pursued as sex in America would provide tremendous gratification. (One might further speculate on the fact that recent American politics shows that "every [white, male Christian] American boy's dream of becoming President" seems to encourage the exploitation of all three sexual platitudes of enjoyment, privacy, and "anything goes.")*

If sexuality does not essentially aim at pleasure, does it have any purpose? Jean-Paul Sartre has given us an alternative to the liberal theory in his *Being and Nothingness*, in which he argues that our sexual relations with others, like all our various relationships with others, are to be construed as *conflicts*, modeled after Hegel's parable of master and slave. Sexual desire is not desire for pleasure, and pleasure is more likely to distract us from sexuality than to deepen our involvement. For Sartre, sexual desire is the desire to possess, to gain recognition of one's own freedom at the expense of the other. By "incarnating" and degrading him/her in flesh, one reduces him/her to an object. Sadism is but an extension of this domination over the other. Or one allows himself/herself to be "incarnated" as a devious route to the same end, making the other his/her sexual slave. Sexual activity concentrates its attention on the least personal, most inert parts of the body—breasts, thighs, stomach—and emphasizes awkward and immobile postures and activities. On this model, degradation is the central activity of sex, to convince the other that he/she is a slave, to persuade the other of one's own power, whether it be through the skills of sexual technique

---

*Cf. H. Kissinger, "Power is the ultimate aphrodisiac."

or through the passive demands of being sexually served. Intercourse has no privileged position in this model, except that intercourse, particularly in these liberated times in which it has become a contest, is ideal for this competition for power and recognition. And no doubt Sartre, who, like Freud, adopts a paradigmatically male perspective, senses that intercourse is more likely to be degrading to the woman, who thus begins at a disadvantage.

Sartre's notion of sexuality, taken seriously, would be one of the great turn-offs in history, comparable (for us straight folks) to a session or two with the works of the now-legitimate *literateur* the Marquis de Sade. Surely, we must object, something has been left out of account: for example, the two-person *Mitsein* that Sartre himself suggests in the same book. It is impossible for us to delve into the complex ontology that leads Sartre into this pessimistic model, but its essential structure is precisely what we need to carry us beyond the liberal mythology. According to Sartre, sexuality is interpersonal communication with the body as its medium. Sartre's mistake, if we may be brief, is his narrow constriction of the message of that communication to mutual degradation and conflict. Nagel, who accepts Sartre's communication model but, in line with the liberal mythology, seeks to reject its pessimistic conclusions, makes a mistake in the opposite direction. He accepts the communication model, but leaves it utterly without content. What is communicated, he suggests, is arousal. But, as we have seen, arousal is too broad a notion; we must know arousal of what and to what end. Nagel's notion of "arousal" and "interpersonal awareness" gives us an outline of the grammar of the communication model, but no semantics. One might add that sexual activity in which what is aroused and intended are pleasurable sensations alone is a limiting and rare case. A sensation is only pleasurable or enjoyable, not in itself, but in the context of the meaning of the activity in which it is embedded. This is as true of orgasm as it is of a hard passion-bite on the shoulder.

This view of sexuality answers some strong questions that the liberal model leaves a mystery. If sex is pure physical enjoyment, why is sexual activity between persons far more satisfying than masturbation, where, if we accept recent physiological studies, orgasm is at its highest intensity and the post-coital period is cleansed of its interpersonal hassles and arguments? On the Freudian model, sex with other people ("objects") becomes a matter of "secondary process," with masturbation primary. On the communication model, masturbation is like talking to yourself; possible, even enjoyable, but clearly secondary to sexuality in its broader interpersonal context. (It is significant that even this carnal solipsism is typically accompanied by imaginings and pictures; "No masturbation without representation," perhaps.) If sex is physical pleasure, then the fetish of the genital orgasm is no doubt justifiable, but then why in our orgasm-cluttered sex lives are we so dissatisfied? It is because orgasm is not the "end" of sex but its resolution, and obsessive concentration on reaching climax effectively overwhelms or distorts whatever else is being said sexually. It is this focus on orgasm that has made Sartre's model more persuasive; for the battle over the orgasm, whether in selfish or altruistic guise ("my orgasm first" or "I'll *give* you the best ever") has become an unavoidable medium for conflict and control. "Unadorned sexual intercourse," on this model, becomes the ultimate perversion, since it is the sexual equivalent of hanging up the telephone without saying anything. Even an obscene telephone caller has a message to convey.

Sexual activity consists in speaking what we might call "body language." It has its own grammar, delineated by the body, and its own phonetics of touch and movement. Its unit of meaningfulness, the bodily equivalent of a sentence, is the *gesture*. No doubt one could add considerably to its vocabulary, and perhaps it could be possible to discuss world politics or the mind-body problem by an appropriate set of invented gestures. But body language is essentially expressive, and its content is limited to interpersonal attitudes and feelings: shyness, domination, fear, submissiveness and dependence, love or hatred or indifference, lack of confidence and embarrassment, shame, jealousy, possessiveness, and so on. There is little value in stressing the overworked point that such expressions are "natural" expressions, as opposed to verbal expressions of the same attitudes and feelings. In our highly verbal society, it may well be that verbal expression, whether it be poetry or clumsy blurting, feels more natural than the use of our bodies. Yet it does seem true that some attitudes, e.g., tenderness and trust, domination and passivity, are best expressed sexually. Love, it seems, is not best expressed sexually, for its sexual expression is indistinguishable from the expressions of a number of other attitudes. Possessiveness, mutual recognition, "being-with," and conflict are expressed by body language almost essentially, virtually as its deep structure, and here Sartre's model obtains its plausibility.

According to Nagel, "perversion" is "truncated or incomplete versions of the complete configuration" (13). But again, his emphasis is entirely on the form of "interpersonal awareness" rather than its content. For example, he analyzes sadism as "the concentration of the evocation of passive self-awareness in others . . . which impedes awareness of himself as a bodily subject of passion in the required sense." But surely sadism is not so much a breakdown in communication (any more than the domination of a conversation by one speaker, with the agreement of his listener, is a breach of language) as an excessive expression of a particular content, namely, the attitude of domination, perhaps mixed with hatred, fear, and other negative attitudes. Similarly, masochism is not simply the relinquishing of one's activity (an inability to speak, in a sense), for the masochist may well be active in inviting punishment from his sadistic partner. Masochism is excessive expression of an attitude of victimization, shame, or inferiority. Moreover, it is clear that there is not the slightest taint of "perversion" in homosexuality, which need differ from heterosexuality only in its mode of resolution. Fetishism and bestiality certainly do constitute perversions, since the first is the same as, for example, talking to someone else's shoes, and the second is like discussing Spinoza with a moderately intelligent sheep.

This model also makes it evident why Nagel chose as his example a couple of strangers; one has far more to say, for one can freely express one's fantasies as well as the truth, to a stranger. A husband and wife of seven years have probably been repeating the same messages for years, and their sexual activity now is probably no more than an abbreviated ritual incantation of the lengthy conversations they had years before. One can imagine Romeo and Juliet climbing into bed together each with a spectacular set of expectations and fantasies, trying to overwhelm each other with extravagant expressions and experiments. But it may be, accordingly, that they won't understand each other, or, as the weekend plods on, sex, like any extended conversation, tends to become either more truthful or more incoherent.

As body language, sex admits of at least two forms of perversion: one deviance of form, the other deviance in content. There are the techniques of sexuality, overly celebrated in our society, and there are the attitudes that these techniques allegedly express. Nagel and most theorists have concentrated on perversions in technique, i.e., deviations in the forms of sexual activity. But it seems to me that the more problematic perversions are the semantic deviations, of which the most serious are those involving insincerity—the bodily equivalent of the lie. Entertaining private fantasies and neglecting one's real sexual partner is thus an innocent semantic perversion, while pretended tenderness and affection that reverses itself soon after orgasm is a potentially vicious perversion. However, again joining Nagel, I would argue that perverse sex is not necessarily bad or immoral sex. Pretense is the premise of imagination as well as of falsehood, and sexual fantasies may enrich our lives far more than sexual realities alone. Perhaps it is an unfortunate comment on the poverty of contemporary life that our fantasies have become so confined, that our sexuality has been forced to serve needs which far exceed its expressive capacity. That is why the liberal mythology has been so disastrous, for it has rendered

186 Part Four: About Love

unconscious the expressive functions of sex in its stress on enjoyment and, in its platitude of privacy, has reduced sexuality to each man's/woman's private language, first spoken clumsily and barely articulately on wedding nights and in the back seats of Fords. It is thus understandable why sex is so utterly important in our lives, why it is sometimes so unsatisfactory, and so often a bond most profound.

26

Incest: The Ultimate Taboo

In 1979, when the sexual revolution was already firmly established, a perfectly normal, heterosexual couple won a headline in the *National Enquirer*. What did they do? They fell in love and got married. The scandal was that Vicky Pittorino and David Goddu were sister and brother, separated from childhood but siblings nevertheless.

The parents were horrified; the couple was indicted, tried, and convicted. They vowed not to have children (he even had a vasectomy), but the charge was not modified. It was not the possibility of giving birth to "imbeciles" that constituted their crime; it was the marriage itself. Legally they were not even siblings, but "nothing," writes James B. Twitchell, reviewing the case in *Forbidden Partners*, "is thicker than blood."

Incest is so serious a violation of both nature and culture, it seems that it is rarely talked about—and then only when accompanied by expressions of unqualified horror. It is something worse than sin or perversion, not suitable for simple gossip or scandal or even, until rather recently, for scientific or scholarly study. It is often contended, without study or argument, that incest is the one clearly universal prohibition—true of all peoples at all times and true of most animals, too. It is assumed that

This review of *The Original Sin: Incest and Its Meaning* by W. Arens (Oxford University Press, 1987) and *Forbidden Partners: The Incest Taboo in Modern Culture* by James B. Twitchell (Columbia University Press, 1987) appeared in *The Philadelphia Inquirer* on Sunday, April 12, 1987. The much-revised version appears here with the permission of the Philadelphia Inquirer.

incest is not just a violation of social convention but a crime against nature, a taboo that is built right into our genes.

But if this were so, why would we need to prohibit it? As Freud argued, there is no need for a taboo against what we wouldn't do anyway. There is ample evidence that it has often been flouted in history by royalty; the pharaohs, who married their brothers and sisters; the Incas; tribal kings in Africa and Hawaii. (Indeed *taboo* does not signify an absolute prohibition but rather an act allowed only to the elite—a king or queen or gods and goddesses.) There is by no means any shared agreement about what counts as incest, and moreover, there is a sense in which incest would seem to fulfill, rather than violate, some of our central romantic ideals: that we express our love through sex and that we love those closest to us.

Accordingly, it is a taboo that is frequently violated in modern Western society, although this is a fact that has only recently become evident. Freud refused to believe the incestuous reports of his female patients and treated them as fantasies. And even Kinsey, in his groundbreaking studies of sexuality in the 1940s, called incest in America "very rare."

The new evidence of incest (a researcher estimates that one of every 100 American women has been sexually molested by her father or stepfather) raises deep questions about our society and about human nature. Are these many violations a sign of the weakening of the taboo, or some sickness and perversion of our natural impulses? The simple theories—that incest is prohibited by nature and that all societies share in universal rejection of incest—are clearly inadequate to explain an extremely complex and disturbing phenomenon.

Forbidden Partners and W. Arens's *The Original Sin* provide a first-rate exploration of the problem of incest and the sources of its prohibition. Arens is an anthropologist at the State University of New York at Stony Brook. His previous book was a refutation of "the myth of cannibalism," though the book under review makes no parallel attempt to deny the frequency of incest. Arens emerges with the surprising view that it is not the incest taboo that is a product of culture but rather incest itself. We have a "natural aversion" to incest, but "it is the nature of human freedom to override nature." The study of incest thus becomes not the study of nature gone wrong but "an anthropology of evil."

Twitchell is a professor of English at the University of Florida at Gainesville. His previous books include a study of vampires and a critical review of horror pictures. His study is focused on the representation of incest in literature in the last two centuries or so, and his thesis is that literature, and language in general, is the "second line of defense" (the first being natural aversion) against incest. Literature provides us with warnings, he argues, from the monstrous consequences of incest implied in our standard fairy tales (e.g., "Little Red Riding Hood," "Beauty and the Beast," etc.) to the more sympathetic but comic treatments in such novels as Herman Melville's *Pierre* and Vladimir Nabokov's *Lolita*.

Against the ordinary view, that incest is simply unnatural, both of these books argue that the case is much more complicated. Twitchell insists that the incest taboo is "uncultural" rather than unnatural. Arens insists that incest, rather than the taboo, is cultural invention. Both agree that there is rampant confusion even in the identification of incest.

For example, incest today is typically conflated with child abuse and narrowly discussed in terms of father-daughter incest. But not all incest involves forcible rape or trickery, and daughters are not always children. Arens mentions the case of one (married) woman who took quite literally and willingly her dying mother's instructions "to take care of your father."

There is also incest between mothers and sons, but most common, and least reported, is sibling incest—for example, a young brother and sister "experimenting" together. Sometimes such relations break out into scandal, such as the couple who made it into the *National Enquirer*, or Lord Byron and his sister back in the early part of the last century. But most of the time such romances and experiments go undiscovered or ignored, and when they are discovered, the discipline and all information typically remain within the family. There need be no threatening of a child by an adult, no abuse or disruption of parental authority, no seduction of innocence (even if both brother and sister are quite innocent themselves). Indeed, some writers on incest separate parent-child and sibling incest as virtually two distinct phenomena.

Moreover, it is clear that what counts as incest is also a source of considerable confusion. Accusations of incest seem to apply to everything from fairly chaste sex play, sexual intercourse, and romantic affection to marriage and procreation. The biological argument against incest (the increased possibility of abnormal children) applies directly to the last of these. But clearly the taboo is not, in that sense, biological, for the horror we feel about a stepfather and his stepdaughter, who are biologically not kin at all, is in no way modified by the fact that they do not share the same genes.

The debate over the incest taboo is partly, perhaps even the key to, the nature-nurture controversy. The question is whether there are some basic human drives and inhibitions that are instinctive, and therefore universal, or whether all human behavior is molded by culture and learning and therefore specific to a given social environment. The biology of sexual desire divides into two traditional theories, usually associated with Sigmund

Freud and Edward Westermarck, who were (more or less) contemporaries. Westermarck argued, against most of his colleagues, that there was a natural aversion to incest, among animals as well as human beings. Freud, on the other hand, argued that there was a natural temptation to incest, which is why he insisted there was such a powerful taboo against it. The two theories provide quite different pictures of the role of biology and, consequently, the role of culture. For Freud, the taboo is cultural against a dangerous natural drive. As in so many aspects of Freud's theories, our actual behavior is explained in terms of two dramatic and opposed forces. For Westermarck, culture echoes and reinforces nature and so the taboo itself is natural, incest is unnatural.

Arens gives careful consideration to recent theories in sociobiology—the view that human social behavior is itself determined by inherited biological factors. He points out various shortcuts and sleights of hand of such theories, but he ultimately agrees with both Westermarck and the sociobiologists that incest is unnatural, based on a "natural disinclination." He, too, points to a tendency to "outbreed" in other species. Primates generally prefer strangers to group members. Female baboons, for example, often take considerable risks to mate with a new arrival rather than take the much safer domestic course of mating with a familiar male. Westermarck's critics objected that this would suggest that married people would grow less inclined to sexual passion after years of marriage (to which Arens replies that, though Westermarck may never have married, he understood a thing or two).

The thesis of "natural avoidance" still leaves open a number of questions. For example, is the basis of the avoidance blood or familiarity? The most challenging research in this area follows the lead of Yonia Talman's familiar kibbutzim study in which *none* of 492 children reared together ended up marrying one another, a dramatic support for "natural avoidance" of sex with those with whom we were reared.

It is still widely believed that it is the avoidance of genetic inbreeding that motivates the taboo. And, indeed, research does show that inbreeding causes genetic defects. In two studies of marriage between siblings, for instance, more than half of the children were either physically or mentally deformed. But scientific grasp of such information has been slow in coming, and the power of the prohibition anticipates it by many centuries.

Explanations of the incest taboo today tend to focus on the functions of the taboo rather than its origins. The great anthropologist Bronislaw Malinkowski suggested that incest was forbidden because it made the socialization of children difficult or impossible. He also points out the serious confusions of kinship that result from incest, and kinship is the basis of many societal structures. (Think of Roman Polanski's movie *China-town,* in which poor Faye Dunaway must navigate her way through the unthinkable confusion of being both mother and sister to her daughter.)

Twitchell, in his book, displays the diversity of incest patterns in literature, treating us at the same time to a feast of literary reminders (in Nabokov's *Lolita,* Humbert was the virgin, not Lolita) and historical tidbits (Anne Boleyn was charged with incest as well as adultery and treason. She supposedly "incited" her brother, but it was rumored that she was Henry VIII's illegitimate daughter.) Twitchell includes some incredible representations of sexual horror from artists Paul Klee, Sibylle Ruppert, Alfred Kubin, and Edvard Munch. Arens explains the diversity of incest prohibitions and their violation with an appeal to human freedom: Whatever nature dictates, we make up the rules, and we can violate them. It is incest, he tells us, rather than the taboo that requires the "ingenuity of our species."

These are two excellent, readable, and thoughtful books that make the case for complexity in a subject that too often has been thoughtlessly ignored as "natural." Both authors, incidentally, state categorically that they think incest is wrong, even if they appreciate the intricacies of its perverse appeal. Perhaps the most striking message of these two books is that however much we may pride ourselves on our liberation from sexual inhibitions, some of those inhibitions are deeply ingrained and not to be overcome. We like to think that we are different from generations past, but in the most fundamental ways, we are not so different after all.

27

A Drop in the Bucket

"As a wound infects the finger, a thought the mind."

—Ethiopian Proverb

For twenty-five cents you can call the weather bureau to satisfy your curiosity about the temperature today, or you can save an Ethiopian child from starving to death tomorrow. (For the price of a call to Dial-a-Joke, you can save two.) We are told that, for a dollar, less than the price of that Big Mac snack, you can feed an African family for a week. For the price of a late-night pizza, you can save an Indian from blindness. These are the thoughts that explode in our complacent minds—and we cannot wait to get rid of them.

One recollects the magazine photo of a two-year-old child—could he really be seven?—the arms and legs as thin as the limbs of a spider, the stomach bloated in the now too-familiar paradox of starvation. But the sinister fact is that even if we are moved—and how could we not be?—we have this obscene ability and readiness to rationalize. A million starving children is a statistic that the mind cannot grasp. (It was Stalin, remember, who pronounced that one death is a tragedy but a million is a statistic.) And statistics are worse than lies, especially when true. They numb us

Originating in a conversation with the novelist Diana Silber, then Diana Henstell, this essay first appeared in *The Austin American-Statesman* and later became part of the preface of my book *A Passion for Justice* (Addison-Wesley, 1990). © Austin American-Statesman, and reprinted with the permission of the publisher.

to the facts even while informing us. They reduce that benign natural impulse, "we have to do something!" to a mere gasp of horror, or worse, an argument about the validity of the methodology of the statistician. Some recent studies of poverty in this country, for example, seem to be intended as weapons in an ideological argument rather than part of an effort to promote justice. Our natural compassion for that single child and others like him is dulled by a meticulous network of figures and theories, and we do nothing.

An acquaintance of mine recently bought a new Mazda RX-7 for the price of 250,000 Ethiopian dinners. He said, "What's the point? Whatever we might give, it would just be a drop in the bucket." The argument (I supposed) was that saving one or five or even a hundred children from the horrible fate of starvation didn't amount to much, considering the millions that were dying and had already died. In fact, those same children we save today would most likely starve next week or next month.

But, of course, he didn't actually say this. (The same sensitivity without the inhibition or tact is illustrated in a high school principal who, upon hearing that one of his five-year-old pupils had AIDS and had been barred from attending school, declared "The kid will be dead in a couple of months. What's the point of a lawyer?" [Fairfax Co., VA] reported in *Newsweek*, January 1988.)

I brought the subject up with a colleague who had just sold a modest house in Austin for a $150,000 profit. She said, "What's the point? The money never goes to the right people anyway."

The argument, I supposed, was that some 30 or 40 percent, or in some cases, even 60 or 70 percent of relief funds goes into administrative costs, inefficiency, and waste, or in the case of Ethiopia, the military expenditures of a hostile, hateful government, instead of relief. That would mean a 5 percent (tax deductible) deduction from her profits on the house would save only 7,000 or 8,000 lives, instead of 10,000 or 20,000.

But of course, she didn't say this.

A politically radical friend replied that nothing short of a revolution would help these people. He wasn't clear about when or how that might happen.

A politically conservative colleague started talking about the virtues of the free enterprise system and the "magic of the market," adding the predictable corollary that "these people brought it on themselves."

These are all good people, considerate at work, generous on birthdays, kind to their friends, just going about their business. But part of their "business" seems to be rationalizing, and the premises are none too pretty. There is the megalomania: if my gift won't make ALL the difference, then what's the point? There is the fear of being ripped off: "But some of my money is going to people I don't like at all. (Why should I accept such a limit to my control?)" There is the nagging but negative image of charity that is so tied to pity and, consequently, to a certain sense of superiority and the idea of being "patronizing." As good egalitarians, therefore, we avoid seeming superior by not giving. Finally, there is straightforward hypocrisy: people who praise "individual generosity" but always leave bad tips (ask any waitress) and find something wrong with every charity.

Our failure is not so much greed or selfishness as it is a stubborn, infantile insistence on blocking out the nastiness of the world, even when our awareness might make some difference. How much of the violence and ugliness on television is designed (not by anyone in particular) to make us more callous and uncaring, in the recognition that the world is so bad that there's just not much that we could do to change it? (Isn't "realism," just another name for resignation, cynicism, and despair?) Then there is that Sunday School lesson that says, "Remember that others are worse off" and even "There but for the Grace of God go I." But these words of wisdom have been reduced to platitudes, simple nonnegotiable facts about the world. And instead of feeling gratitude we just feel lucky, or, we falsely pretend that we have earned our good fortune. Or, we rationalize, even at the cost of considerable self-deception. We blame the victims for their own plight, citing their "laziness" or suggesting the unthinkable, that "they choose to live that way," even "they're happy the way they are." And then we feel put upon. What we don't seem to feel is moved to act with dispatch.

It is true that time spent wallowing in the miseries of the world helps no one, but neither do bad rationalizations and neglect. It may not be a just world, and there is no point in pretending that it is. But in the end, we really are the world, there are no excuses; and justice, if it is to be found anywhere, must be found in us.

28

Righteous Food

"I see dozens of cookbooks and hundreds of articles a year purporting to tackle nutritional issues, and the amount of just plain bunk is staggering."

—Anne Mendelson, "Nutribabble" (*The Nation*, 6/17/91)

I love bran. No, I love to eat bran. It makes me feel good. Well, not exactly, but my doctor *told* me that it would make me feel better, eventually. Or, at least, it would make it less likely that I would feel worse, or suffer certain ailments (I forget which). That is, assuming that I might be afflicted otherwise, which neither he nor anyone else will ever know.

But that doesn't matter, because eating bran, at least this year, is the *right* thing to do.

Bran, you see, is *righteous food,* food that makes you feel better, not because you like it, not even because you know that it's good for you. You feel better just because you know you are eating it.

Actually, I hate bran. The texture is revolting. What taste it has reminds me of the taste of sawdust. (I used to chew on wood as a kid.)

What I wake up excited about is a gigantic piece of double-fudge chocolate cake, the kind Sutter's (now defunct) French patisserie used to serve in New York. (Having never had a grandmother to bestow such flavors, my *gebak-lust* is uncomplicated by nostalgia.) But at the age of thirty-six, I know that all those calories, the starch, the artery-hardening shortening and butter, not to mention the hundred and two different poisons

---

First appeared in *The Daily Texan*, 1980.

they are daily discovering in chocolate, in refined sugar, and no doubt in flour, too, are *bad* for me, especially first thing in the morning. Actually, I don't know that at all, but I have been made to believe it, which amounts to the same thing. And when I did indulge, usually with my brother Jon (now a master baker himself), I remember waddling down Greenwich and 10th Street in a state of gluttonous agony, done for the day, the caffeine from the accompanying cup of coffee almost undetectable through the sludge of my swollen belly. At most, the coffee—itself a righteous food, though certainly not at all healthy—added a tingle of anxiety to my feelings of self-disgust.

Chocolate cake, you see, isn't just not good food—perhaps it isn't even food—but it's the antithesis of righteous food; it's the kind of food that makes you feel bad, not just full, but guilty, just for eating it. Righteous food is the kind of food you learn to love the way you once learned to love sore muscles. It's the kind of food that makes you feel that you're a good person, looking with righteousness at a world full of seductive meats and sinful desserts, overcooked vegetables, and bastardized starches. And bran, for the moment, is one of the most righteous foods of all. A bowl in the morning (with skim milk, of course, and no sugar) and I feel fit enough to go out and give a sermon to my friends eating quarter pounders at MacDonald's.

It is not quite true that "one is what one eats" (a notorious pun in German, *er ist was er isst*). But what we eat is surely a telling indication of what we would like to be. Meat eaters have always correlated their bloody beef and beastly behavior, crunching through sinews, grinding gristle, chewing the fat with virility and strength. Vegetable eaters have always thought of themselves as more serious, peaceful, contemplative, if not, according to some Eastern ideals, vegetative. The Hindus, of course, made quite a point of the relationship between "purity" of food and "purity" of thought. Potato eaters tend to act if not look like potatoes and, who can deny it, the love of dessert has always been rightly associated with decadence (as in "decay"; what in childhood threatened only our teeth now becomes the nemesis of the soul itself). Anyone who loves dessert, no matter how apparently upstanding or unglamorously serious he or she may be, is capable of the most wanton debauchery. (One must except the mere fruit cup and the unembellished slice of melon.) But, instead of the after-dinner orgy—or perhaps in anticipation of it—one has dessert.

(Debauchery is not confined to dessert, however. "Sinner that I am" proclaims Byron's Don Juan in Canto 15, having done no more than spy the *soupe a la beauveau* about to be served.)

Coffee, on the other hand, is not only a sobering influence but itself a mark of sobriety, seriousness, and sociability. The struggling artist who makes himself the seventh cup of *expresso* has to be serious about his work (no matter how much time he spends grinding the coffee beans). Coffee shows character. Coffee is also a medium of communication. Someone drinking coffee alone in public is certainly a sociophobe, if not a sociopath. The lone bourbon drinker is most likely lonely; the solitary coffee drinker is probably plotting a revolution.

But coffee, now is the time to protest, is surely *bad* for you. So it is. Coffee ruins your "nerves." It causes ulcers. It makes for sleepless nights. But health isn't everything. Coffee is a righteous food, too, the drink of sobriety, the work drink, stimulant to serious conversation. Every health food maniac I know drinks enough coffee to kill a sloth. (A few fanatics are supposed to drink barley brew.) The unhealthy aspects of coffee represent a kind of sacrifice—to work, to sobriety, and to friends who cannot converse without caffeine and its rituals.

Coffee rides high on every list of righteous food as well as on the list of sermons: ("You know, I really do drink too much coffee. . . ."), a double virtue, since it allows one both self-criticism and a pronouncement of seriousness at one and the same time.

A long tradition of righteous foods has its best-known and possibly oldest example in the ancient Hebraic laws of "Kosher" foods. These are the prohibitions on pork, for example, which are still felt even by many people who follow none of the other well-defined rules of practice. There is the all but incomprehensible refusal to eat milk with meat, a prohibition powerful enough to once cause months of anguish for one of my friends for whom the common cheeseburger and pepperoni pizza presented moral anxieties of frightening proportions. There are the at least inconvenient restrictions on shops, plates, silverware, and condiments, and a host of dubious distinctions of edible versus inedible foods based mainly on the food's foot, or lack of them. (No hooves of a certain kind, no fish without fins, etc.)

Now the idea has often been taken as self-evident that this strange collection of prohibitions must certainly have been a policy of health and nutrition, the reasoning of which has often been lost or forgotten. Thus eating pork, for example, probably did prove to be dangerous because of trichinosis, and two thousand years before the germ theory of disease, it was no doubt much safer to abstain from eating pig altogether than to try to figure out which parts under what conditions brought about the disease. Similarly, one can surmise that the ban on shellfish was once connected to an outbreak of hepatitis or some such disease. One can only guess at the prohibition on eating a kid boiled in its mother's milk (later generalized to milk and meat in general) or to the restriction on bloody meats. But, the argument goes, there is a more-or-less medical explanation, if only we could find it.

However reasonable this "materialist" theory of the Hebraic dietary laws looks at first, that is, however much we want it to look "rational" in our own present-day terms, the theory doesn't hold up. Kosher food is and was righteous food, and whatever concerns for health may have entered into the authorship of the prohibitions, it was the prohibitions themselves that were their own justification. "Clean" and "unclean" were metaphysical and not medical terms. Jewish food was righteous because it set Jews off from everyone else. (Not insignificantly, one of the major breaks between Christianity and Judaism was in Jesus' declaration that "all foods are clean." [Mark 7:19]) Kosher food is righteous food because it is "clean" food, defined by God precisely in order to mark off "the chosen people." The French "structuralist" scholar, Jean Soler, for example, has gone through the books of the Torah and the Talmud to show in impressive detail how the dietary laws are not at all (or if at all, tangentially) matters of hygiene but of rigid and rigorous religious logic, canonized in the Old Testament, following the ancient ideas of "natural kinds" and "natural order." "Unclean" foods are altered foods (fermented grain, for example) or food that slips between the "natural" categories. (Shellfish are not fish, for example.) Soler argues that the original dietary laws commanded the Jews to be strict vegetarians, but this was amended (by God, after the Flood) to allow certain kinds of meat, so long as it was cleansed of blood and properly blessed and prepared.

Similar rituals of prohibition and preparation are traced by Claude Levi-Strauss, the "structuralist" anthropologist, in his book, *The Raw and the Cooked,* but the point again to be made of these exotic practices, as well as our own, is that health is at most a secondary consideration; propriety and self-righteousness come first. Of course, in our society, health and righteousness have temporarily joined forces. (This was not true even ten years ago. We then called immoral people despicable; now they are "sick.") But there is little evidence that the ancient Hebrews or Levi-Strauss's Amazon tribesmen shared our interest in jogging as a sign of moral rectitude. The Talmud was not an early version of the Scarsdale diet, and there was no claim that eating Kosher food would make you happier or healthier, just holier. Of course you would quite properly get sick when you "broke" Kosher, but that was more guilt than disease.

Among the thousands of items we know to be edible, we choose to call only a small proportion "food." Some edible nonfoods are left out as a matter of "taste," bull testicles, for example ("Rocky Mountain Oysters");

others with genuine revulsion (cats, dogs, and people, for example). Bugs are *verboten,* but in a classy restaurant, ants and grasshoppers can be delicacies. Worms are good for you, but absolutely forbidden. And within the class of "foods," some are "junk" (typical snack "foods" are favorite examples), many are acceptable, others are righteous, i.e., "good" food.

A few years ago, the only foods I didn't eat were politically unrighteous foods—seedless grapes and iceberg lettuce, for instance. (I still don't eat them, so effective was the sense of righteousness that accompanied abstinence.) As a kid, of course, spinach was the ultimate righteous food, mainly, I'm sure, because we didn't like it, which was mainly, I'm sure, because we were told it was "good for us" mainly, I'm sure, because we didn't like it.

The Kosher prohibition on pig meat was bolstered by our modern-day priests at the FDA when it was announced that bacon causes cancer, and eggs, for so long one of the main righteous foods (because they were cheap, of course) all of a sudden joined the ranks of foods to be frowned upon when it was claimed that they seriously raised cholesterol levels. Garlic comes and goes as a righteous food, largely, I'm convinced, according to class distinctions and varieties of snobbery. The new garlic virtue is that it prevents the flu; once it kept away vampires. Shellfish are generally unrighteous, as are most foods that are known best for their gourmet status. (Something can't be both a luxury and righteous.) Chocolate cake loses on almost every criterion, but bran, until recently, wasn't even in the running.

Modes of preparation are more or less righteous, too. Frying is bad, while steaming is good, broiling is ambiguous, and sautéing is snooty. Baking is good; boiling bad. (A show of lack of concern, for example, to Levi-Strauss's primitives as well as our own kitchens. Boiled meats are mutilated meats, and boiled vegetables are vegetables that have not been loved enough.) Most interesting, of course, are what foods can be eaten raw and which only cooked. (Why cucumbers raw and zucchini cooked?) Some shellfish are eaten alive. William James, incidentally, argued that the sight of blood was instinctively repulsive. Could that in fact be a leftover of our common Kosher heritage, including the macho mode of overcooked meats as well as the equally macho mood that takes pride in a steak as bloody as an Aztec sacrifice?

In Bali, eating is a matter of ritual and, because of an intense belief in magic, often a matter of terror. What one eats, with whom, in what order, and where, carries with it the constant threat of a curse, manifesting itself mysteriously in disease and death. Despite our sometimes fashionable admiration of the occult and its horrors, their life seems to us wholly "irrational" and intolerable. If, every time you opened up a pistachio nut, or didn't, you had to worry about the forces of darkness coming down on you or your family, life might indeed be more exciting, but it is a kind of excitement I think we would gladly live without.

But as I listen to today's radio broadcast (it doesn't matter which day—it comes anew everyday), and I hear of yet another common substance believed by someone to be "carcinogenic," our own black magical incantation, I wonder if we are not doing to ourselves just what the Balinese are doing to themselves. The FDA is our new witch doctor, making noises and casting spells over the airwaves. Our voodoo incantations are octosyllabic labels ending in "-izide," "-azode," "-itate," "-imate," "-amine," and "-erol." Our self-proclaimed local ministers rail against artificial preservatives and "chemicals." All of a sudden, I no longer enjoy my broiled hamburger. My favorite fish is loaded with mercury and my carrots are covered with insecticide. Chocolate cake is poison, and no doubt I'll hear by the end of the year that bran causes sterility and worse.

Eating is a political activity. It is not, as we sometimes pretend, the mere satisfaction of an appetite. We do not eat only—or usually—to satisfy hunger or gain nutrition, nor do we eat just for enjoyment. Food provides ceremonies and rituals. Food has interpersonal and symbolic significance, like sex, with which eating is often compared and occasionally confused. And if this is true of what we eat, it is also true of what we do *not* eat, or do instead of eating, for righteous food is largely a matter of prohibition. In ancient Rome, the impoverished poets lampooned the gluttony of the aristocrats—beginning a long literary tradition. And today too, the hallmark of righteous food is "simple" food, often minimal food, and ultimately, even, no food at all.

There was a time when righteousness required a full life of sinless piety—more or less. Today, according to many people, it seems necessary only to eat properly, even if one has just begun to do so. To become a vegetarian and eschew Burger King is to become one of the elect.

Vita Brevis, some old poet once said, and good meals are even shorter. Just let me enjoy mine, will you?

29

What a Tangled Web We Weave

" 'I have done that,' says my memory. 'I cannot have done that,' says my pride, and remains inexorable. Eventually, memory yields."

—Friedrich Nietzsche, *Beyond Good and Evil*

"The average American tells 200 lies a day."

—Arsenio Hall

Throughout the history of philosophy, deception has been assumed to be a vice, honesty a virtue. Of course, one might tactfully suggest that the very nature of the subject—the articulation of (preferably) profound truths—requires such a commitment. If philosophers didn't seek and tell the truth, what would distinguish them from poets and myth-makers, apart from their bad prose? Philosophers seek and tell the truth, the whole truth, and nothing but the truth. Or so they would have us believe. Diogenes strolled the city looking for an honest man, not expecting to find another but never doubting that he himself was one. He would not have fared much better, we suspect, if he had toured the philosophers' hall of fame. His predecessor Socrates insisted that he was telling the truth when he claimed to know nothing, an argumentative strategy that was doubly a lie. For many philosophers and scientists, too, we readily recognize that the search for truth may be something of a cover, a noble facade for working out personal problems, pleasing their parents, or pursuing personal ambition.

Nietzsche suggested that every great philosophy is "the personal confession of its author and a kind of involuntary and unconscious memoir" (Nietzsche, *Beyond Good and Evil,* 1966, i, 6). But unconscious revelation is hardly the same as telling the truth, and some philosophers, among them Nietzsche, have argued that there is, in fact, no truth. What have we then? Refusing to tell the truth would then itself be a kind of truthfulness, and insisting on the truth would be a philosophically venal sort of lie.

And yet, honesty and truth-telling have always been listed high among the greatest virtues. Socrates, we are told, died for it. Epictetus the early Stoic defended above all the principle "not to speak falsely." In more modern times, Immanuel Kant took the prohibition against lying as his paradigm of a "categorical imperative," the unconditioned moral law. There could be no exceptions, not even to save the life of a friend. Even Nietzsche took honesty to be one of his four "cardinal" virtues, and the "existentialist" Jean-Paul Sartre insisted that deception is a vice, perhaps indeed the ulti- mate vice. Sartre argued adamantly on behalf of the "transparency" of consciousness, thus enabling him to argue (against Freud) that all deception is in some sense willful and therefore blameworthy. And today one reads American ethicists—e.g., Edmund Pincoffs—who insists that dishonesty is so grievous a vice that its merits cannot even be intelligibly deliberated. In this, unlike many other matters, philosophy and common sense seem to be in agreement. And whether philosophy merely follows and reports on the *Zeitgeist* or actually has some hand in directing it, it would be safe to say that the philosophical championing of honesty is an accurate reflection of popular morality. Lying, for philosophers and laypersons alike, is wrong.

But what does it mean to insist that lying is wrong, and how wrong is it really? Is a lie told to embellish an otherwise tedious narrative just as wrong as a lie told in order to cover up a misdeed and avoid punishment? Is a lie told in desperation any less wrong than a calculated, merely convenient lie? Is a lie told out of self-deception more or less wrong than a clear- headed, tactical lie? (Is the former even a lie?) Are all lies wrong? Is lying *as such* wrong? Or do some lies serve an important function not only in protecting one another from harm (especially emotional harm) but in developing and protecting one's own sense of individuality and privacy? One could think of lying as diplomatic, as fortification, as essential protection for a necessarily less than candid self. Or, one could just think of honesty as merely one among many of the virtues, not a fundamental virtue at all. It is worth noting that Aristotle, in his catalog of moral virtues, lumped "truthfulness" together with "friendliness" and "wit," important traits to choose in a friend or colleague, to be sure, but hardly the cornerstone without which the entire edifice of morality would fall down. Moreover, what Aristotle meant by "truthfulness" primarily concerned the telling of one's accomplishments, "neither more nor less"—in contemporary terms, handing in an honest resumé. He did not seem at all concerned about social lies, "white lies," or, for that matter, even political lies except insofar as these contributed to injustice or corruption.

Critics have often challenged Kant's analysis of honesty as a "perfect duty," appealing to our natural inclination to insist that it is far more important to save the life of a friend than it is to tell the truth to the Nazis who are after him. But if there is even one such case in which it is right to lie and honesty can be overridden, then the "perfect" status of the duty not to lie is compromised, and the question is opened to negotiation. It is in the light of such dogmatic (*a priori*) condemnation, too, that we can understand the perennial controversy surrounding the seemingly innocent "white lie," the lie that saves instead of causing harm. And, to say the obvious (though it is often neglected by philosophers), lies can also entertain, as theater and as fiction, and not only on the stage or on the page. Indeed, lies can also be useful in philosophy. How many professors are now employed because some Cretan, years ago, declared that "all Cretans are liars"? Was he lying? Is there anything wrong with a lie when it causes no harm? And is it always true that we should tell the truth "even when it hurts"—or refuse to lie when it helps?

Behind the blanket prohibition of lying we can discern the outlines of a familiar but glorious philosophical metaphor—the truth as bright, plain, and simple, standing there as the Holy Grail of Rationality, while dishonesty, on the other hand, is dark and devious, the ill-paved path to irrationality and confusion. In revealing the truth, we think of consciousness as transparent through and through; in deception we detect an opacity, an obstacle, a wall within consciousness. The honest man and the true philosopher know all and tell all (except in Socrates' case, since he insists that he does not know anything). Nevertheless, Socrates' student Plato offers to lead us out of the shadows and into the light, even at great peril. The philosopher illuminates that which the liar and the layperson leave in the dark, including his or her own inner soul. Truth and light are good; deception and darkness are bad or evil, leading not only to ignorance and harm but to the degradation of rationality, the abuse of language, and the corruption of the soul. But philosophy, one begins to suspect, has overrated these metaphors of clarity and transparency. The obvious truth is that our simplest social relationships could not exist without the opaque medium of the lie.

In his novel *The Idiot,* Fyodor Dostoevski gave us a portrait of a man who had all of the virtues, including perfect honesty. He was, of course, an utter disaster to everyone he encountered. More recently, Albert Camus presented us (in *The Stranger*) with an odd "anti-hero" who was also incapable of lying. It is not surprising that he comes off as something of a monster, inhuman, "with virtually no human qualities at all" (as the prosecuter points out at his trial for murder). On a more mundane and "real life" philosophical level, one cannot imagine getting through an average budget meeting or a cocktail party speaking nothing but the truth, the whole truth, and nothing but the truth. If one wished to be perverse, he or she might well hypothesize that deception, not truth, is the cement of civilization, a cement that does not so much hold us together as it safely separates us and our thoughts. We cannot imagine social intercourse without opacity. Steve Braude, a philosopher who works extensively in parapsychology, illustrates the utter importance of deception with a simple experiment. He asks his audience if anyone would take a pill (which he has supposedly invented) which will allow them to read the minds of everyone within a hundred-yard radius. Not surprisingly, no one accepts the offer. We can all imagine the restless thoughts flickering through a friend's mind as we describe our latest trauma or the adventure of the day, the distracted and hardly flattering thoughts of our students as we reach the climax of the lecture two minutes before the classbell rings, the casual and not at all romantic thoughts of a lover in a moment of intimacy.

"What are you thinking?" is an extremely dangerous and foolish question, inviting if not usually requiring the tactical but flatly deceptive answer, "Oh, nothing." In such cases, the truth is rarely interesting or tolerable, the lie virtually required by rules both of civility and utility. The threatening nature of the truth has long been whitewashed by philosophers (Plato and Nietzsche excepted), often under a psuedosecularized version of the religious banner "the truth shall set you free." (It is perhaps not without intentional ambiguity that this originally religious injunction [John 8:32] is engraved on the administration building of the University of Texas at Austin.) But, against the philosophers, we all know that sometimes the truth hurts and the harm is not redeemed; that the truth is sometimes if not often unnecessary; and that the truth complicates social arrangements, undermines collective myths, destroys relationships, and incites violence and vengeance. Deception is sometimes not a vice but a social virtue, and systematic deception is an essential part of the order of the (social) world.

Now it can readily be argued that lying is just not the same thing as deception, and deception is not the same thing as opacity. There is much that one may not know and may not need to know; but to be told what is not true when one asks is, nevertheless, essentially wrong, a lie, and not merely deception. Deception may be nonverbal, and deception (notably in official circles) typically takes the form of a "run around" and not an explicit lie as such. There are true answers that are so misleading that one is nevertheless tempted to call them lies, and there is that protracted silence in the face of questions that even in the absence of an answer cannot be considered anything other than deception. But such complications make it much less obvious what telling the truth is and what is to count as a lie. Not to know what another is thinking is not the same as being intentionally misled or told what is simply not the case. It is one thing to foolishly ask "What are you thinking?" and to be told, "Oh, nothing." It is something quite different to be told a falsehood. Evasion and deception must be distinguished; but when we look at cases, that distinction is not so neat and simple. How literal and explicit does a comment have to be to count as a lie instead of a verbal evasion? Must a lie be an answer to a specific question, whether asked or only implied? Does a lie have to be verbal at all? (We will readily admit an answer in the form of a nod of the head, for example. How about a rolling of the eyes?)

Self-deception complicates this picture even more. It is one thing to self-consciously and intentionally tell what one knows to be a falsehood, but it is something quite different to tell what one sincerely believes and that turn out to be false. But what if the sincerity is superficial and one really knows the truth? Or what if one really doesn't seem to know but nevertheless *ought* to know the truth? The presence of that "ought" suggests that both deception and self-deception have a normative as well as a factual basis. Part of the problem is that lying seems to presuppose that one is clear about the truth oneself and then purposefully and directly misleads the other about its nature. Lying, accordingly, is fully intentional and malicious—at least insofar as it willfully deprives another of something extremely important—the truth. But this presupposes a degree of rationality and transparency that just doesn't hold up to scrutiny. There are, of course, cold-blooded, self-interested lies, knowingly false answers to such direct questions as "Where were you last night?" and "Who ate all the cookies?" But one might consider the claim that such lies are the special case rather than the rule, like cold-blooded murder-for-profit viewed in the bloody complex of accidental, negligent, desperate, and passionate homicides.

Not all lies are responses to a direct question. Not all lies presuppose knowledge. Many lies are dictated by our social roles, where truthfulness becomes a form of rebellion, and many lies are nothing more than a protection of privacy—notably "fine" as an answer to the direct question, "How are you?" Many so-called lies are not only "white" but heuristic and educational: the various modes of fiction, the exercise of the imagination, ritual narratives and myths, perhaps even the whole of religion. Philosophers of science have long argued that the teachings of science are in an important sense fictitious, based on useful explanatory postulates—genes, black holes, electrons, quarks. And what of those researchers who lie and fudge data, in order to more persuasively demonstrate what they believe to be the truth? Such "frauds" include some of the greatest scientists in history. There are instances in which the wrongness of lying is as straightforward as a breach of contract: "You promised to tell me what you knew but what you told me was false." Indeed, most straightforward lies involve some such well-defined context, a direct question or a specific set of expectations. But our fascination with lying and deception will not be satisfied by the straightforward case favored by the philosophers. What we are after is a drama of truth and falsehood in the complex social and emotional webs we weave, compared to which what is often singled out as "the lie" tends to become a mere epiphenomenon, an ethical "dangler" of comparatively little psychological interest. Without rejecting honesty or defending deception, it is time to re-open the question once asked by Nietzsche (in *Beyond Good and Evil*): "Why must we have truth at any cost anyway?" But, then, he was the philosopher who insisted, above all, on being ruthlessly honest.

30

Bioscience as a Social Practice

"Dr. Frankenstein, I presume." So began an earlier meeting between bioscience and society. Mary Shelley's creation (that is, the doctor, not the monster) captures as well as any thirty-second sound-bite from Jeremy Rifkin the fear and fascination with which the ordinary citizen approaches such topics as genetic engineering and ecological intervention. Of course, monsters make great reading and good theater whereas the depiction of a bioscientific paradise would inspire little but envy. (Simone Weil rightly observed that evil and not goodness makes great fiction but only good makes a good life.) From the other side, bioscientists rightly complain of public lack of appreciation for their work and political interference, poor working conditions, erratic and often irrational funding procedures.

And yet, we are, of course, a bioscience society. The fruits of bioscience have virtually doubled life expectancy and (insofar as it can be measured) the material quality of our lives in less than a century—merely a nanosecond in the long history of biological evolution. The ideas and promises of bioscience help define as well as challenge our social policies and our ethical principles. The newest techniques of bioscience provide the topic for endless social and political debates. The average citizen is grateful for bioscience breakthroughs and expects always more—a cure for cancer, a vaccine against

These comments emerged during the course of a week-long conference in bioethics held in Berlin in November, 1990, under the auspices of Silke Bernhard and the Schering Company. Reprinted by permission of Wiley Publishers and the Schering Company.

AIDS, a solution to global warming, an indefinite reprieve from the increasingly receding sentence of the Grim Reaper. And all of this as if by magic. But the bioscientist is no longer the leisurely naturalist, making some great discovery while walking through the woods or taking a tour of the South Pacific. The bioscientist depends upon society for very expensive research labs and equipment, for experimental subjects and, not least but often most difficult to obtain, emotional support and appreciation. The relationship between bioscience and ethics, accordingly, is both symbiotic and mutually antagonistic. Society expects a great deal from bioscience, and yet every innovation is greeted with suspicion: a Jeremy Rifkin conference, an Arthur Caplan rebuttal, and the predictable made-for-television movie.

I would like to mollify the antagonism between bioscience and society, taking their mutual dependency as something of a premise and begin a plea for mutual understanding and the social responsibility of scientists in a free market of ideas. But perhaps the first thing to say is that conflict can be healthy and uninterrupted silence can be dangerous. The easily understandable attitude on the part of some scientists, "give us the money and let us do our research," is no more desirable than political control over science policy. (Brian Winne has wisely pointed out that the absence of social concern, e.g., in the development of nuclear facilities in the 1950s, was hardly a sign of health.) What philosophers call "dialectic" (a sometimes heated conversation that moves from polarized disagreement to increased mutual understanding) is a sign of social health even if annoying and cumbersome to the unwilling dialecticians. In the free market of ideas, it is competition and disagreement that gets rid of bad ideas and establishes good ones. In a democratic society, debate and suspicion about authority— including the admittedly fallible authority of scientists—is essential. We distrust as well as depend on our experts.

In this sense, science is *not* in a privileged position in our society; it, too, is part of the chronic dialectical conflict that (within science) makes science work and (outside of science) is the essence of democracy. But there are healthy and unhealthy dialectics. What is unhealthy is polarization and extremism, those shouting matches in which neither side listens to or responds to the other, in which differences expand rather than contract and the voices that get heard are of the "more Mao than thou" variety rather than the voices of reason (not to be confused with the voices of mere neutrality or disinterest.) When irrational, uninformed, and sometimes insane positions come to dominate the debate, when the debaters are no longer critical of their own presuppositions, when the battle becomes political (literally, decided by power), when there is a total loss of compassion for either scientists or their subjects and the debate degenerates to moral name-calling ("Frankenstein!" and "Philistine!" respectively), we know that the dialectic has derailed and a new "covenant" has to be forged.

Bioscience is a social practice. What this seemingly simple and hardly controversial statement implies, however, is that much if not most of the popular view of science—on the part of most scientists and science students as well as the "lay" public—is deeply flawed. That popular view prefers to take the scientist as a solitary cosmic wanderer (who may just happen to work in a laboratory with other like-minded scientists and just happened to study his or her subject at some more or less prominent university). The activity of science is that of an isolated thinker confronting the comprehensible wonder of the world. It is a rational relationship between a single mind and the Truth. The scientist, according to this popular view, is "dispassionate" and "objective" (though fascinated and enthusiastic, perhaps ambitious, too), working entirely on his or her own with only Nature as a constant companion. It is a heroic picture, but like most heroic pictures it is largely fantasy and inaccurate even as a description of the work of great geniuses such as Darwin, Mendel, and Einstein. True, they may have separated themselves from the world, insulated by the originality of their thoughts, but they were nevertheless very much a part of their times; they inherited their problems and their scientific vocabulary (however they may have subsequently changed it) from their teachers and colleagues. The structure of their discipline, the way they framed their questions, the way they considered their data: these were not personal inventions but part of the practice of science at the time. (This seems obvious to us when we look back at the history of science, and it will be obvious again when future historians look back at us.)

To say that bioscience is a social practice is to say a great deal about its place in and its distance from the larger society in which it thrives. A social practice defines its own little world within the world. One might, without being demeaning, compare bioscience in this regard to American football. Each has its own rules, its definitive roles, its own language, aims and assumptions, its heroes and saints (Nobel laureates and Heisman Trophy winners, respectively). Religious critics of science sometimes enjoy pointing out that science, too, is a "religion," on the grounds that it has its own internal assumptions, and even saints. But the same could be said of any practice, even football (which is also taken to be a religion, for instance, in Texas.) Every practice has its own "internal goods," the goals and satisfactions that make participating in the practice and being "good at it" worthwhile. It is participation that justifies the practice for its practitioners, not its products or results. The thrills of discovery and victory, for example, are internal goods, more aesthetic or even hedonic than "practical."

Practices also have external rewards, of course: the salary one receives for being a scientist or a professional football player, and possibly the fame (more likely for a football player). Practices can and must be justified "from the outside" as well as by the joys of participation. The practice must benefit or at least not harm the surrounding society. Football is entertaining for the public and injuries are restricted to the players. Scientists work in their labs and sometimes produce socially valuable discoveries. But in this distinction between "internal goods" and "external rewards" and between the two sources of justification lies considerable room for misunderstanding. Scientists have difficulty explaining to the public that they are really interested in the questions more than the answers (and every answer leads to yet more questions), and football fans and players have a hard time explaining to the uninitiated why grown men would risk serious injury trying to place a bloated pigskin across an arbitrary line in the grass.

Bioscientists believe first of all in the intrinsic good of "knowledge for its own sake," and that belief, more than anything else, defines and justifies the practice. Those outside the practice, on the other hand, see bioscience and the knowledge it produces as a means, a way to increase crop and milk production, a way to cure or (better) prevent disease. This leads to some odd and uncomfortable consequences. Bioscientists need to seek funding to search for "knowledge for its own sake" by promising (only sometimes truthfully) that such knowledge will yield practical results. The public in turn expects miracle cures as if "by magic," ignoring the process that alone makes such discoveries possible and provides the meaning of the activity for the scientists who engage in it. The current clamor for an AIDS vaccine and cure is but the most visible example of such politically directed "targeted" research. One might also speculate how the misunderstanding between bioscientists and society originates in the process of bioscience education, where theories are presented as prepackaged products and little or no attempt is made to convey the thrill of pursuit and discovery.

One way of utilizing the distinction between internal goods and external rewards of a practice is to make some sense of the often abused distinction between bioscience on the one hand and biotechnology on the other. Bioscientists understandably see themselves as doing "pure" or "basic" research, which may (or may not) result in some usable product for the public. The public, ignoring the process and practice, confuses or simply ignores the distinction, taking science as nothing (significant) other than the process of inventing and producing technology. On the other hand, some very sophisticated commentators on the bioscience scene have similarly objected—in agreement with the public but on much more substantial grounds—that the dichotomy between bioscience and biotechnology is artificial and ultimately insidious, that the very process of testing and experimentation is necessarily "applied" as well as "pure" (e.g., in the search for a vaccine). One very good reason for listening to such criticism is that it rightly rejects the idea that bioscience (unlike its technological cousin) is "value-free" and "noninstrumental," in other words, that bioscience is not a social practice. But one need not (and cannot) make the distinction between science and technology absolute nor should one confuse the two. Biotechnology (which is essential *within* the practice of bioscience as well as a product of the practice) can be understood as the practical significance of the practice, which in turn defines itself not in opposition to such practical significance but nevertheless as distinct from it. But here again we find considerable room of misunderstanding and antagonism. Insofar as bioscience can be defined in terms of its internal goods, there is always the political question: Why should society (which may not share the scientist's pursuit and joy of discovery) fund it? And insofar as the new technology coming out of science serves policies and purposes that are themselves quite independent of science, why should they be given special priority just because they are the fruits of science? For example, there is no doubt that the genome project, an ambitious exercise in pure science, can promise genetic technologies that will alleviate suffering and save lives. But if we are only looking at those results, a fraction of the billions of dollars that fund the genome project would allow public health officials to end much more suffering and save millions of lives through a worldwide public health, nutrition, and vaccination campaign requiring no new science or technology. Why do the more exciting scientific solutions take priority over old, established and now-routine technologies that would, in fact, do much more good? In a world of limited funding, we find ourselves making deep ethical and political choices on behalf of the new bioscience.

In any discussion of bioscience and society the concern for ethics is sure to take a prominent seat at the table. But there is considerable confusion here and, as in the practice of bioscience as such, much room for disagreement and mutual misunderstanding. In many of the discussions we read by bioscientists themselves, the defense of bioscience and biotechnology is couched exclusively in the language of cost/benefit analysis, or in more philosophical terms, a crude form of utilitarianism. Utilitarianism is an ethical view that evaluates actions and policies according to a single, seemingly simple criterion, maximizing "the greatest good for the greatest number." How many people are helped (for example, by a new vaccine or pesticide) and how many people are hurt, and how much are they helped or hurt? (It was stated as a much more sophisticated position by its founders, Jeremy Bentham and John Stuart Mill, but that is not of importance here.) The argument on behalf of bioscience and technology, to be sure, is that its products over the past century or so have clearly led to a vast increase in human welfare, even in the face of nuclear holocaust, germ warfare, global warming, and other potential threats of apocalyptic dimensions. But the arguments against bioscience are typically not of this kind, and so the bioscientists and their critics speak past one another. The language of risk may be prominent (especially with the intrusion of product liability lawyers), but it is not the language in which ethics usually defines itself.

What one hears much more—in more or less primitive terms—are the accusations that bioscientists are "interfering with nature," "tinkering with evolution," and "threatening human integrity." These accusations may or may not be accompanied by religious doctrine. (Aristotle defended such a theory of "natural law" three centuries before Christianity; Thomas Aquinas, following Aristotle, wrote over a millenium later.) But what they point to is a dimension of bioethics (as opposed to bioscience) that is often uncompromising and, for many people, even more important than questions of physical well-being and potential harm. The wild-eyed and sometimes rabid reactions to the wide range of questions and techniques concerning human reproduction are the most obvious examples, and bioscientists often find themselves in a fluster facing seemingly irrational syndromes of attack by those who would outlaw not only abortions but all use of fetal tissue (however derived), embryo experimentation, and assisted fertilization. In the eyes of a cost/benefit analysis, the aim of which is the unquestioned concern for human well-being, those arguments may make little sense, but cost/benefit has very little to do with them. From the perspective of the admittedly obscure notion of human "integrity," however, they are all of a piece, however ill-considered. It is the process of "tinkering," not the results that are in question. On a more sophisticated and abstract plane, one may maintain the thesis that whatever humans do is part of nature, and human integrity cannot be separated from the pursuit of human happiness. But the "gut reaction" of those very basic even if uninformed beliefs is not to be taken lightly, and in more thoughtful form they provide dimensions to the discussion that bioscientists will ignore only at their peril.

What is at stake here is not simply the familiar and often dogmatic confrontation between science and religion (Knowledge and Faith). It is the manifestation of what is probably the singularly most important feature of contemporary democratic society, and that is the *pluralism* of ethics.

It is not just that people don't agree about various issues, such as the desirability of artificially inseminating infertile would-be-mothers or intervening in the genetic structure of a newly formed zygote. There is a clash of ethical frameworks, and where sex, babies, and human bodies are involved—not to mention the suffering of animals that might otherwise be some family's pet or the destruction of an environment that might well be a wall poster in the family dentist's office—one can be sure that much more will be at stake than either the excitement of science or the well-being of the lucky recipients of a new technology. To begin with, even utilitarianism has its obvious fractures, between the well-being of a single individual or a small group and the larger public good. What may well move us in an individual case can look more like a mathematical matrix when millions of people are involved, and the solutions to the larger problem may well offend us if considered individual by individual. Thus epidemiology has with some justice been called "medicine without tears."

The skewed debates and dimensions of pluralism are not confined to the molecular and the global; even where individuals are concerned (no matter how many of them) bioscience and scientists will find that they run up against the all-important conception of individual *autonomy*—a person's right to make his or her own decisions—and the charge of *paternalism*—the tendency of (scientific or political) authority to preempt such decisions. There are questions of human dignity intricately tied to such notions as autonomy and integrity, but also the much more specific and hardheaded language of *rights*. Then there are questions of *ownership,* a concept tied in any number of complex and controversial ways to the notion of rights, including (especially) the odd idea of ownership of one's own body and questions about the ownership of one's children, animals, and, of course, the earth itself (or whatever more or less modest piece of it). There are *cultural* and *aesthetic* values that may (and often do) conflict with these. (The practice of bioscience may be one example of such conflict.) There are complex questions of *justice,* which include some reference to rights, but much more complicated questions of comparative well-being and merit. There are sociopolitical questions about class interests and privileges, accusations of neocolonialism, and ethically loaded distinctions between the "developing" and the "squandering" nations of the world. Then, of course, there are religious concepts and concerns, ranging from Hindu holiness of cows to Greenpeace holiness of whales, from the extremities of Christian Science and EarthFirstness to the more mundane middle-class concern with cholesterol (by no means a merely medical concern).

All of these criss-cross and clash with alarming frequency, giving the false impression to more hysterical society-watchers that we have lost our "values," that "relativism" runs rampant, and "nihilism" waits in the wings. But the truth is that democracy and science thrive on such chaos. The greatest danger, much in evidence on all sides of the literature, is rather an undue fear of the treacherous "slippery-slope," a form of argument that always suggests, "if you let *them* get away with *this* [fertilizing human eggs in vitro, cutting funds for this or that political reason] then it will not stop until it gets to *that* [Frankenstein monsters, no science at all]." The truth is rather that open dialogue and disagreement—what in American constitutional law is gracefully referred to as "checks and balances"—is healthy and productive for both bioscience and society. What is unhealthy and disastrous for both is that mutual suspicion that knows no outlet but avoidance and condemnation, that will not talk and mutually explore possible agreements or compromises not only about risks but about values, too. The debate over the control of bioscience, whether by politicians and people who know nothing about it (How could they make informed and intelligent judgments?) or by the scientists themselves (How many professional groups have in fact shown the ability to "police" themselves?), is based on the wrong-headed assumptions that scientists and nonscientists cannot and will not talk to one another about issues of mutual interest and importance. It does no good if bioscientists see themselves as victims of the irrational whims of society, and society will not benefit if it maintains its "Frankenstein" fear of the bioscientist and his or her ability to convert life into monsters. We need to cultivate a society of bio-Einsteins, not in genius of course but in their ability to appreciate both the wonders and promises of science and its threats and ethical antagonisms. We need citizens who are not only better educated in science (it is by no means obvious that increased knowledge lessens one's fears of science) but properly torn and confused about an enormously complex and unsettled network of issues. Bioscience needs an engaged and not just an appreciative citizenry.

31

Animal Minds

From fables and fantasies, we have become accustomed to ants and elephants and creatures of all kinds who talk and tell us what is on their minds. They scheme, brood, rationalize, and resent their superiors. They become morally indignant, proud, and furious. They fall in love, often with members of other species. (Kermit the Frog and Miss Piggy are our latest *ménage à bête*.) Ants warn grasshoppers of the perilous winter; ducklings are embarrassed about their looks; young elephants complain to crows about the size of their ears. Even those of us who try to be hardheaded in such matters find ourselves, on occasion, telling buoyant and often tedious tales about the intelligence and cunning of our cat, which has the craftiness of a con artist, or the love of our dog, whose devotion puts ancient Greek heroes and Christian saints to shame.

The scientific community, by contrast, puts less stock in the animal mind. Three centuries ago, Descartes declared that animals are mere "machines," without minds or intelligence and devoid of reason and will. The American behaviorist John Watson revolutionized not only the science of animal behavior but human psychology, too, by denouncing "anthropomorphism" wherever it proposed benign but unjustifiable empathy in place of more rigorous methods. B. F. Skinner reduced mainstream American psychology to systematic correlations between stimulus and response,

---

This piece was written while I was a participant in the Dahlem Conference on "Animal Minds" in Berlin in 1981. It first appeared in *Psychology Today,* March 1982.

with no intervening mental way stations. College sophomores may have protested, "Where is consciousness?" but the proscription of nonexplanatory and unconfirmable concepts remained the first rule for the scientific study of animals.

There has always been a hint of absurdity in the unwillingness of humane behaviorists, who fondle, pamper, and converse with their pets at home (and sometimes in the lab), to ascribe the most basic mental properties to their experimental subjects. Fifty years of strict adherence to behaviorist methods have proved that behaviorism is just as limited, scientifically, as the anthropomorphism it replaced. H. S. Terrace, one of Skinner's most eminent students, points out that even in the classic behaviorist experiments with rats and pigeons, it is necessary to postulate something between stimulus and response: memory, for instance, or some form of "representation," or "inner" function. Even the philosophical behaviorist W. V. O. Quine, Skinner's longtime colleague and defender at Harvard, now accepts the necessity of understanding the stimulus as some form of active perception, not merely passive neurophysiological reception.

Contemporary neurological studies have demonstrated a clear continuity between animal and human brain structures and functions that makes it utterly unreasonable to deny to animals at least some of the psychological features that we ascribe to ourselves. Jerre Levy, a University of Chicago neurophysiologist, has concluded from this research that "we have no reason to suppose that there are any unique properties of the human organ of thought." Indeed, Levy observes, much medical research on animals *assumes* the continuity of consciousness from one species to another.

These days, scientists are once again becoming wary of *a priori* or dogmatic limitations on the range of their investigations and conclusions, whether imposed in the name of science or of sentimentality. And speaking of sentimentality, scientific agnosticism concerning the existence of consciousness in animals is intolerably at odds with the recently renewed concern about animal suffering and animal rights, which are supported by many scientists themselves. "The welfare of animals must depend on *understanding* animal suffering," writes biologist Peter Medawar, "and one does not come to this understanding intuitively." Accordingly, it is not surprising that the existence of animal consciousness has again become an open scientific question.

A year ago, just across the street from the Berlin Zoo, a large group of distinguished scientists came together under the auspices of the much-respected Dahlem Konferenzen. The Dahlem Conferences have traditionally been oriented toward the biological sciences, attracting from around the world leading researchers in such fields as molecular genetics and neurology, to formulate "state of the art" reports and to frame new vistas for investigation. More recently, the conferences have adopted a sometimes philosophical stance; a few years ago, for instance, they took a critical look at sociobiology.

In 1981, the purpose of the conference was not only to bring together the current research in one area but also, and more important, to establish the legitimacy of the field itself—in this case, the scientific study of animal minds. The exact title of the conference was "Animal Mind—Human Mind," and its purpose, prominently announced below the familiar *Nicht Rauchen* signs on the wall of every meeting room, was to reintroduce the once *verboten* concepts of "experience" and "consciousness" into the study of animal behavior. Indeed, Donald Griffin of Rockefeller University in New York City stated the question in a particularly scandalous way: "What is it like to *be* an animal of a particular species?" The old idea of empathy had been welcomed back into scientific psychology.

Among the fifty or so conferees were evolutionary biologists, neurologists, animal behaviorists, psychologists, and philosophers. The experimental psychologists and biologists who came were interested in such varied subjects as bees, birds, dolphins, and college undergraduates. The presence of many participants in the recent "ape language" controversies guaranteed at least one lively discussion. Terrace, teacher of the chimp Nim, was there. So was Levy, one of the pioneers in right brain/left brain experimentation. Hans Kummer, Carolyn Ristau, and E. S. Savage-Rumbaugh were the other resident experts on apes. C. G. Beer and Peter Marler, the confidants of gulls and songbirds respectively, were there. Theodore Bullock from San Diego, sometimes in his dolphin T-shirt, represented the Delphinidae. James Gould, the Princeton ethologist, dominated much of the argumentation with accounts of his bee experiments. Philosophers Daniel Dennett, author of *Brainstorms,* and Jerry Fodor, who teaches at the Massachusetts Institute of Technology, kept the larger issues in view.

With such a broad spectrum of interests, there was little likelihood of reaching a consensus. Nevertheless, one could at least be confident that the various issues would be argued. Of course, the old academic wounds were much in evidence. Despite the best efforts of the observer-inmates at the zoo, who provided much of the informal entertainment for the conference, the arguments often put the believers in animal minds on the defensive. Skeptics ignored the evidence of the animals' own antics in favor of the too-familiar philosophical arguments about the "unconfirmability" of all claims about animal minds.

Griffin, the conference director, set the tone for the unusual discussions to follow by noting in his opening remarks "how little we really know about animal minds"—in part, he said, because "scientists have so long ruled out *a priori* the possibility that mental experiences could occur in animals." And yet, perhaps surprisingly, rather clear agreement on the main point was apparent by the end of the conference: that it makes sense to talk about the minds of animals and to investigate, in a scientific context, precisely what kind of mind this or that animal has.

Consider for a painful moment the behavior of a puppy whose paw has just been slammed in the screen door. It is difficult to take seriously any theory or methodological principle that rules out explaining that behavior in terms of the *feeling* of pain. The question becomes less clear, however, as we climb down the phylogenetic ladder. Does a lobster feel pain as it is dropped into the pot of boiling water? Does the inadequately swatted wasp feel pain as it chases us out of the room? Does the bisected worm feel pain, and if so, in both halves? Or are such questions beyond the domain of science?

It would surely be folly to say so. But scientific discussions of the basic features—raw feelings and sensations—of what we might tentatively call consciousness have too long fallen into one of two equally unacceptable patterns. Either all mentalistic terms have been forbidden as nonexplanatory, or, as many people have too easily assumed, whatever squirms or reacts feels pain, just as we do. If the question is whether or not an animal is suffering in a particular situation (*the* dominant question in discussions of animal rights), the first way of thinking is totally unsatisfactory. It is tantamount to the demand that no concern for animal well-being can have scientific justification. The second way of thinking, though perhaps acceptable in Aesop and Walt Disney, is no better. How do we *know* whether an animal has a feeling, and how do we know *what* it is feeling?

The current outcry against the use of animals in unnecessary experiments and against the alleged brutality of the conditions under which animals are mass-produced for food presupposes the potential of animals for suffering. Peter Singer's epochal treatise on *Animal Liberation,* for example, indicted what he called the "concentration-camp methods" of cosmetics manufacturers, who squirt chemicals into the eyes of rabbits until they go blind, and of poultry farmers, who keep chicks cooped up in cages no larger than their bodies. But do we know what constitutes suffering for a chicken?

"Scientists are accused of using 'torture' and 'concentration-camp methods,' " writes Marian Dawkins of Oxford University, a participant in the Dahlem Conference. "Their critics must therefore know how to judge when an animal is suffering." Mere intuition is not always dependable; Dawkins argues that there are conditions under which chickens actually *prefer* small cages. "We have to *find out* about animal suffering, species by species," he concludes. Or as Julian Huxley wryly puts it. "The tapeworm's peptic Nirvana is not for me."

The existence of animal feeling on this basic level, though we can never "observe" the feeling itself, can be tested by experiment. Animals cannot report their pains and preferences, but, Dawkins insists, they can "vote with their feet." Pigs can be taught to use light switches, and by using them can choose their ambience. Hens can choose cages, bees trees, and paramecia their chemical homes. Such studies at least establish the existence of pain and of preferences.

One might well object that the demonstration that an animal feels something certainly does not warrant use of the term "consciousness." This point led to the most often repeated conclusion of the Dahlem Conference: that the traditional question of whether or not a creature is conscious has to be rejected in favor of a broader question about gradations or levels of consciousness. The all-or-nothing question only reinforces the old disputes, Bullock argued. Virtually every animal, he said, has a mind (though perhaps not consciousness) of some degree of complexity. It responds to its environment through sequences of more or less complex behavior, sometimes learning, sometimes calculating, sometimes even thinking. But whether we mean by mind simply the ability to experience sensory input or pain, or the ability to learn and adapt, it becomes clear that we are not talking about degrees of development within the realm of minds.

At the end of the conference, Bullock conducted a survey to find out how the conferees rated the capacity for suffering and the intelligence of forty-odd creatures, from human infants and chimps down to earthworms and paramecia. In one sense, the results reflected the obvious: Rating decreased as the list descended the biological scale. Yet the survey also reflected a new attitude among scientists: There was no precipitous drop-off in ratings from one species to another. Cats scored slightly higher than jackals, mice slightly higher than crows, starfish slightly higher than anemones. Thus it was clear that "conscious or not" was no longer the issue.

The language of mind, unlike the concrete terminology of neurology, is riddled with vague and value-laden terms. To say of a creature that it has a cerebellum is not to pay it a compliment, but to say of someone or something that it is "intelligent" certainly is. We use "having a mind" as a term of praise. (It brings to mind the professor who responded to an athletic-scholarship student's query about his I.Q.: "Why, I didn't know that you *had* an I.Q.") Both "consciousness" and "sensitivity" are desirable attributes as well as psychological descriptions. It is therefore extremely important to recognize the *ethical* edge of these terms, and to be exceedingly cautious in defining them.

There was a kind of absurdity to many of the definitions that conferees proposed. One discussion group used the characterization of consciousness suggested by David Premack, the ape-language researcher, who defined it as the ability to make a true-false judgment. Reaching such a judgment, however, is an extremely high-level reflective and linguistic operation that might well be argued to be within the province of only some human beings. Simple sensitivity was generally rejected as inadequate for consciousness, as was the ability to learn or even to carry out complex calculations.

What too often emerged as a criterion for consciousness was the ability to reflect and articulate the possession of some concept of selfhood and of what we would call "self-consciousness." The effect of setting such high standards for consciousness was to give the animal mind only token recognition, and to save all of the high-level attributes of mind, especially consciousness, for human beings and, perhaps, a couple of apes.

To take the levels-of-consciousness theme seriously, however, is to take seriously not only the presence of a minimal mind but a wide variety of mental abilities and processes. "What is it like to be a bat?" asked philosopher Thomas Nagel of New York University, who had taken part in the Dahlem sociobiology conference. Even at the most basic level of consciousness, it is the empathetic query "What is it like *to be* an *X*?" that marks off the realm of mind and consciousness.

There is consciousness in the sense of organized sensory perception, a rather passive process, and consciousness in the more developed sense of organizing sensory perception, which requires active mental functioning. There is simple pattern recognition, and then there are the far more sophisticated processes of comparison and generalization. There are many levels of learning that include memory and mental representations. Then there is the very high-level process of articulating those representations, a process that divides again into many levels: from the ability to use single words or signs, to the ability to produce distinctive speech, to the ability to employ words or signs with broad semantic meaning (as opposed to more context-bound utterances), to the ability to combine words in a syntax, to the ability to employ syntactic transformations, and finally to the ability to use a metalanguage (literally, a language about language) in which one can not only express one's representations but also talk about the relationships between representations and language, including the use of such metalinguistic terms as true and false.

Between full-scale reflection and simpler communicative consciousness lie other dimensions of mind, including the capacity for interpersonal intrigue. Robert Seyfarth, then at Rockefeller University, who observes monkeys in the wild, told fellow conferees about a monkey that intentionally deceived its peers by giving the "leopard warning cry" (ordinarily used by monkeys to give notice of the presence of an enemy) as a means of breaking up a fight. Koko the gorilla is often reported to deceive the human beings who talk to her. Even dogs and cats sometimes behave as if they had at least rudimentary awareness of the idea of deception, which involves knowing what others believe and how they can be fooled.

With such a range of linguistic levels, the heated debates over whether or not the likes of Nim and Koko actually speak a language strike us as somewhat medieval. Language, too, admits of gradations. We might well balk at the claim that a parrot knows Spanish. But there is certainly some sense in which a dolphin or a gorilla speaks a language while dogs and cats do not, and a further sense in which dogs and cats can at least understand language while fish and clams do not.

Neither is self-consciousness a single concept, with an all-or-none manifestation only in species that have some concept of self. Some animals display interesting behavior in front of a mirror, while others do not. (Chimps do, but dogs don't.) Noticing one's reflection suggests a sense of self, but so, too, does the recognition of one's own smell, or possessing a sense of one's territory.

Biologist Lewis Thomas has argued that even sponges and bacteria might have such a limited sense of self-identity, an idea that leads him to the somewhat suspect thesis that individual self-identity is one of the more pervasive aspects of nature. We do not need to confuse the chemical self-consciousness of single-celled animals with the identity crises of American adolescents, however, to recognize that there is more than one kind of self-consciousness and a ladder of levels upon which the many creatures with minds distribute themselves. Socrates insisted that "the unexamined life is not worth living," but this is an unfair criterion of self-consciousness to apply to a squirrel.

The conferees always came back to the unavoidable question: Granted that an animal is behaving in such and such a manner, how can we know that it feels anything? A basic distinction emerged between what some members of the conference summarized quasi-poetically as "sapience and sentience," or intelligence and feeling. Some participants suggested that the former was clearly within the domain of science, while the latter was not. Virtually everyone agreed that sapience and sentience are not the same, and that they present researchers with different issues. Even remarkable intelligence is not enough to establish the existence of consciousness in the "sentient" sense, a few argued. Indeed, it was even argued that the one renders the other unnecessary.

The elaborate forages, flights, and filial dances of bees provide one of the awesome examples of intelligence and communication in lower species. Gould explained the work done some years ago by Karl von Frisch to demonstrate that bees make very complex calculations of the shortest distance between hive and flower, no matter what obstacles lie between and no matter how circuitous the route they must take. Gould also described his own recent findings. When he moved flowers whose location bees had previously learned to communicate to their sisters, bees returning to their hive at first gave what had become a false description of the flowers' location. But they quickly learned to compensate for their error.

The intelligence of these bees is beyond dispute, but what of consciousness? It is hard, if not impossible, to empathize with a bee, to believe in the consciousness of a species so far away in "the great chain of cuddliness," as one conferee called it. In any case, the intelligence of bees does not provide an argument for bee consciousness, as Gould himself acknowledged.

One might argue that bee perceptions require at least sensations of a reasonable level of sophistication, but the reply is that any theory of information-processing is sufficient to explain their behavior without postulating the existence of consciousness. One might also argue that the learning capacity of bees, although limited, points to a form of intelligence that cannot be attributed to mere mechanism. In this case, the reply is that even computers can be built to adapt themselves to changes. Indeed, that is what a bee is: a remarkably concise and precise organic computer. The slightest deviation from the bee's hard-wired routines results in utter chaos. A drop of oleic acid placed on a healthy, living bee triggers dead-bee removal activity on the part of its sisters, who are oblivious to its frantic struggle.

The assumption in this argument, which unfortunately permeated much of the conference discussion, was that mechanism and consciousness are in opposition; that if behavior can be explained mechanistically (for example, in terms of information-processing and familiar computer operations), the behaving organism is therefore not conscious. Part of the argument was evolutionary: It was said that an organism programmed to its environment does not *need* consciousness, which is essentially a device that allows increased adaptability. The larger part of the argument was an argument that goes back to Descartes: If it is mechanism, it cannot be conscious. (The other half of the Cartesian argument, "If it is conscious, it can't be a mechanism," was notably omitted.)

But even the first half of the Cartesian argument fails. There is no longer much reason to think that we—as paragons of consciousness—might not also be explainable, some day soon, in terms of computer-like mechanisms. Indeed, the argument can even be turned around. Dennett, co-editor of *The Mind's I,* suggested that one might properly attribute mind (though not consciousness) to computers and thermostats, which display "intelligence" in the mechanistic sense.

Intelligence can be measured, and there can be no intelligible doubts about the operational correctness of such questions as "Can an animal learn to do X in Y situation?" If it can, it is to some degree intelligent.

But there is a difference between intelligence and sentience, and establishing one seems to have only minimally to do with establishing the other. Whatever the intelligence of a bee or an octopus, the issue of what it experiences is an open question. Indeed, at what point would we be willing to ascribe even the most rudimentary feelings or experiences to a computer, no matter how superior its intelligence?

There is intelligence, and then there is sentience. The second without the first seems unlikely; the first without the second, whether in a computer or in a bee, is not worthy of the name "consciousness," or, for that matter, the less provocative (perhaps just shorter) word "mind." Information-processing plus sensitivity, whatever the sophistication of the mechanisms involved, are the basic ingredients of both animal and human minds.

However attractive, the distinction between intelligence and feeling only temporarily clarifies some issues, and then it further muddles them. The distinction reintroduces, though covertly, the old separation of those features of animal behavior that admit of observation and experimentation, and those that do not. Given that separation, feeling seems to become the residuum of science—that which is left over, unexplained, after all the more testable results are in. But this is not really the case. Feelings, while not directly observable, are nonetheless demonstrable, usually beyond any reasonable doubt. And feelings, if they are of any complexity, are not easily distinguishable from what we are calling intelligence. Whether or not feelings are learned, they are almost always influenced by learning.

A too-sharp contrast of intelligence and feeling leads too easily to the old behaviorist theory that only testable and measurable behavior counts and that those mysterious "inner" feelings have no standing as far as science is concerned. Rejecting that too-sharp contrast in turn underscores the importance of those new developments in psychology that currently parade under the banner of cognitive science. Unlike behaviorism, cognitive science accepts the need to refer to inner aspects of animal minds to explain all but the simplest reflex behavior.

But the "inner aspect" is no longer considered to be anything so ineffable as a "feeling"; it is a demonstrable "representation," which may be said to be either a function of the nervous system or a function of the mind, depending on one's viewpoint. In either interpretation, it is a function, the series of links between the contingencies of the animal's environment and the animal's behavior. Accordingly, the view thus defended is often called "functionalism," and the various functions are at least sometimes, notably in ourselves, products of conscious awareness as well as operative steps in a logical and perhaps programmable sequence of inferences and reactions.

What is a representation? Jerry Fodor, the MIT philosopher, argued at the conference that virtually all psychological explanation requires talk of representations, and that only sometimes can these be views as internal images, such as our own imaginings. We postulate a representation, a kind of flight plan, in Gould's bees. We postulate a representation, another kind of map, in Terrace's pigeons and in Koko the gorilla, whose representations include (at least) the dictionary for hundreds of signs and their references. To ask whether these representations are essentially conscious is to miss the point—in fact, two points. First, consciousness is a multileveled conception. Second, the consciousness of the representations, in the sense of self-awareness, is a quite different question from the functioning of the representations; they may function in the absence of self-awareness, and often do. Postulating a certain representation does not require that an animal actually feel much of anything, but neither does it rule out feeling.

Discovering or postulating the nature of representations and how they are processed is a matter susceptible to experimental investigation. The representations of bees can be tested by detailed observation and by manipulation of the situations in which bees respond in predictable ways; the adaptability of bee intelligence can be tested by changing circumstances until the "bee computer" breaks down.

In some animals, information-processing can be extremely sophisticated while adaptability is limited. Young birds, according to Peter Marler, need to hear only a brief fragment of their characteristic song to learn it. Without that short sample, however, the bird does not learn the song at all, so the song is not purely instinctive. Within that species's song, however, there is also individual variation, such that every bird's song is clearly distinguishable from that of other birds of the same species. The representation is relatively simple, in this case, but the processing and adaptability are more sophisticated.

In most mammals, representations and their processing and adaptability are much more complex than in birds, most dramatically so when symbols and language are involved. It is a matter of fascinating debate where such representations begin: with the varied communications of monkeys; with the "language" of birds and bees; or with the more basic communication that, it might be argued, takes place even in the microbiological world, even within a single cell. Here again, the only answer worth investigation rather than argument would seem to be that there is a hierarchy of symbols and languages, some more sophisticated than others. We can investigate the language of gulls calling out to each other over the cliffs of Dover, and the sign-language conversations between Francine Patterson and Koko, without falling into the often nasty debates over what counts as a language and what does not.

It is not the existence of consciousness but the nature of conscious experience that remains the open question. Granted that some insects have remarkable ability to communicate, and granted that they must sense something if they are to process any information at all, we can still ask: Do they feel confusion when lost, or patriotic when the hive is attacked? Gulls display remarkable ability to discriminate one another's calls, according to C. G. Beer of Rutgers University. But does it make sense to suppose that they are glad to see each other? When my dog displays his "hangdog" look as I pack my suitcase for a trip, am I justified in saying that he is depressed? To reject that question *a priori* is no longer justifiable—which does not mean (as Watson and Skinner feared) that we are thereby bound to believe everything reported by Aesop and Disney. To open the question is not to give up one's experimental criteria or what we are used to calling (when it is convenient) our common sense.

Several years ago, Cambridge philosopher G. E. M. Anscombe was asked about the implications for our concept of human uniqueness if apes were taught to talk. "They'll up the ante," she replied. Indeed, Justin Leiber, the philosopher who organized the "Apes and Language" conference in Houston last year, referred to the dispute over primate intelligence as a religious debate, concerned as much with the self-image of the human species as with the evidence about primates.

32

Ethical Styles

The recently renewed interest in "applied ethics" has not proved to be wholly flattering to ethics. In the conflict-resolution-minded context of practical problems, twenty-five-century-old disputes do not appear promising, and even given some semblance of a generally agreed upon if banal principle, practical application is often difficult, or at least debatable. Too often, courses in business or medical ethics begin in a vacuum—ethical theories first, cases to follow. But even when such courses are set up in boardrooms and hospitals on a "real life" case basis, there is that awkward sense of the ethicist as outsider, aloofly superimposing abstract and contentious theories on painfully practical problems which call for an immediate decision. Not surprisingly, many of the people to whom our ethical theories are being applied turn out, in the name of efficiency, to be dogmatists or existentialists, in the imminently practical words of a classic gangster movie, "ya takes yus choice and ya takes da consequences."

But where our tradition perhaps fails us most in the realm of practice may be our own sense of dogmatism—our age-old conviction that there must be a "right" (if not "true") way of thinking about ethics, rather than a variety of ways, each of them "ethical." In other words, there are different *ethical styles*.

This essay began as an approach to teaching ethics to business executives and other professionals but developed into something of a general approach to ethics in a book, *It's Good Business* (Atheneum, 1985). This particular version has not been published before.

"Ethical styles" is a phrase and an idea that would have been utterly unacceptable until a few years ago—except, perhaps, to Nietzsche and Oscar Wilde. It smacks of relativism of an odious sort. It suggests not only subjectivism (which at least can be "deep" and supported by extensive reasons and reasoning) but superficiality as well, ethics and ethical behavior as fashion, a matter of personality or worse, a costume of thoughts and actions that may be put aside as easily as it can be put on. Of course, different ethical styles would have very different advantages and disadvantages, and it may well be that an ethical style is no more easily changed than other lifelong traits of character such as thoughtfulness, recklessness or spontaneous generosity. Nevertheless, the idea that the professional philosophers who are "rule utilitarians" or "Kantian deontologists" are just expressing personal differences, rather than arguing—once and for all—about what is really "right" grates against our philosophical sensibilities. Is the categorical imperative really just a Kantian hangup? Does utilitarianism betray a suppressed wish to be an accountant?

But the fact is that promoters of applied ethics have been forced into a recognition of ethical styles, albeit very much against their own philosophical judgment. This is evident, for example, at the beginning of the large majority of applied ethics textbooks, which begin by rehearsing once again—but probably for the first time for the future executives, doctors, engineers, or lawyers in the classroom—the time-honored disputes among and between utilitarians, deontologists and, perhaps, libertarians. With considerable embarrassment, the ethicist seeking to apply these theories will suggest that, "now an act utilitarian would say that. . . ." The "applied" context is not the place to dispute the ultimate superiority of one or another ethical school, to show that deontological arguments do indeed involve utilitarian considerations, or that utilitarianism, despite all clever qualifications, cannot adequately deal with the question of justice, with desert island examples, or with the gleeful sadist. The case itself demands discussion—be it the responsibility of pharmaceutical companies to stop drug abuse in the streets, euthanasia for the dying, bridge bid-rigging, or a lawyer-client confidentiality. The audience wants a resolution, and the perennial philosophical dispute can, quite frankly, be damned. And so they get, "well, a libertarian would no doubt see it this way. . . ."

In the context of that long classical tradition in ethics, which we conveniently but somewhat arbitrarily trace back to Socrates, such answers are indeed inadequate and embarrassing. In the applied context, on the other hand, they are in some equally embarrassing sense necessary. Disputes between utilitarians and deontologists are not restricted to professional philosophy. They are a very real part of the arguments that go on daily in offices and boardrooms across the country. Indeed, philosophers thrown into practical contexts are often surprised—with mixed feelings—to see just how well the "nonphilosophers" have mustered up not only evidence but arguments for their positions. It sometimes appears that all that there is for the philosopher to do is to give these positions their proper names— an exercise of dubious practical importance but in any case considerably less than the traditional view of philosophy as a conceptual peacemaker would prescribe.

And yet, the recognition of such large ethical differences can be of enormous practical importance—even in the absence of a knock-down argument for one ethical position and against all of the others. Philosophers may be frustrated by the lack of resolution to the classical disputes, but they are at least well-informed about what is in dispute, and practiced in the art of clarifying what is at stake in this position or that one. The fact is that a great many practical disputes, in which the relevant evidence has been made available and the prominent arguments have been formulated and exhausted, turn out to be identical to the classic philosophical disputes (if a bit more crude and less filled with jargon). But the philosopher who is waiting for the final solution in ethics is not going to be in an enviable position to resolve practical disputes involving the same unresolved philosophical questions. In practice if not in ethical theory, there are only ethical styles and the perseverence of mutual discussion, not final solutions.

In practical disputes, it is not clear to the participants how differences in ethical style are to be treated, in part because there is usually not the recognition that the dispute is, in part, a clash of ethical styles. Once accounted for, however, differences get treated as options or as possibilities to be resolved through negotiation. What is much worse, however, is when the discussion takes on the same direction as most philosophical debates and stops only with the unacceptable conclusion that "it's a complicated issue." However philosophically gratifying, that conclusion is the worst one possible, if our experience in business ethics is a fair indication. It doesn't teach conflict resolution but rather the importance of ignoring philosophy.

The classic and most familiar clash of ethical styles is the seemingly irresolvable conflict between the deontologist and the utilitarian. It is worth repeating, but in style-minded terms, what the nature of that conflict tends to be in practice. A person who puts rules and duty first (the "deontologist") believes in the letter of the law, and in the office or in the boardroom he or she will very likely cite the rules of the institution or principles from a professional handbook. It may not matter that the rule in question is outdated or impractical. It may not matter that it became a matter of law or policy under another administration now out of office. It may not matter that the rule will no doubt be changed some day. The deontologist or rule-bound person believes that one should obey rules, laws, regulations, and policies, whatever their origins and whatever the consequences. Any other way of thinking, from this standpoint, is amoral.

The utilitarian, on the other hand, is self-consciously practical. Rules serve a purpose, a function, and they are to be obeyed just because— but only because—they serve that purpose or function. A rule that proves to be impractical no longer deserves our respect or obedience. A rule that was formulated under very different circumstances or was legislated by a different administration should be carefully scrutinized and not given too much weight. The utilitarian makes decisions on the sole ground that a certain course of action has the best consequences for everyone involved. If that fits the rules (as it usually does), then so much the better. If it does not, then so much the worse for the rules, and so much too for the deontologist, who because of sheer obstinacy or perhaps for some un-fathomable personal reason refuses to see the point.

We know how this little scenario tends to go, from departmental meetings if not from arguments in ethics: the rule-bound person considers the utilitarian an opportunist, an amoral deviant, a person who does not re-spect authority and the rules. The utilitarian considers the rule-bound person to be utterly unreasonable and impractical if not neurotic and "impossible." When general utility conflicts with an established rule, the utilitarian and the rule-bound person are sure to misunderstand one another. There can be no compromise because each of them considers his or her own position to be beyond negotiation and neither can understand the other, except, perhaps, in the terms of moral pathology.

Some practical disputes get more fine-grained; arguments between rule-bound people and between varieties of utilitarians are not difficult to find. Of course, not every attitude in ethics constitutes an ethical style. There are, however, many ways of being ethical. We have mentioned the two most common of them, rule-bound and utilitarian. Some others are varia-tions on these; some are insightful while others degenerate. More often than some philosophers suppose, "metaethical" theories appear as ethical styles, typically defining normative content as well. But what is most important is that all of these deserve to be called "ethical" and perhaps "moral" approaches to practical problems, though they differ considerably and have different advantages and disadvantages in terms of simplicity, clarity, applicability, and scope. Here I have outlined seven distinct ethical styles of thinking and acting, but without any claim to completeness, in order to give some sense of the sorts of attitudes and approaches that appear to be most prevalent in practical situations (no doubt one could make up many more on an *a priori* basis):

(a) *Rule-bound:* thinking and acting on the basis of rules and principles, with only secondary regard to circumstances or exceptions.

(b) *Utilitarian:* weighing probable consequences, both to the company or the profession and to the public well-being. Principles are important only as "rules of thumb." "The greatest good for the greatest number of people" is the ultimate test for any action or decision.

(c) *Loyalist:* evaluating all decisions first in terms of benefit to the profession, the institution, the company and its reputation. (In business, "the company man.")

(d) *Prudent:* long-term self-interest through identification with the profession, and the institution, the company, or the larger social good, but always aware of the only contingent connection between self-interest and the larger interests one serves.

(e) *Virtuous:* every action is measured in terms of its reflection on one's character (or the profession, institution, or company reputation) without immediate regard to consequences and often without paying much attention to general principles.

(f) *Intuitive:* making decisions on the basis of "conscience" and without deliberation, argument, or reasons. Intuitive thinkers tend to be extremely impatient with more deliberative deontological and utilitarian types. It is a style that flourishes at the top of the decision-making hierarchy, if only because of an obvious history of natural selection. (Errors in intuition, unlike errors in deliberation and calculation, cannot be readily explained or rationalized.)

(g) *Empathetic:* following one's feelings of sympathy and compassion. "Putting oneself in the other's place" is the *modus operandi* of the empathetic style, whether the "other" be a competitor ("How would we like if he . . . ,") or a client ("I can easily imagine how it would feel to be . . .").

Every style has its excesses, however, and an understanding of ethical styles includes some appreciation of their degenerate forms as well:

(a) *Rule-bound* (degenerate form, *compulsive*): being so caught up in principles that even the point of the principles is lost from view.

(b) *Utilitarian* (degenerate form, *cost/benefit compulsive*): an insistence on putting a value on everything, even that which is "invaluable." Also the *perplexed liberal:* finds so many possible consequences and complications that action becomes impossible and inaction ("pending investigation") the only moral course. The source of most committees.

(c) *Loyalist* (degenerate form, *hominoid*): in office circumstances, the " 'Yes'-Man," a technician who has lost all sense of social context and even of his or her own well-being.

(d) *Prudent* (degenerate form, *gamesman*): thinks of a profession solely in terms of self-advancement and treats all rules and laws—including moral principles—as mere boundaries of action. "Free enterprise" rhetoric in business often adopts this stance. Ethical problems for the gamesman are mainly obstacles, opportunities, challenges. (Not uncommon in legal ethics, frowned upon in medicine.)

(e) *Virtuous* (degenerate form, *heroic*): every action is self-consciously a reflection of extraordinary virtues and abilities in which any course of action that is routine or ordinary is not to be seriously considered. Also, *obstinate, stubborn,* and *impossible.*

(f) *Intuitive* (degenerate form, *mystical*): making decisions on the basis of invariably cosmic intuitions, often with cloudy references to "the whole earth" or "cosmic harmony," without further justification and with as little reference to practical realities as possible. Eccentricity is taken to be a virtue (prosaic intuitions are a sign of sheer heteronomy).

(g) *Empathetic* (degenerate form, *sentimental* or *maudlin*): having so much sympathy that it becomes impossible to look after one's own or the profession's (institution's, company's) self-interest. A "bleeding heart" with a very short career in business or law, and a nervous breakdown in medicine. (In the press, often used as a conflict of hard-hearted professionals against ethics and sensitivity.)

Perfectly proper ethical styles can also go wrong. One way is to be inappropriate. Whatever one's preferred style of thinking, there are contexts in which some styles are clearly appropriate, others clearly inappropriate. For example, when speaking to a religious group, a prudential or a utilitarian style will be disastrous. Lecturing at a sales meeting or to a group of young surgeons, on the other hand, a deontological style will sound abstract, pompous, and beside the point. Philosophers sometimes talk as if moral considerations (of the rule-bound variety) are *always* appropriate, in any practical context. The fact is rather that ethical styles—and style of any kind—are context sensitive. The idea that some peculiarly tedious styles are appropriate everywhere has caused many a philosopher to be left off the guest list. (Kant's popularity as a dinner guest in Königsberg makes one wonder.) Whether or not there is a "true" ethical theory, there is always a place or not a place—for certain ethical styles.

The discussion of ethical styles is not intended as a part of—much less to replace—traditional ethical arguments and debates. But for the philosopher who tries to "apply" ethics and for whom that means something more than hanging our laundry in the seminars of professions other than our own, it is a concept of considerable value. To talk about ethical styles is to say, first of all, that many of the positions and arguments that have defined the history of ethics also define practical positions and arguments used by people who have never taken or thought of taking a philosophy course, and, second of all, it is to emphasize the importance of respect for ethical differences, which we may take for granted but are not easily recognized by most people in the midst of an argument. It is in times of conflict or crisis that differences in ethical styles become prominent, and it is in those times that such differences must be understood and negotiated instead of being allowed to make a bad situation that much more explosive.

33

Environmentalism as a Humanism

Does environmentalism have to be explained? Is the visible and olfactorily obvious deterioration of the soil, air, and water around us and the now widespread anxiety (bordering on panic in some quarters) for the quality of these necessities of life a problem whose social significance is really worth subjecting to the acrimony of ideological debate, at just the time when we now have the numbers to cooperate and mobilize for some serious reform? With the emergence of a new consensus and a hitherto unknown solidarity on these vital matters, do we really want to "understand" this social phenomenon in the divisive language of moral self-righteousness, class ideologies, and *ressentiment*? This is what several recent writers, among them Mark Sagoff, it seems, want us to do.

One of the themes—perhaps the main theme—of my own work in business ethics is the self-defeating nature of those overly antagonistic dichotomies between "self-interest" and "altruism," between business values and ethical values, between "the bottom line" and social responsibility, between money and morals. On the subject of corporate policy and environmental ethics, I want to insist that we are talking about one inter-

This paper was delivered as an invited reply to Mark Sagoff at the Center for Business Ethics Environment Conference at Bentley College in Waltham, Massachusetts, in November of 1989 and published in their proceedings. From the Eighth National Conference on Business Ethics, *Business, Ethics, and the Environment: The Public Policy Debate,* edited by W. M. Hoffman, R. Frederick, and E. S. Petry (Quorum Books, 1990), pp. 125–34. Reprinted with the permission of the editor.

nally complex system of interlocking values and not two antagonistic forces. The polemical distinctions, between the love of nature and the exploitation of nature ("reverence" and "utilitarianism") for instance, distort and disguise the complex issues of environmentalism and make mutual understanding and cooperation impossible. For example, those "deep" ecologists who wage war against one another and play "more Mao than thou" in their competition to reject technology and all conceivable technological solutions to environmental problems do the environmental movement no favors but only isolate environmentalism from the very possibility of cooperative reforms (e.g., *The Ecologist,* 1988). It is in response to such divisive polemicizing that the reactionary accusations of environmentalists as "elitists" gain plausibility (e.g., Tucker, *Progress and Privilege*). To attack "exploitation" may also be to reinforce it and to provoke the belligerence rather than invite the cooperation of those who are identified as the exploiters. But competition for the high moral ground and James Watt–type *ad hominem* arguments are not the way to environmental reform. Cooperation and consensus, embracing the interests of the largest corporations as well as the concerns of the ordinary citizen, is the only way to go.

For those of you who know me in my academic life, some of this rage for cooperation and synthesis might be laid at the doorstep of my infatuation with Hegel and Hegelianism, following the great nineteenth-century philosopher in his own attempts to integrate a divided world at war and recapture our already lost rapport with nature. (It was Hegel, we might remind ourselves, who first advanced the optimistic conception of "the end of history" to summarize this grand sense of synthesis.) But in my more practical, para-corporate life, this emphasis on cooperation and consensus serves a vital purpose, to reject the rather belligerent anti-business prejudices of many of my colleagues (as well as the anti-academic attitudes of the executives I work with) in order to recognize the absolutely essential role of the multinational corporations along with more idealistic reformers in any conceivable solution to the urgent environmental problems that confront us and to acknowledge the importance of shared concerns and solutions. This is not to deny that some giant corporations are part of the problem, but it will do no good to promote self-righteously the myth of endemic corporate irresponsibility—even if there are significant instances of it—and turn solvable practical problems into irresolvable differences in "ideology." I thus find myself very much at odds with Sagoff's paper even while I agree with and heartily endorse and appreciate many of his insights and, especially, his central observation that environmentalism is no longer an issue for isolated eccentrics but one of the most powerful populist issues of our times.

Populism and Elitism:
"The Moral Superiority of the Uninvolved"

One of Sagoff's favorite targets is the magazine *Car and Driver*. When I was younger, I confess that I was an avid reader of *Car and Driver*. The feel of a fast car on the open road seemed to me then, as it still seems to me now, one of the great joys of living in a technological, open society. And what I couldn't afford to drive, I read about in *Car and Driver*. I do not remember reading the editorials—like most readers I concentrated on the pictures and the "specs"—but I do remember rather distinctly that, even then, I was not hysterically opposed to government regulation of the roads, give or take ten or twenty miles per hour or so, and though radar detectors were not yet available I am sure that I would have had one if they were. I also seem to remember joining the ACLU and campaigning against the death penalty. I even enjoyed watching birds, though the fetish for imported water was not yet with us. Reading Sagoff's essay, however, one would certainly think that I and every reader of *Car and Driver* was a liberal-bashing, libertarian "redneck." The love of technology gets played off against the love of nature; philistine enthusiasms against effete, innocent pleasures. Is there any reason to give credence to such contrasts?

I do not dispute Sagoff's report of those editorials that I never read, but I do question the use of intentionally loud-mouth monthly columnists to gauge the mood of the country. Indeed, the use of such research to make the "populist" point is, I think, to betray an indefensible distance from the very people Sagoff pretends to understand. It is as if, in accordance with one of our rather longstanding philosophical traditions, he were looking at society (especially "the masses" or *hoi polloi*) down the wrong end of a rather long telescope, from a great impersonal distance. There is a very real problem of *perspective* in his analysis, the distance—and with it the disdain—from which he seems to view the people he talks about, drivers, farmers, utilitarians, businessmen (of course), the wrong kinds of environmentalists, lower middle-class citizens who become environmentally concerned only out of immediate self-interest, the liberal intelligentsia, and, I'm afraid, the undifferentiated populace of populism in general. Against our new and certainly welcome shared enthusiasm for the protection of the environment, Sagoff casts suspicion on our motives as so much self-interest, so much mere utility and risk-aversion, so much hype and political band-wagoneering. In contrast, he insists on taking the "high road" of ethics and morals, explicitly distinguishing this elevated route from mere prudentialism, exploitative utilitarianism, and risk/cost/benefit analysis.

These distinctions reflect what Chemical Bank President Tom Johnson has nicely described as "the moral superiority of the uninvolved." It is all too comfortable to chastise the mean, practical motives of those who have to live with the responsibility and the consequences from a position of considerable abstraction and advantage. But the truth is that the fine distinctions so often belabored by philosophers find virtually no application in day-to-day life, and the distinctions between prudence and morality, self-interest and altruism all but collapse when we look at even the most ordinary case of a working person doing his or her job, whether as a factory worker, a secretary, or a CEO. It is worth reminding ourselves that we find few such distinctions in the classic writings of Plato and Aristotle, who were concerned with the harmonious behavior of citizens rather than the artificial divisions between schools of philosophy. These distinctions may be of some philosophical importance but I believe that they lead to nothing less than disaster in the on-going dialogue between public interest groups, industry, and government that constitutes the promising context of today's environmentalism.

Environmentalism and Exploitation: On Leaving "Nature" Alone

In his defense of a particularly moral, reverential environmentalism, Sagoff attacks or at least disparages all merely utilitarian and instrumental attitudes toward nature. Nature is not just there for our use and exploitation, he reminds us. And to be sure, those of us who still enjoy a daily walk in the woods would agree, but to what is this notion of "exploitation" opposed? The use of our little patch of nature as a garbage dump? Isn't our enjoyment of nature "for its own sake" also an aspect of our "use" of it, and from a long evolutionary perspective it is also a kind of exploitation. Our very footsteps alter the natural ecology, not to mention our efforts to protect and reserve the woods "as is." Aesthetic enjoyment is a kind of "use," and the setting aside of an acre or a half continent for our enjoyment is (by the classical definition of utility) just as utilitarian as our use of it as an oil field. Now, I am not arguing the perverse thesis that all "use" is exploitation, of course, but I do want to argue that the overly self-righteous distinction between utility and reverence is an insidious one that gives a false sense of moral superiority to the leisurely observer and wrongly condemns or belittles all of those whose job it is to provide the material preconditions that make that leisure possible (e.g., the electricity to run Sagoff's PC and his FAX machines).

But if indeed one insists on taking the "larger view," ignoring the necessities and preconditions of human civilization "as we know it," could it not be argued that even our benign insistence on saving a species from extinction is itself a willful and anthropocentric manipulation of nature? After all, millions have become extinct with no help from us. What we consider natural is just what we in our short tenancy have become used to and, perhaps, remember with a certain fondness. (The most recent but not the last self-absorbed and pathos-ridden book in this modern genre is Bill McGibben's "Death of Bambi" attack on everything human coupled with an outrageously sentimentalized Disney version of nature [*The End of Nature*, 1989]. If we insist on enlarging the scope of the argument to cosmic proportions, we must also be careful not to confuse our limited view of "life on planet earth" with mere nostalgia.

Greg Easterbrook has recently written, perversely but wisely, I think, that we do not need to take care of nature, thank you; nature is and always will be capable of taking care of Herself. It is an old Sartrian point: nature cannot be destroyed; what falls under the heading of "destruction" is only what we (or some other conscious beings, including God or gods) have come to care about. What concerns us, in other words, is the conservation of a peculiarly human habitat, a world in which we can live comfortably and in harmony with those aspects of nature we choose to privilege. And, even there, the division between nature and human nature is particularly self-serving. Consider Frederick Turner, echoing David Hume two centuries before:

The theory of evolution implies that human history is also a part of nature, and that nature itself has always been a mess: everything interfering with everything else, everything changing, everything being used up, everything irreversible, waste everywhere—the good old second law of thermodynamics. Life is a mess—sucking, secreting, competing, breeding, dying—and human beings—desirous, aspiring, quarrelsome, proud, acquisitive, and embarrassingly self-conscious—are what nature produced when it had the chance to do so. (*Harper's Magazine*, November 1989)

Whatever else it may be, environmentalism should not be an antihumanism, a rejection of the human perspective rather than an appeal to what is best and most human in us: our aesthetic sensitivities, our ability to step back from our projects and our prejudices and plan, our capacity to empathize and cooperate.

Rather than take such a large, suprahuman view of nature or an overly down-to-earth *Car and Driver* view of our complex interaction with "nature," Sagoff insists on a quasi-religious (almost millenarian) vision of reverence for and love of nature (which he rather oddly couples with "respect for community and reverence for the past"—a very different set of concerns indeed, I would think, and not at all supportive of the kind of environmentalism he applauds). Such phrases are edifying, and no doubt even as we pronounce them you see before your inner eyes one of those glorious images of the unspoiled Alaskan wilderness, though probably not, I would guess, the equally natural swarming of life in an algae pond. But what commerce (I use this word not just ironically) can there be between the merely utilitarian view, so vulgarly stated, and the reverent vision of nature for its own sake? Do either of them provide us with a plausible view of our life in the midst of (and as an integral part of) nature? Is the answer to the environmental crisis a "deep" ecology in which we literally (and no doubt impossibly) reject our entire way of life, or is it a much more "superficial" sense of solidarity in which we mutually negotiate our differences and mutual disadvantages? (It is often suggested, e.g., by Thomas Berry in his most recent sermon on the subject [*Dream of the Earth,* 1988], that we should live more like the original Native Americans, conveniently forgetting about the rather dramatic difference in populations, the enormous suffering endured by those pretechnological peoples, and the often violent, even genocidal confrontations between them. But I think that this neo-Rousseauian romanticism of our own "noble savages" is a study that deserves some attention as a symptom of a certain self-hatred.)

Such considerations do not constitute an argument against environmentalism but only an attack on a false deification of nature in the name of what is (but is rarely recognized as) a particularly virulent form of antihumanism. Current calls for the self-sacrifice of our species for the benefit of nature is only the most extreme version of this virulence. I have heard, hardly believing my ears, that the extinction of the human species (perhaps by way of AIDS) would be quite a good thing. It would not only give the waters, the air, and the ozone a chance to replenish themselves; it would allow the continued existence of thousands of species that might otherwise become extinct in the continued presence of Big Human Brother.* I hope

---

*I use "Big Brother" not just in deference to Orwell but to the volumes of literature now appearing that make it quite clear, in case anyone doubted it, that it is we males and our macho attitudes—no doubt exemplified by our passion for *Car and Driver*—who are solely responsible for the destruction of nature, the female of the species being much more "natural" in the requisite sense (e.g., Susan

such suggestions inspire as much horror in you as they do in me, but without for a moment suggesting that environmentalism as such requires any such species-sacrifice or radical reversion to some fantasized more "natural" life-style. Some serious changes are no doubt in order, but as is so often the case, the most radical suggestions are those that guarantee that necessary changes will be put off indefinitely as cooperation and consensus are eclipsed by self-righteousness and nonsense.

Utilitarianism, Humanism, Morality, and Risk

In the context of environmentalism—as in many other contexts both social and religious—the culturally contrived antagonism between nature and culture promotes prejudice and warfare and provokes insults and mutually defensive, typically vicious, and unproductive arguments. But so, too, in philosophy—as in social and religious contexts—the academically inspired opposition of morality and mere utility produces far more conflict and confusion than understanding. Sagoff's juxtaposition of moral reverence and utilitarianism does damage to his own environmental aims as well as to moral philosophy. In a symposium filled not with ideologues but a mixed audience of sincerely concerned business people and academic ethicists, does such a split between utilitarianism and morality make any sense? To be sure, "utilitarian" justifications of pollution and other antisocial actions are sometimes incredibly shortsighted and self-serving, but do we have to promote an overly abstract and often impractical notion of morality to compensate for the occasional deficiencies and shortsightedness of a vulgar pragmatism and a fraudulent appeal to utility? Indeed, how emaciated a conception of utilitarianism one would have to have in order to eliminate from consideration both the long-term view and all spiritual joys of reverence and aesthetics. John Stuart Mill would turn over in his grave. Utilitarianism, after all, was not originally promoted just as a defense of cost/benefit analysis. It was, and still is, a conception of *moral* philosophy. Utilitarianism is, and continues to be, first and foremost a version of *humanism* (by which I do not mean to question its legitimate employment, from Jeremy Bentham to Peter Singer, in the defense of animals). Humanism, in contrast to a good many religious and political ideologies (but equally in harmony with others), is the insistence that people's interests and well-being, their pleasures,

Griffin, *Woman and Nature* [Harper and Row, 1978]; Gerda Lerner, *The Creation of Patriarchy* [Oxford University Press, 1985]; Carolyn Merchant, *The Death of Nature* [Harper and Row, 1980]).

their pains, their happiness, and not some more abstract criteria—whether the Will of God or the "bottom line"—should dictate our concerns and our actions.

Now I don't accuse Sagoff of being an antihumanist, but I do think that the concept of humanism is seriously distorted in his essay, as in many recent diatribes for and against the environment. One essential aspect of humanism and the human is surely respect for our various biological and basic social needs as well as our more large-minded values, including the ethics of equitable distribution that generally gets misplaced under the heading of "economics." Corporations are neither "inhuman" nor "unnatural" but, rather, an obvious outgrowth of what is most human and natural about us—our need to affiliate, cooperate, and organize in sizable groups. True, purely economic utilitarianism carves out a very one-sided view of human motivation, and the cost/benefit "rational strategies" of *homo economicus* are surely not definitive of what we mean or ought to mean by utility. Some of our interests may be so readily measured and quantified, but most of our more human concerns, such as love and affection, creativity, personal pride and living well, liberty and the pursuit of happiness are not, and it is nonsense and inhuman to treat them as bits of irrationality or as "irregularities in the market." But though *homo economicus* may be inhuman, our economic interests constitute an essential element in human life. Demeaning the bottom line in favor of some "higher" ideal always carries with it the danger that both the high ideal and the bottom line will end up so much the worse for the conflict. Whatever our conception of environmentalism, it will inevitably have its utilitarian and its purely economic aspects, and to deny or dismiss this is to reject the possibility of any successful environmental reform whatsoever.

What Sagoff calls "moral," as opposed to merely utilitarian, is very Kantian (though more of the third "Critique" than the second) and equally narrow and limited. Is detached reverence and hands-off respect really our only proper attitude toward nature? (Is that the way the Indians did it? Or was engagement in nature, including a good deal of killing, an essential part of their reverence?) There is something absurd about a conception of morality that preaches respect for human dignity but abstains from action on behalf of actual human beings and disdains the actual conversations and compromises in which the substance of morality gets actualized. So, too, there is something absurd about conceiving of environmentalism through the eyes of those armchair romantics whose occasional walks in the woods (as opposed to working in the fields or even puttering around the garden) stimulate occasional reveries. Environmentalism involves living and working in nature, not just appreciating it, and morality is nothing if not the way we deal day to day with each other and our environment. To separate these into convenient but antagonistic packages, moral reverence on the one hand and mere utility on the other, demeans the discussion.

One especially hateful aspect of utilitarianism, according to Sagoff is the notion of risk and risk assessment, which he also juxtaposes with the "moral." The hazards of risk and cost/benefit analysis have often been trumpeted in the philosophical literature on business ethics, and of course, the most famous perversions of this sort of thinking have become something of a touchstone for the profession—the infamous Ford Pinto case, for example, and more recent bad behavior on the part of Audi. But risk is not just an actuarial concept; it is also an ethical one. Sagoff rightly comments, at the end of his paper, that it is the *meaning* of risk as well as its magnitude that has to enter into our deliberations. In fairly recent works, Bernard Williams and Martha Nussbaum have talked at length about the all-important concept of "moral luck," and Mary Douglas and Aaron Wildavsky—whom Sagoff rather one-sidedly chastises in his footnotes— have given an admirably balanced view of the cultural determinants of "risk" and its meaning in their *Risk and Culture*. One need not defend or exonerate Exxon, for example, in order to note that the company was the victim (the only sense in which Exxon was the victim) of bad moral luck in its Alaskan spill disaster. (It's follow-up performance, however, has already become the paradigm example of corporate irresponsibility and the self-defeating substitution of public relations for concerted action.) But the recognition that "there but for the Grace of God . . ." ought to be an essential part of the humility that forms the frame of ethical criticism, and the tragedies that accompany technology and the manipulation of vast natural resources should not be subjected to that armchair Manicheanism that so readily divides the world into "good guys" and "bad." For most of us, too, our integrity, I would politely suggest, is to at least some extent a matter of moral luck. This is not to say that we haven't been "caught" in our transgressions (small as they may be) but rather that we haven't been caught up in those circumstances where our flaws and failings are very likely to undermine us, not to mention put us on the front page of the *New York Post*. It is rather to say that risk is an essential part of virtually every human endeavor and our reaction to disaster should thus be one not only of blame but of instantaneous response and cooperation. Calculations of risk are not opposed to moral considerations; they are rather an essential part of moral preparation.

The ancient Greeks talked a great deal about moral luck, and in particular that form of bad luck which they (and we) call "tragedy." The Greek concept of "fate" is, of course, much less in favor today (as the result of a very different paradigm of personal responsibility emerging from the Judeo-Christian tradition, I would argue, exemplified by the story of "the Fall"). But the related concept of an "accident" is still very much with us, and I think that Sagoff is wrong when he so easily juxtaposes risk and religion, "chance and moral concern." It may be true that Americans are too quick today to judge that "someone must be at fault," but I see this as a very recent perversion of our notions of morals, responsibility, and luck, and detrimental both to our notions of civil liability and to our concern for the environment. The result is that we get lawsuits instead of cooperative action, a mess in the courts in addition to the mess on the beaches. Moreover, our fetish with "finding fault" is philosophically quite opposed to the rather Stoical attitude of reverence for nature and to the "dominant paradigm" to which Sagoff so often alludes.

Populism and Ideology

I have always been suspicious of philosophical and political analyses of populism, and diagnoses of other phenomena in terms of populism. It sounds at first so innocent—"populism" like "popular"—but it is clearly a mass reference term with only barely hidden contemptuous overtones. (There is no question, for example, what an academic is saying when he or she accuses a colleague of "popularization," or what kind of snarled expression we expect of a music critic when he or she refers to "popular music.") Sagoff's examples as well as the overall theme of his paper—environmentalism as *ressentiment*—makes quite clear the nature of the bias that lies behind his sociological analysis. Why should it be a puzzle how environmentalism ties in with ideology, unless the point is to undermine its credibility. Why should a real issue have to be part of what Marx rather contemptuously called an "ideology" (that is, any self-defensive political position other than one's own, and it is only fitting that Marx's own views soon became the paradigm case of an ideology in just that same contemptuous sense)? I don't get the problem that seems to motivate much of Sagoff's paper. What presumption of self-interest and political fanaticism is suggested in the question "Why should environmentalism have become so popular among the rednecks?" Why the use of the very term "redneck"? What about the absurdly naive view, which I mention only with some embarrassment, that environmentalism has become a widely shared even populist issue just because, in the past few years, it has become so obviously *important* even to the most unobservant and self-absorbed citizens, not just to heavy-breathing citizens of Los Angeles but to people virtually everywhere: Germans in the Schwartzwald glancing (at 190 k.p.h.) from the Autobahn at the demise of at least a third of the trees written about by their great romantic poets, Japanese urbanites with their portable oxygen masks in downtown Tokyo, Latin American peasants who can no longer drink from their local streams and rivers, fishermen who this year are employed as scrubbers and beachcombers during high season, all televised nightly for those who are lucky enough not to experience the ghastly discomforts first hand. Is the prevalence of environmentalism really such a political paradox?

Let me suggest at the same time that "environmentalism" has become one of those words that has already outlived its usefulness. Why should we think that there is one question or one set of interests at stake here? The "environment" is, by its very nature, all inclusive, everything around us, both natural and "unnatural." It includes the soil on the nation's farms, the air in New York, the garbage dumps in Patterson and Ann Arbor, the beer bottles on Route 10 out of Houston, and the petroleum products hitting the beaches and killing the fish in Galveston. Granted that everyone is concerned to some extent with the need to breathe (more or less) clean air and drink water that won't kill us over time, why should we suppose that the concerns that face the farmer and those that face the urbanite are all of the same sort? Instead of "environmentalism versus" our questions ought to be more subtle and multiple; in different kinds of cases there are different kinds of risks, different kinds of costs, different kinds of gains and losses not just in dollars but in quality of life. The urban environments of our great cities are as important to millions of people as the rustic environments of the great outdoors and to ignore the one in celebration of the other—or to collapse the two into a single paradigm—is to undermine the meaning of environmental concern, which is ultimately a regard for nature and human beings wherever and however they live.

Environmentalism, as an ill-defined rallying slogan for a large family of humanitarian and aesthetic concerns, is undoubtedly a good idea whose time has come. My objection to Mark Sagoff's paper, which I hope will not be confused with my respect for his overall enterprise, is that it is divisive and reinforces just those divisions that any effective environmental movement(s) must overcome. The welcome popularity of environmental issues should not be reduced to "populism," even as a corrective to the (now defunct) thesis that these issues are motivated by elitism. But like so many philosophical essays on "applied" topics, Sagoff's paper is written from too far above the fray. It is, unfortunately, yet another example of "the moral superiority of the uninvolved." To be sure, there is ample room for a particularly moral and even reverential perspective on environmental issues, but there is no need for one more "top-down" social sermon filled with accusations about the ulterior motives of those who are newly involved. I share the view that we need laws with teeth to prevent many disasters and an environmental emergency fund to cope with those that will inevitably happen despite our best efforts. But the too-prevalent conception that such regulation should be based on purely moral considerations, opposed to utilitarian concerns and forced down the throats of the corporations as well as the farmers and freeway drivers is ill-conceived and self-defeating. What we need is a shared sense of responsibility, not interminable courtroom battles. I welcome the populism that Sagoff seems so suspicious of, but I see it as an opportunity for working together rather than an occasion for "moral high-mindedness."

Part Six

Money and Morals

34

The One-Minute Moralist

Once there was a bright young businessman who was looking for an ethical manager.

He wanted to work for one. He wanted to become one.

His search had taken him over many years to the far corners of the business world.

He visited small businesses and large corporations.

He spoke with used-car dealers, chief executive officers of Fortune 500 companies, management-science professors, vice-presidents for strategic planning, and one-minute managers.

He visited every kind of office, big and small, carpeted and tiled, some with breathtaking views, some without any view at all.

He heard a full spectrum of ethical views.

But he wasn't pleased with what he heard.

On the one hand, virtually everyone he met seemed frank, friendly, and courteous, adamant about honesty even to the point of moral indignation. People were respectful of one another, concerned about their employees, and loyal to their own superiors. They paid their debts and resented the lawsuits in which they considered themselves the innocent parties,

This brief parody was solicited in response to a question posed by the editors of *Business and Society Review:* "Can corporations conform in an ethical manner?" and published as the lead article in the Winter of 1984, when a book called *The One-Minute Manager* was on the bestseller list. Reprinted by permission of the *Business and Society Review.*

victims of misunderstanding and antibusiness sentiment. They complained about regulation and the implied distrust of their integrity. They proudly asserted that they were producing quality products or services that truly did satisfy consumer demand, making the world a better, if only a very slightly better, place in which to live.

Their superiors were proud of their trustworthiness.

Their subordinates were confident of their fairness.

But, on the other hand, when they were asked for their views about ethics and business, what all of these people had to say was startling, to say the least.

The answers varied only slightly.

"You have to understand that it's a jungle out there!"

"Listen, I'm a survivor."

"If I don't do it, the other guy will."

"You've got to be realistic in this business."

"Profits—that's what it's all about. You do whatever you have to."

And when our bright young businessman brought up the topic of business ethics, he invariably heard:

"There aren't any ethics in business"; or . . .

"*Business Ethics*—the shortest book in the world."

The latter usually with a grin.

At the same time, however, many executives shook their heads sadly and expressed the private wish that it were otherwise.

He met a few unscrupulous businessmen who admitted cutting corners, who had made a profit and were proud of it.

He met others who had cut corners and were caught. "This is a cutthroat world," they insisted, often contradicting this immediately by complaining about the injustice of being singled out themselves.

He met several self-proclaimed "ethical managers" who insisted that they and everyone who worked for them had to be Perfectly Virtuous, to the letter of the Moral Law.

These managers' subordinates generally despised them and their departments were rife with resentment. More than one employee complained about autocratic management and dogmatic ineffectiveness; a philosophical assistant manager pointed out the difference between morality and moralizing. Almost everyone pointed out that the principles that were so precisely printed out in both memos and plaques above their desks were usually impossible to apply to any real ethical issues. Their primary effect was rather to cast a gray shadow of suspected hypocrisy over everyday business life.

Our bright young businessman was discouraged. He could not understand why the conscientious, sociable, civilized, thoroughly ethical flesh-

and-blood managers he met in the office talked in their off moments like the most cynical prophets of corporate Darwinism.

The flesh-and-blood managers complained that the public did not appreciate them.

The cynical prophets joked, "There are no ethics in business," and then wondered why people didn't trust them.

Our bright young businessman was perplexed: Could there be ethics in the real business world? Were compromises and cut corners inevitable? Did the untrammeled pursuit of virtue have to be either hypocrisy or damaging to the bottom line, as he now feared?

And then he met the One-Minute Moralist.

The bright young businessman presented the One-Minute Moralist with his dilemma. The One-Minute Moralist answered him without hesitation.

"You don't understand ethics," he said. "And you don't understand business either.

"You set up an absurd dichotomy between ethical absolutism and the so-called real world, and then you wonder how ethics can possibly be at home in business, and whether business can function without cutting corners and making uneasy compromises. But cutting corners presumes that there are sharply delineated corners. And talking so uneasily of compromise (that is, compromising one's moral principles rather than compromising with other people) seems to assume that ethics consists of engraved principles rather than relations between people who (more or less) share values and interests.

"But ethics isn't a set of absolute principles, divorced from and imposed on everyday life. Ethics is a way of life, a seemingly delicate but in fact very strong tissue of endless adjustments and compromises. It is the awareness that one is an intrinsic part of a social order, in which the interests of others and one's own interests are inevitably intertwined. And what is business, you should ask, if not precisely that awareness of what other people want and need, and how you yourself can prosper by providing it? Businesses great and small prosper because they respond to people, and fail when they do not respond. To talk about being 'totally ethical' and about 'uneasy compromises' is to misunderstand ethics. Ethics is the art of mutually agreeable tentative compromise. Insisting on absolute principles is, if I may be ironic, unethical.

"Business, on the other hand, has nothing to do with jungles, survivalism, and Darwin, whatever the mechanisms of the market may be. The 'profit motive' is an offensive fabrication by people who were out to attack business, which has curiously—and self-destructively—been adopted by business people themselves. Business isn't a single-minded pursuit of profits; it is an *ethos,* a way of life. It is a way of life that is at its very foundation ethical. What is more central to business—any kind of business—than taking contracts seriously, paying one's debts, and coming to mutual agreements about what is a fair exchange? Ethics isn't superimposed on business. Business is itself an ethics, defined by ethics, made possible by ethics. Two hundred years ago, Benjamin Franklin insisted that business is the pursuit of virtue. If you find yourself wondering or doubting whether virtue is possible in business, I suggest you reexamine your ideas about business.

"If you want to talk about hypocrisy, by the way, it is not just to be found in such bloated phrases as 'the untrammeled pursuit of virtue.' There is just as much hypocrisy in the macho, mock-heroic insistence that business is a tough-minded, amoral struggle for survival and profits rather than a staid and established ethical enterprise.

"Now you've had your minute. When you think about business and ethics, don't worry about whether one is possible along with the other. In America, as least, nothing is more ethical than good business."

35

What Is Business Ethics?

"The public be damned. I'm working for my stockholders."

—William Vanderbilt

Business ethics occupies a peculiar position in the field of "applied" ethics. Like its kin in such professions as medicine and law, it consists of an uneasy application of some very general ethical principles (of "duty" or "utility," for example) to rather specific and often unique situations and crises. But unlike them, business ethics is concerned with an area of human enterprise whose practitioners do not for the most part enjoy professional status and whose motives, to put it mildly, are often thought (and said) to be less than noble. "Greed" (formerly "avarice") is often cited as the sole engine of business life, and much of the history of business ethics, accordingly, is not very flattering to business. In one sense, that history can be traced back to medieval and ancient times, where, in addition to the attacks on business in philosophy and religion, such practical thinkers as Cicero gave careful attention to the question of fairness in ordinary business transactions. But for much of this history, too, the focus of attention was almost entirely on such particular transactions, surrounding the field with a strong sense of the *ad hoc,* an allegedly nonphilosophical practice that was more often than not dismissed as "casuistry." Thus, on the one

This was originally written for Peter Singer, ed., *A Companion to Ethics* (Oxford: Blackwell, 1991). A revised version of the essay appears here. Published with the permission of Peter Singer and the publishers.

hand, business was generally attacked as unethical by some of the greatest philosophers (Plato and Aristotle) and by the great religious thinkers (Aquinas and Luther); on the other, there was the ethics of daily commercial life, which was not deemed sufficiently respectable to be part of the noble field of philosophy.

Accordingly, the subject of business ethics as currently practiced is not much over a decade old. Only ten years ago, the subject was still an awkward amalgam of a routine review of ethical theories, a few general considerations about the fairness of capitalism, and a number of already-standard business cases—most of them disgraces, scandals, and disasters displaying the corporate world at its worst and at its most irresponsible. Business ethics was a topic without credentials in "mainstream" philosophy, without conceptual subject matter of its own. It was too practical-minded even for "applied ethics" and, in a philosophical world enamored with unworldly ideas and merely "possible" worlds, business ethics was far too concerned with the vulgar currency of everyday exchange—money.

But philosophy itself has tilted again toward the "real world," and business ethics has found or made its place in the junction between the two. New applications and renewed sophistication in game theory and social choice theory have allowed the introduction of more formal analysis into business ethics, and, much more important, the interaction with and the submersion of business ethics practitioners in the working world of corporate executives, labor unions, and small business owners has consolidated the once awkwardly amalgamated elements of business ethics into a subject matter, attracted the interest and attention of business leaders, and turned once-"academic" practitioners into active participants in the business world. Sometimes, one might add, they are even listened to.

A Brief History of Business Ethics

In a broad sense, business has been around at least since the ancient Sumerians who (according to Samuel Noah Kramer) carried out extensive trading and record-keeping nearly six thousand years ago. But business has not always been the central and respectable enterprise that it is in modern society, and the ethical view of business for most of history has been almost wholly negative. Aristotle, who deserves recognition as the first economist (two thousand years before Adam Smith), distinguished two different senses of what we call economics; one of them *oeconomicus* or household trading, which he approved of and thought essential to the working of any even modestly complex society, and *chrematisike,* which is trade for profit. Aristotle declared such activity wholly devoid of virtue and called those who engaged in such purely selfish practices "parasites." Aristotle's attack on the unsavory and unproductive practice of "usury" held force virtually until the seventeenth century. Only outsiders at the fringe of society, not respectable citizens, engaged in such practices. (Shakespeare's Shylock, in *The Merchant of Venice,* was an outsider and a usurer.) This, on a large historical canvas, is the history of business ethics—the wholesale attack on business and its practices. Jesus chased the money-changers from the temple, and Christian moralists from Paul to Thomas Aquinas and Martin Luther followed His example, roundly condemning most of what we today honor as "the business world."

But if business ethics as condemnation was led by philosophy and religion, so, too, was, the dramatic turnaround toward business in early modern times. John Calvin and then the English Puritans taught the virtues of thrift and enterprise, and Adam Smith canonized the new faith in 1776 in his masterwork, *Wealth of Nations.* Of course, the new attitude to business was not an overnight transformation and was built on traditions with a long history. The medieval guilds, for example, had established their own industry-specific codes of "business ethics" long before business became the central institution of society, but the general acceptance of business and the recognition of economics as a central structure of society depended on a very new way of thinking about society that required not only a change in religious and philosophical sensibilities but, underlying them, a new sense of society and even of human nature. This transformation can be partly explained in terms of urbanization, larger more centralized societies, the privatization of family groups as consumers, rapidly advancing technology, the growth of industry and the accompanying development of social structures, needs, and desires. With Adam Smith's classic work, *chrematisike* became the central institution and primary virtue of modern society. But the degraded popular ("greed is good") version of Smith's thesis was hardly conducive to the subject of business ethics ("Isn't that a contradiction in terms?"), and moralizing about business retained its ancient and medieval bias against business. Businessmen like Mellon and Carnegie gave public lectures on the virtues of success and the *noblesse oblige* of the rich, but business ethics as such was for the most part developed by socialists, as a continued diatribe against the amorality of business thinking. It is only very recently that a more moral and honorable way of viewing business has begun to dominate business talk, and with it has come the idea of studying the underlying values and ideals of business. We can readily understand how freedom of the market will always be a threat to traditional values and antagonistic to government control, but we no longer so glibly conclude that the market itself is without values or that governments better serve the public good than markets.

The Myth of the Profit Motive

Business ethics is no longer concerned solely or primarily with the criticism of business and its practices. Profits are no longer condemned along with "avarice" in moralizing sermons, and corporations are no longer envisioned as faceless, soulless, amoral monoliths. The new concern is just how profit should be thought of in the larger context of productivity and social responsibility and how corporations as complex communities can best serve both their own employees and the surrounding society. Business ethics has evolved from a wholly critical attack on capitalism and "the profit motive" to a more productive and constructive examination of the underlying rules and practices of business. But the old paradigm—what Richard deGeorge has called "the myth of amoral business"—persists, not only among the suspicious public and some socialist-minded philosophers but among many businesspeople themselves. The first task in business ethics, accordingly, is to clear the way through some highly incriminating myths and metaphors that obscure rather than clarify the underlying ethos that makes business possible.

Every discipline has its own self-glorifying vocabulary. Politicians bask in the concepts of "public service" while they pursue personal power, and lawyers defend our "rights" on the basis of handsome fees, and professors describe what they do in the noble language of "truth and knowledge" while they spend most of their time and energy in campus politics. But in the case of business the self-glorifying language is often especially unflattering. For example, executives still talk about what they do in terms of "the profit motive," not realizing that the phrase was invented by nineteenth-century socialists as an *attack* on business and its narrow-minded pursuit of money to the exclusion of all other considerations and obligations. To be sure, a business does aim to make a profit, but it does so only by supplying quality goods and services, by providing jobs, and by "fitting in" the community. To single out profits rather than productivity or public service as the central aim of business activity is just asking for trouble. Profits as such are not the end or goal of business activity: profits get distributed and reinvested. Profits are a means to building the business and rewarding employees, executives, and investors. For some people, profits may be a means of "keeping score," but even in those cases, it is the status and satisfaction of "winning" that is the goal, not profits.

A more sophisticated but not dissimilar executive self-image states that the managers of a business are bound above all by one and only one obligation, to maximize profits for their stockholders. We need not inquire whether this is the actual motive behind most upper-management decisions in order to point out that, while managers do recognize that their own business roles are defined primarily by obligations rather than the "profit motive," that unflattering image has simply been transferred to the stockholders (i.e., the owners). Is it true that investors/owners care *only* about maximizing their profits? Is it the stockholder, finally, who is the incarnation of that inhuman *homo economicus* who—like a pension fund manager or institutional investor—is utterly devoid of civic responsibility and pride, who has no concern for the virtues of the company apart from those liabilities that might spell vulnerability to expensive lawsuits? And if some four-month "in and out" investors do indeed care only about increasing their investments by 30 percent or so, why are we so certain that the managers of the firm have *any* obligation to these investors other than not to intentionally fritter away or waste their money? The pursuit of profits is not the ultimate much less the only goal of business. Rather, it is one of many goals, by way of a means and not an end-in-itself.

This is how we misunderstand business: we adopt a too-narrow vision of what business is—e.g., the pursuit of profits—and then derive unethical or amoral conclusions. It is this inexcusably limited focus on the "rights of the stockholders," for example, that has been used to defend some of the very destructive and certainly unproductive "hostile takeovers" of major corporations in the last few years. To say this, however, is not to deny the rights of stockholders to a fair return, nor is it to deny the "fiduciary responsibilities" of the managers of a company. It is only to say that these rights and responsibilities make sense only in a larger social context and that the very idea of "the profit motive" as an end in itself—as opposed to profits as a means of encouraging and rewarding hard work and investment, building a better business, and serving society better—is a serious obstacle to understanding the rich tapestry of motives and activities that make up the business world.

Other Business Myths and Metaphors

Among the most damaging myths and metaphors in business talk are those macho Darwinian concepts of "survival of the fittest" and "it's a jungle out there." The underlying idea, of course, is that life in business is competitive, and it isn't always fair. But that obvious pair of points is very different from the "dog-eat-dog," "every [man] for [him]self" imagery that is routine in the business world. It is true that business is and must be competitive, but it is not true that it is cutthroat or cannibalistic or that "one does whatever it takes to survive." However competitive a particular industry may be, it always rests on a foundation of shared interests and mutually agreed-upon rules of conduct, and the competition takes place not in a jungle but in a community that it presumably both serves and depends upon. Business life is, first of all, fundamentally *cooperative*. It is only within the bounds of mutually shared concerns that competition is possible. Quite the contrary of the "every-animal-for-itself" jungle metaphor, business almost always involves large cooperative and mutually trusting groups, not only corporations themselves but networks of suppliers, service people, customers, and investors. Competition is essential to capitalism, but to misunderstand this as "unbridled" competition is to undermine ethics and in so doing misunderstand the nature of competition. (So, too, we should look with suspicion upon the familiar "war" metaphor that is popular in so many boardrooms, the current game metaphor, and the emphasis on "winning" that tends to turn the serious business of "making a living" into something of a self-enclosed sport.)

The most persistent metaphor, which seems to endure no matter how much evidence is amassed against it, is atomistic individualism. The idea that business life consists wholly of mutually agreed-upon transactions between individual citizens (avoiding government interference) can be traced back to Adam Smith and the philosophy that dominated eighteenth-century Britain. Today, most of business life consists of roles and responsibilities in cooperative enterprises, whether they be small family businesses or gigantic multinational corporations. Government and business are partners as often as they are opponents (however frustrating the labyrinth of "regulation" may sometimes seem), whether by way of subsidies, tariffs and tax breaks, or as an intimate cooperative enterprise ("Japan, Inc.," and such grand projects as the National Aeronautics and Space Administration space shuttle.) Atomistic individualism is not just inaccurate in the face of the corporate complexity of today's business world; it is naive in its supposition that no institutional rules and practices underlie even the simplest promise, contract, or exchange. Business is a social practice, not an activity of isolated individuals. It is possible only because it takes place in a culture with an established set of procedures and expectations, and these are not (except in the details) open to individual tinkering.

Accordingly, it is a sign of considerable progress that one of the dominant models of today's corporate thinking is the idea of a "corporate culture." As with any metaphor, there are, of course, disanalogies, but it is important to appreciate the virtue of this metaphor. It is social, and it rejects atomistic individualism. The metaphor recognizes the place of people in the organization as the fundamental structure of business life. It openly embraces the idea of ethics. It recognizes that shared values hold a culture together. There is still room for that individualistic maverick, the "entrepreneur," but he or she, too, is possible only insofar as there is a role (an important one) for eccentricity and innovation. But one problem with the "culture" metaphor is that it tends to be too self-enclosed. A corporation is not like an isolated tribe in the Trobriand Islands. A corporate culture is an inseparable part of a larger culture, at most a subculture (or a subsubculture), a specialized organelle in an organ in an organism. Indeed, it is the tendency to see business as an isolated and insulated endeavor, with values different from the values of the surrounding society, that characterizes all of these myths and metaphors. Breaking down this sense of isolation: that is the first task of business ethics.

Micro-, Macro-, and Molar Ethics

We might well distinguish between three (or more) levels of business and business ethics: from the *micro* (the rules for fair exchange between two individuals) to the *macro* (the institutional or cultural rules of commerce for an entire society—"the business world"). We should also carve out an area that we can call the *molar* level of business ethics, concerning the basic unit of commerce today—the corporation. Microethics in business, of course, is very much part and parcel of traditional ethics: e.g., the nature of promises and other obligations; the intentions, consequences, and other implications of an individual's actions; the grounding and nature of various individual rights. What is peculiar to business microethics is the idea of a fair exchange and, along with it, the notion of a fair wage, fair treatment, what counts as a "bargain" and what instead is a "steal." Aristotle's notion of "commutative" justice is particularly at home here, and even the ancients used to worry, from time to time, whether, for example, the seller of a house was obliged to tell a potential buyer that the roof had had its day and might start to leak at the first heavy rains.

Macroethics, in turn, incorporates those large questions about justice, legitimacy, and the nature of society that constitute social and political philosophy. What is the purpose of the "free market," or is it in some sense a good in and of itself with its own *telos*? Are private property rights primary, in some sense preceding social convention (as John Locke and more recently Robert Nozick have argued), or is the market to be conceived more broadly as a complex social practice in which rights are but one ingredient? Is the free market system "fair"? Is it the most efficient way to distribute goods and services throughout society? Does it pay enough attention to cases of desperate need (where a "fair exchange" is not part of the question)? Does it pay enough attention to merit, where it is by no means guaranteed that virtue will be in sufficient demand so as to be rewarded? What are the legitimate (and illegitimate) roles of government in business life, and what is the role of government regulation? Macro-ethics, in other words, is an attempt to take in the "big picture," to under-stand the nature of the business world and its functions as a whole.

The definitive "molar" unit of modern business, however, is the cor-poration, and here the central questions of business ethics tend to be un-abashedly aimed at the directors and employees of those few thousand or so companies that rule so much of commercial life around the world. In particular, they are questions that concern the role of the corporation in society and the role of the indivdual in the corporation. Not surprisingly, many of the most challenging issues are found in the interstices of the three levels of ethical discourse: for instance, the question of corporate social responsibility—the role of the corporation in the larger society, and questions of job-defined responsibilities—and the role of the individual in the corporation.

The Corporation in Society: The Idea of Social Responsibility

The central concept of much of recent business ethics is the idea of social responsibility. It is also a concept that has irritated many traditional free-market enthusiasts and prompted a number of bad or misleading arguments. Perhaps the most famous of these is the diatribe by Nobel-winning economist Milton Friedman in the *New York Times* (September 13, 1970) entitled "The Social Responsibility of Business Is to Increase Its Profits." In this article, he called businessmen who defended the idea of corporate social responsibility "unwitting puppets of the intellectual forces that have been undermining the basis of a free society" and accused them of "preaching pure and unadulterated socialism." Friedman's argument is, in essence, that managers of a corporation are the employees of the stockholders and, as such, have a "fiduciary responsibility" to maximize stockholder profits. Giv-ing money to charity or other social causes (except as public relations aimed at increasing business) and getting involved in community projects (which do not increase the company's business) are akin to stealing from the stock-holders. Furthermore, there is no reason to suppose that a corporation or its officers have any special skill or knowledge in the realm of public policy, and so they are overextending their competence as well as violating their obligations when they get involved in community activities (that is, as managers of the company, not as individual citizens acting on their own).

Some of the fallacies involved in such reasoning are consequent to the narrow "profit-minded" view of business and the extremely unflattering and unrealistic one-dimensional portrait of the stockholder that we mentioned earlier; others ("pure unadulterated socialism" and "stealing") are excesses of rhetoric. The "competence" argument (also defended by Peter Drucker in his influential book on *Management**) makes sense only insofar as cor-porations undertake social engineering projects that are indeed beyond their abilities; but does it require special skills or advanced knowledge to be concerned about discriminatory hiring or promotion practices within your own company, or the devastating effects of your waste products on the surrounding countryside? The overall rejoinder to Friedman-esque arguments that have recently become popular in business ethics can be summarized in a modest pun: instead of the "stockholder" the beneficiaries of corporate social responsibilities are the "*stakeholders,*" of whom the stockholders are but a single subclass. The stakeholders in a company are all of those who are affected and have legitimate expectations and rights regarding the actions of the company: these include the employees, the consumers, and the suppliers as well as the surrounding community, and the society at large. The virtue of this concept is that it greatly expands the focus of corporate concern without losing sight of the particular virtues and capacities of the corporation itself. Social responsibility, so considered, is not an additional burden on the corporation but an integral part of its essential concerns, to serve the needs and be fair to not only its investors/owners but those who work for, buy from, sell to, live near, or are otherwise affected by the activities that are demanded and rewarded by the free-market system.

Obligations to Stakeholders: Consumers and Community

The managers of corporations have obligations to their shareholders, but they have obligations to other stakeholders as well. In particular, they have

---

*Harper & Row, 1974.

obligations to consumers and the surrounding community as well as to their own employees (see following section). The purpose of the corporation, after all, is to serve the public, both by way of providing desired and desirable products and services and by not harming the community and its citizens. For example, a corporation is hardly serving its public purpose if it is polluting the air or the water supply, if it is snarling traffic or hogging communal resources, if it is (even indirectly) promoting racism or prejudice, if it is destroying the natural beauty of the environment, or threatening the financial or social well-being of the local citizens. To consumers, the corporation has the obligation to provide quality products and services. It has the obligation to make sure that these are safe, through research, appropriate instructions, and, where appropriate, via warnings against possible misuse. Manufacturers are and should be liable for dangerous effects and predictable abuse of their products—e.g., the likelihood of a young child swallowing a small, easily detachable piece of a toy made specifically for that age group—and it is now suggested by some consumer advocacy groups that such liability should not be overly qualified by the excuse that "these were mature adults who knew or should have known the risks of what they were doing." This last demand, however, points to a number of currently problematic concerns: notably, the general presumption of maturity, intelligence, and responsibility on the part of the consumer and the question of reasonable limits of liability on the part of the producer. (Special considerations obviously apply to children.) To what extent should manufacturers take precautions against clearly idiosyncratic or even idiotic uses of their products? What restrictions should there be on manufacturers who sell and distribute provably dangerous products, e.g., cigarettes and firearms—even if there is considerable consumer demand for such items? Should producers be liable for what is clearly a foreseeable risk on the part of the consumer? Indeed, it is increasingly being asked whether and to what extent we should reinstate that now ancient *caveat,* "buyer beware," in place of the runaway trend toward consumer irresponsibility and unqualified corporate liability?

Consumer intelligence and responsibility are also at issue in the much-debated topic of advertising, against which some of the most serious criticisms of current business practices have been directed. The classic defense of the free-market system is that it supplies and satisfies existing demands. But if manufacturers actually *create* the demand for the products they produce, then this classic defense is clearly undermined. Indeed, it has even been charged that advertising is itself coercive in that it interferes with the free choice of the consumer, who is no longer in a position of deciding how to best satisfy his or her needs but has instead been subjected to a barrage of influences that may well be quite irrelevant or even opposed to those needs. And even where the desirability of the product is not in question, there are very real questions about the advertising of particular brand names and the artificial creation of "product differentiation." Then, too, are those familiar questions of taste on the borderline (and sometimes over) between ethics and aesthetics. There is the use of sex, often seductive and sometimes quite undisguised, to enhance the appeal of products (from chewing gum to automobiles); there are the implied but obviously false promises of social success and acceptability if only one buys this soap or toothpaste; and there are the offensive portrayals of women and minorities and often human nature as such, just in order to sell products that most of us could perfectly well do without. But is such superfluous consumption and the taste (or lack of it) that sells it an ethical issue? Is anyone actually expected to believe that his or her life will change with an added hint of mint or a waxless, yellow-free kitchen floor?

Much more serious, of course, is outright lying in advertising. But what counts as a "lie" is by no means straightforward in this world of seduction, kitsch, and hyperbole. No one, perhaps, will actually believe that a certain toothpaste or pair of designer jeans will guarantee your success with the lover of your dreams (though millions are willing to take the chance, just in case), but when a product has effects that may well be fatal, the accuracy of advertising is put under much closer scrutiny. When a medical product is advertised on the basis of misleading, incomplete, or simply untrue technical information; when an over-the-counter "cold remedy" is sold with the promise but without any hard evidence that it can relieve symptoms and prevent complications; when known and dangerous side-effects are hidden behind a generic "with this as with all medicines, check with your doctor," then seemingly simple "truth in advertising" becomes a moral imperative and ethics (if not the law) has been violated.

It has often been argued that, in an ideally functioning free market the only advertising that should be either necessary or permitted is pure information regarding the use and qualities of the product. But in certain circumstances, the average consumer may neither have nor be able to understand the relevant information concerning the product in question. In a great many cases, however, consumers take too little responsibility for their own decisions, and one cannot properly blame advertising for their irresponsibility or irrationality. Corporations have responsibilities to their customers, but consumers have responsibilities, too. As so often happens, business ethics is not a question of corporate responsibility alone but an interlocking set of mutual responsibilities.

The Individual in the Corporation: Responsibilities and Expectations

Perhaps the most abused stakeholder in the pattern of corporate responsibilities is the company employee. In traditional free-market theory, the employee's labor is itself just one more commodity, subject to the laws of supply and demand. But whereas one can sell at "firesale" prices or simply dispose of pins or parts of machinery that are no longer in demand, employees are human beings, with very real needs and rights quite apart from their role in production or in the market. Cramped uncomfortable working space or long, grueling hours for employees may reduce overhead or increase productivity, and paying subsubsistence wages to employees who for one reason or another cannot, dare not, or do not know how to complain may increase profits, but such conditions and practices are now recognized by all but the most unreconstructed Darwinian to be highly unethical and legally inexcusable. And yet, the "commodity" model of labor still holds powerful sway over much business thinking, concerning managers and executives as well as workers, both skilled and unskilled. It is for this reason that much of recent business ethics has focused on such notions as employees' rights and, from a very different angle, it is for this reason, too, that the old notion of "company loyalty" has come back into focus. After all, if a company treats its employees as nothing but disposable parts, no one should be surprised if the employees start treating the company as nothing but a transient source of wages and benefits.

The other side of this disturbing picture, however, is the renewed emphasis on the notion of employee roles and responsibilities, one of which is loyalty to the company. It cannot be overemphasized that "loyalty" here is a two-way concern: employees may by virtue of their employment have special obligations to the company but the company has its obligations to them as well. There is a danger in stressing such concepts as "loyalty" without being very clear that loyalty is tied not just to employment in general but also to one's particular role and responsibilities. A role, according to R. S. Downie, is "a cluster of rights and duties with some sort of social function"—in this case, a function in the corporation. Certain aspects of one's role and responsibilities may be specified in an employment contract and in the law. But many of them—for example, the local customs, patterns of deference, and other aspects of "the corporate culture" (discussed earlier)—may become evident only with time on the job and continued contact with other employees. Moreover, it is not just a matter of "doing one's job" but, as a matter of ethics and economics, it is doing one's job as well as possible. Norman Bowie says in this regard, I think rightly, "a job is never just a job." It also has a moral dimension: pride in one's product, cooperation with one's colleagues, and concern for the well-being of the company. But, of course, such role-defined obligations have their limits (however conveniently some managers tend to deny this). Business is not an end in itself but is embedded in and supported by a society that has other, overriding concerns, norms, and expectations.

We sometimes hear employees (and even high-level executives) complain that their "corporate values conflict with their personal values." What this usually means, I suggest, is that certain demands made by their companies are unethical or immoral. What most people call their "personal values" are in fact the deepest and broadest values of their culture. It is in this context that we should understand that now-familiar tragic figure of contemporary corporate life—the "whistle-blower." Whistle-blowers are not just eccentrics who cannot "fit" into the organization that they threaten with disclosure. Whistle-blowers recognize that they cannot tolerate the violation of morality or the public trust and feel obliged to actually do something about it. The biographies of most whistle-blowers do not make happy reading, but their very existence and occasional success is ample testimony to the interlocking obligations of the corporation, the individual, and society. Indeed, perhaps the most singularly important result of business ethics in the public forum has been to highlight such individuals and give renewed respectability to what their employers wrongly perceive as nothing but a breach of loyalty. But when the demands of doing business conflict with the morality or well-being of society, it is business that has to yield, and this, perhaps, is the ultimate point of business ethics.

36

Abstract Greed

"I don't do it for the money. I've got enough, much more than I'll ever need. I do it to do it."

—Donald Trump

"You can't ever get enough of what you didn't really want in the first place."

—Sam Keen

Two years ago I asked my business ethics students, rather casually, how much money they thought that they could reasonably expect to be earning ten years from now. An economics major asked how she was supposed to know about ten years of potential inflation, so I assured them that 1989 dollars would do. A few thoughtful students confessed that, as they had no idea what they wanted to do for a career or a living yet, they could hardly estimate any expected income. But I told them that at the moment I was more interested in their expectations than I was in their career choices, and I asked for a few volunteers.

"Thirty-five thousand dollars," offered one student in the middle of class. The rest of the class, almost as one, chortled and guffawed.

"Too high or too low?" I asked, tongue in cheek, the answer being obvious.

"You can't even live on thirty-five thousand dollars a year," insisted one perturbed student, "even without a family."

Adapted from chapter 2 of my *Passion for Justice* (Addison-Wesley, 1990).

"Well," I needled them, "how much would it take to live on?"

"A hundred grand," shouted a student at the back of the class, and almost everyone nodded or muttered in agreement.

"And do you think that you will make that much?" I asked.

"Sure," answered the same student, with more cockiness than confidence.

"How?" I asked

"Oh, I haven't the slightest idea. Probably in investments." He answered, with a nervous giggle.

Everyone laughed. I then asked the class (there were about a hundred of them) to write down the figure they "reasonably expected" to be earning in a decade, adjusted for inflation, etc. The class average was well over $75,000 a year, not counting a few visionary millionaires-to-be who were not counted in the averages.

I often do that experiment, and I used to get much the same result and discussion, with almost every one of my classes. I'm happy to say that, with the turn into the nineties, the figures are more modest and the ambitions more along the lines of "doing something worthwhile with my life." But whether this is because of a new social consciousness or because of economic despair foreshadowed by the Wall Street scandals and sackings and an economy deeply damaged by federal deficits, I cannot yet say; of course, it may be both, just as the idealism of the sixties was fueled by an affluent confidence mixed with fear and anger about the Vietnam War. These 1989 students were the last students of the Reagan years, filled with the promises of quick wealth and unhampered (unregulated) power that defined business thinking in those days. Everyone knew about the twenty-five-year-olds making their fortunes on Wall Street, and with that in mind, who wanted to go into teaching or social work or (even worse) manufacturing? These students had enormous expectations, stoked everyday by the media, and very little sense of what to do with their lives—except, of course, for that relatively small number of elite students who managed the Prestige University M.B.A.-Wall Street route (before burning out at twenty-eight or so).

What struck me then and still so impresses me was and is not so much the enormous sums of money these students seemed to think that they wanted, deserved, and needed to live on but their utter naivete about how to get it and their remarkable lack of sense about what to do with it. It is the money—no, not even the money but the sheer numbers themselves—that counted. Of course, there are always enough luxuries to covet and to buy, but there was very little desire for such things themselves, only an abstract desire for the ability to buy them. These business students also displayed almost total ignorance of what business life for most people (certainly most of them) actually involves, despite their three or four years of study of the subject. Somehow they thought that they would get a job (they were anxious about that) and then the money would flow in. There was very little thought or speculation about the social relations that actually define most business communities, little thought about what they would actually do to *earn* the money they made, and virtually no thought whatever (for most of them) about what product or service the company they would work for would actually produce. Once employed, they would do the tricks they learned in business school: "suck up" to an executive or two, the corporate ladder would carry them along, and the money would come, too. All anxiety was focused on getting that first job and starting down the path to wealth promoted on all of those Sunday night television shows and Financial News Network interview-advertisements. The questions about "why?" "what?" and "who?" would just have to wait their turn.

I have called this phenomenon, this greed without desire, "*abstract greed.*" Instead of desire, there is the brainwashed sense that this is what one *ought* to want. (Needless to say, most students would forget about it after a few years of meaningful employment and mortgage payments.) It is obvious that if most of these students actually had the desire and expectation for such fantastic amounts of money, they would be doomed to a life of frustration and (felt) failure, even if, without that desire and those expectations, they might be perfectly well off and quite happy. (As the Talmud says, "the rich man is he who is satisfied with what he has.") In abstract greed it is money, pure wealth, that is wanted, not to obtain anything or even to prove anything but wealth as a goal, given and unquestioned, like "honor" in some other societies and "faith" or "patriotism" in others. It is, to hear us talk, the ultimate good, more important than personal dignity and happiness. Indeed, it *is* our personal dignity and happiness.

Where does this peculiar attitude come from? It is not a "natural" desire, indeed, it is spectacular just in the fact that it is so cut off from any natural desire, our need for other people and for self-respect, our need for relaxation and social harmony, even our need for stimulation and challenge. (The much-touted "challenge" of business is, outside of Wall Street, almost always a challenge of creativity, of hard work and perseverance, of organization and cooperation, of good ideas and keen sensitivity to public needs and moods. It is not the challenge of "making money.") Abstract greed isn't even greed. It isn't desire. And it plays only an artificial, distracting, and destructive role in our ambitions. This is just what I want to argue, of course, about the myth that stands behind abstract greed, the myth of "the profit motive"—the idea that we are all ("naturally") motivated by the desire for (more) money. The very idea that money in itself is desirable and readily convertible into power and prestige is an idea that, in most ages and most cultures, has been condemned as a curse (King Midas, notably) or a sin (of "avarice"). And it has been so condemned just because it is cut off from other essential motives and interests: the well-being of others, the good of the community, the well-being of one's own soul. But, of course, no motive floats alone, without anchorage in our deepest needs and desires; my students' abstract greed is obviously tied to all sorts of natural desires, especially the desire for the approval of their peers, and the desire (if it is conscious enough to become a desire) to fit in with the times and to please their parents (who too often give ill-considered advice based on their own frustrations). They want to fit the images provided by the media, and these are too often dressed in the glamour of wealth. (How could a Miami detective afford a ninety-thousand-dollar sports car?) It is the desire to achieve those dubious virtues that too many business executives, unthinkingly parroting the conventional "wisdom" of the times and their speechwriters, declare again and again to be the driving force of American society: the pursuit of wealth, the importance of unfettered competition, the ruthlessness of the marketplace, the need to be an "individual" and to "rise above" everyone else (while maintaining that we are all equal, of course). Ivan Boesky's "greed is good" speech, paraphrased by Gordon Gekko in *Wall Street,* was only a slight exaggeration.

What gets left out are all of those virtues and values that successful executives themselves obviously recognize and probably practice: the importance of patience, the fact that money ought to be earned and not merely coveted, the need for cooperation and mutual respect, the purpose of the marketplace being not just to test the macho-mettle of its participants but to supply everyone with jobs and inexpensive quality products and services. The purpose of life is not to be rich, and to be rich, in truth, is to have enough.

37

Economics and Ethics

There is nothing wrong with economic theory as such. Economic thinking is essential to everyone's education, not only for business people and politicians.

The problem is that economists insist on thinking of their subject as a "science." Oh, let them have the honorific label, if they want it. It only means "systematic knowledge." But economics (from Greek *oeconomicus* = household trading) is and always has been part of the humanities, the sympathetic understanding of people. You know what people want and how they will behave because you know how you would behave in similar circumstances. It's not like organic chemistry. You don't have to enjoy the company of ketones or sympathize with an aldehyde.

Economic theories, like all theories by people about people, are self-distorting. Suppose I tell you how I think you would behave; whatever you do is in part a response to what I've told you, even if you decide to ignore me. People, unlike molecules, have the annoying habit of changing their behavior when they hear a theory. Linus Pauling didn't worry that the chemical bond market would change as soon as he published his theory. Kaufman or Granville utter an oracle on *Wall Street Week* and it changes the situation that very day.

Economics is a human activity and its theories are part of our economy-

---

This brief essay was written in response to a question posed by the editors of *Business and Society Review:* "Is economic theory hogwash?" and published in the Summer of 1983. Reprinted by permission of the publisher.

minded culture. It is not an academic exercise, although anything can be made into an academic exercise. In a religious society, there will be theologians. We instead have economists. They are part of our conversation; they give us some substance to talk about and a vocabulary through which to express our fears and channel our actions. But their predictions are no more than what we make of them. To think that one can run an economy with economists is like trying to cook a good dinner out of an alchemy book.

What Adam Smith presumed between the lines, and what "science"-minded economists have rejected, is the essential role of ethics in the "dysmal science." The key to our economic thinking is a *fair* exchange. "Supply and demand" are not just quantitative categories; they are measures of *value*. Monetary theory is not just numbers; it is a measure of trust and what people think their time, effort, goods, and money are *worth*. We teach our students about the *free* market as if it were a piece of machinery rather than an ethical commitment and a daring experiment. We analyze international exchange rates and leave out dissatisfaction with the local dictator. Then we get annoyed when "politics" (a revolution) interferes with our fraudulently neat mathematical curves.

Economics is about justice as much as it is about the mechanism of the market. Keynes was surely right—whether his theories "worked" or not—if only because his views required giving work to the needy, an essential demand of justice. Reagonomics is wrong—or worse—if only because it has gotten caught up, not in economic theory, but in a theory that is devoid of (or perverse in) ethical considerations. It had to fail, and one does not have to be—should not be—an economist to see why this is so.

Economics is the disciplined self-examination of our material life as a society. Its concern is justice and fairness as well as wealth and poverty. Economic thinking is essential, but only integrated into the context of everything else: our culture, history, ideas, religion, even our sex habits and table manners. Felix Rohatyn is a good example. He has established himself as an outstanding economist because he knows much more than economics. He writes for people other than other economists; he speaks for concerns that are openly ethical.

Sheared of ethics and culture, economics is a language without an interpretation; it is worse than worthless and very pretentious. There is no gulf between theory and practice, between the classroom and the public market of ideas. There is rather the mistaken idea—which is too easily confused with the ideal of "science"—that an isolated, abstract, and conscientiously amoral discipline has anything to say about human reality. But that isn't economics, and it never was.

38

The New Family Doctor

There are two things, according to one of those many variable proverbs, that you should never see made: laws and sausages. Another would be doctors. Unfortunately, one of the less rewarding ways in which I make my living is to be present at the creation, as a college teacher as well as potential patient who is often asked—at this time of year—to write the recommendations with which our young and aspiring "pre-meds" hope to convince the medical schools that they are, indeed, as desirable as their suspiciously high grade point averages would suggest. And every time I write another one—or refuse to write one—it becomes again clear to me that there is something appallingly wrong with the way we choose, train, and educate the people who may someday hold our lives in their hands.

"Whatever happened to the old family doctor?" is a familiar lament, one among many that accompanies the general attack on medicine these days. But anyone familiar with the procedures by which medical students are selected will have no doubts about that: such people are systematically ruled out from the beginning.

Medicine, once the hallmark of wisdom in the U.S., has been undergoing

---

This is a piece, I am happy to say, that is becoming dated, thanks to a renewed effort to humanize the practice of medicine on the part of medical schools and hospitals—no small thanks to an avalanche of malpractice suits based largely on the resentment of neglected rather than maltreated patients. This was written for *The Texas Observer,* in November of 1980, and reprinted with the publisher's permission.

a beating these days. The American Medical Association (AMA) is viewed by many people as a cartel, dispensing health as the Organization of Petroleum Exporting Countries (OPEC) distributes oil. There are numerous complaints, not all of them justified, about impersonal treatment, unprofessional treatment, lack of treatment, and excessive treatment. There is a terrifying increase in the number of "incompetence" suits being filed. A good friend of mine, a liability lawyer in Houston, estimates that some eighty percent of the cases she sees are based on personal grievances against a doctor who was too cold, too aloof, too inaccessible, or too gruff, rather than malpractice suits as such. Only recently, newspapers have made a noise about what every medical student already knows, that the skills and experience of those recent graduates called "interns" raise the odds on Christian Science, and if that weren't bad enough, the totally senseless practice of forcing them into thirty-six-hour shifts, often without sleep, makes every visit to the emergency room of most major hospitals an even more real danger than the emergency itself. Add to this the common knowledge on the inside that you're probably better off with a witch doctor than with an intern in July, fresh out of medical school and new on the job.

All of this is late in the game. Doctors, with few exceptions, are licensed for life. Interns are already graduates; they've survived the selection and weeding out processes and, with perseverance and a little sleep, are virtually certain to become full-fledged doctors. The students whom I see, on the other hand, are fighting a pitched and belligerent battle for admission to medical school, for they know that that is more than half the battle. Once in, the chance of success is far higher than the likelihood of failure. A small percentage simply flunk out, of course, and a number drop out because of the work. Only a few are asked to leave for nonacademic reasons, usually under a protective excuse, "reasons of health" or "personal problems." But given the expense of even the first term of a medical education (and it costs the school or the state even more than it does the students or their parents), the pressure is to encourage success, even to the point of nursing weak students along. This means that virtually anyone admitted to medical school is already past the selective procedure.

When I was in medical school, there were three students at least— the class clowns (if that can be an involuntary role)—who were clearly incompetent. I don't mean subtly flawed, as in socially stupid, illiterate, or possessing the charm of a tissue specimen. I mean that they were incompetent in the most simple tasks. They didn't just give the wrong answers; they answered the wrong questions. They didn't just miss the vagus nerve; they cut through it. They didn't only fail to find the mitochondria in their slide preparation; they consistently ground down the lens of the microscope right through the slide. They are all doctors now—specialists, of course. One of them, now a gynecologist, used to visit the undergrad library during lunch, to peek up the co-eds' skirts. Another had a doctor-father, on the board. These are special cases, of course, the few frightening exceptions in every profession who can be used by the unscrupulous critic to cast aspersions or worse on the whole profession. But they usurped candidacy for that much admired and coveted degree from someone who would have been much better.

I am asked to write at least a dozen or so recommendations for medical school aspirants each and every term. Typically, the student will be someone I do not know at all. This is not always the student's fault, since classes tend to be large. My first inclination is to decline, and often I do, explaining that I couldn't really write a strong letter of recommendation without knowing the student better, to which the reply is too often, "but you know me better than anyone else I've had!" So I write, as much as is possible, an honest but flattering letter—honest, that is, in a vocabulary that has come to mean: "excellent"-O.K., "outstanding"-not bad, "the best in the class"-worth considering, "the best student I've ever had"-I personally like this one. "Good," of course, means "don't even bother" and "competent" means probably stupid as well as totally unimaginative and not very likeable.

I wonder what such letters can mean to those who must choose from among an army of faceless candidates, all with tediously consistent "A" averages, each armed with two or four equally meaningless letters. Perhaps one may be personal, at least, from the family doctor or a relative who went to the school, but that says little about qualifications and ability. The whole process seems to generate a level of anxiety that produces or selects for a ruthlessness and sense of impatience that is precisely what the medical profession does *not* need. For every student I meet who wants to "do medicine," there are ten who want "to be a doctor." And most of them don't see the difference.

What is so apparent to anyone who teaches these students is that those who are bound to succeed in school are precisely those who are most likely to fail as doctors. In fact, the basis on which they succeed is precisely the basis on which they will probably fail. For example, one of my doctor friends (yes, some of my best friends. . .) has complained almost yearly about the vast number of beginning residents who have spent their lives making grades and learning established theories; but medicine is neither. Medicine is mainly *diagnosis*. Figuring out probabilities given a paucity of evidence, sometimes only the vague complaints of a half-conscious patient and often within a very limited period of time. But, whether or not the medical school itself takes the necessary pains to teach the art (and it is an art) of diagnosis—some schools do, some don't—the decision to admit or not admit a particular student is made without any possible reference to this absolutely crucial ability. And what's worse, those students who tend to succeed and get admitted are most often those who do not have either the taste or the skill for such uncertainties, preferring the cut-and-dried theories of their lower-level science classes. (Very few students have carried out any original research, but even this isn't diagnosis.) Premeds tend to avoid the humanities and other subjects based on interpretation and, consequently (complains my same friend, who was a German major in college), they are constitutionally incapable of dealing with the typical office or hospital situation. They are simply the wrong people for the job.

There is another problem of the same severity; I was too generous when I said it was unfortunate that I did not get a chance to meet many of the students who ask me for recommendations. In fact, I get to know quite a few students, even in classes of a hundred and more, which are largely discussion. But these are students who sit to the rear of the room, interested neither in the topic nor in the other students. They are only concerned with, as they would politely put it, "the material" (that means, the grade). But therein lies a confession of monstrous scope: they are "material-oriented," to use the psychological jargon that's going around in education. They are not people-oriented, or problem-oriented. They don't like an interchange. They deal with their friends as competitors rather than colleagues, and one can expect that they will tend to treat symptoms, causes, diseases, and conditions as "material," at best as "patients," but not as people. That may be less disastrous for a surgeon, but many of these students express an interest in psychiatry and general medicine.

I have not mentioned, nor will I, the suspicion that many of us share about the *honesty* of the work that is motivated by such brutal competition. We all have horror stories, personal tales of dedicated students who really "want to help people" who are turned down because of a "B+" average, and others who are so itching to get into medical school that there is no doubt that they'd be the worst ones to work so intimately with people. With luck, they'll practice far away, or maybe get interested in research or AMA politics.

"What ever happened to the old family doctor?" The answer is that he didn't get admitted.

39

Fate and the Liability Crisis

"My formula for greatness in a human being is *amor fati:* that one wants nothing to be different, not forward, not backward, not in all eternity. Not merely to bear what is necessary, still less conceal it . . . but love it."

—Nietzsche, *Ecce Homo*

Everyone knows that something has gone very wrong in America. Our legal system, by most accounts across the spectrum of political opinion, has all but "broken down." The passion for litigation, the seemingly endless court delays and legal convolutions are nothing new, of course; Dickens described them in *Bleak House* and an eighteenth-century French sculptor mocked them in a famous statue in the "Salle des Pas-Perdus" ("Room of the Lost Footsteps") in the Palais of Justice, where the eminent lawyer Berryer is depicted with his foot on a tortoise. In fact, there are unmistakably contemporary references to the same perverse passion for litigation and legal quagmires in Aristophanes' play *The Wasps,* written in 422 B.C. What is new and apparently unique to the American justice scene, however, is a crisis of potentially disastrous proportions, which has its clearest manifestation in several much-publicized recent liability cases. In a speech on the crisis in 1987–1988, President Reagan mentioned a man who had a

---

Originating in a conversation with liability lawyer Donna Kline, in one of the better restaurants in New Orleans, this piece became a seminar at the University of Texas and is now in process of turning into a book, with Donna Kline and John Schwartz of *Newsweek.*

278

fatal heart attack mowing his lawn. His family sued the manufacturer of the lawn mower and won a million-dollar settlement. In another case, a teenage girl decided to sweeten the smell of her decorative candle and so poured some perfume on the flame. The perfume, of course, caught fire, the bottle exploded, and the perfume manufacturer was successfully sued for not supplying sufficient warning. Elsewhere, a woman emerged from cosmetic surgery with her navel slightly askewed. She sued her surgeon, successfully, for $800,000. In another, even more outrageous case, a burglar fell through the skylight of a house he was about to burgle, and his intended victim was ordered by the court to pay him substantial damages.

Our newspapers, less scandalous magazines, and contemporary folklore are filled with such stories. Some of them turn out to be apocryphal. Others turn out to be partially true. The jury's judgment was in fact a multimillion-dollar settlement but an appeals judge later lowered the amount to a few hundred thousand. (Of course, only the first judgment made the headlines.) Many of the most shocking and most publicized stories have been promoted by the insurance industry itself—they ended up paying the tab—as a preliminary gambit to raising their rates. Consequently, the cost of liability and malpractice insurance has skyrocketed, and so we are regaled as well with stories about such low-risk but essential public enterprises as parks, swimming pools, and day-care centers that must close solely because they cannot afford the insurance that would protect them in the case of some possibly absurd or foolish accident that could occur on their premises. The crisis, accordingly, is not just the absurdity of a few bizarre liability cases. It is the multiplying effect of increased fear and even paranoia, ever more litigation and an overburdened court system, skyrocketing insurance rates, and an end to public conveniences and private generosities that a citizen in a civilized country has something of a right to enjoy.

But in the midst of the public outrage and the predictable finger-pointing by those who may be making the most out of the situation, no one seems to be forthcoming with the needed facts and figures: how many of these bizarre cases are there, and what is the actual amount of losses to the industry? What are the effects—both tangible and intangible—of the fear of liability lawsuits and of the greed that is inspired while watching others profit from seeming misfortune? There is a proliferation of professional studies and corporate position papers in the insurance industry and various legal groups such as the American Trial Lawyers Association, but these are predictably one-sided and in any case not readily readable by or accessible to the larger American public. One gets the sense of politics being played, by the insurance industry, by the lawyers, and, of course, by the politicians.

And, on a more basic level, there are critical questions not being asked, such as, "What is liability?" and "What is the purpose of insurance?" Liability law has been a valuable public weapon in the battle for social reform and justice, and in the punishment and elimination of bad businesses and incompetent practitioners. However, excessive enthusiasm for lawsuits and the sometimes fabulous rewards thereof have turned liability law itself into a public liability, too often at odds with the public good, raising prices and paranoia, threatening and eliminating good products and practitioners along with the bad. Given how tightly the two terms have recently been tied together, it is worth noting that the concept of liability often runs counter to the idea of insurance. If lawsuits are aimed at punishment, then why should the insurance company (and the other premium payers) pay the penalty? (Accordingly, some insurance contracts refuse to pay "punitive" damages, and often insurance cannot be obtained to protect against suits for vicious actions or gross negligence.) What are the reasonable limits of liability, or is the concept of liability too often just a pretense to find someone who can be made to pay? Is insurance, as older insurance executives used to say, to provide "protection for widows and orphans," or is it be a much broader program of compensation and risk-minimalization? Does insurance protect us from shoddy manufacturing and irresponsible behavior or does it, in effect, increase our risk and encourage negligence (because it's insured)? And insofar as the purpose of insurance is to provide a "safety net" for the suddenly needy, why should insurance protection be a matter of supply-and-demand, a projection of personal risk assessment, and the competitive product of private enterprise rather than a government responsibility (providing the largest possible pool of policy holders)? And deeper still: how much should we depend on insurance and how much of our lives should be insured? What does this do to our conception of ourselves, and our view of our role in the world? These are questions that often get buried in the avalanche of accusations of corporate greed, the legal feeding-frenzy, and the consumer's rightful campaign against unsafe products and irresponsible professionals.

Where does the problem lie? Needless to say, every group and participant in the emerging scandal blames the others, although it is just this reflex of blaming that fuels and aggravates the crisis. Manufacturers blame the government and greedy lawyers when they don't blame their own customers. The lawyers and the injured customers blame the manufacturers, and everyone blames the insurance companies—whom they nevertheless expect to pay the costs of the crisis. The one person who is often absolved from blame is the victim, who may be dead or maimed for life and quite rightly attracts our sympathy. But there are many cases in which the victim is nevertheless responsible for his or her own misfortune and the defendants not at all, and many juries' verdicts should be viewed as expressions of sympathy for the victim rather than a judgment about responsibility. Corporations and insurance companies, on the other hand, are too often perceived as limitless resources whose costs are but a few cents per share to the stockholders, and the judgments against them, accordingly, reflect a "deep pockets" mentality (*"Someone* has got to pay!") rather than a judgment of liability and blame. And even where liability is the issue, there are many cases in which the plaintiff is clearly out for revenge rather than mere compensation, and the courts—especially through "punitive damages"—have encouraged liability litigation as a "civil" outlet for personal indignation and vengeance rather than a public vehicle for justice and social control. Lawyers obviously have a great deal to gain from the current system, and "contingency basis" cases have given considerable vitality to potential lawsuits that would never have been considered even a decade or so ago. On the face of it the insurance companies would seem to have the most to lose, since they are the ones who ultimately pay both the lawyers and their clients. There is general suspicion—some of it justified—that the insurance industry is benefiting far more than it is suffering from the crisis, and our (preliminary) research suggests that the industry has been promoting for almost two decades the very crisis that it now claims threatens its survival. The insurance companies in turn tend to blame not only the lawyers but the jury system, and more than a few of the much-publicized cases have been described with mixed lament and bitterness as the fault of an easily swayed jury who "just didn't understand the issues involved."

The real victim, of course, is the American public, who inevitably pays the total cost and suffers the shutdown of basic amenities. To pick a particularly frightening example, pharmaceutical companies and emergency medical services are now terrified of ruinous liability suits, and the consequence is the loss of potential lifesaving drugs and procedures. On a more pedestrian level there are the park and school closings and the cessation of public services that particularly affect the poor, again by virtue of the threat of a lawsuit and the rising cost of insurance premiums. But "the public" is not blameless, and popular feelings about the avarice of corporations and professionals and people's consequent willingness to use the legal system as a vehicle for vengeance and resentment is the essential link in a complex network of responsibilities and expectations. To be sure, manufacturers have responsibilities to the consumer and people have the right to expect professional competence and due care from doctors, lawyers, stockbrokers, and engineers, but the liability crisis is not about dangerous products and irresponsible professionals. They can and should be taken off the market or ejected from their professions, and the law and lawsuits can have a definitive hand in seeing that this is done. But the liability crisis is a crisis about insurance. It is not a question about whether wrongdoers should be punished but a series of questions about compensation and risk. Should victims of chance or, in many cases, of their own stupidity be in a position to blame and to gain from those who are by any reasonable standards faultless? Should we have a complex system of legal liability and insurance to provide that gain, not by way of a "safety net" to protect those who suffer serious misfortune but as a punitive system of blame and compensation, a gambling game in which the seriously (and not so seriously) injured get to try their hand (with the help of a willing lawyer) and some of the fattest jackpots available to the otherwise unlucky.

The real culprit, in other words, is no one of the groups or participants in the crisis so much as the *system* itself, which mutually encourages and reinforces some of the worst aspects of all of us, our cultivated avarice and our insecurities and our resentment, as compensation gets confused with greed, and reparation gets mixed up with retaliation. A system that only recently rested on the twin virtues of individual responsibility and the recognized need to provide "protection for widows and orphans" has now become the financier of a vicious game of "suffer and sue," of getting even and profiting enormously thereby. But the most shocking thing about the liability crisis is its rapid evolution and the new philosophy that has made it possible. The idea behind the concept of liability is that the person (or party) who is responsible for injury to another should pay, both as punishment and as compensation for the victim. But insurance undermines at least one half of that idea, because the guilty party does not pay; the entire pool of subscribers and customers pay (and are "punished") through their premiums and higher prices and payment is thus no longer punishment.

The addition of "punitive damages" (too often inappropriately named) can put the cost of blame far in excess of the actual loss to the victim and in excess as well of the guilty party's own ability to pay. Punitive damages can be a valuable tool in the control of willfully irresponsible corporations (e.g., those who carefully calculate the probable cost of a certain number of injuries and deaths due to their carelessness or poor design) but the further addition of "deep pockets" legislation dulls this tool and undermines the concept of "liability" altogether as "fault" is no longer the issue. And in cases where the victim is primarily the victim of his or her own stupidity or carelessness, the questions of "fault" and "liability" become wholly gratuitous, as the questions "Who will pay?" gets entangled with the question "Who is to blame?" In short, the purpose of the liability system has become less and less the compensation of blameless victims and the punishment of those responsible for their plight and more and more a ramshackle, runaway vehicle that tries to take care of all injured persons in the name of a punishment that no longer punishes but instead encourages fraud and greed in the name of a "justice," which is all the more often revenge.

The liability system has grown up hand-in-hand with the legal tort system, and though the two now seem to be forever at odds they continue to grow symbiotically and feed on one another. It is not hard to find the singlemost powerful factor in the recent explosion of liability law that has brought with it a virtual revolution in the insurance industry and thinking about insurance: namely, the proliferation of cars, automobile traffic and the number of accidents, and the many temptations thus provided not only to the legal profession but to the automobile manufacturers themselves (e.g., by selling inexpensive cars that are easily damaged and then charging much more for the parts and repairs). The liability insurance industry could not have found more fertile ground for its rapid growth and could not have succeeded without its virtual partnership with the automobile industry and increasing antagonism with the consumer it was supposedly protecting. In turn, as the insurance companies (by their own willing agreement) under-wrote the new system, the insured public came to care less and less about the cost of car repairs and so those costs went up and up, and the cost of premiums followed, although "safe" drivers did not much appreciate the inevitable connection between the two.

In a different vein, medical malpractice began as a public response to the "law of silence," which prevented doctors from policing their own profession and punishing or preventing incompetence and wrongdoing. Liability lawyers were quick to see the virtues of tort law in the outside policing and penalizing "butcher" surgeons and incompetent practitioners. But as patients became more and more delighted to sue their physicians even when all due care had been taken and, in self-defense doctors felt obliged to pay increasingly backbreaking premiums for increased liability insurance, the plaintiff lawyers found that they in turn could demand larger and larger damages, further raising the price of insurance, allowing the insurance salesmen to insist on ever higher liability ceilings, and so on. The very possibility of a sympathetic jury and a large reward encouraged the most frivolous suits and the insurance companies stood by to pay. They then increased their premiums further to fund this dangerous game.

Insurance industry executives now speak wistfully of the days not long ago when they provided an essential public service, and liability lawyers talk with some amazement about cases that could not possibly have found their way to a courtroom only a few years earlier. Ronald Reagan, describing the fatal lawnmower case mentioned above, rightly asked, "Whatever happened to common sense?" But "common sense," as any good politician knows, is very much the product of other forces, including the various images and illusions of "public opinion" as well as the more tangible forces of economic exigency and experience. The liability crisis is the product of well-meaning intentions to protect the public and punish the irresponsible as well as the powerful influence of the insurance industry and the legal profession, and to resolve the crisis we need to understand and distinguish those well-meaning intentions and the perversion of common sense by a uniquely disturbing ideology, an overly eager readiness to blame, a greatly exaggerated demand for protection and compensation, and no small amount of plain old greed.

The problem, at bottom, is a philosophical problem. True, practical people may gasp at the idea that the infamously unresolvable "free will problem" might have some vital social and economic relevance to the well-being of society, but the systemic problem that lies at the heart of the current liability crisis has a conceptual core. That core is a very contemporary ethical theory: in its most vulgar form, it is "get whatever you can" and "don't worry, they're insured." But the profundity of the problem in fact raises some of those essentially human issues that go back (at least) to ancient times. The concept of fate and the inevitability of "accidents." The nature of tragedy and the basis of individual responsibility. Oedipus is still very much alive for us, and not just because Freud named a (dubious) nuclear family complex after him. Oedipus was heroic (though tragic) because he acknowledged his own horrible responsibilities, even though he could not have known (and was prevented from knowing) the nature or consequences of his actions. Recognizing his long-predicted but still unwitting crimes of killing his father and wedding his mother, he imposed a horrible but appropriate punishment on himself. Today, one is tempted to hypothesize, he would have called out the Thebian lawyers and sued the oracles for their misleading and incomplete predictions.

What we have lost, in a phrase, is our sense of personal responsibility, and it is no small irony that this has happened in a society where, more than anywhere else in history, we pride ourselves on our individuality. But this pride seems to be confined to our accomplishments. It gets excluded from our recklessness, our foolishness, and our ignorance. And this in turn (another irony) in a society that has the greatest communications and information technology of all time. Thirty years ago, "any fool would know," for example, that an untethered bull in a field may well be dangerous and that an unknown dog might bite. But today, quite explicit in our law, is the presumption that "you can't expect people to know." And so we demand compensation and punitive damages for our own stupidities, and we expect other people to accept the responsibility that we ourselves refuse to recognize.

There will always be "accidents" (the very origin of the word entails both unpredictability and blamelessness) but we have somehow only recently evolved the idea that we should suffer no such misfortunes, that someone must compensate us for our loss and make it come out (more or less, though preferably more) even. The ancient concept of fate, accordingly, is in ill-repute these days, confused as it is with a somewhat primitive belief in something like predestination and the inescapability of some prefigured future. But this in itself has much to say about the philosophical origins of our current crisis. French philosopher Paul Ricoeur has written at some length about the difference between the ancient Greek conception of fate and the more Judeo-Christian notion of temptation. The former placed the inevitability of our lives in the hands of the gods, or in any case, "out there," already written in the annals of Time. What was, was what had to be, and one suffered one's fate because that was what one had to do. But we have been brought up, as those ancient Greeks were not, with a keen sense of our own responsibilities. They instead had duties and divine obligations, of course, which themselves were a key ingredient in fate. But we, on the other hand, do not have fates; we are supposedly responsible for our own destinies. The future is unwritten, and an oracle or a fortune-teller to us is, even if correct, at most surprising or "spooky." But the notion of fate should not be lost, even in this new world of responsibility. Life doesn't always go as planned (or, as one wit has put it, "Life is what goes on while you're planning for the future"). But we are no longer philosophically equipped to cope with accidents, except to vaguely invoke our ignorance and "God's Will" or, preferably, to blame someone. And so we sue, for compensation, to get even, or just to prove that we are still "in charge."

Part Seven

Society and Culture

40

"Our Sick Society"

Every age, wrote the Danish philosopher Søren Kierkegaard in 1846, has its own characteristic depravity. The diagnostic tone of the word "depravity of the age" has its undeniable attractiveness, and so comes the question, "What's ours?"

When I ask that of my students, the answers are shockingly uniform. The word "despair" recurs with monotonous frequency, along with "dullness," "apathy," and "crisis." But most of all, they complain that everyone is "into themselves," that is, self-absorbed, though it is not always clear whether this is itself the depravity of the age or a reaction to it. A profound pessimism grips the class. Optimism is considered to be in poor taste. I ask why, but the answers are singularly unsatisfactory: "the energy crisis," "it's hard to get a job," "inflation," and "there's nothing good on TV." Hardly the earmarks of a sick society, much less the absurdity of the human condition.

Kierkegaard, too, complained that his age was dull and boring, devoid of passion if not gasoline. His equally miserable German contemporary, Arthur Schopenhauer, pondered the pointlessness of human existence in general over glasses of fine wine and between reputedly passionate but

This originally appeared in *Newsweek* magazine as a "My Turn" column, in the September 17, 1979, issue. Some of the themes have changed, but the thesis remains. Just this year, social pathologist Christopher Lasch released another new book but the same old lament: "moral and cultural disorder," "spiritual despair," and "the social fabric is unraveling" (*The True and Only Heaven* [Norton, 1991]). Reprinted by permission of *Newsweek*.

unhappy love affairs. The inventor of the diagnostic *kvetch,* Jean-Jacques Rousseau, couldn't get along in Paris, so he indicted society as such as "corrupt" and "depraved." Nietzsche referred to "the disease called man." And today, the same sensibility has a new champion, Christopher Lasch, whose book *The Culture of Narcissism* contains one more thoroughly pathological diagnosis of our lives as a whole.

What characterizes the diagnostic sensibility is its tenacious fatalism, its insistence on rejecting the whole of our culture, not just a piece of it. We are sick. We are not only unhappy: we are doomed by our own self-indulgence. Lasch's "narcissism" is a thoroughly *pathological* term, like Kierkegaard's "depravity," and it is part of the same self-righteous tradition. Of course, moralistic cynicism and collective self-flagellation are nothing new; even the Bible was full of it. But what gives authority to the diagnostic sensibility is its implicitly scientific appeal to medicine, using categories of health and disease.

A few years ago, we were similarly caught up in a game metaphor (games people play, life as a game, etc.). Now our favorite metaphor is disease, and societies are as prone to diagnosis as individuals. Even Jimmy Carter agrees that there is a "crisis of the American spirit." Thus Lasch strikes out, the diagnostician disgusted with his patient, at our self-indulgence and our consumer materialism, our refusal to sacrifice ourselves, the "waning of the sense of historical times," "fascination with celebrity and fear of competition." It is easy to agree, of course, but here it becomes essential to distinguish healthy criticism from the superior stance of the pathologist. Lasch's attack is not aimed at the lapses, failures, and hypocrisies of our shared social life, a life in which he himself plays a genuinely privileged role. He aims at the system as a whole, as if he were or could stand out of it, aloof from it, looking down in disgust but ignoring whatever virtues and values are there to be enjoyed by its participants.

Lasch sees a "collapse of personal life" in America and "a general crisis of Western culture." He attacks capitalism (of course) as well as our fear of death and aging. In fact, there is very little in the American way of life that is not subject to scorn in *The Culture of Narcissism,* the good along with the bad, our happiness as well as our hypocrisy. The examination is thorough, the diagnosis is serious, the prognosis is poor. The disease of "narcissism" consists in fact of our favorite virtues—"the pursuit of happiness," our search for individual fulfillment, and our insistence on personal expression—and is so basic to our lives that it is certainly "incurable," at least without killing the patient.

The disease metaphor itself deserves a diagnosis. What parades as cultural criticism in fact makes that criticism impossible. (Why worry about the manners of an already moribund patient?) And once one becomes a "patient," the pathological suspicion assures that every act is further proof of depravity; psychiatrists mistaken for patients have found it impossible to prove their sanity. The criteria are slippery; everything becomes a symptom, and the diagnostician cannot be proved wrong.

Behind the metaphor is a method; what seems to be concern betrays itself as self-indulgence, a self-righteous bitterness that declares society "depraved" in order that we may pity ourselves for being "caught" in it. We blame the world for our unhappiness or failures and, at the same time, we appear "courageous" by raising ourselves up "above" it. It is the classic technique of resentment, the two-faced emotion that condemns others in order to mask a sense of inadequacy. Now it picks on this detail, now on that one; it is only important that nothing escapes. Resentment is always ready to condemn other people's pleasures as "empty" or "depraved," and it is always ready to enjoy their misfortunes, "their just deserts," while gleefully predicting that the worst is yet to come. Resentment is insidious because it is infectious, respected, and admired even by those who are eventually mutilated by it.

Every age—if I, too, may be simple-minded—has its own peculiar forms of self-denigration. In a society that emphasizes the possibility of happiness, *un*happiness will appear as a kind of failure. Where privacy is a value, loneliness is bound to be a danger; where youth and mobility are prized, the family will of course be endangered, aging and death will be feared and a degree of social uncertainty will be inevitable. Life isn't perfect but that doesn't make it sick. In fact, to say so is what I would call, given the metaphorical currency, hypochondriacal.

Our so-called depravity is nothing but the deficit side of our chosen form of life, and I for one would want no other, given the plausible alternatives. That is not to deny that we are, as one of our possible presidents would say, in deep do-do, or that our psychological health and philosophical outlook may be due for some self-examination. But "narcissism" is a nasty and unnecessary word. Ever since those earlier days when the diagnosis was damnation instead of disease, our proper desire to promote a decent society has been undermined by those bitter voices demanding nothing less than total change, and thereby making change impossible. Indeed, perhaps the most tiresome depravity of our age is all this talk about the depravity of the age.

41

The New Illiteracy: *Vive les* Books!

He hath never fed of the dainties that are bred of a book
His intellect is not replenished;
He is only an animal,
Only sensible in the duller parts.

So sayeth the bard. But twenty years ago, Marshall McLuhan and other latter-day prophets were circulating the message that books were passé, the print medium moribund. Books and linear type were out. Television and other "hot" media—that leave us passive and cold—were in. Ironically, this thesis was read and accepted by hundreds of thousands of readers, who read McLuhan's book instead of watching television.

Today, the prophecy is becoming true. Best-selling books are more often than not preludes to TV miniseries or written after the movie (with lots of pictures, of course). Most college professors I know would fall over backward if they caught more than a handful of their students doing extra reading. (Indeed, some of them fall over backward when the students bother to do the required reading.) Illiteracy is an established part of American life—not just the obviously tragic illiteracy of those who cannot read at all, but the more subtly tragic illiteracy of those who can read quite well and read all the time—sports-page headlines, the front page of the *National Enquirer* at the checkout stand, food-can labels, billboards, and an occasional

From *The Austin American-Statesman,* December, 14, 1980. © Austin American-Statesman. Reprinted by permission of the publisher.

People magazine photo caption. But they don't read books. Or any article that requires a turn of the page (as in, "cont'd, p. xxx").

A friend in publishing tells me that a best-selling book in this country might reach five percent of the population. And that means *The Scarsdale Diet* or Sidney Sheldon's latest pot-boiler. A "good book," one worth encouraging others to read that perhaps provides some intelligent basis for living a better life or understanding the world, might reach one percent at most.

In a country of almost 200 million readers, serious general-interest magazines such as *Harpers* or *Atlantic Monthly* struggle to keep afloat with a readership of less than 500,000 (.25 percent). I saw an ad last week that began, "If you read only one book this year"—as if reading a book were an activity akin to taking the kids to the zoo, or, for some, making the annual visit to the place of worship of their choice. Indeed, if books are food for thought, our national diet is well below the sustenance level.

Part of the problem seems to be that, in this age of easy, passive entertainment, reading books is an effort, and inevitably, those who make the effort are branded "elitists." Why do something that is more difficult when you can sit back and hypnotize yourself before the tube?

A few months ago, Isaac Asimov warned us in *Newsweek* magazine that we are a nation of illiterates, no longer sufficiently well-informed to participate in a democracy or make intelligent choices about major issues. He was answered with a flood of mail branding him an "elitist" and, of course, accusing him of self-interest, since he is one of the few writers these days who actually makes a living off of those who read. But the counter-argument, that books and linear media have been replaced by the new electronic media, is still so strong (although "Marshall McLuhan" is a name that fewer than three in a hundred of my students can recognize) that it needs to be refuted, if possible, once and for all. Books, in a word, are irreplaceable. They admit of no substitutes, and the "movie version" just won't do.

What is so special about books? What do they give us that TV, even good TV, does not? I think there are two answers, both important. One is that books, not the "hot" media, remain the primary vehicle of our culture and independent, critical thought. The other is that the activity of reading books, as opposed to watching TV, requires imagination and a critical facility that is forcibly suspended in the continuous onslaught of TV programming.

The presupposition of culture as a continuity of images, shared symbols and stories cannot be sustained in a medium that changes its image from season to season. Culture is continuity, and those who complain that today's students and adolescents have no appreciation or respect for our country or their elders ought to take a good look at the transient images, symbols, and stories that are supposed to provide that continuity. When every generation grows up with an entirely new system of symbols and heroes, there is bound to be a "gap" between them. (And a generation, these days, tends to be two to five years, at the most.)

This is not to say that the symbols derived from books are in themselves better than the characters developed on TV. Is Long John Silver really more profound a character than Columbo? Is Captain Ahab really more culturally significant than Sam Malone on "Cheers"? If the answer is yes, that is only because of time and continuity. A culture that no longer shares its symbols is no longer a culture.

This is not to say that only the old literary symbols are the exclusive domain of culture. Given a framework, new symbols are always entering the picture, and the old ones are breaking down. But this, too, requires books and reading. Black symbols and Chicano symbols and Japanese symbols enter our culture first of all through the books we read and only on extremely rare occasions, as in *Roots* and *Shogun,* is this possible through the electronic media. (And they were both "runaway best sellers" before their respective miniseries, of course).

Books not only continue the culture, they also make change and correction possible. Part of their advantage in this is simply political: There are a lot more publishers than TV stations; there are new small and independent publishers every day, and it is far cheaper to print and make available a book than it is to produce even a few minutes of television. Some of this difference is possibly to be corrected by multistation cable television, but for now and in the foreseeable future, it is in books and in print that the new ideas and their details will keep circulating, that uncensored criticism and the heated dialogue of democracy will go on.

But even if television were to become more varied, less subject to political and sensitive moral pressures, more imaginative and critical, the second consideration shows us why the new illiteracy would still be a tragedy. It is the limitation of print, the spaces between the words and the lines that force us to think, to imagine, to supply what the medium itself does not. You can't stop to think about an idea on television unless you shut off the set and miss the rest of the show. (Imagine a talk-show host, suggesting that the audience take five minutes to think about what the guest has just said.)

It is often said that "a good book is one which you can't put down," but I would counter that the best books are precisely those that force you to put them down, to think about them, to absorb the images, to imagine oneself even more a part of the world between those pages. Television can't do that, nor can films. Radio, too, is relentless, in the sense that it demands too little of us except for listening. But books give us only symbols; we have to do the work. Books are exercise for the intelligence. Reading is a form of thinking, a kind of work as well as a pleasure and a responsibility.

At the beginning of this year, I came across a freshman in college who declared himself with some pride to be a "born-again" Christian. I noticed with some curiosity that he was leafing through a set of flash cards with biblical phrases printed on them. I asked him if he had ever read "The Book," and he answered no, without embarrassment. I asked him, as politely as possible, whether he thought that the Bible was indeed "the revealed word of God," and he answered, also politely, that indeed it was. The paradoxical fact that he believed this and had never bothered to read it struck him not at all, but to me it seemed to sum up the temper of the times. Even if The Word is revealed in a book, it seems, reading is just too much trouble.

42

Culture Tells Us Who We Are

In our aggressively egalitarian society, "culture" has always been a suspect word, suggesting the pretentions of an effete and foolish leisure class, like the grand dames spoofed in Marx Brothers' films. But the pretentions of a self-appointed cultural elite notwithstanding, "culture" actually refers to nothing more objectionable than a system of shared symbols and examples that hold a society together. Within a culture we are kindred spirits, whether or not we agree or get along, simply because we understand one another.

A recent and somewhat frightening Rockefeller Foundation study on the state of the humanities in American life reported that the vast majority of even our most educated citizens is ignorant of the common literature and history that reinforce not only cultural identity but also moral choices. Doctors, lawyers, and business executives are in positions of great responsibility, but often have little or no training in the ethical background that makes their critical choices meaningful.

Across our society in general, we find ourselves increasingly fragmented, split into factions and "generation gaps" just because the once-automatic assumption of a shared culture—something beyond shared highways, television programming, and economic worries—is no longer valid.

In our schools, according to the Rockefeller report, the problem lies largely in what has recently been hailed as the "back to basics" movement,

---

This first appeared in the *Los Angeles Times,* August 4, 1980, several years before E. D. Hirsch's best-selling book on the same topic. Needless to say, matters have not improved since. Reprinted with permission.

which includes no cultural content whatsoever, just skills and techniques. Reading is taught as a means of survival in the modern world, not as a source of pleasure and of shared experience. The notion of "great books" is viewed by most educators as an archaic concept, relegated to the museum of old teaching devices, such as the memorization in Greek of passages from Homer.

But are "great books" (and legends, poems, paintings, and plays) indeed the only conduit of culture, or have they been replaced by more accessible and effortless media of transmission: for example, television and films?

Films, to be sure, have entered into our cultural identity in an extremely powerful way; indeed, it is not clear that a person who knows nothing of Bogart or Chaplin, who has never seen (young) Brando or watched a Western, could claim to be fully part of American culture. But these are classics, and they have some of the same virtue as great books; their symbols, characters, and moral examples have been around long enough to span generations and segments of our population, and to provide a shared vocabulary, shared heroes, and shared values. No such virtue is to be found in television series that disappear every two years (or less), films that survive but a season or "made-for-TV" movies with a lifetime of two hours minus commercial breaks.

"Television culture" is no culture at all, and it is no surprise that, when kids change heroes with the season, their parents don't (and couldn't possibly) keep up with them. The symbolism of *The Iliad* and *The Scarlet Letter,* however much we resented being force-fed them in school, is something we can all be expected to share. The inanities of contemporary sitcoms, viewed by no matter how many millions of people, will not replace them.

The same is true of our musical heritage. The Beatles are only a name to most twelve-year-olds. Beethoven, by contrast, continues to provide the musical themes we can assume (even if wrongly) that all of us have heard, time and time again. This isn't snobbery; it's continuity.

A professor recently wrote in the *Wall Street Journal* that he had mentioned Socrates in class (at a rather prestigious liberal arts college) and had drawn blanks from more than half the students. My colleagues and I at The University of Texas swap stories about references that our students don't catch. Even allowing generous leeway for our own professional prejudices and misperceptions of what is important, the general picture is disturbing. We are becoming a culture without a culture, lacking fixed points of reference and a shared vocabulary.

It would be so easy, so inexpensive, to change: a reading list for high school students; a little encouragement in the media; a lot more encouragement from and for the parents; a bit more enlightenment in our college curricula; better teaching; fewer requirements and more inspiration. But then again, I wonder, who cares? I suspect that our leaders like their constituency uninformed and uninspired, our schools would rather require than inspire, and a good many parents, while "wanting the best" for their kids, nevertheless find themselves threatened by a culture that they themselves have not mastered either.

With all this in mind, I decided to see just what I could or could not assume among my students, who are generally bright and better educated than average (given that they are taking philosophy courses, hardly an assumed interest among undergraduates these days). I gave them a name quiz, in effect, of some of the figures that, on most people's list, would rank among the most important and most often referred to in Western culture. What follows are some of the results, in terms of the percentage of students who recognized them:

Socrates, 87%; Louis XIV, 59%; Moses, 90%; Hawthorne, 42%; John Milton, 35%; Trotsky, 47%; Donatello, 8%; Copernicus, 47%; Puccini, 11%; Charlemagne, 40%; Virginia Woolf, 25%; Estes Kefauver, 8%; Debussy, 14%; Giotto, 4%; Archduke Ferdinand, 21%; Lewis Carroll, 81%; Charles Dodgson, 5%; Thomas Aquinas, 68%; Spinoza, 19%; Moliere, 30%; Tchaikovsky, 81%; Darwin, 56%; Karl Marx, 65%; Faulkner, 43%; George Byron, 18%; Goethe, 42%; Raphael, 17%; Euripides, 8%; Homer, 39%; T. S. Eliot, 25%; Rodin, 24%; Mozart, 94%; Hitler, 97%; Wagner, 34%; Dante, 25%; Louis XVI, 25%; Kafka, 38%; Stravinsky, 57%; John Adams, 36%.

A friend who gave the same quiz to his English composition class got results more than 50% lower on average.

I suppose that many people will think the quiz too hard, the names often too obscure—but that, of course, is just the point. The students, interestingly enough, did not feel this at all—not one of them. They "sort of recognized" most of the names and felt somewhat embarrassed at not knowing exactly who these people were. There was no sense that the quiz was a "trivia" contest (as in, "What's the name of Dale Evans's horse?") and there were no accusations of elitism or ethnocentrism. The simple fact was that they knew these names were part of their culture, and in too many cases they knew that they weren't—but should be—conversant with them. That, in itself, is encouraging.

43

Literature and the Education of the Emotions

Why books? The arguments I hear these days, from some very literate and book-loving theorists, make it sound as if the love of books is nothing but self-serving, not just for writers and publishers but for the "elite" who maintain their political superiority with the pretensions of "culture." Literacy is a capitalist device to separate out the advantaged, some Marxists say (on the basis of very wide reading). Literacy is the ploy of a white, English-speaking elite to render "illiterate" peoples from a different culture, with a different language and a different history, say some very learned educators. And, indeed, there is something very right about these arguments: whatever our clumsy attempts at democratic education, there remains a drastic difference in class and racial mobility, a difference that is easily and often measured in precisely those tidbits of knowledge that come from a literary education. Much of what is called "literacy" is indeed cultural pretension, and it is not hard to argue that, in a nation with a nonwhite unemployment rate of well over 20 percent, literature is a luxury that is practically, if not culturally, restricted to the relatively leisurely upper-middle class.

Against such arguments, what can be said in favor of books? There are nonliterate cultures, of course, and they are very much alive. But it is worth asking what they have instead of books, or rather, what it is that makes books so important to us. The response I want to defend here

This study began with a conference on "Literacy" at Simon Fraser University in 1981 and originally appeared in *Literacy, Society, and Schooling* (Cambridge University Press, 1985). Reprinted by permission of the publisher.

is this: Books, not television, remain the primary vehicle of our culture, and not just as the source of our concepts and our ideals and our heroes. What is more difficult to show but just as important, is that books are an important source of shared emotions as well as a means of understanding emotions in other people and providing a safe and central vehicle for having emotions. In other societies, there are other vehicles, and, one might argue, some of them are superior. ("For what?" needless to say, remains the crucial question.) But for most of us, a literacy-deprived life is too often an emotionally limited life, too, for good substitutes are hard to find.

A second part of this answer is that the activity of reading books, again as opposed to watching television or any number of intellectually more passive entertainments, requires an exercise of the imagination and the use of a critical faculty that is forcibly suspended through the continuous onslaught of TV programming. Or for that matter, through the continuous onslaught of words and images from almost any source—lectures and films, for example—that forces our attention rather than our critical and imaginative participation. Emotions are not just reactions; they are social imaginative constructions. Here is the key to a "free people"; a "nation of readers" who know how to enjoy the privacy of a book, in which the wheels of their imaginations can spin at will their private conversations and commentary can be perfected silently with or against the greatest minds of our history. But here, too, is an often unappreciated key to a rich and meaningful emotional life, for emotions, as I shall be arguing, are integral to the imagination and both exercisable and educatable through reading as well.

If you haven't read *War and Peace*, what have you missed? What have you missed if you haven't read Dickens, or Camus, or Borges? Or, for that matter Galbraith, Marx, Mill, or Einstein? One might respond that you've missed a certain pleasure in life, or an evening's entertainment or, in the case of *War and Peace*, a couple of weeks' engrossed involvement. Then there are the more practical replies: "You may have missed some important information," or, perhaps, there is the possibility of blowing a job interview or a cocktail party conversation. And then there are the political answers, though rarely presented as such; not reading certain books excludes you from a literary elite, which also happens to be the power elite, with all of the opportunities and status thereof.

I find all of these answers to be inadequate. Some are self-congratulatory, some are vulgarly pragmatic; most are false in fact and some are just resentment. And yet, the literature on literacy does not always make clear just what a good answer to such a question might be.

Spokespeople for the humanities, full of self-congratulation, often give lectures, invariably reprinted in alumni bulletins if not also in the local newspapers, insisting that the liberal and literary arts will make a person a better human being, solve the world's problems, and enlighten "developing" countries to the wonders of Western life. Indeed, one gets the impression that a student who reads becomes something of a saint in this day of television movies, video games, and drive-in blood-and-gore horror films. If this pronouncement proves to be without foundation (Nero, Mussolini, and the Borgias were all well-read) the same spokespeople will retreat to the contradictory idea that reading is good in itself and "its own reward." (I have philosophical doubts about anything being "good in itself," but let's let that pass.) In any case, however well such speeches succeed in attracting funds for the annual giving campaign, they surely fail as defenses of literacy.

On the other hand, there is a clearly practical problem of literacy in our public schools, which has little to do with the self-congratulatory advantages of a liberal education. Students with high school diplomas can't read or write a coherent sentence. In the best schools, students haven't heard of the Oedipus complex or read the classics, or even classic comic books. Christopher Lasch writes in his *Culture of Narcissism* of students who can't date the Russian revolution within a decade or so, and in a survey I carried out last year for the *Los Angeles Times** I found that a majority of honors college students didn't know the names of Faulkner, Goethe, Debussy, Virginia Woolf (almost everyone knew the phrase "who's afraid of . . . ," but didn't know where it came from). They didn't know who Trotsky was, or Niels Bohr, or Spinoza, or Kafka. A small but frightening percentage didn't really know who Hitler was.

So, on the one hand we have the congratulatory speeches about the liberal arts; on the other we have an admittedly desperate educational situation. Between them, we can see the battle between "the basics" and the need for "elitist" education developing, with the inevitable consequence that the question of literacy becomes a political problem; literacy becomes status and "the basics" become the focus of an education that is conscientiously devoid of anything more than the "basic" ability to read and write.

If we are to cut through such problems, it is important, I would argue, to begin by distinguishing three different kinds of literacy. For the most part, we've been arguing about only two. The first is the ability to read and write—the nuts-and-bolts part of literacy—the skills that everyone in this society *must* learn if they are to have any possible chance at decent jobs, fair treatment, and protection. This is "functional" literacy. It has

*See essay 42.

to do with being able to read a simple contract (despite the fact that most of the contracts that we sign are unreadable anyway). It has to do with being able to write a letter of application or reading a warning label or an advertisement. Its practical importance is unquestionable, and—therefore—usually unquestioned. This is not the realm of philosophical discourse about the nature of the good society or the mind of humanity.

Second, there is "literacy" in the snobbish sense, meaning "well-read." This is the sense defended by liberal arts college presidents, for this is the commodity they sell. It is the sort of literacy that is paraded across the pages of the *New York Review of Books* and is displayed by readers thereof. It is having read not only *Moby Dick* but also *Typee,* having Nietzsche and Eliot quotes at the tip of one's tongue, and being able to recite lines of Chaucer or Shakespeare without pausing for even a moment in one's conversation. Such literacy is unabashedly elitist, often competitive (if not intrinsically so), and a mark of social superiority (which is not, I hasten to add, an argument against it). But between the "functional" and the high-falootin' is a third kind of literacy, which is what concerns me here.

This third kind of literacy is really what one might call "knowledgeability," except that the word smacks too much of mere information and know-how and too little of the affective and the experiential, which is crucial to it. It is a type of literacy that is concentrated in but not exclusive to books, which—today—also involves film and the other arts. It can come from conversations on the street, lectures, and political rallies but, for a variety of reasons, it revolves around the printed word. It has to do with participating in certain basic or even essential experiences, knowing if only vicariously a form of life that touches on our own. In this sense, reading *The Iliad* is not just an exercise in reading (which is what it too often becomes in high school), and it is not a matter of being able to say you've read it or occasionally drop learned allusions. There is a sense in which living through the Trojan War is a part of all of us, expected of us, if only in the safe and bloodless form of newly translated Homeric verses. Reading Einstein or Darwin is not just getting knowledge; it is sharing intellectual adventures that lie at the heart of our civilization. In this sense, literacy is a kind of love, not an ability or an accomplishment. It is participation, education in the classical sense—being brought up to be part of something, not just successful in a career.

Discussions of literacy slip between the three senses with disconcerting ease. Sometimes literacy is compared to utter illiteracy, the inability to even write one's own name. Sometimes illiteracy is ignorance, sometimes social incompetence. Sometimes it is compared in a scholarly way with what is called the "oral" tradition in literature, and accused of imperialism in the demeaning thereof. But, of course, what one says about literacy and what one compares it to depends entirely on what one means by it.

The third kind of literacy is often confused with a type of escapism or merely "vicarious" involvement in life. The experiences one gains from books are said to be not "real" experiences but purely formal, detached, isolated from life rather than a part of it. I think that this is basically wrong, but to show this, I will have to turn to my concern for the emotions in literature. The question of what is a "real" experience and what is not is not nearly so simple as the critics of "vicarious book experience" make it out to be.

Literature is vital to the education of the emotions. One very difficult question concerns what is to count as literature—just *Moby Dick* or *Treasure Island* too? And for that matter, what about "Mork and Mindy" and "Hill Street Blues"? Here's an equally difficult question: If literature is said to serve the emotions, just how can emotions—which are generally considered to be unlearned, instinctual, visceral responses—be educated at all? Perhaps, one might argue, literature can serve to provide models of self-restraint and control of the emotions, but this hardly counts as the education *of* the emotions. Perhaps, in the modern version of an ancient debate between Plato and Aristotle, it can be argued that literature provides an "outlet" for emotions, which might otherwise have their dangerous expression in real life. But as we know from the endless debates about violence and pornography, it is not at all clear from the evidence (and the evidence seems to be one of the lesser considerations) that such literature does not motivate and inspire such behavior instead of sublimating or defusing it. Whether inspiration or sublimation, however, the obvious effect of literature on emotions is hardly evidence of education. One might argue that some literature stultifies and numbs the emotions, but this hardly helps make our case for literature and the emotions either.

What we need, first of all, is a new and better conception of emotion. If an emotion is a physiological response, no matter how complex, then it will not do to talk of education, though we might talk in some limited way of cause and effect. William James, who wrote a classic treatise on the nature of emotions and came back to the theme many times in his career, defined an emotion as the sensation of visceral change, prompted by some unsettling perception. But as James unfolded his global vision of the human mind and its abilities, this physiological view of emotions tended to be weakened, watered down and, finally, ignored. In his brilliant discussion of religious experience—a complex emotional experience if there ever is one—James ignores all but completely his physiological theory of emotion and focuses instead on the imaginative and creative aspects of faith as an emotion. Indeed, in his less transcendental discussions of curiosity and knowledge, the education of emotion is very much in evidence, and even in his writings on emotion as such, there is much discussion about changing one's emotions by way of changing one's behavior, one's thoughts, and one's outlook—in other words, by educating them.

James's retreat from the physiological view of emotions to a view both more flattering and more pragmatic led him and leads us to a realization that is not readily forthcoming so long as one thinks (as James did in his essays) of an emotion as an emergency secretion of adrenalin, as in panic, sudden anger, or "love at first sight." Such emotions are indeed blatantly physiological (though this is surely not all that they are) and difficult to control—much less advise intelligently—given the urgent nature of the circumstances. But the emotions that mean the most to us are not those transient moments of panic, fury, and infatuation; they are such enduring passions as lifelong love and righteous indignation, which are clearly learned and cultivated with experience and which prompt and inspire us to actions far more significant and considered than a start of panic, an "outburst" of anger, or the often embarrassing first flush of love. Here, too, we can appreciate the importance of emotions and their education. It is not mere "control" that concerns us; it is cultivation, development, refinement. True love is not "natural"; it is taught, and learned. Moral indignation is nothing less than the end result of a moral education. Indeed, even fear—the most primitive of emotions—is learned more often than not, and the supposedly obvious examples of "inborn fear" do not make the general education of this emotion any less essential to life.

The most significant emotions are those which play the largest roles in the structuring of our lives. Philosophers sometimes talk as if reason can and should do this, but no novelist or poet could or would try to define a theme or a character through reason alone. The structures of literature as of life are such grand emotions: love; patriotism; indignation; a sense of duty or honor or justice; and the less admirable passions of jealousy, envy, and resentment. One might try to teach such emotions and establish such strictures through general principles or slogans but one is much more assured of success teaching by example or, better still, through experience itself. Where direct experience is not available—as it often is not and is not wanted—"vicarious" experience will do the job. Thus the heart of literature is and has always been *stories*, narratives that provide not only examples of virtue and vice but also the opportunity to enter into a shared and established emotional world. There is and always will be considerable debate about the place of "morality" in literature. Literature is, whatever else it may be, the communication of emotion. But this need not depend on plot or narrative; it can be conveyed through form as well. Indeed, one is tempted to suggest that there may be as much emotion in the formalism of William Gass as in the moralizing of John Gardner.

What is an emotion, that it can be educated? If I may summarize a theory and three books in a phrase, I would say that emotions are essentially a species of judgment. They are learned and intelligent, even if they are not always articulate. They contain essential insights that are often more accurate and more useful—even more "true"—than the much deliberated truths of reason that contradict them. (If reason tells us that our petty loves and desires are of no importance while our emotions proclaim them magnificent, it might well be foolish to be reasonable.) "Every passion," wrote Nietzsche, "has its own quantum of reason." Indeed, more than a quantum; it is its own reason. "The heart has its reasons," insisted Pascal, "that reason does not fathom." Every emotion is a way of constructing the world. It is a measure of place and importance in which we and all things of significance get that significance. Love creates its love, as anger indicts the accused. To enter into an emotion is not to "enter into someone else's brain." It is to participate in a way of being in the world, a way in which things matter, a way charged with shared understandings and obsessions.

To educate the emotions is nothing like the stimulation of a physiological state, though to be sure that can and sometimes does follow hard on certain emotional experiences. To educate others is to provide them with an opportunity to have that emotion, to learn when it is appropriate —and when inappropriate—to learn its vicissitudes and, if the term isn't too jarring, its *logic*. To learn to love is to learn to see another person in virtually infinite perspective, but it is also to learn the dangers of love, the disappointments, the foolishness, and the failures. Some of this one learns firsthand, but it would be a tragic love life indeed that had to go through the dozens of stories of love, lust, and betrayal in the first person illiterate. Not to mention the various wounds and greater injuries that one would have to suffer to learn even a chapter of *War and Peace,* firsthand.

In a rather different context, Israel Scheffler has discussed the breach between emotions and reason as utterly destructive of education.* He caricatures the standard view of emotion "as commotion—an unruly inner disturbance." The "hostile opposition of cognition and emotion," he says, "distorts everything it touches: mechanizing science, it sentimentalizes art, while portraying ethics and religion as twin swamps of feeling and un-

*"In Praise of the Cognitive Emotions," *Columbia Educational Review,* 1977.

reasoned commitment." Education, he goes to say, "is split into two grotesque parts—unfeeling knowledge and mindless arousal."

And emotion, we might add, gets lost, for it is neither unfeeling nor mindless, though it is both knowledge and arousal. It is knowledgeable arousal, one might say, educated through experiences in some sense not one's own, through shared stories, through literature.

The influences of literature on the emotions can be catalogued into four groups, over and above the brute stimulation of passions which, while dramatic and often effective, should not really count as education. A well-wrought example or story may inspire feelings of the strongest sort: of sympathy or compassion, of anger or indignation, but education means learning something, not just repeating a familiar feeling on the basis of an equally familiar stimulus.

1. Literature tells us what other people feel. The great significance of the increasing (if still largely unread) availability of foreign literature, for instance, is that it informs English readers about the circumstances and expressions of passion in people unlike ourselves. The sense of shame in Indian family life; the sense of honor in Samurai Japan. In one sense, such information does not educate our emotions at all, but rather allows us to get some glimmer of understanding about the emotions of other people. But if emotions are judgments about the world, they are also influenced—and partially constituted—by knowledge *about* those judgments and their context. It is of no small value to our own emotional perspective to learn that romantic love is very much a "Western" emotion, for instance, or that other societies have conceptions of family intimacy and attachment far stronger than our own.

2. Literature not only lets us know that *other people have such and such emotions; it also tells us* how *they feel.* It lets us imagine "how we would feel if. . . ." Sometimes, the circumstances are recognizable but there is good reason not to know about them firsthand. The descriptions of the battles of Borodino in Tolstoi's *War and Peace* and Waterloo in Stendahl's *Charterhouse of Parma* give us powerful portraits of "how it feels" to be on one of the great battlefields of the nineteenth century, but these are experiences most of us would gladly accept "secondhand." Few of us would want to actually suffer the remorse of Emma Bovary or Anna Karenina, but it is of no small importance to our emotional education that we have, at a safe distance, understood "what it would feel like if. . . ."

3. Literature allows an actual recreation of an emotion. This may not be true of the descriptions of Borodino or Waterloo, or for that matter, of Emma or Anna's final despairing moments. But tales of injustice, such as *Les Miserables,* do something more than inform us "what it feels like when. . . ." Our sense of outrage and injustice *is* a genuine sense of outrage, not just an understanding or a reflection of it. The Northern sense of moral indignation on reading Stowe's *Uncle Tom's Cabin* was not a vicarious emotion but, in every sense, it was the real thing. Emotions are not isolated feelings but worldviews, and worlds unlike sensations require structure, plot, and details. Literature provides that structure, the plot, those details, and once we have been submerged in them, the emotion is already with us. (It does not follow as a mere effect.)

4. *Literature helps us articulate emotions we already have.* Zola's descriptions of a harsh reality give us a language in which we can express our own sense of discontent, and examples for comparison. Marx is, whatever else, a powerful writer, who gives any sympathetic reader an enormous range of metaphors, as well as facts and theories, to bolster a large sense of dissatisfaction and give it expressions. So too Rousseau. Literature gives us examples, models, metaphors, new words, carefully crafted descriptions as well as whole structures in which and through which we can understand and express our own feelings. The education of the emotions is, in part, learning how to articulate them, learning what to expect from them, and learning how to use them.

It should be clear from the above four categories of "influences" that the education of emotions is at least as involved in learning to appreciate the other people's passions as it is in molding one's own emotions. This seems odd, or merely "empathetic," only so long as we cling to the idea that emotions are our own "inner" occurrences, the private domain of each individual and exclusively his or hers, not to be shared (at most expressed or confessed) with anyone else. But emotions are *public* occurrences. Not only are the expressions and the context of emotion evident to a sensitive observer; the structures and values of emotion are also in and an essential part of a culture. We feel this most dramatically in a mob at a political rally or in a large crowd at a sports event. The emotion is not just "in the heads" of the hundreds or tens of thousands of people present; it is literally "in the air," with an existence of its own, in which the people participate. But much the same is true of more modest emotional gatherings. We sit around with our own family and feel the complex of loving; defensive and competitive passions fill the room. Or, we sit around while visiting with someone else's family, sensing the passion in the air but feeling quite "out of it." Visiting a strange culture gives us the sometimes overpowering sense of being present in the midst of emotions that we not only fail to share but fail to understand. Accompanying visitors to our own society who feel similarly throws into perspective our own emotional atmospheres, which, like the (unpolluted) air, is so familiar and so essential to us that we take it for granted and do not notice it at all.

Emotions are public in the sense that they are shared views, with shared values, based on shared judgments. Such judgments depend, to an extent rarely appreciated, on the particular language of the culture. A culture without an emotion word is not likely to experience that emotion. Certain Eskimo cultures lack a word for anger, for example, and it can be persuasively argued that they do not get angry. One might say that the lack of a word indicates a lack of interest, just as a multiplicity of words suggests an emotional obsession. The French, as we all know, have a multiplicity of words (and distinctions) for romantic love; the Russians have numerous words for suffering; Yiddish abounds in words for despair. American English, it is worth noting, has a high proportion of its emotion vocabulary dedicated to the identification of different kinds of anger, while Oxonian English has a remarkably flexible vocabulary for contempt. Cultural generalizations may always be suspect, but it is worth noting the distribution of emotion words in peoples' own language. Not coincidentally, the language circumscribes values and judgments, and these in turn determine a distinctive outlook on the world.

How does one learn to participate in an emotional culture? In a word, by becoming literate: not necessarily in the nuts-and-bolts sign-your-name read-a-contract sense, perhaps, although it cannot be denied that much of our emotional culture is defined and communicated by the written word, in newspapers and street-corner pamphlets as well as best sellers and subway and highway advertisements. Nor is it necessarily by being part of that elite literary culture that proclaims itself the bearer of the better emotions. To participate in the emotions of a culture is to speak its language; to share its value judgments; to partake in its stories, its history, and its heritage. To have an emotion—even the most exquisitely private and personal emotion—is to be part of an emotional culture. Teenagers in love fervently believe that they alone feel a passion all but unknown in the history of the world—and share this feeling with a million other teenagers (and post-teenagers). They are all part of the world of romantic love, a world promulgated and advertised with a ferocity unprecedented in the history of emotional propaganda. Orwell tried to be terrifying by imagining a society brainwashed by "the Anti-sex league." Far more terrifying may be the present reality of an entire society, awash in love-and-sex sentimentality and so comfortable with it that it even seems "natural."

and discourages jealousy, but our vision of envy is not so clear. It would be a study of no small importance and enormous scope: the place of envy in American literature, and American life.

The kind of argument that is merely suggested here—the ways in which literature defines and teaches emotion—could and should be developed for a spectrum of emotions and a wide body of international literature. But the connection between emotions and literature should be getting clear: it is not just that literature inspires or illustrates emotions and provides us with examples of them. Literature, taken broadly as the shared perspectives and narratives of a culture, actually defines emotions and brings them into being. To teach literature *is* to educate the emotions, although—like any teaching—this can be done consciously or unconsciously, competently or incompetently. To teach literature is to teach how other people feel, and how we would feel if. . . . It is to teach us *to* feel certain emotions, and to articulate and understand the emotions we do have. Literacy is not just good for or food for the emotions; it is, ultimately, what the emotions are all about.

One of our oldest debates concerns a healthy or a deleterious effect of the emotions we experience "vicariously" through literature (including drama and film). Plato fought Aristotle on the desirability of "catharsis" in the theater, and long and varied traditions of moral psychologists throughout the history of Christian theology have argued the acceptability of vicarious experiences of the more sinful emotions as opposed to the actual sins. (Vicarious faith and Platonic love presented very different issues.) Greek comedies presented deception, cowardice, and foolishness but, the question was, did these encourage or discourage these vices in their audience? Medieval morality plays had as their unquestioned intention the discouragement of lust, envy, gluttony, anger, pride, etc., but it was a burning question then as now whether the portrayal of such passions, even unsympathetically, would nevertheless stimulate precisely the sins depicted. Today, the argument regards pornography and violence on television. The question, as ever, is whether such "vicarious" experiences, even if presented or intended in a discouraging light, have a positive or negative effect on the genuine emotions.

The distinction between vicarious and genuine emotions, however, is not at all so clear as the proponents of the various traditional moral arguments would suggest. So, too, the charge that people who read books have thereby only vicarious emotions, not real experiences, does not hold up to examination. Of course, there is an obvious difference that can be granted right from the start: readers of a terrifying or bloody novel (e.g., *Frankenstein, All Quiet on the Western Front*) or viewers of a horrifying movie (e.g., *Jaws, King Kong*) have the luxury of fear, terror, and horror without the real risk of harm. The "willing suspension of disbelief" explains *how* they have such experiences. What is by no means so evident is *why* they choose to have them. Whether they are real experiences of fear or not they are certainly emotions—real as such—of some kind, and this needs to be explained. In this regard it might also be wise to distinguish—as is too rarely done—between the emotions of fear and terror on the one hand and horror on the other. What gets experienced while reading frightening books and viewing "horror movies" is properly horror, not terror. Terror, one might say, is real fear; it believes in the danger of its object. No "willing suspension" here. Horror, on the other hand, tends to be horror regarding an idea, one step removed. We are horrified by the very idea of a war, or the very idea of abortion, or the very idea that a married woman might actually fall in love with a younger man. We do not experience genuine terror reading or viewing a "thriller," but we may well feel genuine horror on reading or viewing a horror tale. Vicarious horror, in other words, is real horror, whether or not vicarious terror is real fear. Both terror and horror should be distinguished, we might add, from mere grossness (a vivid description of an abortion, a close-up of the effects of a gunshot), which grade-B writers and film-makers now tend to employ instead of the more artful skills of suspense and true horror.

Discussions of vicarious emotions (and many discussions of emotion) tend to focus much too heavily on the emotion of fear. Readers of Stendahl, we may readily admit, do not really fear the sudden impact of a bullet in their backs, and it is also extremely debatable that they can literally be said to fear for the fictional hero. But we already mentioned that the emotion of moral indignation we experience while reading *Uncle Tom's Cabin* is the genuine emotion. Indeed, moral indignation, even in "real life" (and in what sense was *Uncle Tom's Cabin* not "real life"?), is an emotion that observes and judges rather than participates. The result of moral indignation may be real action, but the emotion itself is quite real regardless of the possibilities for action. Indeed, *Uncle Tom's Cabin* inspired very real action, even if the events depicted in the book were fictional.

What we just said about moral indignation holds of a great many important emotions. Certainly grief, sadness, amusement, compassion, and pity are real enough whether or not the persons and events on the pages or on the screen are real. So, too, the power of romantic love experienced by the reader or viewer of the hero or heroine. Who would deny that love is often experienced at a distance, directed at persons whom we may know much less than we know that fictional character with whom we have briefly shared a vicarious adventure? Who would deny that the persons with whom we fall in love are often fictional, creations of our own imaginations or Freudian "phantasms" left over from more primal love experiences? What is true is also true of hate, and a dozen other passions besides. Indeed, once we start examining the list, it begins to look as if everything we experience while reading is real—except, that is, the story and its characters.

A proper analysis of vicarious emotions would take us far beyond the limited claims of this essay, but the essence of a theory can be sketched very briefly. It is typically argued that an emotion is vicarious and therefore not a real emotion because its object—what it is about—is not real. Now in this sense very few emotions are "real," since almost all emotions involve a certain subjective reshaping of their objects, whether it is in love, hate, anger, or simple compassion. The attention of every emotion is selective (we look for virtues in love, vices in hate). Most emotions involve a certain distance from their object, even when it seems that we have never been closer to them. Yet every emotion constitutes its own object, as the particular (perhaps peculiar) object of that emotion, even if that same object and emotion are shared by hundreds or millions of people—as the great books may be, and the emotions contained therein. To say that the object of an emotion is fictional (and known to be so) is therefore not necessarily to say that the emotion is not real. To insist on this absurdity would be to either limit the range of "real" emotions to a pathetic and extremely timid group of realistic attitudes, or it would be to deny the reality of emotions almost altogether. The power of an emotion may have very little to do with the reality of its object.

What is critical to the reality of an emotion is the position of its subject, the person who actually feels the emotion. In the case of reading (seeing films, etc.) this has a triple edge; it means, to a certain extent, that the characters or situations in the book (film) already have a certain amount of emotion *in them*—e.g., a frightening situation, a lovable character, a vicious, envy-filled villain. Second, there must be some sense of inference to the emotions of the author, not by way of the infamous "pathetic fallacy" ("Dostoevski must have been really depressed when he wrote this") but it is of no small importance that a story has been composed, or retained, by someone, perhaps an entire community. In oral traditions, the importance of the emotion in the storyteller (perhaps the entire culture) is self-evident. In modern literature, this link is none too evident, and has often been under attack. But my interest here is not the method of literary criticism; it is difficult to deny that the ordinary nonformalist reader is well aware that behind the pages is another human being. The easy separation of text and author is no evidence against this.

Third, and most important, readers (or viewers) have emotions, and these are the passions that concern us. The emotions of the personalities in the pages are more or less given to us, and the emotions of the author(s) are for most purposes irrelevant to us. But the emotions of the readers are determined in part by the text, in part by the readers themselves. Here, perhaps, is the most important advantage of books over film (and other more determinate media): readers of books are free to visualize, no matter how precise the description of a character, their version of that character. Not surprisingly, the envisioned figure almost always bears a striking resemblance (whether recognized or not) to persons of importance to the readers. (Such recognition is usually rare; as so many critics have so often said, much of what Freud said about dreams is certainly true of the literary imagination, but in readers as well as authors.) Readers can "act out" a drama in much more personal terms than the movie viewer, and this same activity of the imagination, we can now say, thereby learns how to enact (and reenact) emotions of an increasingly sophisticated variety. The education of the emotions is, more than anything, the education of the imagination, learning to engage in a variety of emotional roles, in a variety of situations that may never have been encountered in real life—at least, not yet.

What is critical to the education of emotions is precisely the fact that the emotions experienced while reading are not merely vicarious, not unreal, even if the situations and characters of the story may be wholly invented. It is not the reality of the emotion's object that is critical, but rather the reality of the emotion's subject, the reader. But it would be folly of a different kind to think that readers simply *create* their emotional experiences, that the emotions in the novel—including the form and structure of the novel as a whole—do not determine and *teach* emotions to readers. That is the very importance of the great masterpieces of our literary tradition; they teach those emotions which, for better or worse, our collective culture has chosen as the temperament of our age.

44

In Defense of Kitsch

"Kitsch causes two tears to flow in quick succession. The first tear says: how nice to see children running on the grass!

The second tear says: How nice to be moved, together with all mankind, by children running on the grass!

It is the second tear that makes kitsch kitsch."

—Milan Kundera, *The Unbearable Lightness of Being*

I recently attended an exhibit at the Denver Art Museum featuring, among other nineteenth-century French works, a painting by Adolph Bouguereau (1825–1905) and one by Degas, more or less across from one another in the gallery. The Bouguereau is a classically arranged portrait of two very pretty little girls, in rosy pink and soft pastels, set against an expansive sky. The Degas, by contrast, catches one of his dancers in an awkward back-scratching gesture, her body turned away from us, her face unseen. She is framed in a cramped canvas in pale green, ochre, and burnt orange. The Bouguereau is one of those well-painted pieces of sweet kitsch that

Kitsch is always on my mind. I have had many good discussions with Kathy Higgins on the topic and I was inspired by her essay, "Sweet Kitsch" in Halperson, ed., *The Philosophy of the Visual Arts* (Oxford University Press, 1992). My interest was stimulated by Paul Ziff in a conversation at Pier-One Imports over various knick-knacks. A much longer version of this essay first appeared in the *Journal for Aesthetics and Art Criticism* 49, no. 1 (1991). Reprinted by permission of the publisher.

gives French academic painting a bad name. At the same time, it is an almost "perfect" painting. John Canaday writes, in his classic textbook on modern art, "The wonder of a painting by Bouguereau is that it is so completely, so absolutely, all of a piece. Not a single element is out of harmony with the whole; there is not a flaw in the totality of the union between conception and execution. The trouble with Bouguereau's perfection is that the conception and the execution are perfectly false. Yet this is perfection of a kind, even if it is a perverse kind" (*Mainstreams of Modern Art,* p. 154). The Degas, on the other hand, is anything but "perfect" in this sense. It is one of those tiny discomforting treasures that haunts the viewer for hours afterward. But it is the Bouguereau that turns out to be one of the most popular pieces in the museum. The curators of the exhibit comment, "Most of our visitors readily admit they don't know a whole lot about art. So it's only natural for them to look for works that are pretty and easy to understand." And then they add, "novice viewers rarely speak of the Bouguereau's features and aesthetic qualities. Instead, they use it as a springboard to dreams of the future or nostalgic memories of the past. More advanced viewers are soon bored" (from the catalog of the exhibit).

What makes Bouguereau kitsch? What makes it bad art? From an aesthetic point of view it is the "perverse perfection" that is so offensive and cloying, the absence of any interpretive ambiguity or dissonance on the part of the viewer, but most important (for our purposes) it is the manipulation of emotion, the evocation of "cheap," "false" emotions that makes this otherwise "perfect" painting perverse. Clement Greenberg, for instance, complained (in 1939) that kitsch "is mechanical and operates by formulas. Kitsch is vicarious experience and faked sensations. . . . It is the epitome of all that is spurious in the life of our times. Kitsch pretends to demand nothing of its customers except their money—not even their time" (*Art and Culture,* p. 10). Calling a work of (bad) art "kitsch" is not just to condemn the glibness of its technique; it is also to question the motives of the artist and the emotional maturity of the audience. In such cases, sentimentality is the culprit, manipulated by the artist, indulged in by the viewer. It is, we hear from critic after critic, *false* ("faked") emotion. And so, the sentimentality of kitsch becomes not ultimately aesthetic but ethical, a species of dishonesty. Thus Karsten Harries writes, in his *The Meaning of Modern Art,* "to isolate aesthetics from ethics [is] to misunderstand what art is all about" (p. 77).

The very notion of "taste" in art necessitates the existence of "bad taste" and, consequently, bad art. But bad art comes in many varieties and is subject to different kinds of objections. There is sheer technical incompetence, just to begin with (although artistic inability as such is much less fatal than it used to be); there is ignorance of the medium, the tradition and its history, the current fashions, and the tastes of the times. For those outside the bustling art centers, what seems to be bad art may be just bad timing. There is unimaginative imitation and straightforward plagiarism. There is such a thing as having "no eye," the failure to understand color or composition. But there is also an "ethical" dimension to bad art, as in the depiction of the forbidden, the blasphemous, the vulgar expression of the inexpressible, the provocation of the improper, and cruelty. (For example, a bar stool whose legs are actual, stuffed buffalo legs.) Once upon a time, bad art was, above all, such use of unacceptable subject matter, evoking the wrong emotions and provoking the wrong reactions (e.g., visceral disgust and nausea)—but this, too, seems to have recently dropped out of the picture. These days, it is far wiser for an aspiring young artist to offend or disgust the viewer rather than evoke such gentle sentiments as sympathy and delight.

But this is just what is particularly interesting, from a philosophical point of view, about that peculiar variety of "bad art" called "kitsch," and, in particular, that variety of kitsch sometimes called "sweet kitsch." Sweet kitsch is art (or, to hedge our bets, intended art) that appeals unsubtly and unapologetically to the softer, "sweeter" sentiments. Familar examples are the roadside ceramics of wide-eyed puppies and Keen-type paintings of similarly wide-eyed children. Saccharine religious art (so long as it is serious and not sarcastic) would be sweet kitsch, and so, too, perhaps, much of Muzak and Rod McKuen–type poetry. Examples of sweet kitsch are often mentioned as paradigm instances of bad art, but the nature of its "badness" is just what makes kitsch philosophically interesting. The problem is not that sweet kitsch is always badly done. Indeed, some kitsch may be highly professional and keenly aware of the artistic and cultural traditions in which it gains its appeal. Some kitsch seems to be flawed by its very perfection, its technical virtuosity and precise execution, its explicit knowledge of the tradition, its timeliness, and the fact that it stimulates the very best emotions—the "soft" sentiments of kindness and sympathy and the calm passions of delight. But the best emotions seem to be the worst emotions where art is concerned, and "better shocking or sour than sweet," has become something of a rule of thumb for artists and a criterion of good taste for connoisseurs. But why is this? What is wrong with sweet kitsch? Its deficiencies appear to be just what we would otherwise think of as virtues: technical proficiency and a well-aimed appeal to the very best of the viewer's emotions.

What makes Bouguereau kitsch is the one-dimensional purity of the emotion. These girls don't do any of the nasty things that little children do. They don't whine. They don't tease the cat. They don't hit each other. They don't have any bruises. They aren't going to die. The art gives us a false portrait, a carefully edited one that limits our vision and restricts our sense of reality. It "manipulates" our feelings. There is no ambiguity. Above all, there is no discomfort, no ugliness or awkwardness, no sense (as in the Degas) of intruding on privacy. Bouguereau himself writes, "I see only the beautiful in art . . . art *is* the beautiful. Why reproduce what is ugly in nature?" (Cf. Degas: "I show my models deprived of their airs and graces, reduced to the level of animals cleaning themselves.") It is here (though not only here) that ethics meets aesthetics, in the images we are given of human reality, visual theories of human nature, if you like—one a portrait of pure innocence, the other a reminder that we are awkward animals. Sentimentality is "false" because it gives us a picture of ourselves that is too pure, too ethically one-sided. But isn't the Degas portrayal just as "one-sided," as far as its philosophy (its theory of human nature) is concerned? It may be an infinitely better painting (as a painting) but is it better as a *moral theory*? Even if we were to accept the rejection of kitsch as art, why is the sentimentality of kitsch to be condemned, in other words, not just as art but as ethics?

What is wrong with sweet kitsch, first and foremost, seems to be its sentimentality, its easy evocation of certain "sweet" emotions. But what is wrong with sentimentality generally or in some specific case? I think that the heart of the problem lies in our poor opinion of the emotions in general and in particular the "softer" sentiments. When I speak simply of "kitsch," it is to be understood that it is this "sweet" variety alone that I have in mind, though some of my arguments may well also hold where "sour" and "bitter" kitsch is in question. (Is there a "salty" kitsch?)

There is a range of quality to sweet kitsch. On the one hand, there are those "cheap" mass-produced artifacts, disdain for which surely has much to do with economic class distinctions and manufacturing values rather than aesthetic evaluation as such. Much of the literature attacking kitsch is political rather than aesthetic, though ironically much of it comes from Marxists and their kin who despise the mass-marketing origins of kitsch at the same time that they would defend the people who are most likely to purchase such objects. But whether kitsch is attacked because it is cheap and "low-class" or because it is the product of a debased economy, what is wrong with kitsch surely cannot be, philosophically speaking, either the rationalization of snobbery or contempt for its manufacturing and marketing. We should be suspicious about the depth of class prejudices underlying even the most abstract aesthetic argument and the extent to which the charge of "sentimentality" is in fact an attack on unsophisticated taste.

Much of what is called "kitsch" is disdained because it is "cheap" (a word that often performs multiple functions in discussions of kitsch), because it is mass-produced and "plastic," because it is the sort of item that would and should embarrass someone with a proper aesthetic education. There is, on the other hand, some quite expensive and well-produced "high" kitsch, e.g., the academic painting of the mid-nineteenth century exemplified by Bouguereau. High kitsch, whatever else may be said of it, cannot be openly dismissed as "cheap." It is typically very professional, well-made, and expensive. Of course, this opens up a new argument along class lines, an attack on the "nouveau riche" who have money but no taste. Being moved by one's emotions, in contrast to paying attention to the more formal and refined aspects of a work of art, is at best a distraction, if not a "dead giveaway" that one is having a "cheap" emotional experience instead of a cultivated aesthetic response. High-class kitsch may well be "perfect" in its form and composition: the academic painters were often masters of their craft. Thus the accusation that a work is kitsch is based not on lack of form or aesthetic merit but on the presence of a particularly provocative emotional content. (The best art, by contrast, eschews emotional content altogether.)

The term "kitsch" comes from the nineteenth century. One of several suggested etymologies is that the word is German for "smear" or "playing with mud." Toying with this, we might speculate that the "mud" in question is emotion and mucking around with emotions inevitably makes a person "dirty." The standard opinion seems to be that kitsch and immorality go together and that sentimentality is what is wrong with both of them. Thus Harries again: "Kitsch has always been considered immoral." Of course, one culture's or one generation's kitsch may be another's avant garde, and what is obligatory as "compassion" or "sympathy" in one age may be dismissed as mere sentimentality in another. Accordingly, the sentiments that are provoked by and disdained in "sweet" kitsch may vary as well. But whatever the cause or the context, it is sentimentality of kitsch that makes kitsch kitsch and sentimentality that makes kitsch morally suspect if not immoral. Granted, kitsch may be bad art. Granted, it may show poor taste. But why should kitsch be condemned as an ethical defect and a danger to society?

The strong, shared contempt for kitsch and sentimentality is something of a standard for good taste, but there is all too little agreement about "what is wrong" with kitsch and sentimentality to back it up. We can accept, as simply too obvious for our concern here, the claim that kitsch represents "bad taste," but this is hardly a concession given the rarely rational vicissitudes of taste in an art market that now celebrates street graffiti, a pile of bricks, and an artist's dragging himself across broken glass as art. But culling through the literature in both ethics and aesthetics, I think we can narrow down the objections to some tired old charges, none of which holds up to scrutiny. There is the claim that kitsch and sentimentality provoke excessive or immature expressions of emotion and that kitsch and sentimentality manipulate our emotions. There is the claim that kitsch and sentimentality express or evoke "false" or "faked" emotions and that kitsch and sentimentality express or evoke "cheap" or "easy" or "superficial" emotions. There is Kundera's claim that kitsch and sentimentality are self-indulgent, and there is the charge that kitsch and sentimentality distort our perceptions of the world.

The last charge is that kitsch gives us a false and fraudulent, overly "sweet" and benign vision of the world (or certain beings in the world, notably children and puppies) and thus somehow "blocks" our larger, nastier knowledge of the world (children and puppies, too). But what, we should ask in return, is the ethical or aesthetic harm in occasionally seeing the world in such a delightful way? Indeed, underlying all of the above charges is the suspicion that kitsch and sentimentality are modes of distraction and self-deception, shifting our attention away from the world as it is and soothing us instead with objects that are uncompromisingly comfortable and utterly unthreatening. But doesn't that assume that the world is something hateful and not to be enjoyed, and that our genuine emotions are essentially unpleasant and our pleasant emotions essentially fraudulent?

It is true that kitsch is calculated to evoke our emotions, especially those best expressed by that limp vocabulary that seems embarrassingly restricted to such adjectives as "cute" and "pretty" or that even more humiliating, low-octave, downward intoned "aaaaah" that seems inappropriate even in a roadside souvenir shop. It is also true that the emotions provoked by kitsch tend to be unsophisticated and even childlike (as opposed to childish). But is the charge that kitsch provokes too many of these affectionate emotions, or that it provokes them at all? And when the critics of sentimentality call an emotion "immature" or "naive" are they really contrasting it with more mature and knowledgeable emotions, or are they, again, dismissing emotions as such? I would be the first to insist that emotions develop with experience and are cultivated through education, and there certainly is (or should be) a world of difference between the emotions of a seven-year-old and the emotions of a seventy-year-old. But are the emotions of the latter necessarily better or even wiser than the emotions of the child? Indeed, don't we often take emotions to be sophisticated precisely when they are cynical, even bitter, not only controlled but suppressed? There is something charming, even virtuous, about adults who are capable of childlike feelings, and something suspiciously wrong if they can never do so, even in the intimacy of a private apartment, a theater, or an art gallery. To be sure, the ability to be so moved is no sign of aesthetic or artistic maturity but it is not, I want to argue, evidence to the contrary; nor is it an emotional flaw in character. To be sure, we outgrow some of our emotions, but one of the purposes of art is to remind us of just those tender, outgrown sentiments, perhaps even to disturb us regarding their loss. Better yet, art can help us feel them again, and move us to action on their behalf.

I think that our limited vocabulary and expressions indicate a cultivated inability to recognize or publicly express the more gentle emotions. How rich our vocabulary of abuse and disgust is by way of contrast! One can condemn the public expression of emotion as "inappropriate" or as "immature," but it is not excessive or childish expression that is being criticized here. It is the emotion as such, whether expressed or not, and the idea is that sophisticated viewers will be mortified at their emotional response to a piece of high kitsch. The usual cultivated response, accordingly, is a sneer. But if we are embarrassed by the gentle emotions, I suspect that it is because those emotions, in any "amount," make us uncomfortable, and remind us of our own residual naivete.

Of course, it may be that good taste requires subtlety (though one might well object that this is a very cold-blooded and whiggish conception of good taste), and it may be that certain emotions are indeed inappropriate and out of place. (E.g., getting sexually "turned on" by Bouguereau's two little girls—which may in a few troubled souls be difficult to distinguish from more appropriate feelings of affection. This sort of pathology is hardly "immaturity.") But the bottom line seems to be that feeling "cuddly" just isn't "cool." Feeling our "hearts going out" to a painting of two little girls in the grass makes us uncomfortable and indicates incipient poor taste if it is not also a mark of some sort of degeneracy (sexual overtones quite aside). But why should we feel so guilty about feeling good or feeling for the moment a childlike affection? In real children, of course, such gentle feelings may well coexist with irritation, and they may play poorly in the rough-and-tumble world of business outside of the museum. But in such a safe, relatively private context, what would it mean to feel an excess of kindness, even "cuteness"? And why should the unsubtle evocation of tenderness be ethically blameworthy, distasteful, or dangerous? It's bad art, perhaps, but why any more than this? The trumped-up charges against kitsch should disturb us and make us suspicious. These attacks on the most common human sentiments—our reactions to the laughter of a child, or to the death of an infant—go far beyond the rejection of the bad art that evokes them. It is true that such matters provide a facile vehicle for second- or third-rate painters, but if such incidents are guaranteed to evoke emotion, it is because they are indeed a virtually universal concern. The fact that we are thus "vulnerable" may make for some very bad art but this should not provoke our embarrassment at experiencing these quite "natural" sentiments ourselves; nor should it excuse the enormous amount of sophistry that is devoted to making fun of and undermining the legitimacy of such emotions.

Part Eight

On Education

45

Two Cultures, 1990:
Business and the Humanities

At Harvard University the business school is separated from the rest of the university by the Charles River. The symbolism is unmistakable, and it is expressed with some vengeance on both sides.

At the University of Texas, through accident rather than wisdom, the Business Administration-Economics Building is less than thirty feet or so from Waggener Hall, which houses some of the liberal arts departments. And yet, for the amount of commerce between them, they might as well be at opposite ends of the state.

This is a tragedy. Nationwide, the number of students majoring in business has increased enormously, often at the expense of the liberal arts. Some liberal arts departments have simply pretended that nothing has happened. Others, to hold up their enrollments, have yielded to the temptation to become service organs of the business school. This has fostered resentment, not understanding.

At the University of Texas, the liberal arts have become the "dumping ground" for the business school, the last resort for those students not bright enough, not conscientious enough, or not adequately prepared for business

This piece was written for *The Daily Texan* and published on a number of occasions since 1981, once in cooperation with Paul Nelson in the Management Department of the University of Texas at Austin. The "Two Cultures" reference is to C. P. Snow's classic lament about the separation of science and the humanities. Reprinted by permission of the publisher.

courses. What this does to the quality of education in the liberal arts, as well as to the reputation of "business students" in liberal arts courses, is too obvious to mention.

The effect of this has been destructive on both sides: it endangers the integrity of the liberal arts departments, and it turns the business school, as well as the university, into a glorified job shop—the very antithesis of a university. Administrators fight for turf and warm bodies. Business students graduate without even being exposed to the classics of their own culture. Liberal arts students leave the university with contempt for business, despite the fact that most of them will end up in the business world one way or the other.

Let me quickly emphasize that my point here is not to attempt one more defensive plea for the supremacy of the liberal arts; such pleas, in fact, tend to be counterproductive and underscore the problem. Nor is it to demean the business school or its students; indeed, there has been too much of that already, and most of it undeserved.

My concern is the need for more integration as well as respect between disciplines and the right of every student to be encouraged, but not forced, to take advantage of the university as a whole. The present compartmentalization, which exists as much in the minds of the students as in the structure of the university, denies this need and discourages the exercise of this right. Career success and the sensibilities provided by a liberal arts education are *both* goals of the university, and any pressure to choose between them is a perversion of the very idea of the university and "higher" education.

In earlier years, it may well have been the case that students were too readily discouraged from taking "practical" courses; thus the low visibility and often the abysmal quality of business schools, until only a few years ago. Now, the pressures have reversed, and too many students who would be better served in their careers as well as in their university education by a liberal arts or other "impractical" major feel compelled to major in business. This would not be a problem *if* there were more communication and cooperation between the schools. An occasional required course—logic for accounting majors—does not solve the problem.

Too many students in the liberal arts graduate with the regret that they haven't had even a glimpse of practical preparation. Too many students who believe they are "forced" into business believe that they have wasted their years at the university. They find out that they could have gotten the same job and also satisfied their interests in liberal arts subjects. Some do badly in business school, and so deprive themselves doubly. Students who aspire to go on for a master of business administration find out too late that they would have had a *better* chance at the best graduate schools with a major other than business. At Harvard, more than 80 percent of the first-year M.B.A. students are nonbusiness majors; at Texas, 50 to 60 percent are nonbusiness majors.

The point is not that students ought to major in the liberal arts, but neither ought they, in general, to major in business. What is needed, and should be encouraged, is a wider sense of the options and opportunities offered by the university. There always will be liberal arts majors who wouldn't be caught dead in BEB, and there will continue to be many business students who are so absorbed in their business studies that they do not want to distract themselves.

The tragedy, however, are those many business students who do not even know about, or are too intimidated to even audit, any of the excellent courses across Inner Campus Drive, a problem compounded by those in the liberal arts who try so hard to pretend that business doesn't even exist in the university. And what of those many liberal arts students who fret away much of their undergraduate time wondering what in the world they might do once they get "out"?

What is to be done? First, there needs to be more integration and cooperation at the university level, encouraging mutual programs and concerns and discouraging competition between the colleges. It is incumbent on both the liberal arts college and the business school to get to know one another and to encourage their students to do so as well. It means that such crucial concerns as "I'd better major in business if I want to get a job" and "What can I do with a degree in _____?" deserve honest answers. It means that the liberal arts departments must make an effort to make their courses known in the business school, but without "selling out" or taking the easy route by way of required courses, which eventually have the deadly effect of enslaving one department and cheating another.

It means that the business school should encourage its students with electives to look beyond the business school to fill them, and it should consider the motives and interests of its majors as well as their grades and glibly stated ambitions. And finally, much of the task falls onto business itself: employers can encourage well-rounded students by expanding their own searches, recruiting campuswide instead of just in the business school, and have the foresight to hire students who can quickly learn the business as well as those who have had a textbook introduction to it.

Inevitably, some of what I've said will be interpreted as hostile to my friends in the business school, and the same points will be interpreted by my friends in the liberal arts as being much too "pro-business." But my point is precisely to try to get beyond such false antagonisms, so that all students have the opportunity to take full advantage of their four years at the university.

46

Are Ethics Courses Useful?

What is Ivan Boesky doing these days, in his ample spare time? He is studying ethics and his own religious tradition. "Too late" chortles the chorus of critics, but would such studies have made any difference before?

It seems obvious, even to Mr. Boesky, that a modicum of attention to ethics would have interrupted the greedy obsession with gain. Of course, some might still "bend the rules" (or even flaunt them) but most of the wrongdoing that now fills the papers is due to moral myopia, not wickedness.

Yet, we still hear the tiresome complaint that ethics courses are "useless," most recently by Michael Levin in the *New York Times* (11/27/89). He calls them "pointless exercises" that "don't deal with real-life issues" and insists (rightly) that "moral behavior is the product of training, not reflection," that it is a good upbringing, not a late-in-life college course, that teaches the difference between right and wrong. True, as Aristotle told us 2500 years ago, ethics begins with a good upbringing. But it continues and culminates, he also told us, with reflection and deep understanding. It requires experience, including the vicarious experiences provided by literature and what we now call "case studies." Ethics education is, in part, the provision of vicarious experience and the reinforcement of values through reflection.

It is true that "bicyclists don't have to think about which way to lean

This piece was original written under the title "Ethics Courses Are Useful," in direct response to a particularly polemical editorial in the *New York Times*. It was later published in the *Ethics Digest* (1991). Reprinted by permission of the *Digest*.

and honest men don't have to think about how to answer under oath." But even honest men under enormous pressure do have to think about how to answer. Perhaps moral character is a matter of "microchallenges" ("Should you save a Christmas bonus, or go on a spree?") rather than policy decisions ("how should profit be weighed against pollution?"), but the most important of those microchallenges may involve painful choices of personal loyalty and policy as well.

In the not-at-all-uncommon situation in which a middle manager faces conflicting obligations, it is simply not true that "telling right from wrong in everyday life is not that hard; the hard part is overcoming laziness and cowardice to do what one perfectly well knows one should." Professor Levin has evidently never had to "downsize" a staff of good employees because of general cost-cutting above him.

Levin, in short, misses the point. The aim of an ethics course, whether for students or seasoned executives, is not to "teach the difference between right and wrong" but to make them comfortable with the really "hard" choices of management. What gets provided is not new knowledge but practice and ethical edification. The cases are not manufactured for the sake of pedagogy but taken precisely from "real life," preferably from the actual experiences of the participants themselves.

The call for ethics courses does not come solely from an outraged public, the press, and congressional committees. It comes from the professionals themselves: doctors, lawyers, and executives who want the opportunity to think through and clarify the conflicts in which they find themselves on a daily basis. I teach business ethics in university classrooms and corporations, and I must say that I rarely meet a manager who isn't concerned about ethical issues and doesn't want to talk about them, albeit with some discomfort.

The purpose of ethics courses is to provide a forum for reflection, where ethical issues, both personal and those relating to policy, can receive the same concentrated focus that cost/benefit and strategy analyses enjoy in so many other courses.

Every reflective executive recognizes the danger of "tunnel vision," *pleonexia* Plato called it—a sickness of purpose. Michael Maccoby described it as "careerism" in his best-selling book *The Gamesman:* "The individual's sense of identity, integrity, and self-determination is lost as he treats himself as an object whose worth is determined by its fluctuating market value." It is hard to find a manager who does not feel the pressures of careerism or suffer some contradiction between obligations to the company and his or her sense of personal integrity.

That is the "use" of business ethics courses. They do not teach new knowledge. They do not (or should not) dwell on the philosophical disputes over theoretical questions (the relative moral worth of utility versus obligation, or the grounding of "rights"), and they should certainly not encourage that "relativism" suggested by an interminable clash of ethical theories. They are not and should not be limited to those large policy questions that are beyond the control of even most chief executives. They are not intended to "stem the flow of immorality" but to reinforce morality.

I contend that there are no courses that can do more good, so long as one does not have wrongheaded expectations about their intended results or how to go about teaching them. It can, I confess, be frustrating to teach undergraduates and even M.B.A. students, who haven't had the professional experience or had to face their own ethical problems. Yet, even they show enthusiasm and they know that something important is going on—or going to go on—for which they may not be prepared. They've all seen the movie *Wall Street* and watched the fall of Ivan Boesky. They've heard the often self-righteous cries for "more ethics" and, even if they aren't sure what's intended, they know that a preemptive strike isn't going to hurt them.

47

SOTA (Students Older than Average)

When Sarah enrolled at the University of Texas, her first and foremost feeling was that she "didn't belong." She had been a student here once before—a quarter of a century ago. She had performed passably in her classes but earned her "Mrs." degree by the end of her freshman year, when she married the graduating senior whom she had been dating since early in high school.

But now, in her late forties, the last of her three children off to college, surrounded by students her children's age, she could only feel "out of it." She entered my class as inconspicuously as possible; she sat in that anonymous midsection of the room, where all of the faces begin to blur together. She was afraid to open her mouth. After each class, she nervously double-checked the assignment, as if she alone must have missed something essential.

Sarah was a "special student." "Special" in the eyes of the registrar and the administration because she entered with a dubious record, on probation, with a trial period before admission to a regular degree program. In fact, many such students are not interested in degrees; they are here at the university for self-improvement, for stimulation, enjoying themselves immensely. But Sarah and the other "special students" are "special" in another sense too; they are our best students. They work harder, think more, and enjoy their work more than the vast majority of their younger colleagues.

This piece first appeared in *The Denver Post* in 1980 and has since been published on a number of other occasions.

They have a wealth of experience to draw upon and, most important, they have that hunger for learning that is the essence of a good education.

Sarah was not expected to go to college, and so she felt, mistakenly, that the younger students viewed her with some resentment. One brash coed, a friend of her daughter's from high school, had greeted her the first day of registration with "My God, what are YOU doing here?!" And that seemed to sum up her first few weeks. But by the end of the term, she had become the most popular and outspoken student in the class.

She said what the other students could not say. She showed them that college can be something more than an extension of high school, even a rebirth, an exhilaration. From her first weeks as a "special student" who didn't belong, Sarah became a truly "special" student who summarized all of the virtues of education. In fact, she was thrilled with it, if that is not too shrill a term for such a solemn subject. And everyone around her felt it, too.

Sarah is a member of a new and growing class of students. They tend to be in their mid-to-late forties or older; most but by no means all of them are women. With the waning of the baby boom, they will fill an increasing number of places in our higher educational systems. In fact, as enrollments drop, such students are more and more in demand, and some are even being recruited by the university. Some educators predict that, within the next ten years, nearly half of some college populations will consist of these older students. In fact, one of the most active social groups on the UT campus is SOTA, "students older than average." But, because of them, the "average" is quickly beginning to change.

There is a cost, and it is considerable—not in tuition and books so much as in time and energy. There are those nervous weeks of adjustment, overworking on assignments and trying to fit in. Few husbands seem all that willing to start cooking when their wives start college, which they seem to feel is a luxury. So at the end of a long class day, there is the prospect of housework before even more hours of study. There is the feeling "something has to go" but, in fact, it doesn't. Marriages seem to thrive rather than break up for special students. When there are still children at home, they learn to do more for themselves. (Sometimes even husbands do.) Grades stay up as well as the excitement and I've never heard of a student's husband who starved to death. In fact, I remember one remarkably good student at Texas who later told me, "I became Charlie's Phi Beta Kappa key." Another husband called the *Austin American-Statesman* every time his wife made the dean's list, and many of them would eventually show up in class, along with their spouses, trying to share in the new enthusiasm and wealth of information that the university was offering.

We too often assume that the warriors of ideas are the young and open-minded, while their elders tend to be reactionary and anti-intellectual. I think that just the opposite is true, that the older college students tend to be more receptive, less prone to platitude and more willing to give up prejudices—or at least consider the other side. At the same time, they have had more time to develop their convictions, and more experience to support them.

For example, in a weighty class called "existentialism," we were discussing no less a topic than "the meaning of life," and the general attitude among the twenty-year-olds was that life was "absurd" and "meaningless." It was then that Sarah, with her twenty-eight-year advantage and three grown children, turned them inside out, making them see that their profundities were just popular platitudes, and while they listened uncomfortably she lectured them—brilliantly—on the meaning of life as she knew it.

Yet, before she had so proven herself, Sarah had suffered from too many doubts, too many fears. As I got to know her, I wondered how many other students there are like her at Texas right now. Even more urgently, how many other students like her—talented but untried, hungry for what the university can give them but feeling "out of it"—must there be in the Austin area, missing out on an adventure because of their fears?

What we call "higher" education is in trouble. Everyone hears about the financial and political problems, but what is equally serious is that too many students no longer appreciate the point of education; they see school as a means or as a protraction of youthful pursuits, but nothing more. The ideal of self-improvement and cultivation has too easily been replaced by "getting ahead" or just "getting by."

But these students, these "special students," are making the difference. They are excited about the culture they are discovering—which is, after all, their own. They see reading as an adventure and thinking as a challenge. They can appreciate the whole rich tapestry of human experience because they have already lived so much of it. Now they are ready to examine it, understand it, and enrich it still further.

If you would like to be a "special" student too, please drop by the university. Sit in on some classes; look into the various extension and "outreach" programs and, if you are ready to take the plunge, spend a few minutes in the office of admissions.

Socrates once said, "The unexamined life is not worth living." He was already seventy-one, and his best student, Plato, was already "older than average."

48

On Racism and Multiculturalism

I have participated in and listened with considerable concern to the last month's protests and debates about racism and multiculturalism. I have watched as the issues of prejudice, affirmative action, and curriculum reform—which are, unquestionably, interrelated—have nevertheless been confused, one distracting from the others. And it is all too clear how the belligerent opposition, those who like the overly white complexion of the university, are already starting to play the one against the other.

Curriculum reform is an issue guaranteed to keep faculty fighting for years without results, save an occasional emergency course or program designed only to alleviate political pressure, no matter how ill-thought out or designed. Pointless professorial battles now promise to eclipse the issues of racial prejudice and its expression, which have nothing to do with freedom of speech and have no place on (or off) the university campus.

The problems of racism will not be solved or even addressed by courses on multiculturalism. I am not particularly worried, as the conservative National Association of Scholars seems to be, that such courses will be "indoctrination" courses. UT students seem remarkably immune to indoctrination, especially in required courses. If anything, they develop an immunity (combined with a certain self-righteousness) toward the subject matter forced upon them. I suspect that required courses—and the resistance to them—may even increase racism rather than diminish it.

This piece first appeared in *The Daily Texan* at the height of the nationally publicized "multicultural" freshman English course flap during the summer of 1990. It is reprinted here by permission of the publisher.

There is a serious down-side to such courses as well. The Black Studies courses and programs established in the late sixties, for example, succeeded in fostering ethnic pride and providing black and some (already sympathetic) white students the opportunity to focus on black history and experience. But at UCLA, for example, where I was teaching at the time, the establishment of such courses allowed the faculty and administration to wash their hands of the matter, isolate black students even more than before (with their acquiesence and approval), and hire just a few black faculty members to run those few courses and programs.

But it is the lack of black and Hispanic representation on the faculty that is, I believe, the first and most basic problem. There is indeed a "small pool" of minority candidates, especially in such fields as physics, mathematics, and philosophy. The recent move to make deans strong-arm departments is not going to change the demographics. We might compete with a few Ivy League Schools and the several state universities that pay considerably higher salaries than we do, but the likelihood of winning one of those few candidates is exceedingly small. In a few fields there may be only one or two candidates, and they virtually have their pick of the top universities in the nation.

We could loosen our criteria and hire more minorities from less prestigious schools and with less promise for academic success, but this would soon establish a "second tier" faculty that would (like the "new hire" policies in the airline industry) guarantee continued resentment and contempt and do no one any favors. The "bum's rush" demand for hiring more faculty emanating from the administration right now is only going to end in frustration and embarrassment, and the bad situation is going to continue.

What we need is a *long-term* program to develop, not just find, minority faculty who can join the university, not as token or second-class citizens but as fully competent and competitive teachers and scholars. We need to reject these short-term fixes that are being proposed by administration and students alike.

We in the fields that are so underrepresented need to go out and give lectures and lessons in largely minority Texas elementary schools. Before they are deadened by required courses and bad teachers, children readily learn to love almost anything interesting. Children take to philosophy, for example, with an enthusiasm and acceptance rarely found even among our undergraduates.

Many of us on the faculty would gladly do this, as part of our sense of service to the community. We should expose children to academic subjects. We should show them that people actually live their lives doing this, loving it and getting paid for it. Then, the critical role of the university should be to provide minority scholarships so that those students can seriously study such subjects. We can encourage them to stay here for graduate and post-graduate study, supported again by some serious scholarships, or we can send them on to other first-rate graduate schools. But despite all the recent talk of "commitment," our current funding for such scholarships—at both the graduate and undergraduate levels—is pathetic.

It is not in the present "small pool" that adequate faculty representation will be found but in generous planning for the near future. If we were to take it upon ourselves to encourage and develop the faculty we so desperately need, we will not only enlarge the pool of candidates for our own positions but get proper credit for a valuable program that will benefit other universities, too.

Multiculturalism in the university and in the curriculum will then be a natural consequence, for even if these new teachers have been primarily exposed to the same old male white pedagogy, their heritage and political interests will no doubt guarantee just the changes that are now being demanded. As the palette of instructors changes so will the painting.

49

Professors Riot: Kill Moby Dick

News Flash: There is rioting and chaos in the streets of the university. Rebellious gangs of literary critics have declared war on books and authors, and they are encouraging their students to join them.

"It would be considered an act of war," warned the National Commission For Excellence in Education, if some foreign power had done to our educational system what we have done ourselves. The commission did not just have nuts-and-bolts literacy in mind. What is also at stake is our sense of ourselves as a culture and the emotions that give our lives meaning.

It is in the context of this crisis, rather than in my usual spirit of philosophical irritation, that I suggest looking at some of the latest fashions in literary criticism. Some of the theories behind them have merit, and some of the new attention to the reader—the student—is long overdue. Nevertheless, the practical impact is proving to be a disaster. And the frictions and battles engendered are, at best, extremely embarrassing. One might be all too tempted to simply dismiss such teapot tempests if it were not for the fact that they impinge so directly on the current catastrophe.

From Baltimore to Berkeley, professors of English and other literatures can be heard shouting, "There are no masterpieces!" and "Textuality is

---

Deconstruction is now dead, of course, though Derrida is still very much alive and teaching in California. This piece first appeared in *The Austin American-Statesman* April 2, 1985. © Austin American-Statesman. It is reprinted here by permission of the publisher, and with special thanks to Janet Luedtke.

fascism!" They are declaring themselves free from and superior to the texts they are teaching. (The students are dismayed. The text is their anchor.)

What is happening is nothing less than a revolution, and there are few departments of literature that have not been torn apart by it. (It is worth noting that most other departments in the university, however, have barely been touched by it, and may not even know that it is going on. All too often, the public image of the university seems to be occupied by the latest row in the English Department.) On the one hand, there are the traditionalists, like myself, who stubbornly believe that students have to learn to read and appreciate books before they can become critics. On the other hand, there are the revolutionaries, who insist that the students run through very abstract and obscure theories of interpretation before they even know how to walk through the library. What is really at stake, of course, is the status of the professor.

The revolutionary approach is defined, first of all, by the denigration of masterpieces. These are the books that define a culture. They are also the books that students won't read. ("They are too long . . . too hard . . . boring.") How do the new theories encourage these resisting readers? These "smug iconoclasms" (so-called by critic Jonathan Culler, who defends some of them) entreat students not to admire great books but rather to "deconstruct" them.

"Deconstruction" is the favorite weapon of high-level anti-intellectualism in America. (It is already long dead in Paris.) Ironically, it is for the most part the creation of a deep and devoted philosopher, the French philosopher Jacques Derrida. One of the main themes—a very old theme in philosophy—is the indeterminacy of interpretation. Derrida is particularly critical of certain seemingly absolute polarities that pervade much of philosophy and psychology, and he has developed a style—one hesitates to call it a technique much less a "method"—for showing how such seemingly solid foundations of criticism are in fact unstable, and often contradicted within the text itself. So far, so good. But its American practitioners have taken up the banner of deconstruction as "progressive" as opposed to all alternative "reactionary" approaches to literature. Military metaphors run rampant with the language of destruction (though every deconstructionist dutifully points out the three-letter difference between "destruction" and "deconstruction"). Like so many movements that begin as a mark of mental health and end up as symptoms of intellectual illness, deconstruction is often summarized, e.g., by Jonathan Culler, one of its leading advocates, as the thesis that we can know nothing. Every poem, novel, and thesis is vulnerable, and the aim of deconstruction seems to be to run through the lot.

The antiquated target of literary deconstruction, the now-anachronistic "New Criticism" of many decades ago, did warrant the accusation of deifying and uncritically worshipping the great texts. But taking books too seriously is hardly the problem now, and current conservative backlash has to be seen as caused by rather than the cause of the deconstructionist movement. Deconstruction is a devastating technique for undermining emotional involvement and not really reading texts. It begins with the presumption that every work is flawed if not exploitative, and it has now infected probably half of the literature departments in our universities, affecting professors who typically lack any of Derrida's philosophical sophistication to put such theses in perspective. Deconstruction has become, stripped of its self-promotion and paradoxes, a way of not taking texts seriously, of not entering into them but undermining them, "reducing" their emotional context to petty subjectivity and prejudice. Deconstruction is, in one sense, just criticism—but it is criticism of a particularly nasty variety. It goes after weaknesses rather than strengths, searching the margins of the text instead of trying to comprehend the whole. Of particular interest to the deconstructionists are political and cultural biases and inconsistencies and, especially, sexual hang-ups. This is not Norman Mailer they are deconstructing, but Herman Melville and Emily Dickinson.

Consequently, the geniuses of literature are no longer to be admired. Their texts are no longer there to be venerated but rather to be undermined. Their role as vehicles of culture is destroyed and their power to inspire emotion—any emotion except perhaps contempt or pity—is extinguished. And, concerning the general crisis in literacy, the resisting reader cannot help but respond, "Why then read them at all?"

The power and the importance of literature lie in its ability to bring to and submerge the student in a context (and perhaps a culture) that is richer or at least different from his or her own. Teachers sometimes talk sympathetically about "tapping into the student's emotional experience" but, in fact, this is getting it backward. The literature does not "tap into" so much as it informs and ultimately forms students' emotional experiences. It is essential that the book (or film, etc.) provides students with something that they do not already have—a situation, at least. The core of the emotional experience is in the book (film, etc.) and the students enter into it. It is thus with particular alarm that we should look at some new theories of criticism that as a genus have attracted the title "reader response theories," which make deconstruction look rather innocent by comparison.

On the one hand, reader response theory demands new attention to the reader, a valuable suggestion when students are often virgins where reading is concerned and come from many different backgrounds. On the other hand, illiteracy tends to be elevated to a virtue. According to reader response theories, the new heroes of literature—replacing authors and master-pieces—are the barely literate readers, and, of course, their English professors. It was Geoffrey Hartmann of Yale who notoriously proclaimed that the creative baton has passed from the author to the literary critic, which, given the readability and intelligibility of current criticism, philosopher John Searle rightly calls the *reductio ad absurdum* of the movement. Consider, for example, this recent comment from one of the more distinguished professors of literary criticism in America:

> No longer is the critic the humble servant of texts whose glories exist independently of anything he might do; it is what he does, within the constraints of the literary institution (i.e., tenured English professors) that brings texts into being and makes them available for analysis and appreciation (Stanley Fish, *Is There a Text in This Class?*)

In other words, *Moby Dick* is not the masterpiece. Indeed, Melville's masterpiece would not even exist if it were not being taught and written about by English professors. We now learn that Melville in fact contributed very little; the true creator of the work is the student: "the reader . . . supplies *everything*" (Stanley Fish, *Diacritics*, 81; the italics are his).

There is a pedagogical function of reader response theory that should indeed be taken seriously. Janet Luedtke, an Anne Sexton scholar at Texas, has made the very important point that much of the problem with teaching literature today is that there is too little effort on the part of instructors to locate and reach and affect the students. Today's teaching techniques, the worst of which are parodied by some of the deconstructionists, are aimed primarily at those few students who already know and understand (or pretend to) the texts in question, mostly upper- or upper-middle class students who have had considerable educational advantages before they ever enter the university. So interpreted, reader response theory means nothing less than paying attention to the abilities and susceptibilities of the student reader. But when this appreciation for the needs of the reader is abandoned in favor of a pretentious theory about his or her superiority, education is undermined and literature is no longer instructive. The reader simply supplies his or her own emotional reactions—any emotional reaction at all, presumably, sometimes without regard for the details of the text. The "interpretive" community in a large undergraduate class is often each student alone, plus, perhaps, the opinion of the professor. If one wants to be amused by Anna Karenina's suicide or giggle through *Cry, the Beloved Country,* the text and the teacher have lost any authority to insist otherwise.

Literature, I have argued elsewhere,* teaches us to articulate as well as to understand our emotions. What practical advice do the new theories have to offer today's student, who is trying to express an emotion in a proper sentence with at best insecure command of English vocabulary and grammar? One distinguished professor, in defense of the students, proclaims that "it is impossible to write an incorrect sentence." The author, a professor of literature who evidently hasn't graded student essays for a while, calls this "freedom." He goes on to say,

> Since language can no longer produce meanings that allow us to think contemporary experience, we have to look elsewhere—to mathematics, or abstract art or superrealism, or movies, or, perhaps, new languages created by random selection of words. (O. B. Hardison, Jr. [*Sewanee Review,* Summer 82], p. 404)

One need not denigrate mathematics to doubt its ability to express emotion, and one would not have to look further than some student papers to find such a "random selection of words," but it is not at all clear that what is expressed thereby is "contemporary experience"—or any emotion whatever.

Finally, what could be more detrimental in the current situation than to give in to the worst form of student resentment—perhaps the least honorable of all emotions—and those who despise their texts (unread) just because they are required. They blame the author for this injustice. But consider a well-known Marxist literary critic, Terry Eagleton, who, whatever his political views and no matter how brilliant his writings, is also employed to teach students to admire and enjoy literature. He celebrates "the revolt of the reader," who has been "brutally proletarianized, by the authorial class" (*New Literary History,* 1982). He encourages "an all-out *putsch* to topple the text altogether and install the victorious reading class in its place." It seems not to bother him that the class of readers is quickly becoming a null class. "We don't need the authors," he insists, leaving open the question whether we need any readers either. Against the tyranny of literature, he encourages "political intervention," "if necessary by hermeneutical violence" (by which he means deliberate misreadings of books —another timely bit of advice for students who don't know how to read carefully in the first place).

Now none of this should be construed as an attack on the literary theory that lies behind these rash proposals. In many instances it is philo-

---

*See essay 43.

342   Part Eight: On Education

sophically interesting and, not surprising, based on some serious philosophy in turn. Nor should it be viewed as one more reactionary attempt to quash student freedom and reinforce the much-dated "canon" so adored (but rarely read) by conservatives. My concern is with the students, not the polemics, with teaching, not theory. In the current climate of illiteracy and ignorance it seems to me that the last thing we need is an ideological elitism that would leave ordinary students further foundering on their own.

It could and should be objected that education is not just ingesting books and informing emotions; it is also learning to criticize them. Heroes are to be scrutinized. Books—all books—should be criticized. Emotions are to be evaluated. But there is a difference between criticism with respect and criticism that undermines the very possibility of enlightened understanding and emotion. It is one thing to question a book or a passion as an ideal; it is something quite different to reject all ideals.

It might also be objected that it is important to encourage individual interpretations and the application of one's own emotional experience to the text. There is no doubt that a nineteenth-century New England reader of *The Scarlet Letter* inevitably interpreted that book very differently than a contemporary student in Los Angeles. But it is quite different to claim, as it is now claimed with a bravado appropriate to its absurdity, that "there is no text," that there are only readers' individual interpretations and emotions. Hawthorne certainly has something to do with our feelings about Hester, and it is not very likely that her experience has already been duplicated by a typical Beverly Hills sophomore.

It might also be objected that most of our "masterpieces" and consequently our emotions are "ethnocentric," the product and property of a very narrow segment of the world's population. Deconstruction and its allies deflate this pretension. But the answer to this objection should be to broaden the curriculum, to add more books from Africa, Asia, and South America and learn to understand them on their own terms. It is not to eliminate the best works of "Western" literature and pretend that they are of only negative value. To appreciate the emotions of others—including negative emotions caused by one's own society—is extremely important, but it does not necessitate disclaiming or demeaning one's own emotional experience.

Emile Durkheim wrote a century ago that education is primarily concerned not with careers and techniques but with passing along a culture and, we may add, the emotions that are deemed proper to it. Literature is a primary vehicle of that culture and those emotions, and theories of literature are tools to service that vehicle. They help teachers to focus and to criticize, to interpret and to make literature accessible and exciting to students. Inevitably, they will also provoke an entertainment of their own, featuring battles between warring factions of faculty that may make the sectarian disputes in Lebanon seem civilized by comparison. But when fashions and fury among the faculty undermine the very purpose of education, literary theory ought to teach and learn a new emotion—humility. In the face of great literature, even chastised, it is or ought to be impossible not to feel gratitude and awe. To bring to a new generation the ability to appreciate and treasure that experience would seem to be the mission and the immediate purpose of teaching literature. In the current revolution, that mission has been the most serious casualty.

50

Beefeater Goes to College

"I cannot distinguish between the love I have for people and the love
I have for dogs.

When a child, and not watching comedians on film or listening to
comedians on the radio, I used to spend a lot of time rolling around on
rugs with uncritically affectionate dogs we had.

And I still do a lot of that. The dogs become tired and confused and
embarrassed long before I do. I could go on forever.

Hi ho."

—Kurt Vonnegut, *Slapstick*

Love, Freud once commented, is the compromise between lust and "the
ordeal of civility." Civilization, he concluded, is made possible by discipline,
through guilt and fear of punishment, to tame the beast in all of us. I
find it difficult enough to ignore an itch or restrain a fart during a business
lunch, not to mention the unmentionable urges that Freud assures me that
I have as well. But imagine being *all* beast, and sitting before a well-set
table without doing more than drooling and looking lovable. Or being
held on a short leash with a fat squirrel less than thirty yards away. If
that isn't love, nothing is. And if that isn't an ordeal, "civility" doesn't
have a meaning.

It is the beast that loves, and is loved. We love the wildness, that
pure joy in the morning which we can share but not even imagine, the
awesome ability to chomp through a beef bone in eight minutes flat, the
total lack of inhibition and the constant reminder of our own primeval

urges. But living with the beast is impossible, and to tame the beast is to lose him.

Freud: "It would be incomprehensible that man should use the name of his most faithful friend in the animal world—the dog—as a term of abuse if that creature had not incurred his contempt through two characteristics; that it is an animal whose dominant sense is that of smell and one which has no horror of excrement, and that it is not ashamed of its sexual functions."

Beefeater is an eight-month-old pound hound, seventy-five pounds dry and without the mud, half shepherd, quarter chow, and assorted chromosome bits from every breed in Austin, Texas. He had wet and exhausted every dog, squirrel, and pair of pants in the city. He had sent at least ten pairs of shoes to the trash, torn the webbing twixt thumb and forefinger on more than one typing hand, chomped through two leashes, and sprained and developed muscles (in me) that I haven't used since my tug-o-war days at camp. It was obvious that life would be impossible, his growing at the rate of pounds per week, without a little discipline. Not having any ourselves, we decided to call in a professional, and send Beefeater to school.

The wisecracks were inevitable: "Is he getting his Barkalaureate?" "Or his Ph.Dog?" "Is he going to study quantum mechanics or bonology?" "Would he make Phi Beta Fireplug?" And so on. But, in any case, it was agreed that what *we* needed was a "master's" degree.

Pavlov's Problem

The purpose of dog school is to discipline people. Torn as we are between our love of the beast and our demand for absolute obedience, we are inconsistent and therefore incompetent. Primitives were excellent dog trainers; they didn't need to envy the wildness and so could enjoy the discipline. There are people today who enjoy the discipline, too, in pampered pansy poodles whose excretory systems mark their only surviving connection with nature.

The conquest of nature? Some people sure can fool themselves. In France, the children are monsters but the dogs will sit in a high chair at a formal roast beef dinner without wiggling an ear. In Germany, children are spanked till blue while the dogs revert to wolfish mischief. In Russia, a turn-of-the-century psychologist who won the Nobel prize in 1904 "discovered" what the colosseum attendants in Ancient Rome already knew, that a ringing dinner bell could cause a dog to slobber even when the food wasn't ready. The problem was, Pavlov only understood dogs and "operant conditioning." He didn't bother to understand people's fantasies about dogs. But then, the Russians also ate them.

Kathy's K-9 College

Kathy's K-9 College is listed in the Austin phone directory under "Dog Training," shadowed by the top entry for "the Canine Hilton." We dialed the boldface number first, as Ma Bell intended, wanting nothing but the best, of course. At the Hilton, you leave your dog four to six weeks, at $43.50 per week. Visits are discouraged. It is therefore ideal for people who like their kids raised by nannies and packed off to boarding school. I feel guilty just leaving for work in the morning. That foretaste of separation anxiety (on my part) was enough. Then there was the money. The idea of leaving my dog to be brainwashed by strangers was more than unpleasant; it was unthinkable. I fantasized the return of a robot dog, sitting, shitting, and heeling on command, the "Manchurian Candidate (Canine-ate?)." Besides, if there's any brainwashing to be done, I wanted to be part of it. Sense of control is a weighty part of the pet fetish, and paying someone else isn't the same as doing it yourself. Then again, there was the money.

Kathy charges $15.00 for eight sessions and promises results. She directs, but you train your own dog. In effect, she disciplines you. The curriculum, standard: "sit, heel, stay, and come." His personality, I was assured, would remain intact. He would love it. And we would start Tuesday at seven.

The First Session

Actually, we missed the first session. It was 95 degrees; the refrigerator was full of beer and hamburger. "Beefer" was more than satisfied with two Gainesburgers and "Kojak." (I was once a great student myself.)

One Part in a Million

A dog can smell one part of urine in 60 million parts of water.

We arrived at the second session of the class expecting, as one expects of all Texas gatherings regardless of purpose, a party. It was more like a hospital waiting room, sulking puppy-person pairs in isolated couples, waiting to have puppy-pizazz surgically removed.

Even on street corners, as dogs explore pants and tails alike for tell-tail smears, people find it impossible not to meet, smile, exchange pleasantries, dog anecdotes, and possibly a phone number or two. Even in New York, a leper can collect friends, teenyboppers, metermaids, and brown baggers with the help of an adorable mutt on a leash. "Oh, he's just a puppy. What's his name?" or "Wow, look at those feet!" As two dogs assume their 6-9 welcoming position, it is virtually impossible for the two creatures at the other end of the leash, within an already heavily sexual context, to get acquainted. Much better than computer dating.

But not in Zilker Park that Tuesday night. Normally, you can walk with a dog anywhere and no one wonders what you're doing. Or why you're there. Or why you're alone. (Because you're not.) You've obviously got a purpose, a companion, and an excuse. For talking to yourself. (You're actually talking to the dog.) For acting silly. (The two of you are playing.) For being a little extra brash and friendly. (What else do you say to a woman into whose crotch your surrogate nose is nuzzling?)

But not that Tuesday night. Armed service inductees in their shorts are never so embarrassed a lot as the eighteen couples self-consciously dispersed around the polo grounds, waiting for Kathy to show up. The smell of so many puppy bottoms was more than Beefer could stand. He was out of the car and almost strangled before I could get his leash untangled from the gear shift lever. His nose immediately hit the asshole of a very proper samoyed at 10 miles an hour. For the reception he got, he might have hit a fireplug. Neither the samoyed nor its platinum blonde owner deigned to recognize so uncivilized an entrance. The point of all this, after all, was to tame such impulses, and it soon became clear just how very Freudian this whole field of patients actually was. The combination of guilt, facing the prospect of taming the lovable beast, and existential embarrassment, having to face the contrast between dog freedom and human propriety, gave those first few minutes the atmosphere of a wake.

I would have settled for a heated argument between the virtues of Purina and the advantages of Friskies, but there was not a hint of conversation. I could only imagine what the first session must have been like.

How People Became Civilized

People became civilized about 20,000 years ago, if at all. The same year, almost to the day, dogs allowed themselves to become "domesticated." There should be no question at whose initiative. Scientists speculate that a species of wolf with an inferiority complex found it unnecessary to compete with the other wolves in the State of Nature. It was easier to team up and knock over the equivalents of what then functioned as garbage cans. This was the first "social contract," as it soon became clear that there was more than enough garbage to go around.

Among themselves, dogs and wolves have always been social animals. The wolf packs of the Yukon Territories, pariah packs in Ancient Egypt, "bums" on the lawns of New Jersey suburbs; they're all the same. (We call it a social "instinct" only because we seem to have lost it ourselves.) It was an easy matter, therefore, for this already socialized animal to adopt humans into its social world. What was difficult was for the humans, imperfectly socialized at best, to accept the dogs. Thereby, the myth of "domestication" began, and so did dog schools.

The role of dogs in the New World was obvious; to socialize for their own interests an otherwise belligerent species of anti-social animal who knew, however, both how to cook and how to open cans.

It is more than a matter of conjecture, therefore, that human civilization, and dog schools, began when dogs learned how to teach people how to behave.

"Heel!"

Kathy's credentials included years of experience, a warden's voice and manner, and the fact that her own dog was the "Dog Stop Dog" on TV. There was relief among both dogs and humans when she formed the formal circle that would give each of the isolated and assymetric couples something to do. The circle resembled an unbalanced Stonehenge, in warmth of its personality if not exactly in geometric form. The faces of dogs and their attendants resembled students facing a final exam. No eye contact. Not a sound, except for an occasional quizzical whimper. The simplest movements became rigid and self-conscious. When Beefeater bolted after an equally randy terrier, there was more embarrassment than fright.

The demonstration began with Kathy and Beefeater. I was just a little jealous. She showed everyone a "scissor jerk," a brisk yank, calculated to teach a dog that it's better to stay in line than to choke. Unfortunately, the "jerk" caught Beefer off balance, his eye on the terrier, and he was flipped over backwards. No lesson in that. But, from that point of the lesson on, it became "them" against "us," the conniving, sneaky, lusty brutes that we held only tenuously in check, versus the ordeals of civility we were about to impose upon them. Unless they chose to strangle, which they did.

Sol y Sombre

On the first command to "heel!" the circle started in motion. It's seven o'clock in Texas, 94 degrees in the shade, but half the circle is in the sun. Priorities become clear, at least to the dogs, and the circle starts to undulate toward the shade. There is a musical chairs competition before the "halt"; the strategy is, lag in the shade, hurry through the sun. Half the circle cheats. On "halt," they keep walking toward the shadows. The circle has disappeared. The dogs drop into a variety of obscene poses. Beefeater clearly wins the dirty dog award. But no one is watching. I'm laughing. On "heel," he gets hauled to his feet once again and adds his own to a melodic scale of a dozen yelps and complaints. There is the indistinct murmuring of dog names. We repeated this musical exercise for an hour, and then everyone bolted for their cars. No chance to say even "see you."

Spot, Prince Rudolph, and Ups

No parkside psychologist has ever failed to note the deep significance of people's choices of pets. Big dogs for compensation, little dogs for a sense of power, well-trained big dogs to supply both at once, vicious dogs to convey a physical threat, cute dogs to convey cuteness, spoiled dogs to display generosity, rigid dogs to demonstrate discipline, handsome dogs to project class, silly dogs (for entertainment, a sense of superiority, or perhaps to create a sense of humor?) and, of course, pairs of dogs, packs of dogs, pairs of parakeets, cats, hamsters, turtles, and fish. It takes years to begin to express oneself through children; the very choice of pets does it instantly. It is so often said that pets are compensation for loneliness. Not true. They are, however, masks of identity.

Dog names ranks number 176 on Thurber's list of things that amaze and fascinate him. It is slightly higher on my own. He is rightly bored by "the plain and fancy names," e.g., "Spot," "Prince Rudolph" (full name "Prince Rudolph Herzenberg of Rumania"). He disdains names that are "coy"—e.g., "Betsy Bye-Bye" and "Itsy Bitsy," giggles over names that are "witty," —e.g., a pair of dogs called "Ups" and "Daisy," or "Pro" and "Con." (Two turtles named "Cuff" and "Link" are only recent additions to the ranks of "Wit.") Then there are "the cryptics." A friend of mine named her mutt "Dachshund," just because he was not a dachshund.

But whether the names are plain, fancy, or cryptic, the game is the same, to define one's own identity as (1) normal ("Spot" or "Fido," what could be more ordinary?), (2) extravagant ("Prince Rudolph"), (3) cute,

(4) witty, or (5) not only witty but teasing (there is no way to get around asking, of a white ball of fluff named "Dachshund," "Why Dachshund?"). Dog names are virtually never descriptive or functional. Dogs fill their names the way fluid fills a pot, with total indifference. The names are part of the identity game that we all play with pets. The dogs are willing victims; they couldn't care less that their name is ridiculous. But it is our sense of power and projection that is so hard to play with other people. In public, you call your dog "stupid" and "silly" and he responds with a wag and a lick. (Try that with your boyfriend.) Isn't it obvious?

Pets in Cages

I wonder, then, about people who love pets in cages.

The Prettiest Girl

Of course, the prettiest girl had the cutest dog.

A Chinese couple, no more than ten feet in height between the two of them, ordered around a Saint Bernard, in Chinese. Their privacy was envied by everyone else.

A man with a doberman carried a revolver under his jacket. No one ever asked him what he did.

A lady with a tiny poodle *carried* him around the circle, lest he become tired, dirty, or tempted to return to his animal nature. On rare occasions, she would allow him to exercise his nearly vestigial feet, quickly returning him to bosom on any command from Kathy.

A lady with a pug looked like a pug, proving folk wisdom right again.

A woman in a Mercedes (actually two Mercedes, on alternate Tuesdays) and a designer dress matched her bull dog in stubborness. The woman won after changing into blue jeans.

One man sat in his car, with his dog, for the entire seven weeks, watching everyone else march around the circle. I understood that he had participated in the first session but his dog had gotten dirty.

"Stay!"

We missed the fourth class. Beefeater had bitten through a "childproof" safety cap on a bottle of 5 mg. valium, nibbled up the yellow pills one by one (I thought they were tasteless), and spent the day in the animal hospital. (Have you ever tried to "induce vomiting" in a seventy-five-pound dog?)

The fifth session was "Stay." It requires a rare feat of intelligence for a dog: Retention. He has to retain a command without repetition and even without your presence. It seems impossible ⁻or twenty years I've watched sad-faced dogs outside of stores, tails glued to the spot but twitching to break loose and play. (If I couldn't keep reminding myself of the order, I doubt that I could do it.)

The trick, we learned, is to begin with a leash, so that "stay" refers to only a four-foot distance for a few seconds. Then a clothesline is added to the leash, and as the distance increases, the time is increased also. The miracle occurs, unexpected. (It was much like the miracle of house-breaking. Has any dog ceased his messing before the owner had given him up as retarded?)

What dogs put up with. They endure what we will not—frivolous commands and tests of obedience. In the ancient world, overseers referred to their servants as "dogs." It was wishful thinking. Liking the same idea, one of the great philosophical movements of the West began when intelligent slaves referred to themselves as "cynics" (Greek for dogs). Their philosophy, essentially "stay." (There was no reason to do anything else.)

"Man's Best Friend"

"Man's Best Friend" is a revealing commentary on friendship. No one seems to think of a cat as "best friend." As a matter of fact, no one in his or her right mind would think of "owning" a cat. Cats put up with us in return for certain nonessential but welcome services.

Birds are another matter. Freedom observed trapped in a cage.

Like hamsters, turtles, and lizards. Truly "kept" animals.

Cats look at dogs the way that society matrons look at street-corner bums—as clowns.

Try telling a cat to "stay." But dogs enjoy it. They thrive on it. Is obedience the basis of friendship?

By the sixth session, Beefeater loved dog school more than food. He was still choking himself and knocking me over backwards ("forging" and "lagging" respectively). The class was still as friendly as a room full of law school applicants ready to take their entrance exam, but Beefeater, it seemed, was already out of the competition.

On "stay," he pounced on a Japanese beetle, *popillia japonica*.

On "come," the ninety-pound secretary next to us was knocked flat by her obedient Great Dane.

On "Heel!" a teeny woman lost her Yorkshire terrier in a patch of uncut grass. She pulled him up like a fish, and he jumped through in the sinew curves of a dolphin.

The high school jock with the grey shepherd has started to score points with the teenybopper with the brown shepherd. The class is becoming humanized. That is, caninized.

The accountant with the plaid bermudas has already succeeded in training his dog to act like an accountant. Only the occasional flip of the tip of his tail betrays him to be a dog.

Twenty Terrified Freshmen

I had agreed to speak to freshman orientation at the University of Texas. Unfortunately, it conflicted with dog school. With an unusually small amount of red tape (two calls, three offices), permission was secured to bring the dog with me. (I mentioned obedience school, which created the false impression that no trouble would be involved.)

Twenty terrified freshman waddled in. On command, they heeled, stayed, and gave ten-second biographies.

A high-minded professor began his slow rhythmic chant on the virtues of UT, hard work, and their lucky opportunity to meet a real live professor, namely, himself. Freckled and summer-tanned faces showed small quakes of nervousness mixed with impatience when Beefeater, who may or may not have understood the significance of his actions, started a low and long-drawn moan and waved his crotch at the crowd as he writhed on his back in restlessness. This was a campus he had pee-ed upon many times, and he knew it in a different light. He started in counterpoint to the professorial chant, breaking into occasional yips and squeals. I reached down to rub his chest—usually a pacifying gesture—but I succeeded only in regulating, and amplifying, the groan. With a single chomp, he bit through his third leash and went off to sniff out the one part in sixty million in the crotch of a new assortment of pants and skirts. Twenty frosh faces lost their tension and turned to the serious business of restraining vocal guffaws. Forty frosh eyes ceased wavering from prof to dog and settled on dog. The pretentious ordeal of civility had been seen through by the beast, and thoroughly refuted. Twenty students vowed that school would not do to them what dog school had failed to do to Beefer. Ponderous professorial drone had met its competition in the call of the restless wild. UT had been humanized, for the moment.

I was not thanked for coming, but there were double Gainesburgers waiting at home. He never knew why I was so pleased with him.

"Down"

"Down" is the most functional of commands. It keeps dresses clean, dogs in place, and, according to one current theory, recently refuted by Beefeater, it makes it impossible for a dog to bark at full volume.

On the seventh session, Kathy ran a contest for the best "down." You could tell people and dogs had been training for the week. Competition, that most American of virtues, brings out the best in all of us. Supposedly, anyway. Even the dogs sensed that something special was expected of them. (Beefeater had gone "down" so many times that week he sometimes dropped to a crouch when I said anything at all.) The dog that won was the dog that was pushed the least, however. It wasn't Beefeater. His was a sad performance, too embarrassing to tell.

When we got home he did it beautifully. (Like sinking the foul shot after the game, I suppose.)

Graduation

No man is a hero to his valet, according to Oscar Wilde. But then again, no one is ever foolish to his dog. No chance of risk or rejection as such; at worst, divided attention. (Psychiatrists tell of bloody family battles for canine attention, ending in beatings and divorce, not to mention spoiled or spanked dogs.) Dogs listen. You can make a dumb comment to your bird. You can complain to your cat. But only a dog gives a sympathetic ear, in fact, two ears—one up, one down.

Graduation eve. We skipped it. We hadn't come to know a soul in the class. The dirty dog award wasn't official. It was too embarrassingly obvious that the diploma was an ego point for me and not even a chew toy for Beefeater. (I had it mailed to me anyway.) And as the class had progressed, it had become even more uptight. Dogs even stopped sniffing. It was as if the people's shame and guilt had infected the dogs, too. But, luckily, there was only a single case in which the training seemed to be fully effective. The dogs were still dogs, difficult to live with but all the better for it.

When I next write a book about philosophy and human nature, I'm going to start with dogs. And so, too, I am going to end this one.